DOCUMENTING LATIN AMERICA

Gender, Race, and Nation

Volume 2

D1567375

Edited by

ERIN E. O'CONNOR
Bridgewater State College

LEO J. GAROFALO
Connecticut College

Prentice Hall

Boston Columbus Indianapolis New York San Francisco Upper Saddle River
Amsterdam Cape Town Dubai London Madrid Milan Munich Paris Montréal Toronto
Delhi Mexico City São Paulo Sydney Hong Kong Seoul Singapore Taipei Tokyo

Editorial Director: Craig Campanella
Executive Editor: Jeff Lasser
Editorial Project Manager: Rob DeGeorge
Senior Marketing Manager: Maureen E. Prado Roberts
Senior Managing Editor: Ann Marie McCarthy
Project Manager: Debra Wechsler
Operations Specialist: Christina Amato
Cover Designer: Bruce Kenselaar

Manager, Visual Research: Beth Brenzel
Photo Researcher: Nancy Tobin
Cover Photo: Patricio Realpe/Liaison/Getty Images
Full-Service Project Management: Madhavi Prakashkumar
Composition: S4Carlisle Publishing Services
Printer/Binder: R. R. Donnelley/Harrisonburg
Cover Printer: R. R. Donnelley/Harrisonburg
Text Font: Garamond 3

Credits and acknowledgments borrowed from other sources and reproduced, with permission, in this textbook appear on appropriate page within text.

Library of Congress Cataloging-in-Publication Data
Documenting Latin America / edited by Erin E. O'Connor, Leo J. Garofalo.
    p. cm.
    Includes bibliographical references.
    ISBN-13: 978-0-13-208508-3 (v. 1)
    ISBN-10: 0-13-208508-9 (v. 1)
   1.   Latin America—History—To 1830—Sources.   I. O'Connor, Erin.   II. Garofalo, Leo.
    F1410.D63 2011
    980—dc22

                                                           2010017428

10 9 8 7 6 5 4 3 2 1

Prentice Hall
is an imprint of

www.pearsonhighered.com

ISBN 10:   0-13-208509-7
ISBN 13: 978-0-13-208509-0

Contents

Thematic Index

Citizenship:

- And race: Chapters 1, 2, 3, 4, 6, 7, 17, 23, 24, 26, 28, 30
- And gender: Chapters 2, 6, 7, 8, 20, 28, 29

Debates over Civilization:

- Indigenous Peoples: Chapters 5, 15, 17
- Afro-Latin Americans: Chapters 4, 14, 18
- Women: Chapters 5, 18, 19, 20

Gender Norms, Society, and Politics:

- Elite and legally sanctioned gender norms: Chapters 6, 8, 10, 18, 20
- Women's acceptance of dominant gender norms: Chapters 16, 18, 20
- Women's struggles with gender norms: Chapters 10, 11, 12, 19, 21, 22, 27, 29

Land and Labor Conflicts and Negotiations:

Chapters 11, 13, 16, 17, 23, 24, 25, 26, 27

Mass Politics and/or Populism:

Chapters 17, 20, 29, 30

Politics:

- Indigenous: Chapters 3, 5, 7, 13, 17, 23, 24, 25, 26, 27, 30
- Women: Chapters 20, 22, 27, 28, 29
- Afro-Latin Americans: Chapters 1, 4, 9, 14, 28

Relations between "Races":

Chapters 5, 7, 13, 14, 15, 17, 23, 24, 25, 26, 27, 30

Revolution and Warfare:

Chapters 3, 13, 16, 25

Slavery and Emancipation:

Chapters 4, 6, 9

Socialism:

Chapters 19, 21, 22, 23, 25, 28, 29

Preface

Although the numerous ways of analyzing the past are part of what make the study of history interesting, they also make it challenging to create texts and document collections that are both meaningful and accessible. Trying to cover everything can make it difficult for readers to keep track of a book's central purpose, whereas too narrow of a focus fails to provide a broader sense of the course of history. To avoid being either too general or too narrow, *Documenting Latin America* focuses on the central themes of race, gender, and politics and develops them deeply.

The majority of primary-source documents in these volumes have been translated and introduced by scholars who have used them in their research. A few of these sources are from works already published in Latin America, but most of them came from either state or religious archives, and none of the archival documents have ever appeared before in English. These archival sources are the heart of *Documenting Latin America*, uncovering many different ways that race, gender, and politics have intertwined over the course of centuries to make Latin America the complex and fascinating world region it is today. Some of the materials derived from scholarly research explore Latin American history, politics, and culture from the perspective of less-powerful peoples, whereas others address the importance of race and gender from the viewpoints of political and intellectual elites. Additionally, the editors have identified and presented document excerpts that they refer to as *classic* documents that have long been available in English. They have chosen these sources based on their importance to the themes of the volume, their accessibility, and their proven success in stimulating classroom discussion.

The chapters in *Documenting Latin America* offer a broad scope and solid coverage of Latin American history. In each volume, documents presented come from many different regions of Latin America, and they consider themes and challenges particular to different periods of time. However, the editors have not attempted to give equal coverage to all regions and problems in Latin American history. Instead the editors selected documents either to complement others in the volumes or to offer unique perspectives on historical problems. Using these criteria allowed for the inclusion of documents from areas of Latin America that cannot be found in many, if any, other volumes available at the time of this publication. This unique blend of perspectives of history from both above and below, from understudied as well as often-studied regions, and from a combination of archival and classic sources allows readers to engage in a meaningful way with Latin America's past.

To aid readers in the task of interpreting original sources, these volumes are broken down into sections, each of which contains several chapters focused around a central theme or historical development. The introduction to each section defines any unusual or important terms, identifies key issues in a particular era, and relates terms and problems to the documentary history's broader focus on race, gender, and politics. Each chapter also begins with a short introduction that provides the reader with the context in which the document took place. The introduction is followed by a brief list of questions to consider when analyzing the document. The central feature of each chapter is a short document or set of documents. Most of the sources are excerpts from longer documents, but they provide readers with ample text and information to develop their own understanding of Latin American history. Using analytical guidelines from the questions, and context from the introduction, *in conjunction with* evidence from the document helps readers to analyze the document and to form an argument about a given event or problem in Latin American history. Similarly, reviewing the introduction to the *section* in which a chapter appears can help readers to place an individual case within a wider historical moment or trend. The interplay between the details in the documents with the images and broader issues presented in various introductory materials gives the best picture of the dynamics of gender, race, and politics in Latin America.

Each chapter offers key terms, questions for further study, and an annotated list of suggested sources. Italicized terms, institutions, and names are defined in the text or footnotes; if they appear frequently in the volume, they are also listed in the glossary at the end of the book. In addition to facilitating reading comprehension, the glossary also provides information about how some of these terms had distinct meanings in different regions or time periods. The questions offered in each chapter not only help readers to make sense of the document at hand, but these questions also provide potential topics for papers, exams, and in-class discussions. In addition, the suggested sources section at the end of each chapter shows where to find more secondary or scholarly sources, primary documents published in English, and visual and film materials. This section provides a brief description of each item listed, and it is particularly useful for readers who want to explore further the issues raised in the chapter for a research paper, class presentation, or other class activities. The editors and contributors of the volumes have recommended a variety of materials, including, in many cases, Web sites, documentaries, feature films, and literature. Therefore, each chapter can be used to either obtain a solid understanding of one case and a particular point or serve as a springboard for launching a larger project following a reader's personal interests.

Acknowledgments

This document history has been, from its inception, the epitome of collaborative work. We are tremendously grateful to everyone who made it possible for us to see our vision through to publication. First and foremost we thank our contributors, wonderful scholars all, who shared their expertise and time to create a unique and valuable resource. They responded with enthusiasm to our project and with good humor when we pressed them to meet deadlines or make changes. We also wish to thank the many fine individuals at Pearson who made it possible to see this project through to completion. While working on the volumes, Erin O'Connor benefitted greatly from a Bridgewater State College (BSC) for a Faculty and Librarian Research Grant (2009), which provided invaluable course release time. Leo Garofalo appreciates years of generous research support from Connecticut College's R.F. Johnson and Hodgkin Faculty Development Funds.

The following reviewers offered helpful insights and suggestions as the manuscript evolved: Jurgen Buchenau, University of North Carolina, Charlotte; Timothy Coates, The College of Charleston; Paula De Vos, San Diego State University; Kevin Gannon, Grand View College; Erick D. Langer, Georgetown University; Stephen E. Lewis, California State University, Chico; Nichole Sanders, Lynchburg College; Joan E. Supplee, Baylor University; Angela Vergara, California State University, Los Angeles; Rick Warner, Wabash College; and Gregory Weeks, University of North Carolina, Charlotte.

College students remain at the heart of this document history. Striving to make Latin American history come alive for our students led us to create these volumes. We especially thank the students—too many to name individually—who tested all or parts of these volumes in classes. Erin thanks her BSC classes on Colonial Latin America (2008 & 2009), Modern Latin America (2008), and Gender, Race, and Nation in Latin America (2009). Leo thanks his Connecticut College classes on Rebellion and Revolutions in Latin America (2008), Modern Latin America (2008 & 2010), Introduction to Latin American and Caribbean History (2008 & 2010), and Crossing the Ocean: Spain and the Americas (2009).

Finally, we must acknowledge our debts to our families and friends who sacrificed time with us so that we could work on this project, and who put up with hearing about it more than they probably wanted to. Friends, you know who you are. And to Eliana Iberico Garofalo, Natalia Garofalo-Iberico, Howard Brenner, Samuel Brenner, and (last but of course not least) Anya Brenner: You are, as you know, always and forever in our hearts.

Erin E. O'Connor, *Bridgewater State College*

Leo J. Garofalo, *Connecticut College*

Maps

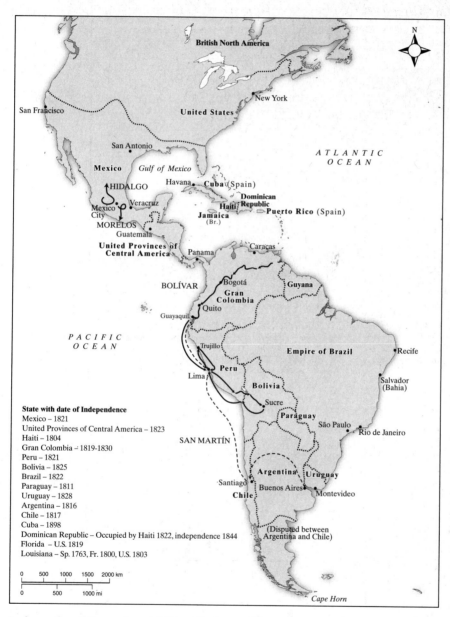

British North America

San Francisco

United States

New York

San Antonio

ATLANTIC OCEAN

Mexico *Gulf of Mexico*

↑HIDALGO   Havana· **Cuba** (Spain)

Veracruz

Dominican Republic

Mexico City   **Haiti** ·

MORELOS   **Jamaica** (Br.)   **Puerto Rico** (Spain)

Guatemala

United Provinces of Central America   Panama   Caracas

BOLÍVAR   Bogotá

Gran Colombia   **Guyana**

Quito

Guayaquil

PACIFIC OCEAN

Trujillo   **Empire of Brazil**   ·Recife

Peru

Lima   **Bolivia**

Salvador (Bahia)

Sucre

Paraguay

São Paulo

SAN MARTÍN   Rio de Janeiro

State with date of Independence
Mexico – 1821
United Provinces of Central America – 1823
Haiti – 1804
Gran Colombia – 1819-1830
Peru – 1821
Bolivia – 1825
Brazil – 1822
Paraguay – 1811
Uruguay – 1828
Argentina – 1816
Chile – 1817
Cuba – 1898
Dominican Republic – Occupied by Haiti 1822, independence 1844
Florida – U.S. 1819
Louisiana – Sp. 1763, Fr. 1800, U.S. 1803

Argentina   **Uruguay**

Santiago   Buenos Aires·

Chile   Montevideo

(Disputed between Argentina and Chile)

0   500   1000   1500   2000 km

0   500   1000 mi

Cape Horn

Independence Struggles and New Nations, 1811–1839

Source: Adapted from John Charles Chasteen, *Born in Blood and Fire: A Concise History of Latin America,* 2nd ed. (New York: W. W. Norton, ©2006), 109, 131.

Countries of Modern Latin America

Introduction

"Doing" Latin American History in the Era of Nation States

There are many different ways of approaching and studying history. To make sense of the past, professional historians not only specialize in particular world regions, but they also focus on specific types of history—such as political, cultural, economic, military, or social history. Historians also differ in their specific focus within a field of study. For example, some political historians might examine history from the perspective of central government officials, whereas others explore how ordinary men and women experienced and influenced politics. Similarly, many economic historians trace how goods were produced and exchanged between different world regions, but there are numerous others who study labor relations. Social and cultural historians often look at history from the perspectives of less-powerful groups in past societies, or the interactions between powerful and less-powerful individuals and groups, and their work often overlaps at least as much with anthropology as it does with other fields of history.

Documenting Latin America focuses on the central themes of race, gender, and politics. These themes are especially important for understanding and evaluating the history of Latin America, where identities were forged out of the conflicts, negotiations, and intermixing of peoples from Europe, Africa, and the Americas. Over time, and due largely to unequal power relations that were central features of colonialism, racial ideologies developed to justify European domination over indigenous and African peoples. Gender, too, played a pivotal role in determining

colonial experiences: Not only were women denied access to political (and often economic) power, but Spanish colonizers also used gender ideas to justify their dominance over non-European peoples. Race and gender inequalities continued to haunt Latin American nations in the aftermath of independence; in fact, one often finds greater constraints on indigenous peoples, Afro-Latin Americans, and women of all classes and races *after* independence than during the colonial period. By the mid-twentieth century, based largely on non-Europeans' and women's own initiatives, state officials began to offer some political rights and social reforms to previously marginalized groups. Today, women and non-Europeans still face serious challenges with sexism and racism, but they have also carved out important niches for themselves in Latin American national politics.

Documentary sources presenting gender, race, and politics, therefore, provide readers with the tools to develop a broad understanding of the course of Latin American social, cultural, and political history. However, the purpose of focusing on a particular theme or angle of history is not to ignore other avenues of exploration. Although historians specialize in particular fields of historical inquiry, every scholar must explain how her or his specialty relates to other fields in order to create a meaningful narrative about the past. The same occurs with chapters in this volume: The histories of race and gender explored in the ensuing chapters also draw on labor, biographical, economic, and military histories to offer a full and balanced picture of Latin America.

Powerful Terms, Terms of Power

Gender. Race. State. Empire. Nation. Subaltern. Elite. All of these are central concepts developed in *Documenting Latin America*. However, none of these terms are simple or static; instead, they are complex and change over time. Furthermore, scholars sometimes disagree on how to define terms and how they function in history. Therefore, it is important to discuss how the editors and contributors of these volumes define, approach, and engage with core terminology throughout the chapters of this collection of primary-source documents.

Politics, Power, and Belonging: States, Empires, and Nations

When one thinks of the state, it is typically state institutions, such as ministries of finance or Superior Courts, that come to mind, or perhaps the state officials who administer these organizations at the central, regional, and local levels. Members of a country, however, sense that the state is more than just institutions and administrators: Many United States citizens, for instance, take particular pride in living under a state that they believe advances the rule of law, equality before the law, justice, and freedom. All states are comprised of two components that operate simultaneously: The *state system* includes government infrastructure, the administrative hierarchy, and policies; equally important, the *state idea* indicates a set of ideologies aimed at legitimizing a given ruling regime.[1] To function, a state system requires a significant portion of the population to accept the state idea, and no state idea can succeed long term if a viable state system is lacking. This description of the state can help readers to understand two central features of Latin American politics since 1500 that are apparent in historical documents. First, the state is made up of a series of practices that institutionalize unequal power relations, whether between local and central government officials, between state authorities and the poor, or between men and women.

Second, although the poor, non-Europeans, and women were excluded from government institutions throughout most of history, the existence of state ideas that required some degree of ideological acceptance gave less-powerful peoples opportunities to interact with, take advantage of, and even shape the state. Many of the chapters in these volumes reveal ways in which both the powerful and the humble played roles in the historical development of Latin American politics and states. Latin America also underwent a shift from *empires* in the pre-Hispanic and colonial periods to *nation states* following independence. As with the broader concept of the state, *empires* and *nation states* are terms that require explicit discussion and definition.

Latin America's colonial history encompasses a period when Portuguese and Spanish emperors ruled almost all of the western hemisphere's territory, population, and wealth (mines, plantations, taxes, and tribute). Even before the arrival of Europeans, imperial rulers dominated the most densely populated regions of the Americas, with the Aztecs controlling the large urban centers of the Valley of Mexico and the Incas presiding over the peasant populations of the Andes. On the most basic level, the term *empire* describes the political organization of a collection of states and territories ruled by an emperor. Empires primarily fostered vertical links between subjects and the emperor, that is, between the ruled and the ruler, rather than favoring horizontal ties that bring together regions, unite competing social sectors, or reconcile the elite groups dominant in each jurisdiction. In fact, a key strength of the Iberian empires was their ability to maintain a level of competition, antagonism, and even distrust among subjects. Competition and overlapping jurisdictions ensured that individual subjects and different sectors or institutions depended on the mediation and favor offered by the imperial administration and, ultimately, the king or queen.[2] The documents collected in Volume 1 of *Documenting Latin America* showed how Spain and Portugal extended their imperial power into the Americas and built institutions by combining European models with local

---

[1]Philip Abrams, "Notes on the Difficulty of Studying the State (1977)," *Journal of Historical Sociology* 1, no. 1 (March 1988): 58–89.

[2]Henry Kamen, *Empire: How Spain Became a World Power, 1492–1763* (New York: Harper Collins, 2003).

indigenous customs and by drawing on the traditions established by Europeans, Africans, and missionary colonizers. Iberian imperial policies simultaneously favored and bolstered the dominance of wealthy European men while still providing the poor, non-Europeans, and women with some ways to protect and advance their interests. Particularly important to the state idea of the colonial period was the notion that the monarch was a compassionate and protective paternal figure who was concerned with the plight of all subjects living within the empire. If monarchies lost this legitimacy and subjects questioned their benevolence, European empires would lose much of their power and hold over Latin American populations.

Contradictory and coercive, the Iberian colonial states were also remarkably enduring. When they finally dissolved in the early nineteenth century, these massive European empires were replaced with (in most cases smaller) *nation states*. Benedict Anderson transformed the study of nations and nationalisms when he identified modern nations as *imagined communities*, a term still frequently used among scholars. Anderson asserted that all modern nations are communities because a critical mass of each nation's members not only identify themselves with a particular territory or government, but they also possess a strong sense of belonging together due to shared language, customs, and values. This community, however, is *imagined* rather than real because all national territories are too large for members to all know each other directly, and because class, race, and gender divisions preclude a natural sense of unity.[3] When scholars discuss *modern nation states* in any part of the world, they are referring to large (usually contiguous) territories governed by a central state, in which a significant or particularly powerful portion of the population is convinced that members of the territory form a single national community. The state system—clear leadership, laws, infrastructure, and monetary systems—is combined with the patriotic sentiment of the nation. In fact, nationalism often provided the state idea through which central government authorities sought to

increase and legitimize their power.[4] Though nations are part of modern history—the earliest date back to the late eighteenth century—they often claim to be ancient and to build on a long-standing and natural cultural identity. Yet the question of national culture is problematic, because all nations are made up of people of many different customs, religions, and even languages. Therefore, one must always ask: Whose culture becomes the national culture? How and why are other cultures excluded, and with what implications for the marginalized groups? The answer to these questions is often the story of interethnic and gender domination. In Latin America, race and gender divisions threatened to undermine nationalistic claims by revealing the exclusive nature of the state and enduring hierarchical social practices, which did not allow women and non-whites full membership in the nation state. The struggle to overcome interethnic and gender divisions in Latin America has been a long process that remains incomplete.

Identity and Power: Gender and Race, Subaltern and Elite

Every individual in the modern world is shaped by his or her race, gender, and relative economic and social power. These forces are so prominent that they often seem natural or straightforward, but they are, in fact, quite complicated. Even some scholars, for example, associate gender only with women, and race exclusively with peoples of non-European heritage. However, men as well as women live gendered lives, and peoples of European descent are influenced by their racial identities—albeit not in the same ways as non-Europeans. Moreover, although one can find consistencies in race and gender ideologies over time, the meaning given to these identities is both culturally specific and historically dynamic. In short, race and gender are constructed identities rather than biological categories.

Genetic studies make clear that biogenetically distinct races do not exist: Races are cultural

---

[3]Benedict Anderson, *Imagined Communities: Reflections on the Origins and Spread of Nationalism,* rev. ed. (New York: Verso, 1992 [1983]).

[4]For a good discussion of the state in the nation state, see E. J. Hobsbawm, *Nations and Nationalism since 1780: Programme, Myth, and Reality* (New York: Cambridge University Press, 1990).

inventions that respond to specific ideologies and historical circumstances (e.g., justifying conquest, coercing laborers, imposing religious conversion). In the most basic sense, race divides humans into distinct groups based on their supposed inherited physical and behavioral differences. Starting in the fifteenth century, Europeans and their American-born descendants developed a notion of race that reflected their attitudes and beliefs about the African, American, and Asian peoples they were encountering. Iberian colonizers typically believed that birth determined a person's physical and intellectual characteristics; they even thought temperament derived from race. However, to establish an individual's race, the state or those around an individual relied on cultural markers like religion, dress, occupation, place of birth, language, marriage partner, and the like.[5] Thus, race functioned more like what one might call ethnicity today. Consequently, by changing or manipulating the emphasis within a combination of these characteristics a person's race might change! By the time Latin American nations achieved independence, modern ideas about race as a biological category had begun to take shape, and peoples of European descent used these notions to identify some so-called races as inherently superior (European or "white") or inferior (indigenous, African, and Asian). Such assertions were problematic in Latin American nation states, however, as the supposedly inferior peoples were also purportedly fellow members in the imagined community of the nation; in some cases these groups even accounted for the majority of the nation's population. The historical figures and authorities presented in these volumes debated and deployed these markers of difference in a variety of ways, and one can trace how the significance of race developed over the course of time.

Gender functions similarly to race in the study of history, as it, too, is socially constructed and has been used to justify unequal power relations. Joan Scott developed a two-tiered definition of gender, which many historians continue to use as a foundation for gender analysis in the twenty-first century.[6] Scott asserted that on one level gender is "a constitutive element of social relationships based on perceived differences between the sexes." This suggests that gender informs both relations between the sexes and also how individuals and societies make sense of assumed sexual differences. Many times, the supposedly inherent differences between men and women were (and are) socially structured—in other words, girls were taught to behave one way, boys another. By the time individuals reach maturity, these behaviors seem natural and timeless rather than learned. Scott's definition of gender also has another important part to it. She argues that gender is "a primary field within which or by means of which power is articulated." Here, she means that gender ideologies (assumptions about male and female qualities, or parental versus childlike qualities) can be manipulated by individuals and groups either to express or try to increase their power over others. Gender often functions this way in politics, and not only when women are involved. For example, when state officials use ideas about manliness to exclude certain adult men from political participation, they are using gender ideas to justify their actions. Gender thus encompasses ideas about how men and women are supposed to act and it influences relationships, including political relationships, between individuals or groups.

Therefore, gender is one of the essential building blocks of all societies and states, and understanding how gender functioned and changed over time is a crucial part of studying history. In Latin America, for example, colonial state officials identified indigenous peoples as *niños con barbas* (bearded children) who, although they might achieve physical maturity, were ostensibly perpetual children in other ways. This gendered racial notion justified the unequal power relations between colonizers and colonized peoples; although this state-sanctioned

---

[5] Magnus Mörner offers one of the fundamental discussions of race in the Americas. His work still represents an important point of departure for any study of ethnicity, class, and social identity construction in the Americas. Magnus Mörner, *Race Mixture in the History of Latin America* (Boston: Little, Brown, 1967).

[6] Joan Wallach Scott, "Gender: A Useful Category for Historical Analysis," in *Gender and the Politics of History* (New York: Columbia University Press, 1988), 28–50.

interethnic paternalism did not always work in practice as it was meant to in theory, as many chapters in Volume 1 show. Women continued to be excluded from politics after independence, but their marginalization held new meaning in the republican era. Denying women political rights helped to define the political nation as a male domain, and excluding women served to obfuscate class and race divisions between men in a given nation. Gender and race, therefore, upheld the politics of exclusion in Latin America just as they did in the United States and other parts of the world. And, just as in other societies, one can still find ways that these notions limit the rights and power of women and non-whites in contemporary Latin America.

Wealthy European men—the *elite*—benefited the most from gender and race ideologies, which helped them to rule over, exploit, and marginalize other groups. In many ways, *elite* is a clear-cut term that refers to those individuals or groups who dominate politics, the economy, and society. However, different kinds of elites existed, and it is important that one avoid the trap of thinking that elites were somehow uniform or homogenous. For example, members of the intellectual elite, whose ideas greatly influenced society and politics, were not necessarily the wealthiest men or those in political power. Different elite groups also competed with each other over economic and political power, and they often had divergent ideas about how society, the economy, and politics should be structured. Another potential division was between political and religious elites: In certain periods and locations, Church and state officials allied closely, whereas in other circumstances these two elite groups were at odds with each other. Even within the Catholic Church, deep divisions surfaced between the regular clergy (who belonged to religious orders) and lay clergy (who ministered to the members of a diocese); in many instances, these different Church officials fought bitterly over the jurisdiction of particular populations. Sometimes elite factions even made alliances (usually brief) with less-powerful peoples in order to beat a competing elite faction.

At the other end of identity and power politics one finds *subaltern* peoples. Although a sophisticated field of subaltern studies exists, in these volumes the term *subaltern* refers simply to those groups that were outside of the dominant power structure.[7] Most obviously, subalterns included indigenous peoples, Afro-Latin Americans, and peoples of mixed racial descent. However, it also included poor people of European descent and women across class and race lines. It is important to note that some individuals could be considered subaltern in some circumstances but part of the dominant power structure in others. Context mattered. An elite woman of European descent was part of the dominant race and class when considering her social status and power over non-Europeans in many ways, yet, throughout most of Latin American history such a woman was excluded from political power and had limited rights to make decisions about the property she owned. Another example would be a male *cacique* (local indigenous leader) during the colonial period: in his case, he would be part of the political structure, at least at the local level, from which the elite woman was excluded. He also enjoyed privileges, exercised power over indigenous commoners, and could participate in commerce. But he was still subaltern because he was excluded from the higher ranks of political power and there were ways that his status was lower than Spanish men of lesser wealth. In cases like these, whether an individual would be considered subaltern or part of the dominant group depended on the nature of one's historical inquiry. The topic being explored, the forms of sociopolitical power under scrutiny, and the broad questions one is trying to answer, for example, determine which groups should be included in the category of subaltern or elite with any given chapters of this documentary history. Furthermore, subaltern groups or individuals did not necessarily share the same problems or goals, and sometimes they clashed

---

[7]South Asian studies groups coined this phrase for history from below. See Gayatri Chakravorty Spivak, "Can the Subaltern Speak?" in *Marxism and the Interpretation of Culture,* ed. Cary Nelson and Lawrence Grossberg (Urbana: University of Illinois Press, 1988), 271–313. A variety of scholars apply subaltern studies to Latin America; see Ileana Rodríguez, ed., *The Latin American Subaltern Reader* (Durham, NC: Duke University Press, 2001). Historians debate how to take Latin America's subalterns into account; a good discussion of this is Eric Van Young, "The New Cultural History Comes to Old Mexico," *Hispanic American Historical Review* 79, no. 2 (1999): 211–247.

and competed with each other. In the short term, an individual might improve his or her life through such contests, but in the long term intrasubaltern competition usually served to keep wealthy European men in power.

All of these terms refer to fluid categories and processes in history. They are complex rather than simple and historically adaptable rather than static. All of the terms also focus on individuals' and groups' relative positions with regard to *power*. Instead of thinking of power as absolute or as something that one *holds*, it is more useful—and more historically accurate—to think of power as something that one *exercises*. This distinction is important because it indicates that even though subalterns were (and are) excluded from most formal positions of power, they might still exercise power in significant ways, particularly in an informal or local level capacity. Power exists in a continuum, with different individuals and groups enjoying different kinds and levels of authority. Chapters in *Documenting Latin America* reveal myriad ways that wealthy European men wielded tremendous power and manipulated gender and race ideas to maintain inequalities. At the same time, many chapters allow readers to explore the numerous and sometimes surprising ways that women and peoples of indigenous or African descent manipulated ideologies that were meant to subordinate them in order to advance their personal or collective interests. These tensions, contradictions, and negotiations over gender, race, and politics were driving forces that moved Latin American history forward; they continue to shape the region today.

Getting the Most Out of Primary-Source Documents

Working with primary sources makes history both exciting and daunting. In the chapters to follow, readers will dive into the archives of Latin America's past alongside the historians who worked to make sense of what are sometimes confusing or conflicting accounts. The primary sources in *Documenting Latin America* offer unparalleled perspectives on the views and lives of real men and women who witnessed

or created key moments in Latin American history; nothing will give readers a truer and more in-depth understanding of the past. Making history is actually a process of giving meaning to the written and visual remains of the past. This book requires readers to evaluate the past and draw their own conclusions, maybe even to question or challenge the editors' or contributing scholars' views of the past.

Primary sources include almost any materials that capture the memories and thoughts of people who lived through particular events or periods in the past. In these two volumes on Latin American history, readers will encounter transcriptions of ships' logs, legal codes, scholarly essays, lists of possessions from wills, testimonial life accounts, portraits, and interrogations from court cases. Each source holds within it useful insights and potential pitfalls; the trick is to extract those insights while avoiding many of the pitfalls. Historians typically employ an array of strategies to recognize what the content of these sources means. A basic strategy is to ask: Who created this source, under what circumstances, for what audience, and with what objective in mind? It is also imperative to consider whose voice, or what combination of voices, one "hears" while reading a document or viewing an image. A written source, or even a visual one, may contain input from one or more creators, speaking for themselves or on behalf of others. It is critical to determine this voice and authorship as accurately as possible. These volumes also present readers with information about people marginalized within Latin American society, many of whom were illiterate. Their thoughts and actions may be hidden within the words, impressions, or descriptions expressed by others, providing readers only indirect access to the voices of the marginalized. This raises questions about an author's viewpoint that may be distorting any given document. Such distortions within a source do not mean that one must discount everything one reads; instead, the challenge is to figure out how an author's perspective affects what a reader gleans from a particular document. A good technique for doing this is to question: What other perspectives might there be on an issue or event being presented in this document? It is critical to read documents or images "against the grain" or "between the lines" to discern and analyze the author's perspective, or to learn something that the author might have been hiding or ignoring. Implementing these methods, as well as others learned in class or on one's own while working with the materials, will enable readers to develop their own ways of engaging with Latin American history and sources.

Questions to Ask When Interrogating a Primary Source

1. What type of source is this?
2. What is known about who created it, when, and where?
3. Whom did the author consider the audience for this piece?
4. What views or perspectives were presented? Were other views silenced or challenged?
5. Is there evidence of distortion in the document? How might this be explained?
6. What can the source tell a reader about an event or period in history? What are the limits to what it can reveal?
7. How does this source fit into a bigger historical picture or period? Does it challenge a bigger picture or narrative in any way?

Volume 2: Modernity and Tradition in Latin America since Independence

Volume 2 of *Documenting Latin America* allows readers to explore how Latin American states and societies have developed and changed from the independence period to the twenty-first century. Latin American independence and nation building coincided with the period in which western Europe (and later the United States) industrialized and *modernized*. The leaders of new Latin American nations sought to shed the vestiges of a colonial past that they viewed as illegitimate or backwards while simultaneously trying to emulate the modernity they associated with western nations. Neither of these agendas proved easy, and Latin Americans today still grapple with the tensions between tradition

and modernity. However, the policies, customs, and meanings associated with traditional versus modern life have changed significantly since the early nineteenth century.

Modernity has many meanings, but at the heart of any modernization effort in Latin America is economic development, particularly industrialization. As Volume 1 showed, Iberian colonies in the Americas produced mainly agricultural and mineral goods for consumption in Europe. Nineteenth-century Latin American politicians and businessmen wished to industrialize, but economic and political disruptions in the period precluded the development of industry in most parts of the region. Even in larger nations, like Mexico and Argentina, there was only limited industrial production, and economic modernization in nineteenth-century Latin America typically occurred due to a new wave of agricultural and mineral exports to the industrialized world. It was not until the early to mid-twentieth century that industrial growth began in earnest in large nations, and in some smaller nations industrialization did not occur until the 1960s and 1970s. Economic modernization did not solve Latin American nations' economic problems. Not only do most Latin American economies continue to center on agricultural or mineral production, but industrialization modernized, rather than alleviated, class inequalities and poverty. However, now the poor are as likely to live in shantytowns on the outskirts of major metropolitan regions as they are to live in remote areas of the countryside. Economic development also occurred unevenly within nations, resulting in renewed competition among regional elites and in wide regional disparities with regard to living conditions. Though problematic, economic modernization changed Latin America's place in the global economy. Brazil, for example, is a leading world producer of ethanol and soy beans, and it boasts one of the world's largest economies. It is possible that large nations in what were once peripheral world regions will play a pivotal role in global development in the near future. Whether this new growth will reduce extreme poverty within these nations, however, remains to be seen.

Modernization has been political and intellectual as well as economic. In the nineteenth century, modernity meant constitutionalism and the rule of law (at least in theory), and it meant valuing empiricism over religion. However, Latin American politicians and intellectuals heatedly debated the value of modernizing at the expense of long-standing traditions. To some extent, one can trace different nineteenth-century stances on modernity versus tradition through the disagreements between *liberals* and *conservatives*. Latin American *liberals* embraced European-style modernity by advocating free trade, individualism, equality before the law, and a secular state. *Conservatives* tended to protect traditions with their support for higher tariffs, the continuation of privileges for the clergy and military, and a role for the Church in politics and society. Of course, it would be misleading to claim that *liberals* wanted to end all traditions from the colonial period or that *conservatives* merely wanted to return to colonial-style government and society. *Conservatives* as well as *liberals* hoped to modernize their economies and infrastructures, and members of both political parties found it difficult to let go of long-standing sociopolitical distinctions between different groups in their nations.

Both *liberals* and *conservatives* held *citizenship* as a revered right and central feature of their new nations. *Citizenship* is a definitively modern term: In the colonial period, all peoples living within the Iberian colonies, whether *creole* elites or poor Africans and indigenous peoples, were *subjects* of the king. After independence, republican governments emphasized that their nations were made up of citizens who shared equal rights before the law and who participated in the political process through voting and office holding. Not all members of the nation were citizens, particularly in the nineteenth century when property and literacy requirements kept the majority of the poor and non-whites from enjoying rights as full-fledged citizens. Moreover, all nineteenth-century nation states denied women the right to vote. In fact, legislators often considered women's exclusion so obvious that they often failed to make specific mention of it in constitutions. Only gradually would marginalized groups gain political rights.

In the twentieth century, socialist and communist parties formed in many Latin American nations, with their leaders criticizing the negative impacts of capitalist modernization. The establishment of the Soviet Union in 1917 (and communist China in 1949) provided leftist leaders with alternative models for modernization. Cuba and Nicaragua even established socialist governments following revolutionary conflicts (in 1959 and 1979, respectively). However, socialist development did not provide an escape from the pitfalls of modernity. For example, the Cuban government replaced economic dependence on the United States with economic dependence on the Soviet Union. Since the fall of the Soviet Union in 1989, the Cuban economy has floundered and the government leaders have had to incorporate some capitalist forms of exchange. Moreover, socialism failed to eradicate poverty, although in some cases it closed the gap significantly between the rich and the poor (often at the expense of certain individual liberties or choices). Still, the fall of the Soviet Union did not crush the appeal of socialism in Latin America, and in the early twenty-first century socialist governments rose to power in nations such as Venezuela, Bolivia, Nicaragua, and Brazil. Unlike many earlier socialist governments, these new socialist leaders gained national political power through elections rather than revolutions.

Although many Latin Americans hoped to resolve racial problems by modernizing, in practice modernization always seemed to create at least as many problems as it solved. In the nineteenth century, modernizers asserted that all men were created equal; yet document evidence shows that they associated modernity almost exclusively with wealthy men of European descent and customs, and they identified Indians and Afro-Latin Americans as backwards groups that inhibited national progress. In the early to mid-twentieth century, this began to change as political and intellectual leaders redefined the roles and value of non-Europeans within their nations. On the surface, intellectual movements from 1900 to 1950 appeared to glorify indigenous and African contributions to national identity, and they were particularly optimistic that miscegenation would strengthen their nations and lead to greatness. At the same time, many Latin American politicians extended voting rights to the poor and non-European men (and sometimes women). However, upon closer scrutiny these theories of racial harmony reveal ongoing, *modernized* racism and allowed elites to justify continuing racial inequalities. Indigenous and Afro-Latin Americans were not simply passive recipients of these changing racial ideologies, and they actively engaged twentieth-century ideals of miscegenation and supposed *"racial democracy"* to advance their own interests. In doing so, they manipulated state-sanctioned rhetoric in ways unanticipated by elites, forcing state officials to concede to at least some of their demands. Most recently, one finds evidence of non-European peoples in Latin American nations taking political matters into their own hands. Especially noteworthy are numerous indigenous activist movements that greatly influenced national politics in Bolivia, Guatemala, and Ecuador. In Bolivia, indigenous activist Evo Morales was even elected president in 2006.

Gender also played a central and contradictory role in the sociopolitics of Latin American modernization. Colonial notions of female honor remained largely unchanged after independence, and women continued to be excluded from politics. Unlike the sociopolitical marginalization of non-white men, women's exclusion from the political nation raised little debate among nineteenth-century politicians. Because women were barred from political participation in modern industrial nations, Latin American statesmen did not feel pressured to incorporate women into politics. Politicians and scholars tended to associate women with traditional values and domestic life and thought of them as incapable of rational participation in politics. Some nations saw the rise of middle-class women's movements in the late nineteenth century, though only a few women's rights advocates challenged dominant gender norms or demanded the right to vote.

The twentieth century brought significant changes in women's lives, but with mixed impacts. Between 1929 and 1961, women in Latin American countries gained the right to vote in national elections, but those who aspired to political careers still faced an uphill battle against gender stereotypes that portrayed women as incapable of political leadership. Women also appeared more often in the formal economy than ever before, with middle-class women filling jobs as teachers and white-collar workers (at least before marriage), and working-class women accounting for a large percentage of the industrial labor force. Still, working-class women had the double burden of wage labor and housework, typically earned less than their male counterparts, and encountered various forms of sexual harassment and discrimination in the workplace. Middle-class women faced criticism for abandoning their feminine and maternal duties if they wished to continue working after marriage.

Political changes since the middle of the twentieth century favored a gradual rise in women's political clout in Latin America, though problems and limitations persist. Socialist governments in Cuba and Nicaragua proclaimed that they would eradicate sexism as well as class inequalities. However, no government can enforce changes in attitudes, and despite important advances, especially in Cuba, gender inequalities persist in socialist as well as capitalist nations in Latin America. Feminist movements in nonsocialist countries, still made up mainly of middle-class women, have advocated women's political, economic, and reproductive rights with varying degrees of success. Many working-class and non-white women, however, have been wary of aligning themselves with middle-class feminists, instead choosing to join their male peers to fight for better wages, better living conditions, political voice, and dignity. As with non-white men, women's achievements can be measured in terms of political positions and power: One can find numerous examples of women who held (or are holding) high political office in Latin American nations. In Argentina, Nicaragua, Panama, and Chile, for example, voters have elected female presidents, something that has not occurred in the United States at the time of this writing. Yet even these high-achieving women's careers show how the pressures of maternal womanhood make political careers difficult: Most women politicians are either single and childless or older women whose children are already grown.

Volume 2 of *Documenting Latin America* takes readers on a journey to explore how social and political rights have expanded in Latin America over the last two centuries. This process was contentious, inherently uneven, and deeply contradictory; to date, it is a struggle that remains incomplete. Even so, the achievements of women and peoples of non-European descent over the past two centuries have been remarkable. Once barred from participation in even local politics, it is now possible to find women, indigenous peoples, and Afro-Latin Americans in the halls of national governments. Those who find themselves in positions of power face the daunting challenge of moving from the politics of protest, in which they criticized governments, to the politics of power, in which they themselves are responsible for enacting changes that they promised to the majority of their constituents. They must balance loyalty to their subaltern support bases with the necessity of representing all members of their nations. And they must do so within the confines of political systems which are still dominated by white elite men. How well they will succeed is, at this writing, unclear. What is certain, however, is that the historical legacies of race and gender politics still resonate strongly in Latin America today and likely will continue to shape the region for a long time to come.

Section I

The Age of Transformation and Revolt, 1780–1825

The age of transformation and revolt stretched from 1780 to 1825, beginning with peasant and slave revolts that offered radical alternatives to the European colonial systems (best represented by slaves taking over in the new nation of Haiti). The era culminated with *creole*-led forces seizing power in one region after another in order to establish independent republics and forestall a complete overthrow of the political, economic, and social systems. Imaginings of nationhood, citizenship, and political rights began to appear, and they motivated debate, new leaders, and mass movements. Over the course of decades, people from a wide array of class and ethnic backgrounds chose to replace centuries-old empires with nations and imperial subjects with citizens. However, not everything changed: Iberian-descended *creoles* retained many of the colonial-era hierarchies in the new republics, and the economies continued to depend on the exploitation of indigenous people, *castas*, and slaves. In fact, access to courts and legal rights to land, property, and control of children declined for indigenous people and women with the creation of independent nation states in Ibero-America.

This era of change and warfare sprang from a prolonged period of rising class-race tensions and economic hardship. Between 1772 and 1776, Spain's Bourbon monarchy raised the *alcabala* (sales tax) from 2 percent to 4 percent and then to 6 percent. Furthermore, tax collectors installed new customs houses along the Spanish colonies' principal trade routes and began to collect these levies more vigorously. Officials ignored local exemptions and extended the taxes to indigenous-style products—like corn and textiles—angering most colonial residents. Royal courts and officials failed to resolve vigorous protests over the new fiscal measures and tax collectors and magistrates' increasingly frequent practices of imposing their cronies and other outsiders on indigenous communities. Indians, *castas*, and even Spanish *creoles* began to unite more frequently in revolt against what they all denounced as "bad government." Peasant rebellions also increased in both New Spain (Mexico) and Peru: In central Mexico, at least 142 short-term uprisings occurred, mainly in native villages, between 1680 and 1811, and native Andean people rose violently against colonial authorities over a hundred times between 1720 and 1790.

As revolts intensified and grew in size toward the turn of the century, a sense grew within both elite and popular sectors that the government should be responsive to the demands of the populace. Dissatisfied subjects often identified their primary loyalties with administrative regions that would later become nation states. They imagined different ways that politics might be structured, and some envisioned breaking away from Spanish rule altogether. Some of the earliest examples of the potential of these new movements and ways of thinking appeared in Peru. North of Potosí, an illiterate Aymara Indian peasant leader, radicalized by repeated abuses, drew on democratic communal customs of decision making to fight back. In Cuzco, Tupac Amaru II, an educated and Hispanicized indigenous elite, and his wife, Micaela Bastidas, drew on a colonial revival of enthusiasm for the pre-Hispanic Incas to rally Indians and non-Indians to fight the imperial state's impositions. Divided loyalties, however, led royalist Indian nobles, terrified *creoles,* and Spaniards to combine forces to defeat the rebels. Nevertheless, Andean peoples continued to imagine alternatives to foreign domination. Even in the very regions where indigenous leaders and their allies were defeated in the 1780s, Marión's chapter demonstrates that non-elite Andean peoples continued participating in politics and rejoined the fight against foreign rule in later struggles.

Along with the revolt that Tupac Amaru II and Micaela Bastidas started in Peru, the Haitian Revolution (1791–1804) exemplified the potential and transformative nature of these early movements. The revolution in the French Caribbean plantation colony of Saint Domingue (later Haiti) played a huge role in how Iberian *creoles* and people of African heritage viewed independence. With the outbreak of the French Revolution (1789), French colonists fell to fighting each other over the ideas of The Revolution. These divisions provided slaves and ex-slaves an opportunity to revolt in 1791; they cast off their chains of servitude and demanded rights as French citizens, destroying the plantation system in the process. Eventually the military and political leadership of Pierre Dominique Toussaint L'Ouverture and Jean Jacques Dessalines helped definitively end slavery, defeat slave owners and a succession of European powers, and secure full independence. In 1804, Haiti became the second republic in the Americas and the first one ruled by non-Europeans (albeit mostly those of middle or elite sectors). For slave owners and *creoles,* Haiti represented the explosive potential of revolt from below and the danger of elite divisions, opening the way for radical revolution. Throughout the Americas, including the United States, these hopes and fears influenced political and economic decisions. These first anticolonial rebellions proved to be the most radical, and they shook the colonial world.

The wounds were barely healed from these wars when new events in Europe shattered Iberia's hold of its colonies and forced people of varying ethnic and class backgrounds across the Americas to act decisively. Napoleon Bonaparte occupied Portugal in 1807 and Spain in 1808, forcing out the Bourbon monarchs in both kingdoms and placing his brother Joseph on the Spanish throne. *Creoles* rejected Joseph and claimed that sovereignty reverted to the people. Resistance grew in places like Buenos Aires and Caracas, where provisional governments were set up in 1810 claiming to govern for the deposed king. In Caracas the famous *creole* leader, Simón Bolívar, persuaded an 1811 congress to declare full independence; for the next fifteen years he fought and defeated royalist forces, setting up *creole* rule in the republics that would eventually become the nations of Venezuela, Colombia, Ecuador, Peru, and Bolivia. Chapter 2 in this section examines Bolívar's pronouncements and plans for government and nationhood. These documents allow readers to follow Bolívar's thinking about how to treat different groups in society, which influenced several republics' new "social contracts" with their citizens.

In Mexico, the 1808 Napoleonic invasion sparked rebellion and loyalist reaction. On the one hand, royalists seized control of the colonial government on behalf of the deposed king. On the other hand, critics of monarchal rule began to plot. One group of plotters included the *creole* priest, Miguel Hidalgo y Costilla; when his fellow conspirators were detected and captured, he rang his church bells and called on his parishioners to join him in launching a rebellion. Mexican *campesinos* (rural farmers and agricultural workers), long frustrated with late colonial policies, were primed to come together under a leader and take advantage of the apparent divisions among *creoles.* Thus, in 1810, central Mexico's indigenous and *mestizo* peasants rose up first under the banners of Father Hidalgo y Costilla and then continued fighting under the command of a *mestizo* parish priest, José María Morelos. The opening chapter on Morelos focuses on his vision for an alternative to Spanish rule; he appealed to

Dated July 20, 1810, this watercolor depicts *creole* revolutionary general and statesman Simón Bolívar (1783–1830) literally liberating slaves. Initially, Bolívar saw no contradiction between independence from Spain and continuing slavery, but he changed his mind by the second half of the 1810s. Bolívar offered male slaves liberty if they joined his rebel army, but many slaves refused to pursue this perilous route to freedom. After the independence, he expressed fears that Afro-Latin American demands for equality would impose non-white rule and exact revenge on *creoles*. Nevertheless, Bolívar advocated gradual emancipation, resulting in abolition in Venezuela, Peru, and Ecuador in the 1850s. Full emancipation required an extended struggle, involving slave resistance, to overcome the opposition of slave owners and merchants. How is the liberation of the slaves portrayed here? What is the relationship between the slaves and the liberators? What message might this work of art have conveyed in 1810? How does that message relate to the actual progress of slave emancipation in Ibero-America?

Source: Casa-Museo, 20 de Julio de 1810, Bogota, Colombia/The Bridgeman Art Library International.

both progressive *creoles* and poor *campesinos*. *Creoles* and Spanish officers commanded a coalition of militias that eventually suppressed the revolt in 1815, although resistance in many areas was never fully stamped out.

Brazil followed a different path to independence. First, the colony provided a refuge for the Portuguese monarchy and court, fleeing Napoleon; from 1807 until 1821, the Portuguese Crown ruled its empire from Rio de Janeiro. During this time, commerce flourished with the opening up of trade, and the colony developed key institutions like banks, universities, and printing houses. Brazilian *creoles* welcomed these changes, although they resented Britain's domination of trade. When in 1808 the French were driven from Iberia, an assembly of Portuguese *liberals* wrote a new constitution demanding the return of the monarchy, the reinstatement of Lisbon's trade monopoly, and rolling back Brazilian autonomy. Brazil's landowners and urban professionals opposed this "recolonization" and succeeded in persuading the prince regent, Dom Pedro, to remain in Brazil. They convoked a Constituent Assembly and created an independent monarchy in Brazil (1822–1889). In the following years, debates over many issues continued, among them slavery and the status of free people of color. Schultz's chapter brings to life one of the assembly debates in 1823 over race and citizenship in the Empire of Brazil. Although some fighting occurred, Brazil avoided the protracted and destructive wars fought in Mexico and the Andes.

Furthermore, Brazil's *creoles* prevented any fundamental change in the socioeconomic structure in the new nation.

The letters, decrees, and accounts collected in this section reveal how political thought and actions functioned at many levels of society and how many people within these American societies ceased to think in terms of subjects and empires and began to think and act as citizens of nations. Military service in *creole*-led independence movements allowed many *mestizo* men to secure status as citizens alongside their *creole* commanders. Indians, women, and blacks, however, fared much worse, because colonial-style hierarchies endured and became central organizing principles in the new Latin American republics. As the colonial period waned and anticolonial and independence struggles spread, indigenous, *creole,* and *mestizo*

elites began to envision politics and society after European rule. Race relations loomed large in their thoughts, and most independence leaders called for an end to colonial racial divisions and the establishment of equality before the law. In practice, however, independence prolonged legally sanctioned racial inequalities, despite the existence of more egalitarian alternatives. The groups that defended alternative national visions continued their struggles by resisting elite impositions. Historian John Tutino summed up this shift by stating "As the colonial rule ended the contested process of nation-building began."[1]

---

[1]John Tutino, "The Revolution in Mexican Independence: Insurgency and the Renegotiation of Property, Production, and Patriarchy in the Bajío, 1800–1855," *The Hispanic American Historical Review* 78, no. 3 (August 1998): 367.

Chapter 1

Father José María Morelos and Visions of Mexican Independence

Erin E. O'Connor, Bridgewater State College

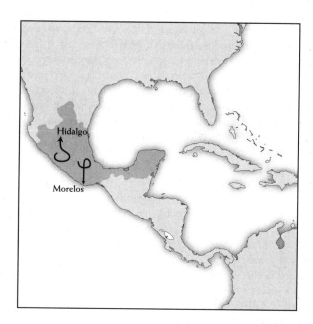

Parish priests leading a violent, multiethnic uprising to overthrow the Spanish colonial government might surprise many readers. Officially, the Catholic Church was supposed to support colonization and keep the populace loyal and obedient to the Crown and its colonial administrators. Fathers Miguel Hidalgo y Costilla and José María Morelos of New Spain (soon to become Mexico) did just the opposite, and their bid for independence earned them enduring fame as the first leaders to imagine and fight for a Mexican nation. Although the priests' actions may have been more extreme than those of other religious officials in the colonial era, there was a long history of priests in colonial Spanish America who were concerned with the plight of the poor and exploited. Still, Hidalgo and Morelos adhered to a more radical vision than other socially concerned priests, calling for an end to slavery and *tribute*, and reforms that would establish Mexico as an independent and representative government. This chapter introduces readers to one of the most important surviving documents from this first struggle for Mexican independence: Morelos's 1813 "Sentiments of the Nation," in which he outlined his vision for the national government he hoped to establish.

The Hidalgo-Morelos movement resulted from a complex set of political, economic, and social factors in early nineteenth-century New Spain. Initially, *creole* responses to the 1808 Napoleonic takeover of the Spanish throne were mixed. Although some powerful Mexico City *creoles* remained loyal to the Crown, other *creole* elites plotted to rise up against the colonial government. One such plot was underway in the Bajío region north of Mexico City in 1810. When authorities discovered the plot, one of the main conspirators, Father Miguel Hidalgo y Costilla, made a preemptive call to arms in his now-famous *Grito de Dolores* (Cry of Dolores) on September 16, 1810. A well-educated *creole* parish priest in the town of Dolores, Hidalgo expected other *creoles* to join his protest when he made his call to arms. Instead, indigenous and *mestizo campesinos* answered his call, and his army quickly swelled to tens of thousands.

The agrarian poor in the Bajío consisted mainly of workers on large estates with some autonomous peasant communities mixed in. Racially, this was mostly a *mestizo* region, and even indigenous peoples living there were fairly Hispanicized in their language, customs, and dress. Although it had not been one of the more tumultuous regions during the colonial period, eighteenth- and early nineteenth-century changes made the Bajío potentially volatile. Eighteenth-century population growth put pressure on peasants and rural workers, who competed with each other for limited land and jobs. These problems were compounded in the early nineteenth century when estate owners expelled some resident workers following a series of crop failures. Former estate workers resented both regional elites and the colonial system that failed

to provide them with relief. Hidalgo's proposals offered a more tolerable government system that would provide tangible benefits for the poor, such as the abolition of slavery and *tribute,* and land reform. For *creole* elites, the Hidalgo insurrection brought to life their greatest fears: that the exploited majority might rise up against their so-called superiors. *Creole* and Spanish elites set aside their differences and banded together to defeat the insurgents. In March of 1811, loyalist forces captured and executed Hidalgo, but his army marched on.

Father José María Morelos took charge of the movement after Hidalgo's death until his own capture and execution in 1815. Morelos, sometimes referred to as a *mestizo* and at other times as an Afro-*mestizo*, was born to a poor family and worked as a muleteer before studying to become a priest. He joined Hidalgo's cause in 1811 and rose to prominence as an intelligent and able leader. Morelos tried, with some success, to bring greater order to the committed but largely undisciplined rebel forces. Less effectively, he also attempted to draw more middle- and upper-class *creoles* into the movement. *Creole* elites considered the insurrection an unruly "Indian" mob, despite Morelos's attempts to win them over with familiar political ideals. In December 1815, loyalist forces caught and executed Morelos, bringing an end to the first phase of Mexican independence. When independence finally came to the nation in 1822, under the military and political leadership of the Spanish officer Agustín Iturbide, it was a profoundly *conservative* movement that proposed to establish a monarchy and maintain the colonial social hierarchy.

The document "Sentiments of the Nation" allows readers to explore the political ideals through which Morelos attempted to broaden his support base. Although Morelos failed to win over moderates with "Sentiments," and royalist forces defeated the uprising, Hidalgo and Morelos strongly influenced the course of Mexican history. The central issue of land reform that drew so many poor *campesinos* into their armies remained unresolved throughout the nineteenth century, and land conflicts worsened over the long term. Nineteenth-century presidents and Mexico's congress focused on ideals of equality before the law and emulation of European models in politics and the economy while simultaneously pursuing policies that allowed large estates to expand at the expense of indigenous and *mestizo* peasants. Rising *campesino* frustrations with unresponsive governments resulted in a true social revolution in Mexico from 1910 to 1940. Though the 1910 Mexican Revolution fell far short of its promises to the rural poor, it produced land and labor laws that, at least initially, benefited the Mexican poor.

As Mexican politics and society changed from 1821 to 1940, the images of Hidalgo and Morelos also transformed. In order to claim Hidalgo and Morelos as rightful heroes of the independence period, yet without questioning the elitism of nineteenth-century nation state formation, nineteenth-century artists played down the more radical elements of the movements. They often portrayed Hidalgo and Morelos alone, rather than with the poor followers who made up the majority of the movement. They also presented the two leaders in poses similar to those in portraits of more *conservative* independence leaders in Latin America. Consider the first image of Hidalgo, an 1895 etching from the publication *Patria e independencia*. Hidalgo is standing at a desk, surrounded by books and papers to emphasize his scholarly background. In the second image, a "Mexican School" painting of the nineteenth century, Morelos was presented in a calm pose in full and formal attire. In contrast, the image of Hidalgo from Mexico's era of revolutionary state building emphasized the radical and insurgent nature of these movements and heralded the leaders as avenging. It was also painted by one of the most famous muralists in early twentieth-century Mexico, José Clemente Orozco. The mural in which the Hidalgo image appears is located in Guadalajara's Palacio de Gobierno (government palace). Hidalgo appears quite different in the twentieth-century image than in the nineteenth-century portrait, for it was precisely his role in leading Mexico's poor in a radical movement that made

him an ideal hero during the process of revolutionary state building.

The document and images in this chapter capture the complexity of Mexican independence. In particular, they show that Mexico's rural poor were neither fully included in this radical independence movement nor were they summarily defeated at its conclusion. In Mexico, as elsewhere in Latin America, poor non-Europeans were aware of politics and engaged with the struggles and ideals of their times, but they would have to wait at least a century to see elements of their own versions of liberty and justice implemented.

Questions to Consider:

1. What kind of government did Morelos envision? How did he propose that citizenship, rights, and obligations be determined in the new nation?

2. Historians often comment on ways that Morelos infused this document with elements of colonial-style hierarchy. Where do you find such elements in the document? What do you make of the tension between equality and hierarchy in the document?

3. Morelos led a very different kind of movement than Bolívar. How similar or different were his political ideas? Did the two leaders' ideas correspond clearly to the kinds of movements they led? Why or why not?

4. Look carefully at the painting of Morelos. To what extent is Morelos's Afro-*mestizo* heritage apparent in this nineteenth-century portrait? Why?

5. Consider the radical messages of the revolutionary-era painting of Hidalgo. To what extent do you see this radicalism reflected in "Sentiments of the Nation"?

José María Morelos, "Sentiments of the Nation"[2]

1. That America is free and independent of Spain and of all other Nations, Governments, or Monarchies, and it should be so sanctioned, and the reasons explained to the world.
2. That the Catholic Religion is the only one, without tolerance of any other.
3. That all the ministers of the Church shall support themselves exclusively and entirely from tithes and first-fruits (*primicias*), and the people need make no offering other than their own devotions and oblations.
4. That Catholic dogma shall be sustained by the Church hierarchy, which consists of the Pope, the Bishops and the Priests, for we must destroy every plant not planted by God: *minis plantatis quam nom plantabir Pater meus Celestis Cradicabitur*. Mat. Chapt. XV.
5. That sovereignty springs directly from the People, who wish only to deposit it in their representatives, whose powers shall be divided into Legislative, Executive, and Judiciary branches, with each Province electing its representative. These representatives will elect all others, who must be wise and virtuous people . . .
6. [Article 6 is missing from all reproductions of this document.]
7. That representatives shall serve for four years, at which point the oldest ones will leave so that those newly elected may take their places.
8. The salaries of the representatives will be sufficient for sustenance and no more, and for now they shall not exceed 8,000 pesos.
9. Only Americans[3] shall hold public office.
10. Foreigners shall not be admitted, unless they are artisans capable of teaching [their crafts], and are free of all suspicion.
11. That the fatherland shall never belong to us nor be completely free so long as the government is not reformed. [We must] overthrow all tyranny, substituting *liberalism,* and remove from our soil the Spanish enemy that has so forcefully declared itself against the Nation.
12. That since good law is superior to all men, those laws dictated by our Congress must oblige constancy and patriotism, moderate opulence and indigence, and be of such nature that they raise the income of the poor, better their customs, and banish ignorance, rapine, and robbery.
13. That the general laws apply to everyone, without excepting privileged bodies, and that such bodies shall exist within accordance with the usefulness of their ministry.
14. That in order to dictate a law, Congress must debate it, and it must be decided by a plurality of votes.
15. That slavery is proscribed forever, as well as the distinctions of caste, so that all shall be equal; and that the only distinction between one American and another shall be that between vice and virtue.
16. That our ports shall be open to all friendly foreign nations, but no matter how friendly they may be, foreign ships shall not be based in the kingdom. There will be some ports specified for this purpose; in all others, disembarking shall be prohibited, and 10% or some other tax shall be levied upon their merchandise.
17. That each person's home shall be as a sacred asylum wherein to keep property and observances, and infractions shall be punished.
18. That the new legislation shall forbid torture.
19. That the Constitution shall establish that the 12th of December be celebrated in all the villages in honor of the patroness of our liberty, the Most Holy Mary of Guadalupe. All villages shall be required to pay her monthly devotion.
20. That foreign troops or those of another kingdom shall not tread upon our soil unless it be to aid us, and if this is the case, they shall not be part of the Supreme Junta.

---

[2]*Source:* From Gilbert M. Joseph and Timothy J. Henderson, eds., *The Mexico Reader: History, Culture, Politics* (Durham: Duke University Press, 2002), pp. 189–191.

[3]*Source:* This article referred to the fact that Morelos did not want *peninsulares*, or men born in Spain, to hold public office in the new nation.

21. That there shall be no expeditions outside the limits of the kingdom, especially seagoing ones. Expeditions shall only be undertaken to propagate the faith to our brothers in remote parts of the country.

22. That the great abundance of highly oppressive *tributes,* taxes, and impositions should be ended, and each individual shall pay five percent of his earnings, or another equally light charge, which will be less oppressive than the *alcabala* [sales tax], the *estanco* [crown monopoly], the *tribute,* and others. This small contribution, and the wise administration of the goods confiscated from the enemy, shall be sufficient to pay the costs of the war and the salaries of public employees.

23. That the 16th of September shall be celebrated each year as the anniversary of the cry of independence and the day our sacred liberty began, for on that day the lips of the Nation parted and the people proclaimed their rights, and they grasped the sword so that they would be heard, remembering always the merits of the great hero, señor don Miguel Hidalgo y Costilla, and his *compañero,* don Ignacio Allende.

Chilpancingo, 14 September 1813

Father Miguel Hidalgo y Costilla.
Source: Picture Desk, Inc./Kobal Collection.

Father Miguel Hidalgo y Costilla mural by Jose Clemente.
Source: PhotoEdit Inc.

Father José María Morelos.

Source: Museo Nacional de Historia, Mexico City, Mexico/The Bridge-man Art Library International.

Suggested Sources:

There are few primary source documents available by either Hidalgo or Morelos beyond "Sentiments." A short (paragraph-long) series of reforms that Hidalgo decreed in 1810 is available in Benjamin Keen, Robert Buffington, and Lila Caimari, eds., *Latin American Civilization: History and Society, 1492 to the Present,* 8th ed. (Boulder, CO: Westview Press, 2004),

267. Other short documents can be found in Joseph M. Gilbert and Timothy J. Henderson, eds., *The Mexico Reader: History, Culture, Politics* (Durham, NC: Duke University Press, 2002) in the chapter on independence, including conservative views, such as Iturbide's "Plan of Iguala" and Lucas Alamán's description of the Hidalgo followers' siege of Guanajuato.

There are excellent scholarly studies of Mexican independence viewed from below. See John Tutino's pioneering study, *From Insurrection to Revolution in Mexico: Social Bases of Agrarian Violence, 1750–1940* (Princeton, NJ: Princeton University Press, 1989), in which he discusses how threats to *campesino* security led to their support for the Hidalgo-Morelos insurrection. For an update of some of Tutino's analysis that discusses the role of gender in the insurrection, see his article "The Revolution in Mexican Independence: Insurgency and the Negotiation of Property, Production, and Patriarchy in the Bajío, 1800–1855," *Hispanic American Historical Review* 78, no. 3 (1998): 367–418. For the foundations of agrarian protest in early nineteenth-century Mexico, see Eric Van Young's *The Other Rebellion: Popular Violence, Ideology, and the Mexican Struggle for Independence, 1810–1821* (Stanford, CA: Stanford University Press, 2001). Although independence benefited mainly *creole* elites, Mexican peasants were actively involved in the transition from colony to republic. For more information on peasants and politics in early nineteenth-century Mexico, readers should refer to the works of Peter Guardino, including *The Time of Liberty: Popular Political Culture in Oaxaca, 1750–1850* (Durham, NC: Duke University Press, 2005).

Chapter 2

The Many Views of Simón Bolívar

Erin E. O'Connor, *Bridgewater State College*

Simón Bolívar not only played a pivotal role in achieving independence for his Venezuelan homeland, but he also led armies to free Colombia, Ecuador, and Peru from Spanish rule. During and after the wars, Bolívar helped establish new governments, and scholars remember him partly for his broad and idealistic goals for the new nations. Despite the plethora of information about him, it is difficult to connect Bolívar to a clear set of political or social commitments. For example, similar to Thomas Jefferson in the United States, Bolívar initially advocated the abolition of slavery, but he backed away from the proposal when plantation owners resisted. Some of Bolívar's ideas or policies appear so deeply contradictory that it is difficult to feel certain of exactly what "The Liberator" (as many called him) sought to achieve with independence. This chapter allows readers to explore firsthand some of Bolívar's ideas and policies.

Bolívar hailed from Venezuela, a region that was not initially one of the most profitable colonial centers but which had a strong economy by the eighteenth century thanks to its many cacao and sugar plantations. As with all Latin American plantation economies, Venezuelan planters' profits derived from the labor of African and African-descended slaves. By the independence era, race and class deeply divided Venezuelan society with a large slave population and an ever-growing (and frustrated) population of free blacks and *pardos* (dark-skinned peoples of mixed racial descent). Eighteenth-century *creole* elites were at once irritated by Crown policies and wary of upheaval from the so-called lower orders of society. Meanwhile, many free blacks and *pardos* were increasingly stymied by a racial system that set limits on the status and positions to which they could aspire.

Although not the first region in which *creoles* rose up against the colonial state, Venezuela's rebels were among the first to declare independence, in 1811. This declaration, however, marked the beginning rather than the end of the politico-military struggle in Venezuela. The Spanish military in Venezuela replenished its forces from the nearby garrison in Puerto Rico, and most *conservative creoles* remained loyal to the Spanish Crown. Moreover, many *pardos* initially supported Spain because the new constitutions failed to abolish slavery, and its property and literacy requirements left many *pardos* without a direct political voice. These divisions resulted from a colonial social hierarchy that left its mark on both the independence wars and on the new nation.

Bolívar himself was from a wealthy plantation-owning family in the Caracas region. As a boy, he received a *liberal* education, much of it in Europe. Well versed in Enlightenment ideas, Bolívar became one of the first *creoles* to join the struggle against the Crown when Napoleon's armies took over Spain. After initial defeats, he eventually began to win over many *pardos* and *llaneros* (cowboys from the interior, typically of mixed racial descent), which made victory possible against loyalist forces. His combined charisma, intelligence, and military ability explain why he successfully led independence armies throughout much of Spanish South America.

As South American nations achieved independence, Bolívar shifted his role from military leader to

Many paintings of Simón Bolívar portrayed him in military garb. How might Bolívar's pose, clothing, and facial features in this portrait have suggested that he embodied both military ability and the refinement that elites associated exclusively with European origins?

Source: Library of Congress.

statesman, and he helped forge several constitutions and national policies. Although his military campaigns and lofty ideas inspired many *creole* statesmen in the newly independent nations, Bolívar achieved few of his political goals. Originally he wanted a grand confederation of American nations, but in the end he only succeeded in establishing the republic of Gran Colombia in 1822, which later splintered into Venezuela, Colombia, and Ecuador due to regionalism, economic problems, and intraelite competition. The failures and limitations of his grand visions left Bolívar searching for ways to establish enduring political systems. As time passed, Bolívar's political ideas mixed radical Enlightenment ideals with *conservative* plans to continue many colonial practices. His "Message to the Congress of Bolivia," the first document excerpt in this chapter, captures one of Bolívar's attempts to adapt his political visions to meet what he viewed as the obstacles to establishing stable representative governments. Bolívar had just finished drafting a constitution for the new nation of Bolivia (named after him), and this speech recommended a government structure for Bolivia.

The legacy of colonial racial structures also haunted The Liberator. In addition to failing to abolish slavery, Bolívar was unable to terminate Indian *tribute,* the central feature of the colonial System of *Two Republics* in which adult indigenous men paid a head tax to the state. In order to establish equality before the law, Bolívar abolished the tax briefly in Gran Colombia, but the government's financial dependence on the *tribute,* combined with popular resistance to its elimination, left him with no option but to reinstate the tax in 1828 under the title "personal contribution of indigenes."

Although Bolívar made numerous references to racial matters, he never directly addressed gender issues in his public statements. In some ways, this was at odds with his private life: Simón Bolívar had a long-term and open affair with Manuela Saenz, a married woman from Quito. Saenz, considered a great beauty in her youth, had languished in an unhappy marriage from a young age. She and Bolívar became the great loves of each other's lives. Saenz also provided Bolívar with crucial political support: She spied on his opponents and even saved his life on two occasions, earning her the nickname *La Libertadora del Libertador* (The woman liberator of The Liberator). Despite his well-known affair with Saenz, Bolívar rarely made known his views on women's roles in politics and society. This chapter offers two statements that he made about women in his private letters. Although Bolívar rarely discussed gender matters in public, the excerpts suggest that gender ideologies typical of male political leaders of his time informed his ideas about citizenship.

Together, the documents in this chapter, like all of the documents in this section, reveal that the independence era was one of both profound changes and compelling continuities. Military and political officials of the independence period aspired to make a clean break with Spanish rule and to prove that they were capable of putting an end to the colonial inequalities that they identified as unjust, even

This painting of Manuela Saenz hung in Simón Bolívar's house in Caracas. Even though Saenz was both Bolívar's lover and confidant, she spent the last 25 years of her life despised and destitute, selling tobacco and living on Peru's northern coast. She died during a diphtheria epidemic in 1856, and her body was dumped into a mass grave. Her belongings—including most of Bolívar's love letters—were burned. A century and a half later, Saenz is regarded as one of South America's independence heroes.

Source: AP Wide World Photos.

tyrannical. Yet colonial legacies proved harder to transcend than men like Bolívar would have liked. In the realm of race, class, and gender relations, some of the most enduring and troublesome obstacles to the proclaimed goals of independence remained.

Questions to Consider:

1. How did Bolívar define "good government" in these documents? How did he justify his views? Can you find contradictions in these documents about what government should be like or what it should do?

2. What seemed to be Bolívar's greatest concerns when establishing social and political order?
3. How did Bolívar define citizenship, rights, and obligations within these documents? How

did race and gender shape citizenship or citizens' rights and obligations? How different were the documents on citizens' rights and duties?

Simón Bolívar's "Message to the Congress of Bolivia"[1]

Lima, May 25, 1826

. . . Legislators! Your duty calls you to resist the blows of two monstrous foes that do battle with each other reciprocally, both of which will attack you simultaneously: Tyranny and anarchy form a vast ocean of oppression surrounding a tiny island of freedom that is perpetually pounded by the violence of the waves and hurricanes that seek unremittingly to sink her. Behold the sea you hope to traverse in a fragile boat, its pilot utterly unskilled.

This draft of a constitution for Bolivia proposes four Political Powers, one having been added, without thereby complicating the classical division of all previous constitutions. The Electoral Power has been given powers not encompassed in other governments considered among the most *liberal*. These powers approach those commonly featured in a federal system. It has seemed to me to be not only convenient and practical but also easy to grant to the immediate representatives of the people the privileges most sought by the citizens of that particular department, province or canton. There is no higher priority for a citizen than the election of his legislators, magistrates, judges, and pastors. The electoral colleges of each province represent their specific needs and interests and serve to expose infractions of the laws and the abuses of magistrates. I dare say, with some conviction, that this system of representation features the rights enjoyed by local governments in confederations. In this way, government has acquired additional guarantees, renewed popular support, and new justifications for being regarded as preeminent among the most democratic governments.

Each ten citizens appoint an elector, so that the nation is represented by a tenth of its citizens. All that is required is ability, nor is it necessary to own property to exercise the august function of sovereign, but the electors must know how to write down their votes, sign their names, and read the laws. They must practice a trade or a craft that will guarantee an honest living. The only disqualifying factors are crime, idleness, and total ignorance. Knowledge and honesty, not money, are the requirements for exercising public authority.

The Legislative Body is constituted so as to guarantee harmony among its parts; it will not stand forever divided for lack of a judge to provide arbitration, as happens where there are only two chambers. Since there are three branches, conflict between two is resolved by the third, the question being argued by the two contesting sides, with an impartial third side deciding the issue. In this way, no useful law will be rejected, or at least it will have been tested once, twice, and a third time before this happens. In all negotiations between two adversaries, a third is appointed to settle disputes. Would it not be absurd, in matters so crucial to society, to dispense with this provision dictated by imperious necessity? The chambers will thus observe toward one another the mutual respect necessary to preserve the unity of the entire body, which must conduct its deliberations calmly, wisely, and with restrained passion. You will tell me that in modern times congresses have been composed of two houses. This is because in England, which has served as the model, the nobility and the common people had to be represented in two chambers. And if the same procedure was followed in North America, where there was no nobility, it is likely that their habit of being under English rule inspired that imitation. The fact is that two deliberating bodies will inevitably lead to perpetual conflict . . .

[1]*Source:* From *El Libertador: Writings of Bolíva*, translated by Frederick H. Fornoff, edited by David Bushnell, 1900w from Chp. "The Bolivian Constitution," p. 54 © 2003 by Oxford University Press, Inc. By permission of Oxford University Press, Inc.

Under our constitution, the president of the republic is like the Sun, immovable at the center of the universe, radiating life. This supreme authority should be permanent, because in systems without hierarchies, a fixed point around which magistrates and citizens and men and events revolve is more necessary than in other systems. Give me a fixed point, said an ancient, and I will move the earth. For Bolivia, this point is a president for life. In him, all order originates, even though he lacks the power to act. He has been beheaded so that no one will fear his intentions, and his hands have been tied so that he can harm no one.

The president of Bolivia is endowed with powers similar to those of the American executive, but with restrictions beneficial to the people. His term of office is the same as that of the presidents of Haiti. I have chosen as the model for Bolivia the executive of the most democratic republic in the world . . .

The president of Bolivia will be even less a threat than the president of Haiti, since the mode of succession offers surer prospects for the health of the state. Moreover, the president of Bolivia is denied all influence: he does not appoint magistrates, judges, or ecclesiastical dignitaries at any level. This reduction in executive power has never been tried in any duly constituted government . . .

The constitutional restrictions on the president of Bolivia are the severest ever known: his meager powers only allow him to appoint the ministers of departments of the treasury, peace, and war, and to command the army. That is the extent of his power . . .

The president of the republic appoints the vice president to administer the state and be his successor. This provision avoids elections, which produce the scourge of republics, anarchy. Anarchy is the instrument of tyranny and the most immediate and terrible of dangers in popular governments. Compare the orderly succession of rulers occurring in legitimate monarchies with the terrible crises provoked by these events in a republic.

The vice president must be the purest of men. This is crucial, because if the president does not appoint a righteous citizen, he must fear him as an enemy incarnate and suspect even his most hidden ambitions. This vice president must strive to win through his good services the credibility he needs to exercise the highest functions and to merit the greatest award given by the nation—supreme power. The legislative body and the people will demand high skills and abilities of this official, as well as blind obedience to the laws of freedom.

Heredity being the principle perpetuating monarchical regimes, and this is so throughout the world, how much more useful would the method I propose be for determining the succession of the vice president? What if hereditary princes were chosen by merit, and not randomly, and instead of squandering their lives in idleness and ignorance, they were placed at the head of the administration? They would without a doubt be more enlightened monarchs and bring prosperity to their people. Yes, Legislators, the monarchies that govern the earth have been validated by the principle of heredity that makes them stable and by the unity that makes them strong. Thus, even though a sovereign prince may have been spoiled as a child, cloistered in his palace, educated by flattery, and driven by every passion, this prince, whom I would make so bold as to call the travesty of man, has authority over human beings because he preserves the order of things and the subservience of his subjects through the uninterrupted exercise of power and consistent action. Then consider, Legislators, that these great advantages are embodied in the *president for life in the hereditary succession by the vice president*.

The Judicial Power that I propose enjoys absolute independence: nowhere else does it enjoy as much. The people present the candidates, and the legislature chooses the individuals who will make up the courts. If the Judicial Power does not come into being in this manner, it cannot possibly maintain its integrity, which is the safeguard of individual rights. These rights, Legislators, constitute the freedom, equality, and security that are guaranteed in the social contract. True *liberal* constitution rests in the civil and criminal codes, and the most terrible tyranny is that exercised by the courts through the all-powerful instrument of the law. . . .

It was to be expected, according to the sentiments of modern times, that we would prohibit the use of torture to attain confessions and that we would reduce the time allowed for motions in the intricate labyrinth of the appellate courts . . .

The responsibility of government officials is written into the Bolivian constitution in the most explicit language. Without responsibility, without some coercion, the state is chaos. I will be so bold as to ardently urge the legislators to enact strong, definitive laws concerning this important matter. Everyone speaks of responsibility, but it goes no further than the lips. There is no responsibility, Legislators. The magistrates, judges, and other officials abuse their powers because there is no rigorous procedure for controlling the agents of the administration. Meanwhile, it is the citizens who are the victims of this abuse. I would recommend a law prescribing a strict and formal annual accounting of the actions of each official.

The most perfect guarantees have been written into this draft: *Civil liberty* is the only true freedom; the others are nominal or of little importance insofar as they affect the citizens. The *security of the individual* has been guaranteed, this being the purpose of society and the source of all other guarantees. As for *property rights*, these will depend on the civil code that in your wisdom you will compose with all dispatch for the happiness of your fellow citizens. I have left intact the law of all laws—*equality*. Without this, all guarantees, all rights perish. To ensure equality, we must make every sacrifice, beginning with infamous slavery, which I have laid at her feet, covered in shame.

Legislators! Slavery is the violation of every law. The law that would seek to preserve it would be a sacrilege. What possible justification can there be for its perpetuation? From whatever perspective you consider this crime, I cannot persuade myself that any Bolivian could be depraved enough to want to legitimize this most abominable violation of human dignity. One man owned by another! A man regarded as property! One of God's images hitched to the yoke like a beast! Let someone tell us, where do these usurpers of men file their titles of ownership? They were not sent to us by Guinea, because Africa, devastated by fratricide, can only export crime . . .

Legislators! I will now make reference to the matter my conscience forbade me to include. In a political system there should be no preference for one religion over another, because according to the wisest doctrines, the fundamental laws are guarantees of political and civil rights. And since religion has no relevance to these rights, it is inherently indefinable in the social order, belonging rather to the moral and intellectual order. Religion governs man in his house, in his private space, and in his heart. Religion alone has the right to examine his conscience. The laws, on the other hand, observe the surface of things; they have jurisdiction only outside the citizen's home. Applying these considerations, is there any way the state can govern the conscience of subjects, enforce the observation of religious laws, and offer reward or punishment, when the courts are in Heaven, when God is judge? Only the Inquisition could stand for them in this world. Do we want to see a return of the Inquisition[?] . . .

. . . popular sovereignty [is] the sole legitimate authority of nations . . .

{T}he Sovereignty of the People [is] the sole legitimate authority of any nation.

Bolívar's Statements on Women, Independence Movements, and Politics[2]

Bolívar's description of female combatants in the wars for independence

. . . even the fair sex, the delights of humankind, our amazons have fought against the tyrants of San Carlos with a valor divine, although without success. The monsters and tigers of Spain have shown the full extent of their cowardice of their nation. They have used their infamous arms against the innocent feminine breasts of our beauties; they have shed their blood. They have killed many of them and they loaded them with chains, because they conceived the sublime plan of liberating their beloved country!

[2]*Source:* From Evelyn Cherpak, "The Participation of Women in the Independence Movement of Gran Colombia, 1780–1830," in Asuncion Lavrin, ed., *Latin American Women: Historical Perspectives* (Westport: Greenwood Press, 1978), pp. 222, 229–230.

Bolívar's letter to his sister, María Antonía, regarding women and politics (1826)

I warn you not to mix in political business nor adhere to or oppose any party. Let opinion and things go along although you believe them contrary to your way of thinking. A woman ought to be neutral in public business. Her family and her domestic duties are her first obligations. A sister of mine ought to observe perfect indifference in a country which is in a state of dangerous crisis and in which I am viewed as the point at which opinions meet.

Suggested Sources:

Readers generally interested in the independence era could start by exploring John Lynch's classic study of the period, *The Spanish American Revolution, 1808–1826*, 2nd ed. (New York: W.W. Norton, 1986); or Jaime E. Rodríguez O., *The Independence of Spanish America* (New York: Cambridge University Press, 1998). Both books offer overviews of important themes and issues.

For an English-language translation of major sources by Bolívar that includes both public statements and private letters, see David Bushnell, ed., *El Libertador: Writings of Simón Bolívar*, trans. Frederick H. Fornoff (New York: Oxford University Press, 2003). For a biography of The Liberator that includes a discussion of developing historiography around this pivotal figure who looms so large over Spanish American Independence, see John Lynch, *Simón Bolívar: A Life* (New Haven, CT: Yale University Press, 2007). To consider South American independence from female perspectives, see Evelyn Cherpak, "The Participation of Women in the Independence Movement of Gran Colombia, 1780–1830," in *Latin American Women: Historical Perspectives*, ed. Asuncion Lavrin (Westport, CT: Greenwood Press, 1978), 219–234. Sarah Chambers provides a probing analysis of Saenz's political views, focusing on the years following Bolívar's death, in her article, "Republican Friendship: Manuela Saenz Writes Women into the Nation, 1835–1856," *Hispanic American Historical Review* 81, no. 2 (May 2001): 225–258.

Chapter 3

Forging a Guerrilla Republic

Javier F. Marión, Emmanuel College, Boston

When still a teenager, the adventurous José Santos Vargas joined the anticolonial struggle as a guerrilla combatant and rebel scribe. He later wrote about those tumultuous years when he and other rural people from humble backgrounds helped establish a guerrilla republic and drive the Spanish out of the Andes. The Spanish American wars for independence were seminal moments in the history of the nations they created. Besides establishing political boundaries, the *revoluciones*, as they were called, served as a sort of crucible that legitimated the existence of the new nations and provided ideological parameters that informed their respective citizens of who they were as a people. The process of creating these nations has often been misconstrued as an exclusively *creole*[1] affair, engineered by the urban, well-to-do classes

---

[1] *Creoles* were American-born individuals normally of upper social rank.

with little impetus from popular groups. As with all things that characterize Latin America, however, the real story is much more complex and fraught with the contradictions of its colonial legacy.

The independence wars represented an unusual opportunity to bring about social change and reforms that resonated with concerns at local levels. As such, they attracted a multidimensional pool of participants who fought for different reasons as members of patriot and royalist armies or as affiliated guerrilla units. But their contributions were rarely acknowledged by historians and politicians, who either downplayed their significance or ignored them altogether. The first generation of national historians eulogized the war's military leaders, such as Simón Bolívar, José de San Martín, and Agustín de Iturbide, as responsible for Spain's defeat and, in varying degrees, as de facto, *creole* founding fathers. Subsequent generations of historians reinforced the relationship between the liberator classes and their respective nations in part because they relied on the personal letters and official correspondences and royalist and patriot officers' accounts of the war.[2] These writings mentioned Indians, *castas*, and displaced peasants as participants in the conflict, but they provided only superficial explanations on the origins, motivations, and guiding ideologies behind these groups' mobilization. It seemed that the popular masses served only as cannon fodder or as passive actors in a conflict they knew little about. Moreover they assumed that these groups lacked a meaningful sense of *patria* (nation), and, thus they were incapable of participating in representative forms of government. With few exceptions, this *creole* version remained the dominant independence narrative until the second half of the twentieth century when different sources were consulted.

In the following passages, readers can attempt to reach broader conclusions about the nature of popular politics by exploring rural sources from Bolivia's independence period (1809–1825). These include excerpts from the *diario* (journal) of José

Santos Vargas, a combatant from the remote and mountainous districts of Ayopaya and Sicasica. José Santos Vargas was a rebel scribe, drummer, soldier, and guerrilla leader in the Sicasica and Ayopaya valleys between 1814 and 1825.

Vargas's account offers the unique perspective of a rural, *mestizo* combatant written in the period's common vernacular. Born to a family of modest means in 1797 and orphaned at age eight, the fourteen-year-old Vargas witnessed insurgent forces enter Oruro in 1811. He followed them through the countryside to Cochabamba and eventually found his way to the Indian community of Cavari (Sicasica district) where his brother Andrés Vargas served as a priest and became a wanted man because he was a rebel chaplain. After royalists captured Andrés in 1816, the young Vargas remained in the region as a member of the Cavari Indian community, eventually marrying an *Aymara* woman. In 1815, Vargas joined the rebel forces in 1815 under commander Eusebio Lira, who valued the boy's ability to write, appointing him scribe and drummer. Vargas enjoyed the arrangement. His proximity to Lira and his inner circle provided a special vantage point. It was Lira who gave him the sobriquet, *"El Tambor Vargas"* ("the drummer, Vargas").

Vargas recorded the actions and motivations of his compatriots in remarkable detail during the war years of 1814–1825. During this period, the insurgency was disconnected from urban independence movements in Buenos Aires, Cochabamba, La Paz, and Salta. The relative inaccessibility of the rugged regions of Sicasica, along with the adjacent district of Ayopaya, had attracted rebel groups seeking refuge during the anti-Spanish Katari rebellion (1780–1783),[3] and the districts again emerged as the epicenter in this new round of widespread resistance and guerrilla activity. By the end of the colonial period, Sicasica remained a predominantly "Indian" district where traditional corporate communities known as *ayllus* predominated and *Aymara* was the lingua franca. By contrast, *mestizaje* in Ayopaya had been commonplace,

---

[2]For example: Daniel Florencio Oleary, *Bolivar and the War of Independence* (Austin: University of Texas Press, 1970).

[3]The Katari rebellion was the Alto Peruvian (Bolivian) Bolivian phase of the anticolonial movement known as the Tupac Amaru rebellion.

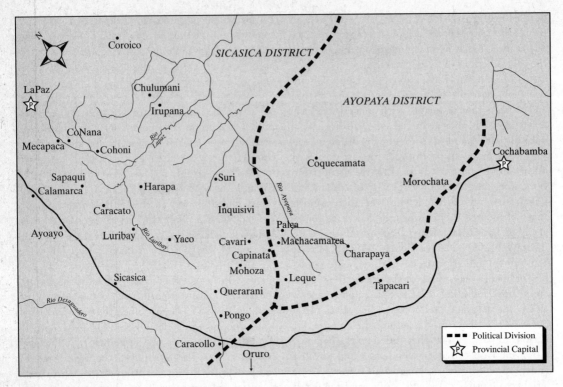

The Colonial Districts of Ayopaya and Sicasica.

and by the nineteenth century, *ayllus* had long disappeared, replaced by *haciendas* and Hispanic towns.

Independence fighters carved out an elongated rebel territory, oftentimes referred to as a *republiqueta* (mini republic) by contemporaries. Geography coupled with guerrilla tactics gave the republiqueta a distinct advantage in resisting colonial authority. When Bolivia achieved independence in 1825, the republiqueta was under the authority of José Miguel Lanza, a *creole* guerrilla leader. It was thus presumed that the Ayopaya-Sicasica republiqueta adhered to the same political precepts that guided Lanza and the *creoles* dominating the new Bolivian republic. However, according to Vargas's *diario*, Lanza did not emerge as leading rebel commander until 1821, and, even then, Lanza was met with stiff opposition from those who envisioned a very different notion of *patria*. The overarching figure in Vargas's account was not Lanza.

Instead, Eusebio Lira, a large, charismatic, and domineering individual of mixed descent from the Indian town of Mohoza, stands out. Lira presided as supreme commander over the republiqueta between 1815 and 1817, when he was murdered by members of another rebel faction. Vargas depicts Lira in almost messianic terms as a native son and indomitable guerrilla leader.

Vargas drafted two versions of his account of these events (in 1825 and 1852). He intended to have it published, but it only reached publication in 1982. The excerpts in this chapter were transcribed from the more complete 1852 manuscript. Vargas's diary reveals that the partisans articulated a highly localized concept of nation that privileged Andeanized notions of honor, kinship, and political legitimacy. The diary also suggests that war temporarily blurred social distinctions and created new forms of upward mobility for Indians and *mestizos* in the mid- to lower social ranges. They developed a highly flexible political culture indicative of Andean-Indian preoccupations with balance, reciprocity, and community. Vargas offered his version because "our political leaders here [in Bolivia] do not know of the events that occurred here, nor do the political leaders in Buenos Aires or in Salta. They do not know the names of those who fought, how they did it, in what time frame, and under whose leadership. They understood vaguely that troops dedicated to the *patria* existed in these parts but only as hearsay. They do not truly understand that the cause of American liberty was deeply rooted in every region."[4] Vargas directly contested the *creole* version of the war because he sensed that he and his compatriots were being excluded from the nation-building process. A variety of people imagined a life without Spanish overlords. They mobilized in large numbers and fought on many fronts to realize these alternatives to colonial rule. However, few of the commoner folk saw their visions turned into reality, and few left

accounts of their efforts and their dreams. Vargas is one who did.

Questions to Consider:

1. What did Vargas and his compatriots mean when they used the word *patria*? Are they referring to the territorial boundaries of Bolivia, all of Spanish America, or the confines of their rebel *republiqueta*?
2. To what extent did the rebels practice and understand participatory forms of government, and whom did they consider their countrymen? How do these definitions of countrymen and forms of government compare to those proposed by Morelos and Bolívar in other chapters?
3. What was the relationship like between the rebel leaders and indigenous peasants? What does that relationship suggest about the extent to which the independence movement did (or did not) help to break down social barriers?
4. What motivated Vargas and his compatriots to participate as combatants? To what extent were these motivations uniform?

[4]Archivo y Biblioteca Nacional de Bolivia (A/BNB), Directorio (DIR), 44B, fol. 5v.

Journal Entries by José Santos Vargas, Combatant in Bolivia's Independence War[5]

José Santos Vargas is Reunited with his Brother

1814 [exact date uncertain]. After three years I came in search of a brother I had. . . . don[6] Andrés Vargas, a clergyman. I found him in Pocusco, near the town

[5]*Source:* "Diario Historico de todos los sucesos ocurridos en las provincias de Sicasica y Ayopaya durante la Guerra de la independencia Americana, desde el año 1814 hasta el año 1825. Escrito por un comandante del partido de Mohoza, el ciudadano José Santos Vargas," Archivo y Biblioteca Nacional de Bolivia (A/BNB), Directorio (DIR), A/BNB, DIR, 44B, fols. 5, 165–168, 177v–185v, 209v, 288.
[6]This was an honorific title in Spanish for men (Don) and women (Doña) of high social standing or commanding respect in a community.

of Cavari. . . . He stretched out his arms to welcome me and he asked me in our conversations about everything I had seen during my travels. I first told him about my days as a school boy but later we talked about the war. He urged me to always embrace the cause of the *patria* and of the liberty of America: This is a just cause. The most just of all. It is the same cause being defended by the *porteños* (troops from Buenos Aires). God will always defend them because the king of Spain was not our legitimate sovereign. We need to defend the liberty of the *Patria* at all costs. We are obligated by God and by nature itself to defend our liberty from Spain's government because they only govern through the use of force and without the slightest interest to act on our behalf.

Eusebio Lira Pardons Marcelino Castro

November 20, 1817. Lira ordered his second lieutenant, Ignacio Borda, and others to Cajuata to arrest don Marcelino Castro. They arrested him in his home and he was brought to the town of Inquisivi. This Castro was once surprised by royalist troops who broke into his home and . . . the governor of La Paz, Juan Bautista Sánchez Lima had him conscripted into his army . . . he was brought to the city of La Paz and later . . . to the town of Sicasica where he was ordered to join the royalist commander, don José Castro Navajas. He followed Navajas everywhere. . . .

When he was brought before commander Lira, Castro explained that when he was first caught, the governor of La Paz, Juan Bautista Sánchez Lima, saw that he had large family and took pity on him. . . . He realized that Castro was poor and that his family could not survive without him. Lira's officers corroborated his story and urged Lira to pardon him. . . . To prove his own innocence, Castro reaches into his pocket pulls out a letter that describes his service to the *Patria*, particularly his role in helping a certain patriot named Juan Crisóstomo Gutierrez, a resident of Inquisivi. But he also [perhaps inadvertently] pulled out another document; a certificate of recommendation from the governor of La Paz, Juan Bautista Sánchez Lima that described the services he had provided to the royal crown . . . it was signed by Sánchez Lima himself.

At this point Lira read the documents and then handed them over to his secretary, don Juan Crisóstomo Osinaga. He sent me to muster the rest of the officers. They all arrived and the secretary read aloud the letter that Castro had presented of his own volition. The officers were left mute as was Castro who could not articulate a single word in his defense. Lira addressed the gathering:

Señores, distinguished officers, compatriots, and brothers in arms, I supported your judgment (concerning Castro's innocence) . . . but it now appears as though we've been deceived. We have an enemy to our cause in these territories and in our midst. I present to you this certificate of recommendation that was in his possession which retraces in detail his whereabouts over a long period of time during which he served various enemy officers. If he were a true defender of the *Patria* he would have separated himself from the royalists at his first opportunity. . . . According to Sánchez Lima he never attempted to escape. This individual was with enemy troops on various occasions. He was with them at Curupaya on the 8th of January, acting as a guide; he was with Navajas at Lirimani and helped the enemy escape on March 8th. . . . Should we, señores and distinguished officers, considered these to be of service to the *Patria*?

Castro responded and claimed that he never served as a guide . . . other men served as guides but not him.

At this point the second lieutenant of the first company, don Manuel Patiño, requested permission to speak. He said that Marcelino Castro was a virtuous person and that he did not willingly communicate with the leaders serving the king. . . . He claimed that the certificate of recommendation written by Sánchez Lima should not be considered as sufficient evidence for him to be treated as a traitor. He continued saying that if Castro was a royalist he would have remained with the king's troops and not return to his home. He did not remain with them even though he was receiving a good salary to do so. Everyone knows that the king and his officers pay well. . . .

Lira again spoke:

If this man did not return to be with his royalist troops it is because he is acting as a spy among us. How do we know that he is not being paid? . . . This man will be jailed and watched by an armed guard.

On the 21st it was determined that he was to be executed and the number of guards increased to include twenty-five men. They called for the priest, doctor don Juan Gutiérrez to accompany him and to act as his confessor. Many of Inquisivi's residents called for Castro's release but to no avail. That night he received a visit from the sister of the priest, Juan Gutierrez; a woman named doña Petrona. She left Castro her *polleras*.[7] Other officers also visited and left him with women's accoutrements. Between two or three in the morning Castro escaped from jail

---

[7] Dress worn by some *mestizas*.

dressed as a woman and left his bed sheets bundled up to make it appear as though a person was sleeping there.

At four in the morning Lira learned of Castro's escape and this caused him to leap from his bed and act greatly disturbed. He summoned the Indians to pursue and capture him. . . . The Indians refused and told Lira that Castro should instead be pardoned. Lira was incensed. He threw the Indians from his home and ordered his men to scour the countryside in search of Castro.

By November 22nd, Lira's heart was calmed. That afternoon, after running some drills, he invited his officers to dinner at a local ranch. During dinner Lira proposed a toast wherein he expressed empathy for Castro's predicament. He feared that he may have unwittingly pushed Castro to the side of the enemy and against the *Patria*. He proclaimed that if Castro presented himself he would be exonerated in the name of the *Patria*.

Reaction to Eusebio Lira's Death

December 19, 1817. We broke camp at three in the afternoon. We monitored the countryside on the way to Palca. We discovered that the more than 3,000 Indians had gathered in highlands; their numbers covered the mountains as we approached the town. They were armed with lances, slings, and cudgels. We entered Palca at six in the afternoon. We learned that the Indians had at least eighteen firearms of all types. They had come from every town from both districts (Sicasica and Ayopaya), as far as Tapacari, Arque, and Paria and they had come to mourn the death of commander Lira. They threatened to destroy the division if it was indeed true that Lira was not alive. All night long they disturbed our sleep. They blew their horns and other war implements. Their noise making made for a very uncomfortable night.

On December 20th at eight in the morning we ascended the heights to meet with the Indians, directly above Palca to a place named Chuñavi. . . . We met with six *indios principales*[8] and they wanted

us to explain Lira's death. [Commander Santiago] Fajardo spoke with them and told them Lira was executed because he was a traitor. . . .

On December 24th . . . a large contingent of Indians descended to again speak with Fajardo; they wanted him to turn over the men responsible for Lira's death: sergeant major, don Pedro Marquina; the captain; the (insurgent) governor of Paria district, don Agustín Contreras; captain, don Eugenio Moreno; cavalry officer, don Santiago Morales; the ensign, don Pedro Granados; officer don Antonio Pacheco, sergeant don Manuel Miranda; and the soldier and Lira's personal escort, José María Torres. The Indians were convinced that these men were accomplices to Lira's murder. After a long dispute, Fajardo realized that he was completely surrounded by throngs of Indians. Realizing his danger . . . he promised to deliver three of the men in question once he returned to town. The Indians accepted. Commander Fajardo entered the town . . . upon being reunited with his men, however, he reneged on his promise. He instead ordered the Indians to tend their fields and to their livestock and to mind their own affairs. He insisted that Lira's death was none of their concern and that the appropriate authorities in Buenos Aires and Salta would soon settle the matter. . . . Some of the Indians obeyed but others wanted to raze the town unless they saw Lira alive. . . . Fajardo announced:

Listen Indians, if my prudent reasoning does not persuade you to leave then I will have to disperse you forcibly.

Listening to this, the Indians responded in *Aymara*, "*Maya amparaqui Maya amparaqu*,"[9] Fajardo ordered his men to open fire. . . . The division fired into the air which caused many of the Indians to disperse. . . . Some sought asylum in the church where the town's women had already taken refuge. This caused quite a commotion. . . . The sight of these Indians entering the temple with lances and cudgels alarmed these women greatly.

On the 25th of December a large number of Indians arrived from Yungas with forty firearms. With them came captain don José Calderón, Rafael

---

[8]*Indios principales* exercised political and economic influence in their communities.

[9]"An eye for an eye." They were also willing to use force.

Copitas and the commander, don José Manuel Chinchilla. Gandarillas had not yet arrived but he was a short distance away. All of these arrived in the town of Machacamarca.

Having received this news, we left Palca for Machacamarca at six in the morning. At ten in the morning we were in the mountains overlooking Machacamarca below us. At eleven the Indians sent a certain Pedro Zuñiga a person of great patriot sentiment from the city of La Paz; The captain commander of Indians from the town of Mohoza, Mateo Quispe; captain commander of Indians from Ichoca, Benito Arguello; captain commander of Indians from Cavari, Mariano Lezcano; captain commander of Indians from Leque, Marcelo Calcina. These men told Fajardo who had arrived with armed escort that it was the people who should nominate the next leader who would govern them. They claimed to represent twenty different communities. They then demanded an election should take place or else they would not be held responsible for what would follow. Fajardo alone would be held responsible before God, before the *Patria*, and before the leadership in Buenos Aires. Fajardo agreed to proceed to Machacamarca and turn the division over to whomever the people choose. He wanted to retire to his house and rest. . . .

On December 26th . . . commander Fajardo joined the gathering and gave a brief speech:

Señores, distinguished officers, compatriots, and brothers in arms, you all know that I've been a patriot from the beginning, a soldier of liberty who never tainted his honor in regards to my convictions. I don't aspire to anything else, given my advanced age. . . . Those who represent the given towns should choose the leader of these territories. You can deliberate in any manner you wish but I don't wish to be included among the names that you will choose from. I don't aspire to that charge. I am a patriot and I will die for the *Patria* despite whatever course destiny brings because I have consecrated my life and blood to her cause.

After a while, don José Buenaventura Zárate spoke up:

. . . given that don Santiago Fajardo stepped down from his position we will need, on this occasion, to name a president and secretary to preside over this meeting. . . . Everyone unanimously agreed with this

course of action. Fajardo nominated don José Buenaventura Zárate to act as president and captain don Ramón Rivero to act as secretary. When the votes cleared, Zárate emerged as president and Rivero as secretary . . . Zárate took his seat and said: Señores, are you willing to obey the leader that you yourselves will name? Will you blindly follow his orders?

He ensured that the *caciques,* mayors, and other officials who spoke in Indian dialects [*Quechua* and *Aymara*] understood what he was saying by speaking to them in their own languages. They all replied that they would respect and obey whatever orders came from their elected leader. Zárate insisted that everyone take an oath to that end and they all did so enthusiastically.

They then proceeded to the business of voting for the leader. The [insurgent] governor don José Manuel Arana voted for commander Fajardo, then sergeant major Marquina voted for Fajardo, followed by captain don José Calderón who also voted for Fajardo.

Fajardo responded:

We should not have held this meeting or these elections if we were to reach the same results.

President Zárate interrupted:

Silence, señores! You should all submit secret votes in writing. The Indians who cannot write should choose a trusted person to write and vote in your place.

Everyone agreed with this idea and did as they were told. At two in the afternoon the final tally was made and commander don Santiago Fajardo was chosen. Despite his words to the contrary it was of no use. He eventually accepted their decision and was sworn in. He then declared,

Señores, I already told you that I am an old man and this presents a problem. To complete the charge you've given me I will need a *compañero* [partner]; someone who will serve as my second in command. He would have the same responsibilities as myself but subject to my orders. . . .

Everyone approved of the idea. Fajardo then told everyone that his personal choice for the position was [insurgent] governor don José Manuel Arana. The president then instructed everyone to do another secret vote in writing. Everyone did as they were told and the vote went to José Manuel Chinchilla despite the presence of many who aspired to be second in command. . . .

Administrating Lira's Republiqueta

December, 1817 [exact date uncertain]. Lira did not pay the men in his division because he did not have the means to do so. On certain Sundays he distributed a small ration of two reales to those of all classes, without exception. On rare occasions he handed out two pesos. He did reserve productive agricultural lands for the troops where he arranged to have them fed and he ate alongside them. He provided clothes as best he could, mostly made with local textiles woven by the locals. He was able to purchase a variety of armaments. . . . Firearms were purchased from merchants in Oruro, Cochabamba, La Paz, Irupana, and Sicasica. Others were taken from the enemy in battle. He arranged for powder to be mined from local sources. Saltpeter from Mojsu-uma and the flats of Oruro was purchased clandestinely by his Indian allies. . . . Horses and mules were donated from Indian communities and local townsmen. His government lacked a tax base because he did not force the Indian communities to pay *tribute* [Indian head tax] nor did he collect the *alcabala* [sales tax]. The local priests regularly contributed with small loans and with whatever donations they could collect. Even some of the *haciendas* opposed to the *patria* contributed the costs of maintaining the troops. *Hacienda* owners as well as Indians from both districts provided the *Patria* with food, they never declined to help. Those who owned the least amount of grains were among the first to contribute. The towns and their inhabitants willingly took turns monthly in providing what the troops needed. . . . The townspeople served through their own energies, their own lives, and with their own interests in mind. . . . In this manner, the people supported commander Lira in his defense of the *Patria*, liberty, and American independence from Spain.

Arrangements were made to lease out lands in order to meet specific costs incurred by the division. In the district of Sicasica specifically, all of the lands and farms that belonged to the Marquee of Santiago, who was absent because he resided in Lima where he served the viceregal court; all of these lands were leased out to others.

In the district of Ayopaya Lira parceled out the hacienda of Punacache which had been abandoned by don Agapito Achá who was very opposed to the liberty of America. These lands were parceled out to 100 pairs of plowmen. . . .

These were the material goods claimed by the *Patria*. Some have falsely accused us of being robbers, thieves, and thugs. The fact that these things occurred cannot be denied and can be attributed to some of the Indians who joined the division as captains, commanders, or as commissioned agents; these were the same individuals that victimized travelers along roads and engaged in other unfortunate activities. But these things normally occurred along the fringes of the territory controlled by the cause of liberty and independence. At the same time, it should be mentioned that those who committed these crimes were pursued and punished.

News from the Outside

On the 24th of March, between Panduro and Aroma they encountered a party of 30 royalist infantrymen escorting the mail from La Paz to Oruro. . . . There we opened the mail and read it aloud. We discovered the state of affairs in Lima, Chile, and Colombia. It was the first time we had heard of Colombia and of general Bolívar and everything that had transpired. We learned everything then. Everything!

Suggested Sources:

For scholars writing peasants and *non-creoles* back into the history of the wars for independence in Latin America, see Peter F. Guardino, *Peasants, Politics, and the Formation of Mexico's National State, 1800–1857* (Stanford, CA: Stanford University Press, 1996); and Eric Van Young, *The Other Rebellion: Popular Violence, Ideology, and the Mexican Struggle for Independence, 1810–1821* (Stanford, CA: Stanford University Press, 2001). For the Andes, see Cecilia Mendez, *The Plebeian Republic: The Huanta Rebellion and the Making of the Peruvian State, 1820–1850* (Durham, NC: Duke University Press, 2005). A classic account of how liberal-republican ideas meshed with pre-Columbian expressions of political legitimacy after independence is in Tristan Platt, "Simon Bolívar, the Sun of Justice and the

Amerindian Virgin: Andean Conceptions of the *Patria* in Nineteenth-Century Potosí," *Journal of Latin American Studies* 25 (February 1993): 159–185. The Túpac Amaru Rebellion can be fruitfully compared with *creole*-dominated independence movements in the Peruvian highlands. See Charles Walker, *Smoldering Ashes: Cuzco and the Creation of Republican Peru, 1780–1840* (Durham, NC: Duke University Press, 1999). Rebecca Earle outlines the various Indian-oriented political programs described as "Indianesque" and employed by both royalists and insurgents in her essay, "*Creole* Patriotism and the Myth of the "Loyal Indian," *Past and Present*, no. 172 (August 2001): 125–145. Lastly, a novelistic account of the independence wars can be found in Nathaniel Aguirre, *Juan de la Rosa: Memoirs of the Last Soldier of the Independence Movement* (New York: Oxford University Press, 1998).

Chapter 4

Slavery, Race, and Citizenship in the Empire of Brazil: Debates in the Constituent Assembly

Kirsten Schultz, Seton Hall University

In 1822, Portuguese-born Prince Regent Dom Pedro I, son of Portugal's king who had come to Brazil 14 years earlier to escape a Napoleonic army's invasion of Portugal, declared Brazil's independence from Portugal. The royal nature of the gesture notwithstanding, elite and popular support for the declaration had been forged the previous year within an emerging political culture of constitutionalism. In the wake of a successful rebellion in the city of Porto, Portugal, a provisional government gathered to draft a written constitution. Supporters on both sides of the Atlantic claimed that a written constitution would guard against the tyranny of absolute monarchy and replace a corrupt old regime with virtuous national sovereignty. Initially constitutionalists also claimed that constitutional government would renew the ties between Portugal and its colonies strained by Napoleon's invasion and the transfer of the royal court to Rio de Janeiro in Brazil (1807). Accordingly, they included representatives from all of the territories of the Portuguese Crown.

By August 1821, however, with Brazilian delegates a minority (75 representatives out of 250), and before many of them had even arrived in Lisbon, the constitutionalists passed measures viewed in Brazil as contrary to Brazilian interests. Brazilian merchants' privileges were curtailed; the judicial courts established in Rio following the transfer of the court were abolished; and the heir to the throne (Dom Pedro) was ordered to return to Portugal, as his father (King Dom João) had been in 1821. The ideal of constitutionally sanctioned representation that had promised to preserve the unity of the Portuguese empire began, instead, to serve as the basis of rupture.

Following his declaration of independence in 1822, the prince Dom Pedro affirmed his support for constitutionalism and summoned to Rio de Janeiro representatives from Brazil's provinces to draft a constitution for the new Empire of Brazil. The elected representatives were well qualified for the task. Half had been educated at the University of Coimbra, Portugal, and many had subsequently served in imperial government and military service. They included lawyers, magistrates, clergymen, physicians, merchants, and landowners. Eighteen had been elected earlier to represent Brazil in Lisbon.

By April 1823 enough representatives were in Rio de Janeiro for formal proceedings to begin. As in other former European colonies in the Americas, one of the main tasks of the Assembly was to render a legal framework for the exercise of the popular or national sovereignty that had displaced the sovereignty of the king in the process of gaining independence. Thus, the representatives sought to define a balance of legislative, executive, and judicial powers as well as the scope of nationhood and citizenship. The first draft of this framework, the "Project of [a] Constitution for the Empire of

A fundação da Patria Brazileira
(7 de Setembro de 1822)

Titled *The Foundation of the Brazilian Nation* (September 7, 1822), this allegory of the Brazilian nation, made well after independence, represents the three races: the African slave, the native Indian, and the Portuguese. A São Paulo landowner and architect of independence, José Bonifácio Andrada e Silva, a Brazilian-born elite (1763–1838), sits with a banner draped over his knees, while the young Portuguese prince and first Emperor of Brazil, Dom Pedro I (1793–1834), who supported the declaration of independence, clutches a sword to his chest. Among Brazil's elites, Silva supported slave emancipation early on; he asked how a newly freed people could steal the freedom from others. How are the three races portrayed in this image? What does the allegory suggest about the author's view of the relations among these groups and their respective roles in an independent nation? How closely do these images of race and nation correspond to the ideas and problems debated in the 1823 Constituent Assembly?

Source: Private Collection/The Bridgeman Art Library International.

Brazil," written by a committee of representatives, was presented to the Assembly in September 1823.

What follows are excerpts from the Assembly's draft constitution and debates on the definition of citizenship in the Empire of Brazil contained in the draft. As many representatives agreed, "to attend to constituting ourselves, and giving the honorable title of Citizen" was a matter of forging an explicitly, and primarily, political identity. Yet the criteria for citizenship were various. Certain exclusions, such as those based on age, gender, and lack of wealth, did not generate discussion. Others were subjected to intense scrutiny and elicited the expression of passionate differences of opinion from members of the Assembly. These hotly debated criteria for citizenship included: legal status; perceptions of cultural, ethnic, and physical difference; and place of birth.

Of particular concern in these debates were articles of the draft constitution that recognized the existence and legacies of slavery. Slavery dominated early nineteenth-century Brazil's economy and society, and at least half of the population was of African descent (free, freed, and enslaved). In some regions of Brazil, patriots had encouraged slaves to enlist in the armed forces to fight for the cause of independence, promising freedom in return. Indeed, throughout the tumultuous 1810s and 1820s, slaves expressed hopes that challenges to the empire and the old regime would lead to an overthrow of the institution of slavery as well. In the wake of the transfer of the royal court to Rio in 1807–1808 and faced with internationalist abolitionist diplomacy, some Brazilian elites, including several representatives to the Assembly, expressed concerns about the moral, political, and economic consequences of slavery. However, preoccupied with the social and economic disorder that they imagined an immediate end to slavery would produce, these elites considered only the possibility of a gradual abolition at some point in the future. As a result, the drafters of the constitution had to reckon with the continuation of slavery in an independent Brazil. In Title II, Article 6, the draft constitution defined "Brazilians" as including "Slaves who obtain a letter of manumission." The law also recognized these former slaves, known as *libertos*, in articles of the draft constitution concerning voting rights.

In November 1823, confronted with the nativist (anti-Portuguese) speeches of some of its members

and what he perceived to be the increasing disorder of the assembly's sessions, Dom Pedro ordered military units to disband the Assembly. The use of such unconstitutional measures (as defined by the draft constitution itself) to protect constitutionalism signaled Dom Pedro's willingness to forego liberal principles in order to maintain his power. Nevertheless, despite this move, the Assembly, its deliberations, and its draft constitution became the "principle source" of the 1824 Constitution, drafted by a council of statesmen appointed by the Emperor, including former members of the disbanded Assembly. Indeed, the Constitution of 1824 both bore the marks of the draft constitution and the earlier assembly discussions; it attested to efforts to clarify ambiguities and resolve conflicts that had surfaced in the past. In contrast to the draft constitution, however, the Constitution of 1824 did not recognize the institution of slavery, the existence of slaves, or the possibility of abolition. Perhaps these purposeful omissions reflected the counsel offered by one representative at the beginning of the citizenship debates that there were things "that were better repressed." This constitution formed the legal foundation for the Brazilian Empire until its overthrow in 1889.

Questions to Consider:

1. Why was the question of manumitted slaves so heatedly debated? What did their status mean to the nation?
2. How did the members of the Assembly define citizenship? What were the grounds for inclusion or exclusion from Brazilian citizenry and society? Was citizenship related to other forms of identity and allegiance? How does the scope of citizenship and voting rights defined in the draft constitution ("Project") compare with those of the Constitution of 1824?
3. To what kinds of principles and authorities did the representatives appeal in making their arguments?
4. What were the main points of disagreement among the members of the Assembly over the definition of "Brazilian"? Do these disagreements affirm or challenge historical understandings of the way elites viewed the poor and people of color in the nineteenth century?

Project of a Constitution for the Empire of Brazil, 1824[1]

Title II: Of the Empire of Brazil

Chapter I: Of the Members of the Society of the Empire of Brazil

Article 5: Brazilians are

I. All free male inhabitants of Brazil, and in Brazil born.

II. All Portuguese residents in Brazil before October 12, 1822 [the date of Dom Pedro's Acclamation to the throne].

III. Children of Brazilian parents born in foreign countries, who come to establish residence in the Empire.

IV. Children of Brazilian parents who were in a foreign country in service to the Nation, even though they do not establish residence in the Empire.

V. Illegitimate children of a Brazilian mother who, having been born in a foreign country, come to establish residence in the Empire.

VI. Slaves who obtain a letter of manumission.[2]

VII. Children of foreigners born in the Empire, as long as their parents are not in the service of their respective nations.

VIII. Naturalized foreigners, regardless of their religion. . . .

Title V: Of Elections

Article 122: Elections are indirect, the mass of active citizens electing electors, and the electors the Deputies [representatives], and equally, Senators in this first organization of the Senate.

Article 123. Those who are active citizens to vote in the Assembly primaries, or the parish:

I. All freeborn Brazilians, and *libertos* born in Brazil.

II. Naturalized foreigners . . .

Article 124: Exceptions:

I. Minors under the age of twenty-five years, not including those who are married, military officers who are twenty-one years old, recipients of higher degrees, and clergy of Holy Orders.

II. Sons of families who are under the power and in the company of their fathers, except if they serve in public office.

III. Servants, not including in this class foremen.

IV. Freedmen who are not born in Brazil, except those who have military commissions or [are in] Holy Orders.

V. The religious and whoever lives in a cloistered community, not including in this exception the religious of military orders or the secular clergy.

VI. Clerks, not including bookkeepers.

VII. Day laborers.

Article 127: *Libertos* born in any parts cannot be electors even if they have military commissions or [are in] Sacred Orders. . . .

Title XVIII: Of Public Instruction, Charitable Establishments, Correctional Houses, and Work

Article 254: There will be equal care to create establishments for the catechism, and civilization of the Indians, the slow emancipation of the Blacks [*Negros*], and their religious and vocational education.

[1]*Source:* "Project of [a] Constitution for the Empire of Brazil," in *Diario da Assemblea geral constituinte e legislativa do Imperio do Brasil* (Rio de Janeiro: Imprensa Nacional, 1824) 1: 689–700.
[2]The term used here is *carta de alforria*, the legal document that established that a slave had been freed or manumitted.

Sessions of September 27 and September 30[3]

. . . There began a discussion of article six . . . "The slaves who obtain a Letter of Manumission."

Mr. Costa Barros: I will never be able to accept that the title of Brazilian citizen is given indiscriminately to every slave who obtains a Letter of Manumission. Recently arrived blacks,[4] without a trade, without benefits, are not, in my understanding, deserving of this honorable prerogative; rather I see them as harmful members of society for which they are a burden [even] when they do not cause evil. I judge it is necessary to limit such a generality, conceiving this article in the following terms: "Slaves &c. who have employment or a trade."

It was supported.

Mr. França: This article six could pass if all of our slaves were born in Brazil because, having the right of territorial origin to be considered citizens as long as the civil impediment of the condition of their parents is removed, they would be restored *pleno jure* [with full authority] the benefit of this right, which was suspended by captivity; but since it is not the case, because a great number of our *libertos* are foreigners from different Nations of Africa . . . it is clear that being coherent in our principles, that this article can pass regarding that which pertains to *libertos crioulos* [born in Brazil], but never to African *libertos* . . . I offer an amendment so that we understand the article in the following terms: "The *libertos* who are native to Brazil."

It was supported. . . .

Mr. Moniz Tavares: . . . I judge that it is best that this article passes without discussion; [this] reminds me that some speeches of the celebrated orators of the Constituent Assembly of France produced the dreadful events of the Island of São Domingos, as some writers who have impartially written of the French Revolution affirm;[5] and perhaps among us some representatives, carried away with excessive zeal in favor of humanity, have expressed ideas (that are best repressed), with the intention of stirring up the Assembly's compassion for this poor race of men, so unfortunate only because nature created them tanned. I will say only that in the old system a slave had only to obtain a Letter of Manumission, and he could assume a military post in a corps, he had entrance to the sacred priestly ministry, without questions of whether he was or was not born in Brazil. . . .

Mr. França: . . . In the last session in which this subject was discussed I offered an amendment with the intention of limiting the privileges of the citizen to *libertos crioulos* only; and this was not due to less philanthropy than the authors of the Project [the draft constitution] appeared to have when they wanted to make [it] extend to *liberto* natives of Africa. I am philanthropic when it comes to providing the protection which they need, as the miserable persons that they generally are; but the force of my devotion does not lead me to a demented course [and] speech such that, without regard, the privileges of the citizen, which are denied to [those of] other parts of the world, are lavished on foreigners of Africa. . . .

Sr. Alencar: I am of a contrary opinion to that of the illustrious deputy, and I say that the article is consistent with the principles of universal justice, and that the amendments seem to me to be unjust, contradictory and impolitic. I say that the article is consistent with the principles of universal justice because it still seems that we should make all inhabitants of the territory of Brazil Brazilian citizens, although we cannot rigorously follow this principle, without offending the supreme law of the salvation of the state. This is the law that prevents us from

---

[3]Source: *Diario da Assemblea geral constituinte e legislativa do Imperio do Brasil* (Rio de Janeiro: Imprensa Nacional, 1824) 2, no. 10: 130, 133–140.

[4]The term used here is *Negros buçaes*. At the time, *boçal* referred to a recently arrived African and connoted an inability to speak Portuguese and unfamiliarity with Luso-Brazilian culture. The word also came to mean stupid and crude.

[5]Moniz Tavares refers to The Haitian Revolution (1791–1804) on the French colony of Saint Domingue. After the French Revolution began in 1789, and as the French National Assembly debated the status of the colonies and the institution of slavery, a massive slave insurrection began that culminated in the independence of Saint Domingue as Haiti in 1804.

making slaves citizens, because besides being the property of others, and so we offend [this] right [of property] if we take away the patrimony of these individuals to whom they belong, we would diminish agriculture, one of the principle sources of the wealth of the nation, and we would open a hub of disorder in society, suddenly introducing into it a bunch of men who, having left the state of captivity, can hardly be guided by principles of well conceived liberty. . . . The illustrious authors of the amendments do not want those who only by virtue of being freedmen should be indistinctly Brazilian citizens; but what will they be, these who are excluded by the amendments? They are certainly not foreigners; because they do not belong to any society, nor do they have any *Pátria* (homeland)[6] that is not ours, nor do they have a religion that is not the one which we profess. . . . Furthermore, if by the principles of sound politics, we should curtail as much as we can the slave trade so that we may end it, it seems that we go more directly towards this end by granting to *libertos* the privileges of the Brazilian citizen, than by demanding that for this that certain conditions be verified. That a *liberto* has to have some trade or employment to acquire such a condition [citizenship] seems to me unjust; it is enough that he has worked all his life, without making him have to overcome one more obstacle. I see that the Indian who quickly enters our society, savage that he is, is a citizen; he does not know how to read nor write, he does not have a trade or a job, and nevertheless none of this impedes the recognition of him [as a citizen]; but it is understood that the slaves, who I judge to be in worse circumstances, should not be admitted even though in terms of customs they are much closer to our own, because they acquire them from their owners in the time of their captivity. . . .

Sr. Carneiro de Cunha: . . . I would add only that the slave who obtains his liberty has in his favor, generally speaking, the presumption of good behavior and industriousness; . . . and because of this

I think that such men well deserve the privileges of the citizen, without the obligation of having a trade or employment . . . Mr. França also excludes slaves from Africa: but I do not know why those born in our territory will be at an advantage over those [African-born] on this point, after being almost always enslaved, as the African has no one who protects him, from the time when he arrives he is always wretched, while the *crioulo* born into the bosom of a family enjoys some comforts, and has, generally, more respect. It does not seem just to me that the less fortunate are offered less assistance. . . .

Mr. Almeida e Albuquerque: . . . How is it possible that by the simple fact of obtaining a Letter of Manumission one acquires the right of citizenship? . . . Won't the fact that they [the African-born] are pagans or idolaters disqualify them? . . . How is it possible that a man without *pátria*, without virtue, without customs, torn, by way of an odious commerce, from his land, and brought to Brazil, may by way of a simple fact, by the will of his owner, suddenly acquire such important rights in our society? If Europeans, born in civilized countries, having customs, good education, and virtues, may not acquire the benefit of the rights of Brazilian citizen without obtaining a letter of naturalization, and this same naturalization requires that they profess the Christian religion, according to the Project [the draft], how can the African slave, devoid of all qualities, be of better condition? . . .

Sr. Costa Barros: . . . I know that there is no more wretched and horrific condition than that of the slaves, but not even for this [reason] should we understand that to indemnify them for the evils which they suffered should we receive them under circumstances that would be damaging for us. . . . Thus, I demand that they have a job or a trade. . . . Mr. Carneiro da Cunha says that the slave who acquires a Letter of Manumission shows with this proof of occupation and good conduct. . . . I am not persuaded of this; Letters of Manumission are almost always given because of love, and most slaves are poorly raised. . . .

José da Silva Lisboa: . . . When it is the *Liberal* Cause that is in question, it is not possible to remain silent, rather I should say with the classic Latin [author] "I am a man; nothing pertaining to

---

[6]*Pátria* was a key word in political discourse at the time. Although in the 1810s it could refer to Portugal, in the process of independence it was invoked in reference to feelings of allegiance to Brazil or to more local regional identities.

humanity should be strange to me."[7] It seems to me that it is right to make the article simple or broad, to get rid of any doubt, declaring to be a Brazilian citizen not only the slave who obtains from his owner a letter of liberty, but also he who acquires liberty by any legitimate entitlement. . . . I am opposed to the amendments. . . . I have as a guiding light the author of *The Spirit of the Laws*,[8] who advises legislators to maintain, when possible, simplicity in legislation. . . . Why will they make arbitrary distinctions among *libertos*, by place of birth, and service and trade? As soon as they [*libertos*] acquire the condition of *civil person*, they deserve the equal protection of the Law. . . . To be a Brazilian citizen is indeed to have an honorific title, but it is only civic rights and not political rights that are dealt with in the chapter under discussion [. . .] civic rights are limited to giving to the free man the *jus* [right] to say – I have a *pátria*; I belong to such a city or village; I am not subject to the will of anyone, but only to the empire of the Law. . . . When I link the article in question with articles 245 and 255 [sic],[9] it seems to me that they completely address the objections, in which some have insisted, by establishing a basis for the regulated benefits to slaves, proposing only their slow emancipation, and moral instruction. Africans themselves, notwithstanding the accusations of paganism and brutality, are susceptible to mental improvement, and for this reason can be called *tabulas rasas*.[10] Mr. President, in the era of liberalism, will the legislature be less equitable than in the time of *despotism*? . . . Enough, Gentleman, of the odious distinctions of castes, of differences of color. Now diversity[11] is an almost indestructible attribute of the population of Brazil. Politics cannot end such inequalities, [rather] it should take advantage of all elements for our regeneration, but not add new inequalities. The class of

slaves will henceforth look upon this august Assembly with the proper confidence in the hope that it will attend to their fate and the improvement of their condition, having in sight the general good, as much as humanity inspires and politics may allow. . . . This consideration alone would be enough to sanction the controversial article, which to me seems to need only the following amendment . . . "The *libertos* who acquire their liberty by whatever legitimate entitlement."

It was supported.

Mr. Maciel da Costa: . . . Does a nation have an obligation to admit foreigners into the union of its society? No. Naturalization is a type of favor, and this favor is always regulated by motives of national interest. . . . If we agree that the admission of foreigners into the union of our society is a favor, if for this favor we demand conditions that political calculation induces us to impose; if upon the same individuals in whose veins runs Brazilian blood, and only because they were born in a foreign country, we impose the condition of residence, considering them half-foreigners; it frightens me to see that the African has only to obtain a letter of manumission, which is a deed that simply authorizes him to dispose of his time, and he enters ipso facto into the union of the Brazilian family, becomes our brother. . . . Not having doubt that the children of an African mother and father should be considered Brazilian because their birth in this country makes them ours, and they have this link to the country, the Africans, because they were born in a foreign country, because we cannot suppose that they have affection for the country in which they lived as slaves, should not be admitted to the union of our family without marrying a Brazilian woman and having a type of industry from which they live. . . .

Mr. Henriques de Resende: . . . As long as they were manumitted, *libertos* used to enlist in the appropriate corps and occupy military posts. . . . Why then in a system of liberal government are they to remain in a worse condition than they were in the era of despotic government? . . .

Mr. Maciel da Costa: . . . political security rather than philanthropy should be the basis of our decisions on this matter. Philanthropy laid the ground for the loss of the flourishing French Colonies. As

---

[7] The Roman author, Terence (185 B.C.–159 B.C.).
[8] The French Charles de Secondat, Baron de Montesquieu (1669–1755), published the widely read *The Spirit of the Laws* in 1748.
[9] The article to which he refers is 254. See above excerpt.
[10] The concept *tabula rasa* (blank slate) suggested that people are not born with innate ideas.
[11] Silva Lisboa uses the Portuguese word *variegado*, which means "diverse" as well as, more specifically, "multicolored."

soon as the declaration of the so-called rights of man[12] was heard there, spirits were enflamed and the Africans served as the instrument of the worst horrors that can be conceived.[13] . . . To diminish gradually the traffic in men and in the meantime treat those who are slaves humanely, this, Gentlemen, is all that we owe them.

Mr. Henriques de Resende: . . . The scorn with which owners or the whites treat the *libertos* will give rise to the aversion that both feel for each other. . . .

Mr. José da Silva Lisboa: . . . A more reasonable fear is that we perpetuate the vexation of the Africans, and of their offspring, showing scorn and hate, with a fixed system of never improving one's condition. . . . Let us leave behind, Gentlemen, the controversies over the color of peoples; they are physical phenomena that vary according to the degrees from the equator, the influx of the sun's rays and geological dispositions and other more profound causes that are not the subject of this discussion. The French were very white when they invaded Egypt and half-black when they left.[14] . . . Good institutions, with correct education, are what make men have the dignity of the species regardless of their color. . . .

---

[12]This is a reference to the French "Declaration of the Rights of Man," approved by the revolutionary National Assembly of France in August 1789. The first article reads "Men are born and remain free and equal in rights. Social distinctions may be founded only upon the general good." For the full text, see http://www.yale.edu/lawweb/avalon/rightsof.htm.

[13]Haitian Revolution.

[14]Napoleon Bonaparte led the French invasion of Egypt, then an Ottoman territory, in 1798.

Political Constitution of the Empire of Brazil, 1824[15]

Title II: Of Brazilian Citizens

Article 6. They are Brazilian citizens

I. Those who have been born in Brazil, whether they are freeborn, or freed persons, even if their father is a foreigner, as long as he does not reside in Brazil in service to another nation. . . .

Chapter IV: On Elections

Article 90. The nominations of Deputies and Senators to the General Assembly, and of members of the General Provincial Councils, will be made by indirect elections, the mass of active citizens in Parochial Assemblies electing electors of the province, and these the representatives of the nation and province.

Article 91. [Those who] vote in primary elections

I. Brazilian citizens who enjoy their political rights.

II. Naturalized foreigners.

Article 92. [Those who] are excluded from voting in Parochial Assemblies

I. Minors under the age of twenty five years, not including those who are married, military officers above twenty one years, recipients of higher degrees, and clergy of Holy Orders.

II. Sons of families who are in the company of their fathers, except if they serve in public office.

III. Servants, not including in this class bookkeepers, principal clerks of commercial houses, servants of the Imperial household [who do not wear a certain uniform], and administrators of rural estates and factories.

IV. Clergy, and whoever lives in a cloistered community.

V. Those who do not have an annual income of 100 *milreis*[16] from landed property, industry, commerce, or employment. . . .

---

[15]*Source:* "Political Constitution of the Empire of Brazil" (1824), from "Political Database of the Americas," at Georgetown University, http://pdba.georgetown.edu.

[16]*Milreis* was a unit of currency. The income requirements for voting were viewed by many as low. A wage laborer typically earned enough to satisfy the requirement in 100 days. See Graham, *Patronage and Politics* (pp. 103–104) in Suggested Sources.

Article 94. All those who can vote in parochial Assembly can be electors, and vote in the election of Deputies, Senators, and members of the Provincial Councils. The following are exceptions:

    I. Those who do not have an annual income of 200 *milreis* from landed property, industry, commerce, or employment.

    II. *Libertos* [freed persons].

    III. Criminals indicted in a judicial complaint or inquiry. . . .

Suggested Sources:

Roderick Barman provides an overview of Brazil's political independence in *Brazil: The Forging of a Nation: 1798–1852* (Stanford, CA: Stanford University Press, 1988). Emilia Viotti da Costa's *The Brazilian Empire: Myths and Histories* (Chapel Hill: University of North Carolina Press, 2000) offers analysis of social and cultural transformations and theories and practices of liberalism. On nineteenth-century political practice, see Richard Graham, *Patronage and Politics in Nineteenth-Century Brazil* (Stanford, CA: Stanford University Press, 1990). For emancipation in the United States and Brazil, see Celia M. Azevedo's *Abolitionism in the United States and Brazil: A Comparative Perspective* (New York: Garland, 1995). On defining citizenship, see Hilda Sabato, "On Political Citizenship in Nineteenth-Century Latin America," *The American Historical Review* 106, no. 4 (October 2001): 1290–1315; and Marcia Regina Berbel and Rafael de Bivar Marquese, "The Absence of Race: Slavery, Citizenship, and Pro-slavery Ideology in the Cortes of Lisbon and the Rio de Janeiro Constituent Assembly (1821–1824)," *Social History* 32, no. 4 (November 2007): 415–433.

Among the most extensive primary sources in English on nineteenth-century Brazil are those of the British merchant John Luccock, *Notes on Rio de Janeiro and the Southern Parts of Brazil; Taken during a Residence of Ten Years in That Country, from 1808–1818* (London: Samuel Leigh, 1820); and Maria Dundas Graham, *Journal of a Voyage to Brazil and Residence There during Part of the Years 1821, 1822, 1823* (1824) (New York: Praeger, 1969). Documents on Brazilian and Latin American slavery and its legacies can be found in Robert Edgar Conrad's *Children of God's Fire. A Documentary History of Black Slavery in Brazil* (University Park, PA: Penn State University Press, 1994); and Sue Peabody and Keila Grinberg, eds., *Slavery, Freedom, and the Law in the Atlantic World. A Brief History with Documents* (Boston/New York: Bedford/St. Martins, 2007).

A number of Internet sources also shed light on the problem of slavery. "Slave Movement during the Eighteenth and Nineteenth Centuries" can be found at the Data and Information Services Center of the University of Wisconsin (http://www.disc.wisc.edu/slavedata/). "The Atlantic Slave Trade and Slave Life in the Americas: A Visual Record" (University of Virginia) offers images of enslaved Africans in nineteenth-century Brazil. The "Political Database of the Americas" at Georgetown University (http://pdba.georgetown.edu) provides links to online constitutions.

Section II

Nineteenth-Century Elite Views of the Nation

Although the poor, non-Europeans, and women were often active participants in Latin American independence movements, *creole* elites dominated the new states. State officials claimed that they would end centuries-old racial systems, replacing them with governments that would ensure equality before the law. In practice, although some wealthy *mestizos* or mulatos gained equal footing with men of European descent, white-*mestizo* political and economic elites were generally uninterested in overturning racial and gender systems from which they benefited. Long-standing gender and racial ideologies and stereotypes provided justification for excluding women and non-whites from the formative nation state. Although these views of gender and race derived from colonial-era ideologies, nineteenth-century statesmen and scholars adapted them to address the new processes and problems of state formation, making the nineteenth century a critical transition period between colonial formations of race and gender and twentieth-century modernization of relations between subalterns and the state.

Intraelite struggles in the early nineteenth century further complicated attempts to create unified nation states. Presidents in early nineteenth-century Latin America rarely served their full terms in office, and legislators continually redrafted constitutions. In the absence of the rule of law, *caudillos* (politico-military strongmen) often dominated regional—and occasionally national—politics. Political instability was, in part, the result of disagreements between *liberals and conservatives* about how to structure governments or grapple with colonial legacies. *Liberals* rejected colonial-style corporatism[1] in favor of individualism, and they advocated equality before the law (at least in theory). Most *liberals* wanted to establish secular governments and put an end to the privileged position of the Catholic Church in politics, and most sought to reduce or eliminate protective tariffs. *Conservatives* often accepted ongoing corporatism within the new nations, favored high tariffs, and sanctioned Church influence in politics. Yet, like their *liberal* counterparts, nineteenth-century *conservatives* advocated the rule of law, and many of them argued that they, too, were establishing equality before the law through representative governments and the abolition of legalized racial distinctions.

Regionalism also plagued the new Latin American states. Commoners and elites alike tended to think in terms of regional objectives and concerns, and it took time for national commitments to develop. Complicating all of this was the harsh reality that national economies floundered in

---

[1] The term "corporatism" suggests a system in which one's rights and duties are determined according to group identity. In the Spanish American colonies, for example, the *System of Two Republics* granted greater rights and powers to Spaniards, placing indigenous peoples in an inferior and dependent juridical position. Corporatism also afforded special privileges to members of the Church and the military.

the decades following independence. Most Latin American governments came out of the wars for independence saddled with foreign debts and struggling export economies. Without reliable revenue sources, statesmen were unable to establish stable governments or shed colonial political legacies. For example, from about 1820 to 1850 Peru, Bolivia, and Ecuador had so little government revenue that they continued to collect *tribute* from indigenous peoples. Although perpetuating the *tribute* system aggravated both *liberals and conservatives,* they saw no means of abolishing *tribute* until other forms of revenue were available.

In the mid- to late nineteenth century (ca. 1850/1870–1900), a new wave of economic growth made more meaningful state formation possible. Demand for consumer and goods and raw materials in Europe and the United States led to a new wave of Latin American agricultural and mineral exports. Middle and working classes in industrialized nations could by then afford items that were once luxuries, such as coffee. The growth of industry and urban living meant that industrialized nations sought fertilizers to make their own agricultural fields more productive—leading to the guano boom in Peru and later exports of nitrates from Chile. By the end of the century, the development of electricity made Chilean copper a valuable commodity on the world market. Although booming export economies resulted in greater government stability, they reinforced Latin America's position as a supplier of raw materials to industrialized nations.

Export booms led to the growth of large estates at the expense of peasant populations. First, landed elites used the court system to wrest land from peasants, whose claims to property were often based on custom rather than legal documentation. Second, many Latin American governments in the era privatized indigenous communal lands, and in many cases it was owners of large estates rather than peasants who gained access to former communal lands. The particular nature of peasant crises varied throughout Latin America, and sometimes within a single nation. Consider the rise of coffee exports in Central America: In El Salvador, coffee estates' quick expansion throughout the country immediately threatened all peasants, leading to frequent peasant rebellions.

Guatemalan coffee estates expanded more gradually, and only in particular regions of the country, resulting in fewer peasant rebellions; yet, by the early twentieth century, most Guatemalan peasants had lost access to lands necessary for their subsistence. In a few cases, owners of middle-sized estates suffered from modernization and large-estate expansion, as occurred in northern Mexico, where *rancheros* (owners of middle-sized livestock estates) lost land to railroad development, oil companies, or landed elites.

Economic growth provided the financial stability necessary to allow political elites to begin nation state formation projects in earnest. With money available from exports, state officials could build roads and railroads, open more schools, and create new administrative offices in some of the more remote regions of their countries. Central state authorities undertook such projects in order to link different regions of their countries together, raise the next generation of citizens with a sense of loyalty to the nation, and assert the presence and power of the central state over all areas of the nation. Documents in this section allow readers to explore how and why racial and gender ideologies were central to the development of elite nation-making projects in the nineteenth century.

Political leaders sought the respect of men who ran powerful western nations, and as a result they identified strongly with a very specific definition of "Progress" focused on emulating western-style political practices, economic policies, and cultural achievements. Progressive elites believed that such imitation would lead inevitably to industrialization, effective rule of law, and international respect for their countries. Advocates of this particular path to progress thought of themselves as creating modern nations, and in the quest for modernity they embraced railroad construction over social welfare and individual over communal rights.

Although nineteenth-century state officials prided themselves on constructing nations in which law ruled supreme and individuals enjoyed equality before the law, Latin American nations, like all nations of the period, were founded on policies of exclusion. Least controversial was the denial of women's citizenship rights, because European model nations also denied women a political voice

These photographs are of a cotton hacienda in the Chincha region south of Lima, Peru. The top image shows the grand architecture and grounds of the hacienda house. Beside it is a photograph of the *cepo*, or dungeon, where estate workers were chained as a form of punishment. The cepo was located directly under the corridor pictured above. Although slavery and Indian *tribute* were abolished in Peru (in 1855), indebted Chinese, Afro-Peruvian, and indigenous workers continued to keep this cotton *hacienda* productive in the late nineteenth century, and they were just as likely to be punished physically as their enslaved predecessors had been. What do these images, both of the same estate, suggest about the nature of economic progress in the nineteenth century? How does the continuity of estate life undermine central state officials' proclamations that all citizens enjoyed the same rights and shared the same obligations? Given that the estate is now a museum and hotel, what do you see in these photos to suggest how and why these spaces are remembered today?

Source: Photographs by Leo J. Garofalo.

and limited their economic rights. Elite gender ideologies simultaneously provided state officials with a means to justify the nature, extent, and limits of political rights within their nations. For example, Jordana Dym's chapter on marriage and citizenship in El Salvador and Erin O'Connor's chapter on changing marriage laws in Ecuador show that marriage and marriage laws were essential to defining citizens' rights. Gender exclusions were not limited to women: Mexican *liberal* Guillermo Prieto's writings, presented by John Tutino, allow readers to explore elite concerns regarding manliness and citizenship.

Although late nineteenth-century constitutions typically asserted equality before the law, in practice peoples of indigenous and African descent were socially and politically marginalized, and in Brazil the slave system continued until 1888. The contradictory position of non-European men worried state officials, as two chapters in this section make clear. Passages from Argentine Domingo Faustino Sarmiento's *Civilization and Barbarism* offer examples of how the desire to emulate all things European often came at the expense of rural dwellers. The closing chapter offers excerpts from a debate over one of the many stages of the abolition of slavery in Brazil. It presents the complexities of abolition and shows how late nineteenth-century notions of progress influenced the arguments on both sides of the debate.

Less-powerful individuals and groups did not necessarily accept their subordinate positions, as document excerpts in Section III reveal. Yet, even when women or non-European peoples sought to advance their own interests, they had to either work within or struggle against the racial and gender assumptions embedded in national laws. Examining elite views of race, gender, and politics, therefore, reveals the limits of national belonging in the nineteenth century and helps readers to analyze the strategies that subaltern peoples developed in their encounters with state officials.

Chapter 5

Argentine Domingo Faustino Sarmiento's Views on Civilization and Barbarism

Erin E. O'Connor, Bridgewater State College

Argentina

Argentine scholar and politician Domingo Faustino Sarmiento (1811–1888) was an important figure whose ideas about national progress had a significant impact both in his own nation and throughout Latin America. Sarmiento was a political *liberal* who thought of himself as advancing the cause of individual rights and liberties. Deeply patriotic, he aspired to have Argentina recognized as one of the modern, advanced nations of the world. His best-known work, and the source of the document excerpt in this chapter, was his book *Facundo: Or, Civilization and Barbarism*, which he wrote while in political exile in Chile. Ostensibly a biography of Juan Facundo Quiroga, a *gaucho* (cowboy) and provincial governor, *Facundo* was, in fact, a treatise on the problem of *caudillos* (politico-military strongmen) in Argentine politics, and in particular a barely masked criticism of Juan Manuel de Rosas (r. 1829–1852).

Sarmiento was also distressed by regional, class, and cultural struggles in Argentina. The greatest political struggle in early nineteenth-century Argentina reflected the deep regional divides and suspicions among the nation's Federalists and Unitarians. Whereas Unitarians wanted a strong central government based in the city and province of Buenos Aires, Federalists wanted greater political autonomy for the provinces. Political elites also argued over the best economic policies to promote and strengthen the Argentine nation—should they embrace protectionist policies as Rosas did, or drop high tariffs and engage in free trade? Did the future lie with cattle raised in the vast grasslands (*pampas*) or with other forms of agricultural, and eventually industrial, production? Finally, there were deep class and racial divides in Argentina. Though Argentina's indigenous and African populations were small when compared with non-European populations in many other Latin American nations, the conflicts between elites and working classes, or Europeans and non-Europeans, intensified.

In *Facundo*, Sarmiento discussed Argentina's failures and promoted a very specific agenda for national growth. He advocated rule of law rather than *caudillo* rule, modernity rather than tradition, agriculture and industry rather than heavy dependence on cattle farming. He envisioned, through European immigration, the rise of a robust middle class of yeoman farmers in Argentina who would become the backbone of an economically strong and politically stable nation. He was deeply critical of the gaucho culture in the Argentine countryside, not only because he thought gauchos uncouth, but also because they often provided *caudillos*' most crucial support. Sarmiento believed

that gauchos and other poor Argentines backed *caudillos* out of ignorance and coarseness, with the strongmen taking advantage of their simplicity and backwardness. Accordingly, Sarmiento argued that widespread education was necessary to strengthen the nation and achieve political stability. Recent scholarship has shown that neither were *caudillos* as dismissive of the rule of law as was once believed, nor were subaltern peoples mere pawns of the strongmen. Instead, *caudillos* offered security in times of upheaval and poverty, and they sometimes provided better functioning administration than civilian authorities did. The poor, likewise, were not simply brainwashed; they knew that any benefits they received served to increase the power of the *caudillo*. They accepted this tradeoff as the best of their available options.[2]

Sarmiento and other progressive elites often clashed with indigenous, Afro-Latin American, and working-class peoples within their societies. The expansion of export agriculture typically came at the expense of the rural poor, often peoples of indigenous or mixed racial descent. Similarly, low tariffs that encouraged increased trade with Europe hurt small-scale artisans and traders who could not compete with European manufactured goods. Governments often recruited poor people of non-European descent to build the roads and railroads that represented progress and modernity, but the poor seldom benefited from improved transportation, which was mainly aimed at facilitating export production and connecting the central government to all regions of the nation. Simultaneously, progressive governments continued to marginalize indigenous and Afro-Latin American peoples, using property or literacy requirements to deny them voting rights. In Argentina and Chile, modern military institutions emerged in part as a by-product of wars and land seizures against indigenous peoples. Progressive

---

[2]For two excellent discussions of the complexities of *caudillismo*, with particular attention to *caudillo*-subaltern relations, see Charles Walker, *Smoldering Ashes: Cuzco and the Creation of Republican Peru, 1780–1840* (Durham, NC: Duke University Press, 1999); and Christon Archer, "The Young Antonio López de Santa Anna: Veracruz Counterinsurgent and Incipient Caudillo," in *The Human Tradition in Latin America: The Nineteenth Century*, ed. Judith Ewell and William Beezeley (Wilmington, DE: SR Books, 1989).

elites took quite seriously the tensions and con-tradictions of their relationships to marginalized peoples. Many of them used ideas similar to those expressed in this chapter's document excerpt to ex-plain why, in their view, it was necessary to trans-form poor, indigenous, and Afro-Latin American populations before incorporating them into the na-tion. To understand both elite and marginalized peoples' views of nation state formation in the nine-teenth century, one must understand the dominant discourses that maintained elite control and subal-tern exclusion in Latin American nations. Reading excerpts from Sarmiento's *Facundo* provides a useful starting point.

Questions to Consider:

1. Why did Sarmiento think that Argentina was caught in a struggle between civilization and barbarism? What were the implications of this clash?

2. How did race seem to shape Sarmiento's ideas about civilization and barbarism? In particular, how did he describe peoples of European versus indigenous descent?

3. In what ways did Sarmiento play on notions of *manliness* and manly duties when he described the gaucho? What purposes did these descriptions seem to serve?

4. Consider the document evidence presented here alongside the document evidence introduced in chapters by Schultz on the Brazilian constitution, Dym on citizenship in Central America, and O'Connor on both marriage laws and indigenous murder. How can you use these chapters to more broadly identify and evaluate the elite views of citizenship and national belonging in nineteenth-century Latin America? Why do you think political leaders spent so much time and energy defining (and refining) the meaning of citizenship at the time?

Civilization and Barbarism[3]

The people who inhabit these extensive districts [of Argentina] belong to two different races, the Spanish and the native; the combinations of which form a series of imperceptible gradations. The pure Spanish race predominates in the rural districts of Cordova and San Luis, where it is common to meet young shepherdesses fair and rosy, and as beautiful as the belles of a capital could wish to be. In Santiago del Estero, the bulk of the rural population still speaks the *Quichua* dialect, which plainly shows its Indian origin . . . The negro race, by this time nearly extinct (except in Buenos Ayres), has left, in its *zambos*[4] and *mulatos,* a link which connects civilized man with the denizens of the woods. This race mostly inhabiting cities, has a tendency to become civilized, and possesses talent and the finest instincts of progress.

With these reservations, a homogeneous whole has resulted from the fusion of the three above-named families. It is characterized by love of idleness and incapacity for industry, except when education and the exigencies of a social position succeeded in spurring it out of its customary pace. To a great extent, this unfortunate result is owing to the incor-poration of the native tribes, affected by the process of colonization. The American aborigines live in idleness, and show themselves incapable, even under compulsion, of hard and protracted labor. This suggested the idea of introducing negroes into America, which has produced such fatal results. But the Spanish race has not shown itself more energetic than the aborigines, when it has been left to its own instincts in the wilds of America. Pity and shame are excited by the comparison of one of the German or Scotch colonies in the southern part of Buenos Ayres and some towns of the interior of the Argentine Republic; in the former the cottages are painted, the front-yards always neatly kept and adorned with flowers and pretty shrubs; the furniture is simple

---

[3]*Source:* From *Facundo: Or, Civilization and Barbarism* by Domingo F. Sarmiento, introduction by Ilan Stevens, translated by Mary Mann, copyright © 1998 by Ilan Stevens, introduction. Used by permission of Penguin, a division of Penguin Group (USA) Inc.
[4]A zambo was a person of both indigenous and African heritage.

but complete; copper or tin utensils always bright and clean; nicely curtained beds; and the occupants of the dwelling are always industriously at work. Some such families have retired to enjoy the conveniences of city life, with great fortunes gained by their previous labors in milking their cows, and making butter and cheese. The town inhabited by natives of the country, presents a picture entirely the reverse. There, dirty and ragged children live, with a menagerie of dogs; there, men lie about in utter idleness; neglect and poverty prevail everywhere; a table and some baskets are the only furniture of wretched huts remarkable for their general aspect of barbarism and carelessness. . . .

The Argentine cities, like almost all the cities of South America, have an appearance of regularity. Their streets are laid out at right angles, and their population scattered over a wide surface, except in Cordova, which occupies a narrow and confined position, and presents all the appearance of a European city, the resemblance being increased by the multitude of towers and domes attached to its numerous and magnificent churches. All civilizations, whether native, Spanish, or European, centers in the cities, where are to be found the manufactories, the shops, the schools and colleges, and other characteristics of civilized nations. Elegance of style, articles of luxury, dress-coats, and frock-coats, with other European garments, occupy their appropriate place in these towns. I mention these small matters designedly. It is sometimes the case that the only city of a pastoral province is its capital, and occasionally the land is uncultivated up to its very streets. The encircling desert besets such cities at a greater or less distance, and bears heavily upon them, and they are thus small oases of civilization surrounded by an untilled plain, hundreds of square miles in extent, the surface of which is but rarely interrupted by any settlement of consequence.

The cities of Buenos Ayres and Cordova have succeeded better than the others in establishing about them subordinate towns to serve as new foci of civilization and municipal interests; a fact which deserves notice. The inhabitants of the city wear the European dress, live in a civilized manner, and possess laws, ideas of progress, means of instruction, some municipal organization, regular forms of government, etc. Beyond the precincts of the city everything assumes a new aspect; the country people wear a different dress, which I will call South American, as it is common to all districts; their habits of life are different, their wants peculiar and limited. The people composing these two distinct forms of society do not seem to belong to the same nation. Moreover, the countryman, far from attempting to imitate the customs of the city, rejects with disdain its luxury and refinement; and it is unsafe for the costume of the city people, their

Above is a photograph of an Argentine gaucho from 1868, albeit not a typical one (the style and condition of his clothing suggest that he was far wealthier than most of the pampas "cowboys"). What markers in the photograph correspond with Sarmiento's discussions of both the supposed barbarism and manliness of the gauchos?

Source: Courtesy of the Library of Congress.

coats, their cloaks, their saddles, or anything European, to show themselves in the country. Everything civilized which the city contains is blockaded there, proscribed beyond its limits; and anyone who should dare to appear in the rural districts in a frock-coat, for example, or mounted on an English saddle, would bring ridicule and brutal assaults upon himself. . . .

Nomad tribes do not exist in the Argentine plains; the stock-raiser is a proprietor, living upon his own land; but this condition renders association impossible, and it tends to scatter separate families over an immense extent of surface . . . Society has altogether disappeared. There is but the isolated self-concentrated feudal family. Since there is no collected society, no government is possible; there is neither municipal nor executive power, and civil justice has no means of reaching criminals. I doubt if the modern world[5] presents any form of association so monstrous as this. . . .

In the absence of all the means of civilization and progress, which can only be developed among men collected into societies of many individuals, the education of the country people is as follows: The women look after the house, get the meals ready, shear the sheep, milk the cows, make the cheese, and weave the coarse cloth used for garments. All domestic occupations are performed by women; on them rests the burden of all the labor, and it is an exceptional favor when some of the men undertake the cultivation of a little maize, bread not being in use as an ordinary article of diet.[6] The boys exercise their strength and amuse themselves by gaining skill in the use of the lasso and the bolas, with which they constantly harass and pursue the calves and the goats. When they can ride, which is as soon as they have learned to walk, they perform some small services on horseback. When they become stronger, they race over the country, falling off their horses and getting up again, tumbling on purpose into rabbit burrows, scrambling over precipices, and practicing feats of horsemanship. On reaching puberty, they take to breaking wild colts, and death is the least penalty that awaits them if their strength or courage fails them for a moment. With early manhood comes complete independence and idleness.

Now begins the public life of the gaucho, as I may say, since his education is by this time at an end. These men, Spaniards only in their language and in the confused religious notions preserved among them, must be seen, before a right estimate can be made of the indomitable and haughty character which grows out of this struggle of isolated man with untamed nature, of the rational being with the brute. It is necessary to see their visages bristling with beards,[7] their countenances as grave and serious as those of the Arabs of Asia, to appreciate the pitying scorn with which they look upon the sedentary denizen of the city, who may have read many books, but who cannot overthrow and slay a fierce bull, who could not provide himself with a horse from the pampas, who has never met a tiger alone, and received him with a dagger in one hand and a poncho rolled up in the other, to be thrust into the animal's mouth, while he transfixes his heart with his dagger. . . .

Country life, then, has developed all the physical but none of the intellectual powers of the gaucho. His moral character is of the quality to be expected from his habit of triumphing over the obstacles and the forces of nature; it is strong, haughty, and energetic. Without instruction, and indeed without need of any, without means of support as without wants, he is happy in the midst of his poverty and privations, which are not such to one who never knew nor wished for greater pleasures than are his already. Thus if the disorganization of society among the gauchos deeply implants barbarism in their natures, through the impossibility and uselessness of moral and intellectual education, it has, too, its attractive side to him. The

---

[5]Readers at the time would understand that a reference to the "modern world" meant western Europe and peoples of western European origin.

[6]Bread was made of wheat, a European product, and, therefore, it indicated higher status than the maize (corn), a product native to the Americas and the staple food of most native peoples. Jeffrey Pilcher has a superb discussion of the relative value of these foods in nineteenth-century Mexico in *Que Vivan Los Tamales! Food and the Making of Mexican Identity* (Albuquerque: University of New Mexico Press, 1998).

[7]Since the colonial period, beards were a symbol of virility.

gaucho does not labor; he finds his food and raiment ready to his hand. If he is a proprietor, his own flocks yield him both; if he possesses nothing himself, he finds them in the house of a patron or relation. The necessary care of the herds is reduced to excursions and pleasure parties; the branding, which is like the harvesting of farmers, is a festival, the arrival of which is received with transports of joy, being the occasion of the assembling of all the men for twenty leagues around, and the opportunity for displaying incredible skill with the lasso. . . .

{In another chapter, Sarmiento described how and why gauchos so often ended up in taverns, and with what results.} The men . . . set forth without exactly knowing where they are going. A turn around the herds, a visit to a breeding-pen or to the haunt of a favorite horse, takes up a small part of the day; the rest is consumed in a rendezvous at a tavern or grocery store. There assemble inhabitants of the neighboring parishes; there are given and received bits of information about animals that have gone astray; the trace of the cattle are described upon the ground; intelligence of the hunting-ground of the tiger or of the place where the tiger's tracks have been seen, is communicated. There, in short . . . the men fraternize while the glass goes round at the expense of those who have the means as well as the disposition to pay for it.

In a life so void of emotion, gambling exercises the enervated mind and liquor arouses the dormant imagination. This accidental reunion becomes by its daily repetition a society more contracted than that from which each of its individual members came; yet in this assembly, without public aim, without social interest, are first formed the laments of those characters which are to appear later on the political stage . . . The gaucho esteems skill in horsemanship and physical strength, and especially courage, above all other things, as we have said before. This meeting, this daily club [in taverns], is a real Olympic circus where each man's merit is tested and assayed. . . .

The gaucho boasts of his valor like a trooper, and every little while his knife glitters through the air in circles, upon the least provocation, or with none at all, for the simple purpose of comparing a stranger's prowess with his own; he plays at stabbing as he would play at dice. So deeply and intimately have

these pugnacious habits entered the life of the Argentine gaucho that custom has created a code of honor and a fencing system which protect life. The rowdy of other lands takes to his knife for the purpose of killing, and he kills; the Argentine gaucho unsheathes his to fight, and he only wounds. To attempt the life of his adversary he must be very drunk, or his instincts must be really wicked, or his rancor very deep. His aim is only to *mark* his opponent, to give him a slash in the face, to leave an indelible token upon him. The numerous scars to be seen upon these gauchos, accordingly, are seldom deep. A fight has begun, then, for the sake of shining, for the glory of victory, for the love of fame. A close ring is made around the combatants, and excited and eager eyes follow the glitter of the knives which do not cease to move. When blood flows in torrents the spectators feel obliged to stop the fight. If a *misfortune* has resulted, the sympathies are with the survivor; the best horse is available for his escape to a distant place where he is received with respect and pity. If the law overtakes him he often shows fight, and if he rushes through the soldiers and escapes, he has from that time a wide-spread renown. Time passes, the judge in place has been succeeded by another, and he may again show himself in the township without further molestation: he has a full discharge. . . .

Before 1810, two distinct, rival and incompatible forms of society, two differing kinds of civilization existed in the Argentine Republic: one being Spanish, European, and cultivated, the other barbarous, American, and almost wholly of native growth. The revolution [meaning independence] which occurred in the cities acted only as the cause, the impulse, which set these two distinct forms of national existence face to face, and gave occasion for a contest between them, to be ended, after lasting many years, by the absorption of one into the other.

Suggested Sources:

Primary sources on the issues raised in this chapter are often difficult to find aside from Sarmiento's famous book. However, novels offer an important window into a variety of elite views on the topic of civilization and barbarism, and one can read them to evaluate how both race and gender ideas were central to the development of nineteenth-century progressive ideas. Argentine novelists, for example, sometimes described the gaucho as a hero. The two most famous novels to do this were José Hernández, *The Gaucho Martín Fierro* (New York: State University of New York Press, 1975 [1872]); and Ricardo Guiraldes, *Don Segundo Sombra (Shadows on the Pampas)*, trans. Harriet de Onis (New York: New American Library, 1966 [1926]). There are also several novels that capture typical elite views of the poor in the late nineteenth century. See, for example, Rómulo Gallegos, *Doña Bárbara*, trans. Robert Malloy (New York: Peter Smith, 1948); Joaquim Machado de Asis, *Quincas Borba*, trans. Gregory Rabassa (New York: Oxford University Press, 1998); and Clorinda Matto de Turner, *Torn from the Nest*, trans. John H. R. Polt (New York: Oxford University Press, 1998).

Among the important secondary sources on the theme of civilization and barbarism is Bradford E. Burns's now classic discussion of nineteenth-century progress and its impact on less-powerful peoples in *The Poverty of Progress: Latin America in the Nineteenth Century* (Berkeley: The University of California Press, 1980). For studies of the gaucho that focus on perspectives of the rural poor themselves, see Ricardo Salvatore, *Wandering Paysanos: State Order and Subaltern Experience in Buenos Aires during the Rosas Era* (Durham, NC: Duke University Press, 2003); or Richard Slatta, *Gauchos and the Vanishing Frontier* (Lincoln: University of Nebraska Press, 1992). On the complex problems of land and liberal reforms in the era, see Robert H. Jackson, ed., *Liberals, the Church, and Indian Peasants: Corporate Lands and the Challenge of Reform in Nineteenth-Century Spanish America* (Albuquerque: University of New Mexico Press, 1997). Those who wish to further explore the links (and tensions) between race and nation in modern Latin America should read Richard Graham's now-classic edited volume, *The Idea of Race in Latin America* (Austin: University of Texas Press, 1990); or the more recent book by Nancy P. Appelbaum, Anne S. Macpherson, and Karin Alejandra Rosemblatt, eds., *Race and Nation in Modern Latin America* (Chapel Hill: University of North Carolina Press, 2003).

Chapter 6

Citizenship through Marriage: De Facto Naturalization in 1840s El Salvador

Jordana Dym, Skidmore College

El Salvador

Who qualifies as a citizen in a country? Many in the United States now take for granted that one's country of birth provides nationality, and adulthood brings full citizenship and rights to elect representatives and run for office. During the Age of Revolutions, however, defining citizenship in republics was something countries were still experimenting with. The qualities that legally determined an individual's citizenship in- cluded a complex calculus of age, gender, marital status, economic position, race, and residence, which varied from country to country and changed over time.[1] Sometimes this complex matrix of qualifica- tions led to disputes, as it did for Bertrand Save, a French resident in 1840s El Salvador, who rejected Salvadoran citizenship for many reasons, including fear of losing his French nationality. As a result of Save's determination, France's diplomatic archives hold a trail of laws and also letters by Salvadoran and French officials that reflect how new republics were in- venting the guidelines for nationality and citizenship. Save had married a Salvadoran woman; therefore, the case also reveals the indirect but important role of women in integrating new members of society.

Perhaps because millions of people of African and Indian origin made up most of Spanish America's population, and foreigners in most countries num- bered in the hundreds, scholars have written more about the role of race than immigration in defining who were citizens and nationals in the independent Spanish American republics.[2] Still, looking at inte- gration of foreigners helps one understand who was considered capable of becoming a full member of both local and national society, and what factors demon- strated the new arrival's ties to the community. The roles that class and gender played in defining who was part of the new national community, and who was not, come through in both official texts, such as con- stitutions, and in correspondence due to disputes over such laws, as seen in the case of Bertrand Save.

In Central America, starting in the 1820s, several hundred Britons, Italians, and Frenchmen farmed, practiced medicine, ran bakeries, and traded. Although they were few, the immigrants attracted lo- cal and official attention because of their education, occupation, and sometimes deep pockets. Central

American leaders believed that foreign farmers would settle model communities and improve agricultural practices, and that investors would buy coffee, indigo, and other exports and loan funds to build roads, bridges, and maybe even a canal. The federal consti- tution was as optimistic about integrating foreigners into the new body politic as it was about its multi- ethnic majority, and provided generous naturalization rules that allowed different kinds of foreigners—those from the Americas, Spain, and other places—to natu- ralize by procedures ranging from swearing an oath to making a formal request. By 1838, due in part to the violent upheavals that led to Central America's sepa- ration into five countries, many settlers had returned home and most foreign residents had not naturalized. Central American governments responded by revisit- ing the way their legal systems treated foreigners; their constitutions of the late 1830s and early 1840s redefined the role of foreigners in society.[3]

In 1840s El Salvador, Luis Bertrand Save found he required consular help when he learned that El Sal- vador's government defined him as a national and cit- izen. In December 1841, voters in Sonsonate, the town where he lived, elected Save as *alcalde* (city magistrate). Despite the local governor's insistence that he take office in January 1842, Save refused, stating that he was not a citizen of El Salvador even though he had lived there for over a decade, had married there, and ran his business there. Save cited both French and Sal- vadoran laws to back up his point. The reason he listed in one letter was very practical: Under Article 17 of the French Civil Code (1803), he could lose his "quality of being a Frenchman," that is, his nationality, by accepting a post in a foreign government. The Sal- vadoran authorities did not care about Save's possible problem, citing their 1841 Constitution and later an 1844 law, to claim that he was a citizen. Several issues were in dispute, as the documents show. First was retroactivity: The laws that El Salvador wanted to apply were passed after Save had entered the country, so should they apply to him? A second issue was juris- diction: The Salvadoran laws affected Save because they were supposed to take effect automatically

---

[1]Peter Riesenberg, *Citizenship in the Western Tradition: Plato to Rousseau* (Chapel Hill: University of North Carolina Press, 1992).
[2]Hilda Sabato, ed., *Ciudadanía política y formación de las naciones* (Mexico City: FCE, 1999); Nancy P. Appelbaum, Anne S. Macpherson, and Karin Alejandra Rosemblatt, eds., *Race and Na- tion in Modern Latin America* (Chapel Hill: University of North Carolina Press, 2003); Nancy Leys Stepan, *"The Hour of Eugenics": Race, Gender and Nation in Latin America* (Ithaca, NY: Cornell Uni- versity Press, 1991).

[3]See Constitution of Nicaragua, 1838, Articles 15, 20; Constitu- tion of El Salvador, 1841, Art 6; El Salvador laws of 1844/1845, and Nicaragua Laws of 1844/1845.

without requiring any specific act. Was this legal? Save (and the French consul) said no, El Salvador's government said yes. The dispute stretched over several years and a second election of Save as Sonsonate's alcalde for 1844, when once again the governor insisted he take office, leading to a second spate of correspondence and, eventually, El Salvador's modification of its naturalization laws.

The laws' provisions and prefaces explaining their motivation, and the correspondence between Save and the Sonsonate governor in 1844, provide insight into the many factors that went into determining who was a member of a local and a national community in a time when states could try to make naturalization automatic and foreign residents could reject those claims. In Save's case, it was not just one but many factors that all parties discussed when justifying whether or not he should be considered a *vecino* (resident) of Sonsonate or a national and citizen of El Salvador—as well as or instead of as a Frenchman. No one disputed that Save had been born in France, had resided for years in Central America, had married a local woman, or ran a retail shop in Sonsonate. What they did argue over was how the law appropriated each of these characteristics to attempt to define Save's place in Salvadoran society. Of which republic was he a citizen? And who decided? Bertrand Save's predicament had local, national, and international implications.

Save's problem also reveals ways women integrated foreign men into society. In the nineteenth century, many countries—including the United States, Argentina, Italy, and Japan—declared that a woman who married a foreigner acquired his nationality and citizenship and lost that of her native land—whether she wanted to or not![4] In

Central America at this time, there seemed to be another story playing out. Constitutions and laws from El Salvador seemed to expect their immigrants to be only foreign men and for those men to marry Central American women and then settle in the region. Instead of forcing the women to take on their husband's nationality, the laws passed by Central American governments underlined that once these foreign men had married and settled in the region, they were expected to become citizens—whether in law or simply in practice. So although Mme. Save does not seem to have written any documents defending her husband and does not appear as an actor in his confrontation with El Salvador's laws and officials, she was a "daughter of the country" (*"hija del país"*), and in this alone was very important not only to Save himself, but also to the government officials with whom he dealt.

Questions to Consider:

1. How did Central Americans define and distinguish between nationality and citizenship? Why do you think they did this?
2. What evidence, either explicit or implicit, can you find in the constitutions about how race, class, gender, and naturalization affected whether or not one was a citizen in the Central American republic(s) in the nineteenth century? How and why did these requirements change over time?
3. Do you agree with Luis Bertrand Save that he should not have been elected *alcalde* of Sonsonate? Why or why not? Was he either a *vecino* or *ciudadano* of El Salvador in 1841? In 1844?
4. What do these descriptions and debates over citizenship reveal, in conjunction with other chapters in this section, about how one's identity shaped his or her rights and obligations before the law?

---

[4]Kif Augustine-Adams, "She Consents Implicitly": Women's Citizenship, Marriage, and Liberal Political Theory in Late-Nineteenth and Early-Twentieth-Century Argentina," *Journal of Women's History* 13, no. 4 (2002): 8–30; Nancy Cott, "Marriage and Women's Citizenship in the United States, 1830–1934," *American Historical Review* 103, no. 5 (1998): 1440–1474.

Central American Federal Constitution of 1824[5]

Section II

Article 13: Every man is free in the Republic. He who welcomes its laws cannot be a slave, nor can he who traffics in slaves be a citizen.

Article 14: All inhabitants of the Republic, natural or naturalized in the country, who were married or older than 18 years old, as long as they exercise a useful profession or have known means of subsistence, are citizens.

Article 15: The Congress will grant letters of *naturaleza* (nativeness) to foreigners who inform local authorities of their interest in settling in the Republic:

1. For services relevant to the nation and designated by law.

2. For any useful invention, and for the exercise of any science, art or office not yet established in the country, or notable improvement of a known industry.

3. For five years' *vecindad* (residence).

4. For three years' *vecindad*, for: those who came to settle with their families; those who contracted marriage in the Republic, and those who acquired real estate of the value and class determined by law.

Article 16: Children born in a foreign country to Central American citizens, whose parents were in the service of the Republic, or when their absence

is not greater than five years and known to the government, are also natives.

Article 17: Spaniards and any foreigners who, having settled in any point of the Republic's territory, swore [an oath of loyalty at] its independence when it was proclaimed, are naturalized.

Article 18: Anyone born in the American republics who comes to settle in the Federation, will be held as naturalized in it from the moment that he expresses his intent before the local authority.

Article 19: Citizens of one state have the exercise of citizenship issued in any other [state] of the Federation.

Article 20: Losing the status of citizens are:[6]

1) those who accept a job or pensions, distinctions or hereditary titles from another government or personnel, without Congress' authorization;

2) those sentenced for crimes which according to the law merit a serious punishment, if they have not obtained rehabilitation.[7]

---

[5]Available in Spanish at the Biblioteca Virtual Cervantes: http://www.cervantesvirtual.com/servlet/SirveObras/13516121092351052976613/index.htm   and   http://www.honduraseducacional.com/Leyes/1824.pdf.

[6]The original Spanish of "calidad" I translate as "status." The Spanish comes from the French, "qualité de citoyen" (French Constitution, 1791, Article 6). A literal translation would be "quality," but "status" seems more faithful to the original sense of the term.

[7]A 1993 Nicaraguan judgment referred to late nineteenth-century crimes as "más que correccional" and "correccional"; the former were crimes meriting three years or more of jail time, the latter were lesser sentences. The judgment was that "correccional" could be understood to mean "lighter or less serious" and "más que correccional" as "serious" crimes, which I used in the translation. Other than El Salvador and Nicaragua, I find no legislation using these terms. Available at: http://www.poderjudicial.gob.ni/bijun/2002/Sente_fmto_web/1990_1997/1993/BJ015055.htm.

Constitution of El Salvador, 1841[8]

Article 4: *Salvadoreños* (Salvadorans) are all the sons of natives of El Salvador, born on its territory: to

sons of other States of the former Union, who are vecinos in it; to naturalized foreigners; and to the sons of salvadoreños born in a foreign country, who[se parents] have a Government assignment, [or] the objective of mercantile speculations or [are] temporarily exiled.

---

[8]Available in Spanish at: http://www.asamblea.gob.sv/constitucion/1841.htm.

Article 5: Citizens are: all salvadoreños over 21 years old who are parents or heads of household, or who know how to read and write, or who have the property designated by law.

Article 6: Foreigners naturalize: 1) by acquiring real property in the country that has the value established by law and have 5 years' vecindad; 2) by marrying a salvadoreña (Salvadoran woman) and have 3 years' vecindario [residence] in El Salvador's territory, and 3) by acquiring a letter of naturaleza from the Legislature.

Article 7: Foreigners, resident at any point in El Salvador, owe all ordinary taxes and duties that the natives bear and in the case that they are unduly bothered in their persons and properties, they will have the same guarantees as citizens to pursue a judgment against the attackers and offenders; and they will be heard and attended to like [citizens] in the courts.

Article 8: A citizen's rights are suspended for a criminal trial in which a court order of prison has been provided for a crime that, according to the law, merits a serious punishment; to be a legally declared fraudulent debtor, or a debtor to the public revenue and judicially required to pay; for notoriously corrupt conduct, or being without a legally-certified honest occupation; for insanity, dementia or mental alienation; and for being a domestic servant close to the person.

El Salvador, Decree 1 (1844)[9]

[A decree of 6 April 1844, issued in El Salvador, by the Deputies, sanctioned by the Senate, and issued by the President]

[The Government of El Salvador] Considering:

1. That the Constitution and state laws on the status of foreigners are few and obscure, and have occasioned abuses of much importance, regarding both natives and foreigners;

2. That for lack of clarity, the laws have become illusory. . . . and it is an obligation to even out rights and duties . . .

Decrees

Article 1: Naturalization is required of: those who have acquired real property in the country whose value reaches 2000 pesos and have 5 years as residents [*vecindario*]; those who have contracted matrimony with a salvadoreña and have 3 years as residents in the territory of El Salvador; and with the issuance of a letter of naturaleza by the Congress, all per article 6 of the Constitution, [he] loses his natural nationality, and is understood to tacitly renounce the *fueros* [privileges] that for his status as a foreigner were in his favor in the infractions and those that merit more than correctional/reformatory penalty.

Article 2: The foreigner who after five years has not acquired real property, nor contracted marriage with a salvadoreña, nor requested a letter of naturaleza, loses all the same his natural nationality, and it is understood that he tacitly renounces the fueros that, for his status as a foreigner, would have been in his favor in crimes and in crimes that merit a more than correctional penalty.

Article 3: Every foreigner at the moment of disembarking will provide his first and last name to the port commander when he disembarks; [the commander] will mark it in a record that will be sent to the Government, with a specific account of his lineage and where he is coming from, and his having taken an oath of obedience to the Constitution and laws.

Article 4: In consequence, the Government will extend in his [the foreigner's] favor, a Letter of Security so that, while he remains a foreigner in the State's territory for 5 years, he can conduct his business and labors, enjoying the same guarantees that

---

[9]*Source:* Archives Diplomatiques Françaises, Ministère des Affaires Etrangères (Paris), Correspondance Consulaire et Commerciale, Guatemala (MAE, CC-G), vol. 2, 1844–1845, fols. 67–68.

the laws concede to the *hijos del pais* [sons of the country], but subject to the obligations imposed by article 7 of the State Constitution.

Article 5: These Letters of Security will be valid for only the 5 years referred to in the previous article; they must be revalidated each year, and after this period, [the foreigners] will have the status of natives, as Article 2 of this law holds, and with the option of posts that the Constitution does not exclude them from holding. . . .

Article 12: When a foreigner complains about any authority, observing in the complaint that which is accorded by State laws regulating administration of justice, he will be promptly attended to; and if he legally proves his petition,

the authority who caused the offence will be treated with the rigor of the laws and repay the foreigner his expenses and damages.

Article 13: Excluded from the former case are Spaniards from overseas who have resided in the Republic's territory at the time of the declaration of independence, and who have sworn the oath to adhere to it [the Republic], or who have contracted marriage with a salvadoreña.

Article 14: This law is obligatory from the moment of its publication for foreigners who have been in the State; from 2 months after publication for those who come from other States of the Republic; and in six months for those who reintroduce themselves from outside Central America.

El Salvador, Decree 2 (1845)[10]

[Decree, 7 June 1845, signed by VP Joaquín Guzmán Dueñas]

{NOTE: *In its introduction, the decree begins by stating that it responds to complaints by consuls and intends to prevent misinterpretation of Article 6 of El Salvador's 1841 constitution regarding naturalization of foreigners.*}

The Vice President of El Salvador, as the Chamber of Deputies has decreed and Senators sanctioned:

3. . . . That the evils that foreigners cause will be inevitable as long as there is no strong national government to contain them and fix by treaties an international law

4. That naturalization should not be forced since according to the laws of some European nations, their nationals cannot lose the qualities of a Citizen except by certain explicit acts

5. That no inconvenience follows from a foreigner being one as long as [he] observes the laws of the country and that the real property that [he] acquires is subject to the same obligations as those of *Hijos del Estado* [sons of the state]

6. Equally that the consuls base their complaints on laws issued with no experience, for the powerful reason that they speak in the name of strong nations, disregarding in the States the faculty of repealing the inconveniences that only a National government can resolve

Decrees

Article 1: Foreigners in conformity with Article 6 of the Constitution naturalize when they have the qualities expressed in the said article; but not precisely by right [*Derecho*], but when they themselves ask for it, in which case the property that the article mentions will be at the value of 2000 pesos.

Article 2: Foreigners can acquire real property in the State in conformity with Article 6 of the Constitution, but the property is not then exempt from legal obligations that should be charged against it if they were in the hands of sons of the State.

Article 3: The decree of 28 February 1844 is abrogated.

Given in San Salvador, 4 June 1845, Senate

---

[10]*Source:* MAE, CC-G, vol. 2, 1844–1845, fols. 477–477v.

Bertrand Save Letters (1843–1844)[11]

Sonsonate, 26 December 1843 (Copy and transcription by Consul Alphonse Huet)

Bertrand Save, of the French Nation [. . .] states:

That the Electoral Committee [*Junta*] of this city has done me the honor to name me *alcalde primero* [municipal justice] to function in the year 1844. This proof of confidence places upon me extreme gratitude that I of course recognize; but I cannot in return accept the election because I am not suitable to fulfill it, most of all because the law does not permit it, for it demands indispensably for such posts the circumstance that the elected [person] be a citizen of the country. I, while I am a vecino, am not a citizen, because, as a foreigner, I have no naturalization letter, neither de facto nor by law am I naturalized, having come into this country long after the oath of independence, as is public and notorious, [and also because I am] relying on a grave illness that I had which the doctor has begun to cure. All has been in vain for me. Separated from my family and my interests, both mine and of others, these principles are all contrary to international laws and principally overseas [laws].

Roman history presents us with an example worthy of attention: there has never been in ancient and modern times a king and emperor more absolute and despotic than Nero; but he always respected the law of nations, he always respected foreigners. All these reasons and rights combined lead me to implore the Governor to repeal the sentence given to make me take up the rod of a judge[12] of Sonsonate; I ask for Justice and swear not to be acting maliciously.

G[od], U[nion], L[iberty][13]

Signed: Bertrand Save

Sonsonate, 5 January 1844

[Copy and transcription by Consul Albert Huet]

[Excerpt]

Bertrand Save, of the French nation, registered in the chancellery of the Consulate General of France in Central America, resident in Guatemala, In the year 1841, the Supreme Government of El Salvador complained in its newspapers and weekly digest that foreigners, in their representations of offenses, were not contacting the Government directly, and that it would hear them with all possible attention. And that they [the foreigners] should not contact their consuls directly. So I, as a lover of order and tranquility, and above all of the Salvadoran people, have directed myself to [the Government's] authorities, so that, as a French national, my resignation of the position of Alcalde Primero of Sonsonate be admitted, which request was entirely refused . . .

[The letter continues with the assertions about Roman law in *Save's letter of 26 December 1843*]

---

[11]*Source:* MAE, CC-G, vol. 2, fols. 240–240v. Bertrand Save to Departmental Governor of Sonsonate, 26 December 1843; fols. 40v–241v: Same to same, 5 January 1844.

[12]Note: Since colonial times, when undertaking their official duties, city justices carried a *vara,* or rod, often gold-tipped, that indicated their position.

[13]"Dios, Union, Libertad" was the official motto of the Central American Republic (1824–1838).

Governor's Response (1844)[14]

Note of the Governor to the Alcalde Primero of Sonsonate

Santa Ana [El Salvador], 8 January 1844

---

[14]*Source:* MAE, CC-G, 2: fols. 241–242v. Governor of Sonsonate, Santa Ana, 8 January 1844, to José Antonio Ramos, Alcalde Primero, Sonsonate.

With the presence of [your] note dated the 6th, I must tell you: that you have complied with Article 561 of the State Penal Code by putting under arrest and imprisoning the Alcalde Primero elect, Mr. Bertrand Save, French merchant in Sonsonate, and [Mr. Save] will continue to be imprisoned until he takes up his post, without prejudice to [also] a 50-peso fine demanded of him. Mr. Save lives in society, and for this must serve the post that today he refuses. For this reason and for articles 6 and 7 of the Constitution of the State [of El Salvador], his resignation was not accepted, and while Mr. Save does not fancy the title of citizen of El Salvador, and we see today with what contempt, he has the capacities [required] by the law to do it, and the obligation to bear communal obligations [*cargas comunales*] . . . If Foreigners after having lived the time that the State Constitution demands, welcome it (the state) to keep their lives and goods out of danger from aggressors, it is very just that they offer their services because, on the contrary, it would be to sustain an injustice and to seek to hold themselves in a better condition than Central Americans [not to do so].

In light of the afore stated, I think that Mr. Save, according to the law, must be obliged to take possession of his post and that, until that time, he remain in jail, without prejudice to demand from him the above-mentioned fine of 50 pesos.

G[od], U[nion], L[iberty]
[Castillo]

Suggested Sources

Many of Spanish America's constitutions can be found in Spanish in the Biblioteca Cervantes Virtual, http://www.cervantesvirtual.com/portal/Constituciones/. Although few constitutions have been translated into English, the Political Constitution of the Spanish Monarchy (1812) (also known as the Constitution of Cádiz) is available in translation at the Biblioteca Cervantes Virtual, http://www.cervantesvirtual.com/servlet/SirveObras/12159396448091522976624/index.htm, and in Arnold R Verduin, comp. *Manual of Spanish Constitutions, 1808–1931* (Ypsilanti, MI: University Litho-printers, 1941). So, too, is the Mexican Constitution of 1824, http://www.tamu.edu/ccbn/dewitt/constit1824.htm. (There are some important translation errors in this version. The Spanish text can be consulted at: http://www.constitucion.es/otras_constituciones/espana/txt/constitucion_1812.html.)

To understand women's constraints in terms of political action, see *Camilla* (1984), an Argentine film that highlights the constraints on women's citizenship in the early nineteenth century. Joseph Conrad's *Nostromo, A Tale of the Seaboard* (New York, NY: Oxford University Press, 2007 [1904]) is a gripping novel that ties together a study of democracy, capitalism, imperialism, and revolution in a fictional South American country (Costaguana).

For treatment of foreigners and respect of laws, see the longer version of this study in Jordana Dym, "Citizen of Which Republic: Foreigners and the Construction of Citizenship in Central America, ca. 1808–1845," *The Americas* 64, no. 4 (2008): 477–510; Lauren Benton, "'The Laws of this Country': Foreigners and the Legal Construction of Sovereignty in Uruguay, 1830–1875," *Law and History Review* 19, no. 3 (2001): 479–512; and Hans Vogel, "New Citizens for a New Nation: Naturalization in Early Independent Argentina," *Hispanic American Historical Review* 71, no. 1 (1991): 107–131. For the French in nineteenth-century Central America, see *The French in Central America: Cultural and Commerce, 1820–1930* (Wilmington, DE: Scholarly Resources, 2000); and William J. Griffith, *Empires in the Wilderness: Foreign Colonization and Development in Guatemala, 1834–1844* (Chapel Hill: University of North Carolina Press, 1965). For the transition from *vecinos* to *ciudadanos* more broadly, see Tamar Herzog, "Communities Becoming a Nation: Spain and Spanish America in the Wake of Modernity (and Thereafter)," *Citizenship Studies* 11, no. 2 (2007): 151–172. For women and citizenship in nineteenth-century Latin America, see Kif Augustine-Adams, "'She Consents Implicitly': Women's Citizenship, Marriage, and Liberal Political Theory in Late-Nineteenth and Early-Twentieth-Century Argentina," *Journal of Women's History* 13, no. 4 (2002): 8–30; Arlene Díaz, *Female Citizens, Patriarchs, and the Law in Venezuela, 1786–1904* (Lincoln: Nebraska University Press, 2004); and Sueann Caulfield, Sarah Chambers, and Lara Putnam, *Honor, Status & Law in Modern Latin America* (Durham, NC: Duke University Press, 2005).

Chapter 7

Liberalism and Its Limits: Guillermo Prieto on Patriarchy, Politics, and Provincial Peoples

John Tutino, Georgetown University

Nineteenth-century *liberals* promised to liberate Latin Americans while guiding the creation of national states and societies. They proclaimed individual rights and demanded popular political participations—yet they clung to exclusions that kept large numbers, often majorities, from sharing in those rights and participations. After independence, *liberals* offered prescriptions that aimed to transform societies rooted in Iberian colonialism and struggling to become nations. Hispanic *liberalism* was rooted in the eighteenth-century Enlightenment and became a concrete program amid the Spanish struggles to defeat Napoleon and simultaneously preserve the American Empire. It culminated in the Cádiz Constitution of 1812 that offered expanded electoral participations that included indigenous communities yet also challenged the right of those communities to hold corporate lands. That foundational charter aimed to reform Spain and its Americas; it became a model for reformers in Portugal's Atlantic domains.[1] During the nineteenth century, with inevitable adaptations and permutations, *liberals* and *liberalism* offered visions that promised to surmount colonial legacies and forge nations by promoting popular sovereignty, market economies, and individual liberties—while challenging the right of Church institutions and native communities to hold lands.[2]

Yet what is promoted as new is rarely entirely new, what is proclaimed as liberating is often laden with limits. There was never one *liberal* vision: Some reformers primarily promoted provincial and municipal rights; some adamantly resisted the power of the Church and the influence of the clergy; some pressed most to privatize property held by Church institutions and indigenous communities; many worked to promote free trade. Nearly all framed their emphases in visions of popular sovereignty and citizenship, equality, and the rule of law. Yet all excluded women, and many insisted that indigenous peoples required education, designed and implemented by *liberals*, before they could effectively hold the rights of *liberal* citizenship.

Guillermo Prieto was a leading Mexican *liberal* intellectual, writer, and office holder. Born in 1818, he never knew colonial life. His grandfather was a merchant and, had not the wars for independence intervened, the family might have gained wealth and landed estates. Instead, Prieto's father managed

Molino del Rey, a wheat mill and estate just west of the capital. Prieto's mother came from a less-favored background, with kin among Mexico City shopkeepers. When his father died in 1831, Prieto faced life without monetary resources—but with family connections in every sector of the city except among the very rich and truly poor. He would live by gaining an education and by the contacts he made in schools and public parks, political meetings, and intellectual soirees. Exalted aspirations for himself and the Mexican nation, both constrained by uncertain prospects, internal conflicts, and limited means, shaped Prieto's *liberalism*.

Prieto became a political journalist and activist in the 1840s. When the United States invaded and occupied Mexico City in 1847, he fled with the government to Querétaro. He was a partisan of continuing the war to prevent the loss of vast northern territories; he acquiesced in a view that saw the fight, the territories, and much of Mexico's national potential as lost. In 1850 General Mariano Arista became president. Arista was a moderate *liberal*, committed to equal rights and electoral rule, open to accommodation with the Church and clergy, and respectful of the nation's deeply Catholic culture. Guillermo Prieto was Arista's last treasury minister, holding that pivotal but challenging portfolio from September 1852 to January 1853, when Arista was toppled by *conservatives* who brought Antonio López de Santa Anna back to the presidency in a government crafted by Lucas Alamán, the ideological and political leader of postindependence *conservatism*. Santa Anna was proclaimed His Most Serene Highness; he and Alamán attempted to bring deeply religious monarchical visions to the heart of national government. Members of the deposed *liberal* cabinet were exiled from the capital, and Prieto departed under armed guard to live in the city of Querétaro. Once a center of trade and textile production that linked the silver-rich north to Mexico City and the Atlantic world beyond, in the 1850s, it was a provincial capital facing economic decline. Later, Prieto was forced to the famously *conservative* town of Cadereita, at the edge of the rugged Sierra Gorda, where indigenous peoples were historically independent, deeply resistant, and often more loyal to the Church than the nation. He was only about 100 miles from the capital, yet isolated in another—just as deeply Mexican—world.

[1]On Cádiz and New Spain as it became Mexico, see Antonio Ávila, *En nombre de la nación* (Mexico City: Taurus, 2002). On the impact of Cádiz in Portugal and Brazil, see Kirstin Schulz, *Tropical Versailles: Empire, Monarchy, and the Portuguese Royal Court in Rio de Janeiro, 1808–1821* (New York: Routledge, 2001).
[2]The best analysis of Mexican liberalism remains Charles Hale, *Mexican Liberalism in the Age of Mora, 1821–1853* (New Haven, CT: Yale University Press, 1968).

Prieto kept detailed diaries. His chronicle of growing up in newly independent Mexico City, his difficult personal life, and his rise to intellectual and political prominence was published after his death as *Memorias de mis tiempos* (Memoirs of My Times).[3] The sketch of his life here is taken from that autobiographical narrative, which also offers sharp portrayals of key personages of the years from the late 1820s to the early 1850s, friends and foes. Prieto continued to keep diaries during his months in Querétaro and Cadereita. He published the chronicles of exile in serial form in a Mexico City newspaper in 1857, while far more radical *liberals* took power and wrote a constitution that set off another decade of conflict. A war to defeat *conservative* and clerical opposition from 1858 to 1860 was followed by a struggle to liberate Mexico from French occupation and the imposed Empire of Maximilian of Hapsburg. Only in 1867 did radical *liberals* reclaim rule under President Benito Juárez, born a Zapotec Indian. Prieto's *Viajes de orden supremo* (Travels on Order of the Supreme One), published under the pen name Fidel (the faithful one), details his encounters with provincial Mexico. Both chronicles offer insight into the goals, limits, and contradictions of nineteenth-century Mexican *liberalism*.[4]

The documents that follow are excerpted from Prieto's urban memoirs and provincial travels. The selections divide into three sections: the first outlines Prieto's visions of the good in society; the second offers his views of the challenges of politics in the 1850s, *liberal* and *conservative*; the third offers sketches of provincial peoples. Although Prieto's views, particularly of rural peoples, may seem less extreme than Sarmiento's, his writings present a *liberalism* that was privileged, patriarchal, and political. Prieto exalted liberty, appreciated Christianity, and presumed patriarchy. In political life, he promoted *liberalism* as the cure for Mexico's ills. His encounters with independent women, indigenous people, and a homosexual man suggest commitments to a moral order that remained deeply traditional and laden with exclusions.

Questions to Consider:

1. What emphases shaped Prieto's vision of the good in Mexican society? How did his preference for patriarchy relate to his *liberalism*?
2. How did Prieto understand the challenges of political life in Mexico in the 1850s?
3. What troubled Prieto about women's employment at Querétaro? What does his concern suggest about *liberal* views of women's roles in Mexico?
4. How did Prieto see the Church as a problem but the priest as a solution? How could he see the people as sovereign, yet worry so much about the indigenous majority?
5. Why was Prieto so troubled by the cook in Cadereita? What does his anger suggest about his *liberalism,* his definition of manhood, and his understanding of politics?

---

[3]Guillermo Prieto, *Memorias de mis tiempos* (1906: repr. in vol. 1, *Obras completas*, Mexico City: CONACULTA, 1992). Translations are mine.
[4]Guillermo Prieto "Fidel," *Viajes de orden suprema* (1857; repr. in 2 vols, Querétaro: Gobierno del Estado, 1986). Translations are mine.

Prieto's Visions of the Good

On Patriarchy and Family[5]

The family of don Manuel Cosío offered a picture of patriarchal happiness. All admired its perfect harmony, the paternal kindness and majesty, the respect given the home, the constant happiness, the meals enjoyed with contentment, and the solace of simple family pleasures.

---

[5]*Source:* Guillermo Prieto, *Memorias de mis tiempos* (1906: reprint in Vol. 1, *Obras completas* (Mexico City: CONACULTA, 1992). Translations are mine. p. 330.

On Patriarchy and Society[6]

My father was so fine, so sincerely a friend of the poor, that the peons adored him. As master, his name was magical, generating contentment, ending troubles, . . . creating comfort and pleasure.

---

[6]*Source:* Guillermo Prieto, *Memorias de mis tiempos* (1906: reprint in Vol. 1, *Obras completas* (Mexico City: CONACULTA, 1992). Translations are mine. p. 56.

On Privilege and the People[7]

But for me, everything false, everything artificial and pretentious has been not only repellent, but impossible. . . . Such ideas have always exaggerated in me the contrast between my internal habits, my domestic customs, and my aristocratic way of living with my family, keeping the traditions of my parents, and my love for the people, my desire to study them despite their lack of civilization, their inconsequential ways, and their vices.

On the Nature and Necessity of Indians[8]

The Indian is accused of laziness, yet no one lives more actively . . . He is portrayed as inert, yet without him what would become of our everyday commerce? Who more than he is dedicated to supplying our most urgent needs? Cultivation, the essential source or our well being . . . the root of life for all people, what would it yield among us without the Indian?

On the *Liberal* Dream[9]

We will found this *raza* [race, with an implication of nation] by creating a community of interests; by

Portrait of Benito Juárez by the artist Diego Rivera. Juárez was an acculturated Zapotec Indian, committed *liberal*, and president of Mexico from 1861 to 1872. How does this image caputre Juárez's ethnic identity? How does it downplay that identity, and why?

Source: Private Collection/The Bridgeman Art Library International.

transforming the legacies of colonization; by bringing all equally under civil rule; by recovering the good in Christian evangelism; and by progress, light, and the proclamation and practice of every liberty, protected by order, morality, and justice.

---

[7]*Source:* Guillermo Prieto, *Memorias de mis tiempos* (1906: reprint in Vol. 1, *Obras completas* (Mexico City: CONACULTA, 1992). Translations are mine. p. 297.

[8]*Source:* Guillermo Prieto "Fidel," *Viajes de orden suprema* (1857; reprint in 2 volumes: *Querétaro: Gobierno del Estado*,1986). Translations are mine. p. 191.

[9]*Source:* Guillermo Prieto "Fidel," Viajes de orden suprema (1857; reprint in 2 volumes: Querétaro: Gobierno del Estado,1986). Translations are mine. p. 308.

The Challenges of *Liberal* Politics

On Becoming Treasury Minister in the Cabinet of President Arista[10]

The revolutions inflaming every village, the diplomatic pacts threatening our government, the

insubordination in the barracks, the hunger bewildering with its pains and spreading discontent, the savages devouring our frontiers, the usury and speculation that greedily devour those condemned to misery. Such in outline was the fragile reality of the nation when President Arista kindly gave me charge to lead the Ministry.

---

[10]*Source:* Guillermo Prieto, *Memorias de mis tiempos* (1906: reprint in Vol. 1, *Obras completas* (Mexico City: CONACULTA, 1992). Translations are mine. p. 494.

On the Conservative Program of Lucas Alamán[11]

With subtle insight, Alamán sent . . . a kind of charter program for the new government. It can be reduced to the annihilation of every popular institution, the centralization of power, the exaltation of the clergy, and the preponderance of the army; the

[11]*Source:* Guillermo Prieto, *Memorias de mis tiempos* (1906: reprint in Vol. 1, *Obras completas* (Mexico City: CONACULTA, 1992). Translations are mine. p. 504.

distribution of all funds by the dictator's hand, even to the municipalities; the destruction of freedom of trade, adopting a system of prohibitive tariffs—in a word, hate for all liberties, the trampling of all rights of men, and the revival of legacies of the worst times of the colony and the viceroys. And despite the absurdity, the inconceivability of the program, the influence of the clergy, the speculators, the rootless, and the politicians without principles, not only does the project appear feasible, it finds partisans across the republic—with a few honorable exceptions.

The Discomforts of Provincial Exile

On Women in the City of Querétaro[12]

The misery of the unfortunate classes, the residue of lost people in the gateway to the North, and above all the frightful ignorance of women and the inattention generally given to their education, has produced in Querétaro examples of sadly precocious deterioration and prostitution among women. The tobacco factory and textile labor have offered them *fementido* [false, implying feminine] gains, making women accustomed to certain liberties, a certain neglect of domestic duties. The result is that when unemployment spreads, their only recourse is prostitution.

On a Good Priest and His Miserable Parishioners[13]

I must mention here the resident vicar of Vizarrón, Father Albino Montes, one of those creations who . . . are dispensers of celestial consolation on earth. Living in one of the most miserable towns in the republic, truly speaking in a ruin of a town, amid

[12]*Source:* Guillermo Prieto "Fidel," *Viajes de orden suprema* (1857; reprint in 2 volumes: *Querétaro: Gobierno del Estado,* 1986). Translations are mine. p. 165.
[13]*Source:* Guillermo Prieto "Fidel," *Viajes de orden suprema* (1857; reprint in 2 volumes: *Querétaro: Gobierno del Estado,* 1986). Translations are mine. pp. 314–315.

swarms of natives in whom barbarity competed with misery in an improbable degradation of our species, Father Montes personified the consolation, the torch of Christian civilization, the promise of mercy, carrying his august mission to his parishioners with sensitivity and love. . . . Amid rains, on roads impassable on foot, where every path clings to the edge of an abyss and any misstep could lead to death, Father Montes traveled without rest, carrying the treasures of compassion and the Eucharistic bread to huts full of the most nauseating diseases and the most repellent barbarism, seemingly united under the protection of Satan to fend off the benefactor of the spirit.

His life was a perpetual labor, the remuneration of his toil was converted into alms, his rest was teaching children, his solace a holy intervention to calm discord through preaching. Tied to his flock by links of the spirit, involved in the most important memories in their lives and those of their neighbors, joining in the most important events in the lives of his children, as he called them, his presence was a blessing, his title God's mediator. In distant hamlets, they recognized the hoof beats of his proud horse, children ran from their huts to hug his legs, women and the old stopped him to consult about their afflictions. Father Montes, a young man of excellent literary education . . . gave advice to farmers, shared the rules of hygiene with the infirm, and offered pure and simple moral lessons to all who consulted him.

On a Cook Presumed Homosexual in Cadereita[14]

I arrived in town, at high noon, with all the appearance of a criminal. Amid the clamor of the armed soldiers who escorted me and the curious townspeople who gathered around, I stopped at the inn on the plaza, taking a room as narrow and dark as the mind of a contemporary nobleman, so disheveled it must have been kept by the national treasury.

Soon after arriving, we asked about a restaurant. As a guest of the inn, I conveyed my appreciation so fully that one of the proprietors of the most celebrated establishment in town came to place himself at my service. I struggle to relate to my readers the profound disgust, the intense discomfort, the uncontainable passion that took control as I faced the cholera produced in me by the sight and first words of the cook.

He was a little man of medium stature, his complexion so dark that my name [Prieto] would fit him well; his hair shined with grease, divided like a woman's, his brilliant curls held behind his ears; his earrings and necklace of coral; his shirt impudently open, hidden under a silk shawl tied like a woman's with ribbons of veil at the waist, its fringe hanging in the back with obvious coquetry; his tight cotton trousers were stylish, his shoes low, and in his shirt lace and feathers like a ranch girl dressed up to go out. In a word, he was what they call in the north a *marica*, an effeminate man. Such beings are prodigies of degradation, apostates of the male sex, sacrilegious transfigurations, unfortunately well known and for me and every man who keeps common cause, detestable, loathsome, and insulting in the extreme.

I cannot describe what I felt when without prior greeting, without precedent, strutting, winsome, and with the most melodious voice, the ambiguous cook said to me:

"*Mi vida* [My life], what do you wish?"
"Go away, get out of my presence!"

"My God, why so scornful, fair one? We have green and red *mole*, roast chicken, and beans refried with chopped onion."
"Man! I will not eat. Go to hell!"

The counterfeit man was about to continue when the soldiers in the lodging ended the repugnant scene.

Suggested Sources:

Rarely do indigenous people, poor women of any origin, and homosexuals (who remain nearly invisible) offer their voices and visions in texts remaining from the nineteenth century. We are left to seek the diversity of Mexico and other Latin American societies through the eyes of the powerful and the privileged, often foreign visitors, all of whom must be read carefully and critically. Among the most revealing narratives is Fanny Calderón de la Barca's *Life in Mexico: The Letters of Fanny Calderon de la Barca, with New Material from the Author's Private Journals*, ed. Howard T. Fisher and Marian Hall Fisher (Garden City, NY: Doubleday, 1966). She was the Scottish wife of Spain's first ambassador to independent Mexico. She lived in Mexico City and toured much of the country during the late 1830s and early 1840s; her letters and journals provide revealing detail. Brantz Mayer was United States consul in Mexico City at about the same time. He studied Mexican history, lived its politics (with mostly *liberal* friends), toured the country around the capital, and wrote *Mexico as It Was and Is* (Baltimore: W. Taylor, 1846)—a text laden with insight and bias. After the war that claimed the huge northern territories of Mexico for the United States, Mayer published the larger *Mexico, Aztec, Spanish, and Republican: A Historical, Geographical, Political, Statistical and Social Account of That Country from the Period of the Invasion by the Spaniards to the Present Time*, 2 vols. (Hartford, CT: S. Drake, 1852). For a Mexican perspective parallel to Prieto's, there is Manuel Payno's *The Bandits from Río Frío: A Naturalistic and Humorous Novel of Customs, Crimes, and Horrors*, 2 vols., trans. Alan Fluckey (San Francisco: Heliographica Press, 2005). Payno was also a moderate *liberal* and government official, a close colleague

---

[14]*Source:* Guillermo Prieto "Fidel," *Viajes de orden suprema* (1857; reprint in 2 volumes: *Querétaro: Gobierno del Estado*, 1986). Translations are mine. pp. 308–309.

of Prieto. He wrote his long descriptive account of Mexico and its nineteenth-century customs as a novel, in many ways as revealing as Prieto's chronicles. In *Mexico during the War with the United States*, ed. Walter Scholes, trans. Elliott Scherr (Columbia: University of Missouri Press, 1950), José Fernando Ramírez compiled numerous accounts of the wartime challenges that led to the political conflicts of the 1850s. Both Prieto and Payno are represented in the collection.

Charles Hale, *Mexican Liberalism in the Age of Mora, 1821–1853* (New Haven, CT: Yale University Press, 1968), remains the classic analysis of the politics and ideological debates of Mexican *liberalism* leading up to the 1850s. Steve Stern in *The Secret History of Gender: Women, Men, and Power in Late Colonial Mexico* (Chapel Hill: University of North Carolina Press, 1995) provides a wide ranging analysis of gender relations in diverse regions of Mexico at the end of the colonial era with suggestive insights on the national era that

followed. In *Peasants, Politics, and the Formation of the Mexican National State: Guerrero, 1800–1855* (Stanford, CA: Stanford University Press, 1996), Peter Guardino brought relations with peasant communities to the center of analysis of the emergence of *liberal* power, focusing on regions south of Mexico City. Florencia Mallon's *Peasant and Nation: The Making of Post-Colonial Mexico and Peru* (Berkeley: University of California Press, 1995) analyzes interactions among *liberal* state builders and peasant communities, always with an eye toward gender relations, during the middle and later decades of the nineteenth century, while Mexicans faced international, national, and social conflicts. I know of no analysis of homosexuality, nor of views of homosexuality, in nineteenth-century Mexico. Given the pivotal importance of patriarchy to colonial legacies and *liberal* visions, the (supposed) homosexuality described and vehemently rejected by Prieto remains a key topic awaiting a historian.

Chapter 8

Marriage Laws and Nation in Ecuador, 1860–1911

Erin E. O'Connor, Bridgewater State College

Throughout the nineteenth century, Latin American women—from the humblest servants to the wealthiest landowners—lacked basic political and civil rights. Nowhere in Latin America did women have the right to vote, and in most countries married women's rights were quite constrained. Yet women's marginalization in politics and society did not produce the same heated debates in the nineteenth century that one finds over the position of Indians, Afro-Latin Americans, or even foreigners. Instead, most central government officials agreed that women should be excluded from political affairs and remain under the watchful protection of their husbands. Most nineteenth-century constitutions, in any part of the world, did not even specify that women were excluded from the right to vote, because central-government officials considered their disqualification to be self-evident. Like their peers in other world regions, the elite men who ran Latin American nations assumed that most women would marry and raise children and that their husbands would provide for them. Many historians have noted that women's rights, and the gender norms behind them, changed least of all in the transition from colony to republic. When women's status did change, it was often for the worse, with laws that gave husbands even tighter control over women and children than they had enjoyed in the colonial period.[1]

The documents in this chapter invite readers to explore the importance of marriage and gender laws in nineteenth-century Latin America by presenting how these laws changed in Ecuador from 1860 to 1911. They offer concrete evidence of the many ways that women's rights were severely constricted through the manipulation of gender ideologies. Government-generated marriage laws and debates also show how and why statesmen found gender a useful tool for advancing their political agendas. Though the document excerpts presented in this chapter are from Ecuador, they provide evidence of a broader pattern in Latin American women's history, because similar laws and changes occurred in most other Latin American nations during the period.

Excluding women from politics and identifying them with the private sphere offered statesmen a tool with which to address several political problems. National political leaders claimed to create representative governments in which all men were equal before the law, yet as other chapters in this section show, poor non-white men were systematically marginalized in nineteenth-century politics. Excluding women from politics and placing them under their husbands' control helped to resolve some of the tensions among men over race and class inequalities. Although poor and non-white men had to answer to their so-called race and class "superiors," the law allowed all of them to enjoy patriarchal authority in their own homes. Furthermore, state officials developed and changed marriage laws to reflect and reinforce their own political objectives, and sometimes marriage laws had as much to do with seemingly unrelated political concerns as they did with regulating the relationships between husbands and wives. For example, the document excerpts presented in this chapter reveal how the changing relationship between Church and state in Ecuador was reflected in marriage laws.

The first document excerpt in this chapter is from the 1860 Ecuadorian Civil Code. As with any civil code, it was designed to identify the rights and obligations that everyone living within the nation had in business matters, social interactions, inheritance, and personal disputes. The 1860 civil code was the standard law code, particularly for marriage relations, for decades to come.[2] It was in effect during the *conservative* rule of Gabriel García Moreno, who dominated Ecuadorian national politics from 1860 until his death by assassination in 1875. Marriage, family, and morality were particularly important to García Moreno, who proposed to use Catholicism to forge Ecuador into a strong and unified nation. In fact, during the second phase of his rule, from 1869 to 1875, Catholicism was a requirement for citizenship, and concubinage was a punishable crime. The document taken from this period gives one a sense of how and why gender ideas and marital relations were critical to his proclaimed goals.

Other document excerpts are from the *liberal* period (1895–1925) and include the civil marriage law (1902), a debate over female suffrage (1910), and the law defining the civil rights of married women (1911). *Liberals* sought to expand and strengthen the presence of the central government throughout Ecuador, so that peoples of all

---

[1]Evelyn Cherpak, "The Participation of Women in the Independence Movement in Gran Colombia, 1780–1830," in *Latin American Women: Historical Perspectives,* ed. Asunción Lavrin (Westport, CT: Greenwood Press, 1978), 219–234; Sarah C. Chambers, *From Subjects to Citizens: Honor, Gender, and Politics in Arequipa, Peru, 1780–1854* (University Park: Pennsylvania State University Press, 1999); Elizabeth Dore, "One Step Forward, Two Steps Back: Gender and the State in the Long Nineteenth Century," in *Hidden Histories of Gender and the State in Latin America,* ed. Elizabeth Dore and Maxine Molineaux (Durham, NC: Duke University Press, 2000).

[2]There was, for example, an 1889 civil code, but it simply reiterated the marriage laws presented here. See República del Ecuador, *Código Civil de la República del Ecuador* (New York: Imprenta de "Las Novedades," 1889).

regions, classes, and ethnicities would be aware of and loyal to the state in their daily lives. *Liberals* also aimed to establish a strong secular government, and they were often at odds with Church officials, whose power was on the decline with the passage of *liberal* laws. Finally, *liberals* purported to advance individual rights and equality before the law much more adamantly than García Moreno had done. However, *liberals'* commitment to this ideal was more often theoretical than practical, as poor and non-white Ecuadorians remained exploited and marginalized. Within this broader aim of upholding and extending individual rights, many *liberals* were adamant in their quest (as they saw it) to "liberate" married women and "modernize" gender relations in Ecuador—topics that emerge in the document excerpts on the period. Readers can decide for themselves the extent to which *liberals* achieved their proclaimed goal of liberating married women, and the purposes that changing marriage laws served within the broader *liberal* agenda.

Although the marriage laws outlined here parallel those found in other Latin American nations during the nineteenth century, Ecuador also has a special place in Latin American women's history: In 1929, it was the first country in the region to allow women to vote in nationwide elections. This did not mean that suffrage rights were widespread, let alone universal: Literacy requirements for voting were maintained until 1979, and these kept the majority of Ecuador's poor, particularly indigenous, peoples politically alienated.

Questions to Consider:

1. What limits did Ecuadorian law place on women? How did the law change over time?
2. What was the relationship like between Church and state in these documents? How did it change over time?
3. How—and how much—did legislators' views about women's proper role(s) and place in society change over time?
4. In what ways did laws (and lawmakers) assert that the institution of marriage was important to the well-being of society and to the nation in these documents? What purposes might it have served them to "legislate the domestic sphere"?

Excerpts from the Ecuadorian Civil Code, 1860[3]

Art. 98: Marriage is an indissoluble solemn contract between a man and a woman which unites them for life, with the aim of living together, procreating, and helping each other.

Art. 99: It falls upon ecclesiastical authorities to decide whether a proposed marriage contract is or is not valid. [. . .]

Art. 124: Spouses are obligated to guard the faith, and to offer each other mutual help and assistance in all of life's circumstances.

A husband owes his wife protection, and a wife should obey her husband.

Art. 126: A husband has the right to require his wife to live where he does and to change her residence with him.

This right ceases when its execution would endanger the life of the wife.

A wife, on her part, has the right that her husband will receive her in his house.

Art. 128: Marriage consolidates the goods of the married couple, and a husband administers his wife's goods.

Art. 130: A wife cannot, without her husband's authorization, celebrate any kind of contract . . . nor remit a debt, nor accept or reject a donation, inheritance or legacy, or acquire any onerous or lucrative title, nor dispose of, mortgage, or pawn goods.

Art. 132: A wife does not need her husband's authorization to dispose of that which is hers in her will.

Art. 136: A judge's authorization can replace a husband's in cases when a husband denies it without just cause, as well as in cases of his real or apparent

[3]*Source: Código Civil de la República del Ecuador* (Quito: Imprenta de los huérfanos de Valencia, 1860).

absence, when the delay would cause [his wife] harm.

Art. 149: A judge will decree the separation of goods[4] in cases of insolvency or fraudulent administration [of goods] on the part of a husband.

Art. 153: A wife who has separated goods from her husband does not require his authorization for acts and contracts relative to the administration and enjoyment of the things that she administers separately. [. . .]

But she does need his authorization, or a judge's in substitute, to engage in a trial, even in cases concerning that which she administers separately, saving those exceptions in article 129 [which stipulates that a wife does not need her husband's representation in criminal cases].

Art. 159: The legal re-establishment of a husband's administration of marital goods returns things to their previous state, as if the separation of goods had never happened. But acts executed legally by the woman, during the separation of goods, will be validated. [. . .]

Art. 162: A trial for *divorcio*[5] falls under ecclesiastical authority. The civil effects of *divorcio* (that is, all that concerns conjugal goods, personal liberty, the upbringing and education of children), are regulated privately by civil laws.

A civil judge will regulate and decree a husband's provision for woman's food and housing, and litigation expenses, during the *divorcio* trial.

Art. 167: A "divorced" woman administers, independently of her husband, the goods that she took from his control, or that she acquired after the *divorcio*.

Art. 168: A husband who caused the *divorcio* is still required to contribute to the decent maintenance

of his "divorced" wife.[6] A judge will decide the amount and form of the contribution, attentive to the circumstances of both spouses.

Art. 169: Even if the wife was the cause of the *divorcio*, she will have the right that her husband provide her with [a stipend] necessary for modest maintenance, and a judge will decide what the contribution should be, as in the case of the previous article, giving special attention to which goods the husband still controls for his wife, and the conduct that he has observed in a wife both before and after the *divorcio*.

Art. 170: A husband who finds himself in a state of indigence has the right to his wife's help, insofar as he needs it for his modest maintenance, even if he was the cause of the *divorcio*; but in this case the judge, who regulates the contribution, will take into account the conduct of the husband.

Art. 172: If the couple reconciles, all the goods, related to marital society and the administration of goods, will be return to the state they were in before the *divorcio* occurred, as if the *divorcio* had never taken place. [. . .]

Art. 1734: A husband is the chief of marital society, and as such he administers freely all marital goods and those of his wife, subjected, however, to the obligations that this present [law code and] title places upon him and [any limits] which he has contracted through marriage agreements.

Art. 1735: A husband is, with respect to third parties, owner of the marital goods, as if they were his own goods obtained under his own patrimony, in such a manner that during [marriage] his creditors can persecute a husband for all his goods . . . without prejudice or compensation for those which he has within or outside of marital society.

[4]A separation of goods was when a couple remained married, but officially set up separate households due to some marital conflict. It was distinct from the *divorcio* discussed next.
[5]*Divorcio* was a formal separation dispensed by ecclesiastical authorities, with the goal of reuniting couples whenever possible. Because the Church considered marriage indissoluble, a *divorcio* did not permit either a husband or wife to remarry. This would change in Ecuador with the passage of new marriage laws in 1902 and 1910. Because of the changes over time, I have used *divorcio* rather than the English term divorce, and put the term "divorced" in quotation marks, when translating from nineteenth-century documents.

[6]The Catholic Church only granted *divorcios* under specific circumstances, such as adultery on the part of either spouse, a husband's failure to provide for his wife, domestic violence, or a spouse being forced to either commit a crime or do something contrary to Church teachings. Most of these stipulations meant that *divorcio* was largely a female prerogative, and both religious and secular officials saw it as a means of protecting married women from abuse.

Draft of the Civil Marriage Law, and Senate Debates, 1902 and 1910

Draft of the Civil Marriage Law from the Transcription of Senate Proceedings on August 19, 1902[7]

The Congress of the Republic of Ecuador,
DECREES

Art. 1: To establish civil matrimony in the Republic

Art. 2: That in order for marriage to produce civil effects it is necessary that it be celebrated in accordance to the prescriptions of the law.

Civil marriage will precede any religious ceremony . . . ministers of any religion who proceed with the nuptial benediction without [the couple] having had a civil ceremony, will . . . be fined two hundred sucres or imprisoned for three months, and in cases of repeat offenses, they will be fined five hundred sucres or imprisoned for one year . . .

Art. 6: Marriage can be dissolved by divorce.

Art. 7: The causes of divorce are:

1. A wife's adultery.
2. The corruption of one spouse by the other.
3. The attempt of one marriage partner against the life of the other.
4. If one of the spouses is the author, instigator, or accomplice in a crime perpetrated against the honor, life, or goods of his/her spouse, or of their children.
5. An attempt by the husband to prostitute his wife or his children.
6. A wife's refusal, without just cause, to live with her husband.
7. Abandonment of the couple's shared home.
8. Impotence.
9. Absence of more than five years, without just cause.
10. Resisting compliance with marital obligations, without justifiable motive.
11. Excessive gambling.
12. Habitual drunkenness.
13. Dissipation [meaning disappearance of one spouse?]
14. One spouse being sentenced to four years confinement, or other penalty of equal or greater gravity.

Excerpts of Senate Discussion of the Civil Marriage Law on September 15, 1902

{Senator} Banderas: As a Catholic, I cannot contribute even the remotest cooperation with the creation of a law that my conscience tells me is anti-Catholic in all facets . . . marriage is considered a contract and a sacrament, it falls exclusively under the rule and authority of the ecclesiastical jurisdiction . . . radicals have tried to establish [a distinction] between the contract and sacrament of matrimony, considering one independent of the other, in order to conclude that marriage is a purely human contract, subject only to civil jurisdiction and that the Church has no reason to intervene . . . this ill-fated distinction [is false].

{Senator} Riofrío: By opening the door to divorce, one opens it a little more each time to the most frightful corruption. It degrades woman who is redeemed by Christian marriage; it deprives children of the sweetness and love of the home, it annuls parental [or paternal?] rights, and it destroys the family. . . . [As one senator put it] 'I am a *liberal* . . . but I declare that the project of Civil Marriage, sent here by the house of Deputies, is a monstrosity and an absurdity'. . . We should not uproot the rocks that form the foundation of the social edifice, and that which we would [tear down] with this proposal would be not a single stone but an entire wall . . . In effect, sirs, between law and social institutions there is a wall of separation, and between those institutions the one which forms the foundation stone, sustaining all else, is Christian marriage.

{Senator} Andrade Marín: Mr. President, I am an Ecuadorian and moreover a legislator . . . I think, Mr. President, that as an Ecuadorian I am under the

---

[7]*Source*: República del Ecuador, *Anales de Senadores*, 1902— Congreso Ordinario (XXXV).

strictest obligation to procure by all means possible that Ecuador will fit into the rest of the civilized nations of the world . . . [and the rest of the civilized world] says that civil marriage is a vindication of the rights of men . . . If this contract is celebrated now, I say it will result in gains, with respect to spouses, to the legitimacy of children and their right to be raised and educated, their right to inherit goods from their parents, and the right of woman to be provided for by her husband . . . and who should regulate such cases? Undoubtedly the Civil Authorities.

{Note: The civil marriage law passed in 1902. It was revised in 1910 to allow couples to divorce by mutual consent, rather than having to list a specific grievance that led to the dissolution of the marriage.}

1910 Congressional Debate over Whether to Give Women the Right to Vote[8]

Representative Borja Cordero, September 7, 1910: It is notable, Mr. President, that never in the Republic has there been such a strict fulfillment of the free right of suffrage, and out of this a decree has been conceptualized that makes a bloody joke of citizens' rights. If there are men for whom voting is not possible, how can we permit a woman to do so? I insist that this proposal is a joke, and we cannot let it pass to a second debate.

Colonel López, September 7, 1910: Woman is called upon to share responsibility for the family in the home, therefore why would she not enjoy equally in civil and political rights with man? Can the *liberal* party deny this right, against the text of the Constitution, which dictates . . . that to be a citizen, one simply has to prove a capacity to read and write, without referring to sex?

Representative Barrera, one of the authors of the bill, on September 7, 1910: Why have we denied woman the right to exercise her political rights? . . . [Ours is only] a theoretical *liberalism;* when it is time to put it into practice, we back away from it. By what manner is woman less than man in the realm of ideas? *Liberalism* establishes that we should uphold woman's dignity.

Representative Borja Cordero, September 9, 1910: Woman is under the direct power of man, such as her husband, her father, her brother, and it is natural that she, deprived of her independence . . . suffers from the immediate influence of [men] . . . thus in a home where there are five or six daughters, all of them and their mother, will reflect the father's mode of thinking. And what will be the result? The opinion of the father will be apparent in five or six or seven votes. This is nothing other than establishing corruption in the Legislation.

{Note: The bill failed to pass.}

[8]*Source:* República del Ecuador, *Anales de Diputados*, September 7–22, 1910.

Law and Congressional Debates Pertaining to Civil Rights of the Married Woman, 1911

Draft of the Law on "The Civil Rights of the Married Woman"[9]

The Congress of the Republic of Ecuador
    DECREES

Art. 1: A married woman can throughout the time of her marriage maintain total or partial control of her own goods and administer them independently . . .

In this administration, a married woman has the legal capacity to act or enter into contracts of sale or mortgage real estate and to present herself in trial.

Art. 2. The goods that a woman excludes from marital society must be publicly documented . . . and if a husband is not involved in [creating] the document, he will be notified of its contents.

[9]*Source:* República del Ecuador, *Anales de Diputados*, September 25, 1911.

Art. 3. Any problems between the couple that are stirred up by the handing over the goods [to] the wife, or any other issue relative to the said goods, will be discussed in a summary trial.

Art. 8: A wife will administer for herself the capital she holds separately or that comes from her own work or industry. It will be respected by third parties as the exclusive property of the wife.

From Congressional Debates over the new law[10]

Senator Vela, one of the bill's authors, on Sept 9, 1911: It is well known that the family gives birth to society and therefore to the Nation . . . We who have opened the doors for woman to be a citizen, to have the same political and social rights as we have . . . how can we not concede to her equality in the matter of civil rights? . . . I have seen the need for woman to seek a door of escape in order to free herself from the cruelty of a husband without honor, without conscience, and who many times gets married because he is interested in a woman's goods . . . [and] after a while, sunk in misery, he abandons her and lives in public concubinage, while . . . his own wife and her legitimate children, die in poverty.

Senator Andrade, on Sept 9, 1911: The Ecuadorian woman . . . cannot independently manage her goods as occurs in other countries. Here it would occur that, separated from her husband, the wife would look to her priest [to tell her how to handle her money], because woman is essentially religious.

Senator Andrade, September 11, 1911: Woman is, in marriage, obliged to obey her husband at all times, as a result of which is that the wife cannot proceed freely [regarding her own property.]

Senator Peñaherrera, September 15, 1911, summarizing resistance to the proposed law: [The change

proposed by Sr. Intriago] appears at first glance to be absurd and is a system in which the relation between the spouses lacks an authority figure; and, in a certain way, it makes marriage into a union of two husbands, instead of a husband and a wife.

Suggested Sources:

Primary sources on women and nation making for the nineteenth century are few, and there are none available in translation for nineteenth-century Ecuador. For an interesting novel that is available in translation, in which a nineteenth-century Peruvian feminist raised women's problems without questioning basic gender norms, see Clorinda Matto de Turner, *Torn from the Nest*, trans. John H. R. Polt (New York: Oxford University Press, 1998). Also see translation of works by Juana Manuela Gorriti, in Francine Masiello, ed., *Dreams and Realities: Selected Fiction of Juana Manuela Gorriti*, trans. Sergio Waisman (New York: Oxford University Press, 2003). For collections of sources that include some documents on women in the nineteenth century, see Gertrude M. Yeager, ed., *Confronting Change, Challenging Tradition: Women in Latin American History* (Wilmington, DE: SR Books, 1994); and June E. Hahner, ed., *Women in Latin American History, Their Lives and Views*, rev. ed. (Los Angeles: UCLA Latin American Studies Series, vol. 51, 1980). For western women's views of Latin American women in the nineteenth century, see June E. Hahner, ed., *Women through Women's Eyes: Latin American Women in 19th-Century Travel Accounts* (Wilmington, DE: SR Books, 1998).

Several monographs treat the issue of gender and nation in nineteenth-century Andean nations. For Ecuador, see Erin O'Connor, *Gender, Indian, Nation: The Contradictions of Making Ecuador, 1830–1925* (Tucson: University of Arizona Press, 2007). Top-quality studies of gender and politics for Peru are in Sarah C. Chambers, *From Subjects to Citizens: Honor, Gender, and Politics in Arequipa, Peru, 1780–1854* (University Park: Pennsylvania State University Press, 1999); and Christine Hunefeldt, *Liberalism in the Bedroom: Quarreling*

---

[10]*Source:* República del Ecuador, *Anales de Senadores*, September 9–15, 1911.

Spouses in Nineteenth-Century Lima (University Park: Pennsylvania State University Press, 2000). For other areas of South America, see Arlene J. Díaz, *Female Citizens, Patriarchs, and the Law in Venezuela, 1786–1904* (Lincoln: University of Nebraska Press, 2004); and Elizabeth Dore and Maxine Molineaux, eds. *Hidden Histories of Gender and the State in Latin America* (Durham, NC: Duke University Press, 2000). A provocative collection of essays on the role of honor in nation state formation is in Sueann Caulfield, Sarah Chambers, and Lara Putnam, eds., *Honor, Status, and Law in Modern Latin America* (Durham, NC: Duke University Press, 2005).

Chapter 9

Debating the "Free Womb" Law in Brazil, 1871

Erin E. O'Connor, *Bridgewater State College*

In 1871, Brazilian legislators heatedly debated whether to pass legislation freeing children born to slave mothers in order to end slavery within a generation. Brazil holds an important place in the history of chattel slavery in the Americas: It was the first, the largest, and the last of the slave societies. In the aftermath of independence, the slave question loomed large over the young nation: Kirsten Schultz's chapter, for example, shows that centuries of slavery and its resulting population of free blacks and *mulatos*, made it difficult for legislators to define citizenship as they drafted the first constitution in 1823. As the century progressed, Brazilian statesmen were under increasing international pressure to abolish first the slave trade and then slavery itself. Unlike the United States, where slavery came to a sudden end after failed attempts at political compromise, abolition occurred gradually in Brazil, and only after legislators considered the potential social, economic, and political ramifications of terminating the slave system.

Slavery presented a legislative conundrum for several reasons. Many Brazilian elites worried that without slave labor the economic foundation of the nation would crumble, because the Brazilian economy was based on agricultural exports grown on large plantations with slave labor. Though there was a large and varied free black and *mulato* population by the nineteenth century, slavery remained the exclusive labor supply on export estates. Slavery permeated every aspect of the Brazilian society and economy: Although the vast majority of African slaves lived and worked on plantations, slaves could be found in virtually every trade and location. A final obstacle was that most Euro-Brazilians (and some peoples of mixed heritage), even humble shopkeepers and poor widows, owned at least one or two slaves. Despite dynamics that made politicians wary of abolition, nineteenth-century European governments often made the abolition of the slave trade a prerequisite for continuing to trade with them. In 1831, the Brazilian government yielded to international pressure and abolished the transatlantic slave trade. However, from 1831 to 1850, thousands of slaves continued to arrive from Africa every year in a thriving contraband trade. Only in 1850 did Brazilian officials put enough force behind the law to make it effective, after the British government threatened a blockade if they did not.

Brazilian planters and politicians also worried over the potential social and political impact of abolition. Planters had a great deal of control over their slaves' personal lives, and they feared that a shift to wage labor would undermine their control of large estates. Furthermore, estate owners who dominated local politics and trade were uncertain about the impact that abolition would have on their political power. Finally, many planters and politicians believed that slavery was less brutal in Brazil than in other areas of the Americas and believed it was possible to combine slavery with republican government.

Yet plantation owners were divided on the subject of abolition. Planters in the northeast sugar-growing region, who had already experienced a decline in numbers of slaves along with waning profits, often supported the gradual movement toward abolition. Slavery was expanding in the coffee-producing southern region of São Paulo, however, and planters there ardently resisted abolition. Among Brazilian abolitionists, some sought the end of slavery for exclusively moral reasons, whereas others opposed slavery due to political and international pressures. Brazilian elites, like their counterparts in other parts of nineteenth-century Latin America, wanted European governments to recognize Brazil as a peer, "civilized" nation. Slavery increasingly carried a stigma of barbarism not only for the enslaved but also for the people and nations who enslaved them as well. Some state officials were further troubled by the contradiction between slavery and constitutional guarantees of equality, a dilemma that became more intense in Brazil with rising interest in shifting from a constitutional monarchy to a republican government.

Though most abolitionists hailed from the middle and upper classes of whites and *mulatos,* slaves themselves played important roles in the buildup to abolition. Slaves were aware of, and responded to, the rising conflict and debate over slavery in Brazilian politics. Waves of slave revolts occurred in the 1830s and 1870s—both periods when elites appeared particularly divided. Other slaves lashed out individually against cruel overseers. Yet, instead of running away, many of the slaves who attacked overseers turned themselves in to the police as means of airing their complaints against overseers. Finally, many slaves took advantage of the new laws allowing them to bring grievances against owners and overseers to court, asserting that the slave system itself was a form of injustice. Slaves often called upon *liberal* notions of individual liberty and equality before the law in order to demand either freedom or better treatment. In the 1880s, with abolition in sight, many slaves simply abandoned plantations.[1]

The 1860s were the turning point in the long path toward abolition in Brazil. Before 1863, using the United States as their model, Brazilian elites harbored some hope that they might successfully combine republicanism and slavery. When the United States' slave system crumbled in the 1860s, that hope was dashed. Around the same time, Brazil entered into a territorial war with Paraguay (1865–1870), and the government offered freedom

---

[1]George Reid Andrews, *Blacks and Whites in São Paulo Brazil, 1888–1988* (Madison: University of Wisconsin Press, 1991), chap. 2.

to any slaves who joined the army and fought in the war. Slave men responded in droves, willing to risk their lives for the promise of freedom. Brazilian elites and statesmen finally faced the fact that Brazilian slavery had to come to an end. By the 1870s, even the monarchy supported the abolition cause and accepted the inevitable turn to republicanism in Brazil.

The next important stage of abolition came with the passage of the 1871 Rio Branco Law, also known as the "Law of the Free Womb." Although the law granted freedom to all children born to slave mothers after the its passage, it contained significant limits. For example, when the children reached the age of eight, their mothers' owners could either free them and receive government compensation or have the children labor for them, without pay, until age twenty-one. Despite these stipulations, the Free Womb law was pivotal in the abolition process: Because slave owners could no longer buy slaves from Africa and they could no longer add to the number of their slaves through reproduction, eventual abolition was inevitable.

In the 1880s the legislature passed further laws to press forward the cause of abolition. An 1880 law made it illegal to trade slaves within Brazil, making it yet more difficult for slave owners to prolong slavery by getting replacements for slaves who died or were freed. The Sexagenarian Law of 1885 freed all slaves age sixty or older, though it required them to stay and work for their former owner until they were sixty-five. In 1888 the Golden Law abolished slavery altogether. With the slave question finally resolved, Brazil became a republic in 1889.

Many plantation owners breathed a figurative sigh of relief when abolition did not undermine the old social and economic order. Though many freed slaves left the plantations on which they had worked as chattel, most remained within the plantation system because they lacked skills to work elsewhere, so planters maintained a readily available labor supply. Similarly, the abolition of slavery did not result in uprisings or other forms of social unrest that former slave owners feared. Begun under international pressure, developed gradually to alleviate elite concerns, and finalized through both law and slave actions, the long process of abolition had finally come to an end in Brazil. It would not, however, settle problems of racial inequalities or racism in the nation, as later chapters show.

Questions to Consider:

1. What economic impact did Barros Cobra think that the Free Womb law would have on Brazil? How did Torres-Homem respond to this claim?

2. Why did Barros Cobra argue that the Free Womb law was contrary to good government and the rule of law? How did Torres-Homem suggest that passing the law would advance the cause of good government and rule of law?

3. Why did Barros Cobra think that the Free Womb law would threaten civilization and encourage barbarism in Brazil? How did Torres-Homem suggest that passing the law would advance civilization in Brazil?

4. Despite their opposing views, how did *both* Barros Cobra and Torres-Homem engage with and support general notions of "progress" in the nineteenth century that are discussed in the introduction to this section and that are evident in chapters such as the one with Sarmiento's writings on civilization and barbarism?

"Slave Property Is as Sacred as Any Other": A Chamber Member Opposes Free-Birth Legislation (1871)[2]

Mr. Barros Cobra: . . . Gentlemen, it is true that in this country there exists a point of view that demands a solution to the great problem of slavery.

The existence of this opinion is undeniable in the abstract, in principle; fortunately there is not one Brazilian who wishes the permanent preservation of slavery in the Empire; in this sense there is unanimous agreement: the cause of abolition is definitely decided upon.

[2]*Source:* Robert Edgar Conrad, ed., *Children of God's Fire: A Documentary History of Black Slavery in Brazil* (University Park: The Pennsylvania State University Press, 1984), pp. 438–446.

To the honor of the Brazilian Empire, we do not need to overcome the difficulties, prejudices, and animosities against which the legislators of France and the United States had to struggle; the natural generosity of the Brazilian character, the religious spirit and the principles of morality and civilization decided the theoretical question a long time ago.

But, if we can be proud of the existence of that unanimous opinion in respect to the humanitarian and civilizing idea, there is no doubt that public opinion does not reveal itself equally in favor of the ideas contained in the government's bill, or in favor of the solution that it calls for [. . .]

The servile institution unfortunately appeared as a main element of our social organization, and for three long centuries it sank deep roots into our laws and soil; it represents immense and important capital investments, and almost the only instrument of agricultural labor. Agriculture is practically our only industry, and so almost the only source of our wealth and public revenue, of our prosperity and credit; as a result, the interests associated with slavery are extensive and complex; they are the interests of the entire society that relies on them.

Almost all the other nations found themselves in quite different circumstances; slavery was localized in the colonies, at great distances, and therefore its abolition could have no effect upon the metropolises. Even in the United States the difference was great, because also there slavery was localized in the southern states, which made up a small part of the republic; so that the solution to the problem there, if fatal to the South, did not damage the greatness and general prosperity of the republic. Besides, those countries were energetic and rich, with resources sufficient to overcome the crisis, and agriculture was not practically the only source of income; and, most important, none of them chose the least opportune moment, the most critical combination of circumstances, as our government did, to attempt to abolish slavery. (*Hear! Hear!*) . . .

Mr. President, from all the known methods leading toward emancipation, the government's bill selected as the best solution that of liberation of the womb, or, more accurately, the liberation of those born from the date of the law, with indemnification of the masters of those same newborn children, once they have reached the age of eight. Depending upon the master's choice, this indemnification will be either monetary, that is, in the form of bonds valued at 600$ each, maturing in thirty years, with a 6 percent annual interest rate, or they will take the form of the freed children's services until the age of twenty-one.

This solution, which the government and the bill's supporters have called the wisest and most agreeable solution, is, I repeat, the most dangerous of them all (*hear! hear!*); and, saying this, I am not guided by reason alone, but also by the example of other nations who were forced to make similar reforms.

In all those nations this measure had to be followed at once by others more decisive, which precipitated the final solution to the crisis. And why should this be so? Do we not observe that the mere introduction of this proposal has already brought agitation and that, still more important, the enforcement of such a law will arouse false expectations among the slaves, desires for freedom, optimistic feelings of impatience which will become a source of great dangers and—who can predict?—of great catastrophes for the society and for the slave owners. (*Hear! Hear!*) [. . .]

Mr. President, Article 2 of the bill now under discussion foresees a situation that constitutes one of the defects of the bill's main idea, which has been pointed out by the opposition: the abandonment of the liberated minors by their patrons.

Mr. Gama Cerqueira: Hear! Hear!

Mr. Barros Cobra: Doing justice to the generosity and natural humanity of the Brazilian character, I do not expect the law to produce a slaughter of innocent children. [. . .]

Concerning abandonment, however, it may be anticipated that it will take place on the greatest imaginable scale; since the promised indemnification is not adequate, as I will demonstrate, and because it is dependent upon many chance events and circumstances, there will be a complete loss of the incentive that otherwise would encourage masters to accept the efforts and burdens involved in rearing and educating the children of the slave women, along with the loss of the latter's services during the time they are burdened with pregnancy and motherhood. The law cannot, must not, rely upon charity, which is certainly a very beautiful thing, but cannot be relied upon when legislating for human beings. And what will the government do, with what methods and resources is it prepared to provide for at least half of the children who are born each year, that is, twenty or thirty thousand, according to the least exaggerated claims? The organizations [intended to care for children] which are mentioned in Art. 2 have not been established, and when they are they will be a very small remedy compared with what will be needed.

Yet this is not the principal or even greatest defect which I find in the bill; there are others which I request permission to examine quickly.

Above all, I must point out that the bill, as now conceived, is unconstitutional: 1st, because it disrespects the right to property; 2nd, because it grants political rights to a class which, according to the Constitution, cannot possess them.

However unjust, inhuman, and absurd the domination of one man by another, that is, slavery, may be, it is certain that this condition was legally established by civil law, which created and regulated the master's property right over the slave. Therefore, for good or for evil, slavery became a legal institution among us more than three centuries ago, authorized and protected by law and strengthened by its antiquity, and therefore slave property is as sacred as any other, though illegitimate in principle.

The law cannot impose upon the present generation the expiration of a guilt which was not its own, and in which the state itself is an accomplice. It is enough to remember that the present owner of a slave was not the owner in the past and may not be in the future; he found this property established in the society into which he was born, and he obtained that property by purchase, trade, or inheritance, by some means, that is, for legally acquiring property. Therefore, this property is as sacred as any other, and to deprive the owner of it is a violent and evil act. [. . .]

Once the fact is accepted that slavery is legal, if not legitimate, equally legal is the right to ownership over the present slaves, as well as ownership of the slave womb and the children who may emerge from that womb. Our national law, the Portuguese as well as the Brazilian, always honored and acknowledged the Roman principle *partus sequitur ventrem*, and it was constantly and uniformly respected by the legal wisdom in our courts. Therefore the fruit of the slave womb belongs to

the owner of that womb as legally as the offspring of any animal in his possession. However much this conclusion may offend our humanitarian feelings, it is undeniably logical and in conformity with the law. [. . .]

However, the government's bill attacks and disregards this right, proclaiming the freedom of children of slave women born from the date of the law, and thereby expropriating from the citizen that which is legally in his possession, without prior compensation in compliance with the Constitution.

In fact, gentlemen, the bill refers to indemnification, but, whether it means monetary indemnification or indemnification through the services of the person freed, I look upon both of them as unreal and in no way sufficient. (*Hear! Hear!*) [. . .]

Furthermore, these freed people, who will remain in the houses or on the establishments of their patrons, receiving the same status and treatment as the slaves, living among the latter and bound to them by family ties, at the age of twenty-one will enter into society infected with all the vices of slavery, ignorant, brutalized, despising work, with no education whatsoever, with no comprehension of human dignity, which only freedom awakens. What future is being prepared for our society which thirty years after the law goes into effect will annually receive into its bosom a least 30,000 freedmen, 30,000 new citizens—illiterate, emerging from a brutalizing captivity—but *ingenious* nevertheless, possessing, that is, full political rights. Will this not be a cause of anarchy, a permanent source of grave perils and tremendous misfortunes? . . .

Public order, security, the peace and tranquility of families, conditions even more sacred than the right to property, will obviously be upset and threatened; and the government will lack even minimum resources to protect and reassure them. [. . .]

Gentlemen, continuous or gradual emancipation by indirect methods, aside from being the easiest way, is also the one which will serve us best for the accomplishment of this important reform . . . To endeavor by means of a well-synthesized system of indirect measures, to aid and encourage private initiative, to facilitate manumissions, to establish an emancipation fund as large as possible, and meanwhile to undertake a careful and complete census of the slave population, to encourage and favor agriculture, to provide for a substitute of slave labor by free labor; this is our great mission, a difficult one obviously, but more meritorious than raising the banner of the slaves' redemption above the ruin and destruction of the nation. (*Hear! Hear!*) By the wise and continuous application of this combination of measures, in less than twenty years, without threatening public order, without significant setback to our wealth and production, the abolition of slavery could be achieved, because by then the slaves will be diminished [by deaths and emancipation] to a third of their present number . . .

I thank the chamber for the attention with which it has honored me, and ask your pardon for having abused your patience for so long. (*Very good; very good.*)

The speaker is complimented by many of the honorable deputies.

30. Propaganda against the Free Birth Law of 1871: The Blindfolded Figure Symbolizes Agriculture (*Lavoura*) Menaced by the Hand of the Government Lighting the Powder Keg of the "Servile Element"

This is an image of propaganda against the Free Birth Law of 1871. The blindfolded figure symbolizes Agriculture, menaced by the hand of government, which lights the powder keg of the "servile element." How did this image play upon both elite fears and aspirations? What parallels can you find between this image and the assertions that Barros Cobra made about the Free Womb law?

Source: Robert Edgar Conrad, ed., *Children of God's Fire: A Documentary History of Black Slavery in Brazil* (University Park: University of Pennsylvania Press, 1984).

"As If It Were a Crime to Be Born": A *Mulato* Senator Passionately Defends the Free-Birth Law (1871)[3]

Mr. Salles Torres-Homem: . . .

Gentlemen, after a long age of obscurity and blindness in which all of us were involved, there came a time when the institution of slavery appeared before the conscience of the Brazilian people as it really is, enveloped in a new light which illuminated every aspect of the tragedy, producing in our minds and sentiments a gradual revolution which has never ceased, which has constantly moved forward, acquiring new strength along the way.

Mr. F. Octaviano: Hear! Hear!

Mr. Salles Torres-Homem: It was this moral revolution that twenty years ago effectively contributed to the successful suppression of the traffic, which neither the cruisers nor the resources of the world's first maritime power had been able to suppress.[4] That revolution is the same one which today raps on the doors of parliament demanding an instant completion of the work of civilization.

There were two ways to perpetuate slavery . . . : the [Atlantic] traffic and reproduction, that is, the bearing of children. The power of public opinion which destroyed the first of these ways will destroy the second, because both are equally nefarious and inhuman. [. . .]

If [the slaveholders] are asked why the legislator who can reform and amend laws cannot amend laws that deal with property, they will doubtless reply that property is inviolable because it is based upon natural law that existed before civil law, and it is derived from an immutable principle of justice, which sanctifies and affirms for each man the fruit of his own labor, a principle without which society could not exist. We are thus transported to the realm of law and justice, where the rational basis for the inviolability of property in general is to be found.

But, gentlemen, if it is proved that ownership of a human being, far from being founded upon natural law, is on the contrary its most monstrous violation, if instead of being supported by justice it is sustained only by the evil of coercion and force, then the alleged basis of the inviolability of that special property disintegrates and disappears; and the law that supported it is seen as nothing more than an error, or a social crime, and is subject to amendment like any other law that does violence to the nation's interests.

Mr. President, I should not have to demonstrate before this august assembly that intelligent creatures, endowed like us with noble qualities, facing the same destiny, should not be compared, from the point of view of property, to the colt, the calf, the fruit of the trees, and to the living objects of nature that are subjects to human domination. An absurd, detestable doctrine! [. . .]

Listening to the [pro-slavery petitioners] speak so loudly about property rights, one is surprised that they have so soon forgotten that the greater part of slaves who work their lands are the descendants of those same people whom an inhuman traffic criminally introduced into this country with an affront to laws and treaties! They forget that during the period from 1830 to 1850 more than a million Africans were thus surrendered to our agriculture, and that to obtain that quantity of human cattle it was necessary to double and triple the number of victims, strewing their blood and their bodies over the surface of the seas that separate this country from the land of their birth. (*Very good.*)

And since human and divine laws were trampled upon in this way, how can such laws be invoked to support the future enslavement of the children and grandchildren of the victims of that hateful commerce?

The petitioners also oppose indemnification, which they would like to see increased to the price equal or even superior to that of the child, to whom they possess no claim whatsoever. What is the purpose of this indemnification? The costs, it is said, of bringing up the children.

---

[3]*Source:* Robert Edgar Conrad, ed., *Children of God's Fire: A Documentary History of Black Slavery in Brazil* (University Park: The Pennsylvania State University Press, 1984), pp. 446–451.

[4]Conrad notes that this is "a reference to Britain's long campaign against the international slave trade."

But these unfortunate people are nursed by their mothers, nourished by the crumbs of coarse food which their mothers help to plant and harvest: the milk from the maternal breast given to her own child, the mother's sweat that allows them to survive and covers their nakedness, this is what the masters will possess to sell to the treasury!

Mr. President, I regret that this provision is included in the bill; it blemishes it just as it disgraces the proprietors, because it appears to be designed to safeguard against their barbarity; there is concern that they will abandon the children to hardship and death, if their inhumanity is not offset and controlled by greed. However, even in this case, it is not gold that rightfully should be given to such men; it is the Gospel that they should receive, so that they may learn to comply with their sacred duties of charity toward the children of those people who labor endlessly and without pay to produce their masters' wealth and that of their descendants. (*Hear! hear!*)

Meanwhile the petitioners insist that they favor the reform, that they do not argue with the necessity of it, but only disagree on how to achieve it. Let's take a look at the terms they agree to.

They accept the reform, without the freedom of the newborn; without the indemnification, which does not represent the whole value of the slave; without the slave's right to his personal savings; without obligatory manumission; without the protective intervention of the public authority to prevent the law from becoming a fraud; without the essential precautions against abuse; without any rest whatsoever from the prisons of captivity; without the immediate implementation of the law, and with no implementation for as long as a complete slave census has not been taken; without, finally, anything that directly or indirectly, at distance or near at hand, may be contrary to their habits or cause them the least discomfort! (*Hear! hear!*) Otherwise they are in complete agreement. (*Laughter. Very good.*) Incomparable reformers.

How sad it is that they have not been well understood. They accept the reform with the condition that Roman legal regulations regarding slavery are to be retained in all their genuine and classic purity . . .

Mr. President, one of the most distinguished members of the other chamber, for his talents and prospects, did not hesitate to praise the benefits of the institution of slavery and to deplore the fact that the government was trying to put an end to an arrangement essential to the production of the country's wealth. I might reply that the production of wealth is not the single and paramount aim of society, which is not made up only of creatures who are born, consume, die, and are buried in the furrows of the earth which nourishes them, that their destinies are higher, their circumstances, needs, intrinsic makeup, and civilization more complex.

But, moderating my argument in the face of opposition and granting the production of wealth all the importance it deserves, I will add that here, like everywhere else, in antiquity as in modern times, slavery was and should be recognized as a powerful source of backwardness and degradation . . .

Gentlemen, the secret of wealth lies not only in the variety of climates, in the soil's fertility, in natural advantages; it is also to be found mainly in the innermost being of each person, in his energy and talents, and in the laws that protect and develop him. (*Hear! hear!*) The moral order creates the material order in its own image. Brazil, visibly held back by slavery on the road to prosperity, will not soar off into the future of greatness and opulence to which it is destined, except when on its free soil no plant grows moistened by the sweat and blood of the slave. (*Hear! hear!*)

Suggested Sources:

For a primary source by one of the most famous Brazilian abolitionists, see Joaquim Nabuco, *Abolitionism: The Brazilian Antislavery Struggle*, trans. Robert Conrad (Urbana: University of Illinois Press, 1977). An excellent, and now classic, source of documents on Brazilian slavery is the collection from which the debate presented here was taken, Robert Edgar Conrad, ed., *Children of God's Fire: A Documentary History of Black Slavery in Brazil* (University Park: Pennsylvania State University Press, 1984). For a more recent, and comparative, documentary history of slavery and abolition, see Sue Peabody and Keila Grinberg, eds., *Slavery, Freedom, and the Law in the Atlantic World. A Brief History with Documents* (Boston/New York: Bedford/St. Martins, 2007). For an excellent collection of both primary sources and secondary readings on Brazilian history, see Robert M. Levine and John J. Crocitti, eds., *The Brazil Reader: History, Culture, and Politics* (Durham, NC: Duke University Press, 1999).

For a classic and still excellent discussion of slavery in nineteenth-century Brazil, see Stanley J. Stein, *Vassouras, a Brazilian Coffee County, 1850–1900: The Roles of Planter and Slave in a Plantation Society*, rev. ed. (Princeton, NJ: Princeton University Press, 1985). Also see Mary C. Karasch, *Slave Life in Rio de Janeiro, 1808–1850* (Princeton, NJ: Princeton University Press, 1987). For a comparison of abolition processes in the United States and Brazil, see Celia M. Azevedo, *Abolitionism in the United States and Brazil: A Comparative Perspective* (New York: Garland, 1995). A fascinating discussion of how slavery complicated and protracted the development of a civil law code in Brazil is Keila Grinberg's "Slavery, Liberalism, and Civil Law: Definitions in the Elaboration of the Brazilian Civil Code (1855–1916)," in *Honor, Status, and Law in Modern Latin America*, ed. Sueann Caulfield, Sarah Chambers, and Lara Putnam (Durham, NC: Duke University Press, 2005), 109–130.

Section III

Ordinary People and State Officials in the Nineteenth Century

The last section explored why gender and race relations were central to elite nation state formation projects in nineteenth-century Latin America. Yet nineteenth-century elites embraced narrow and self-serving notions about women, indigenous peoples, and Afro-Latin Americans; to accept their accounts uncritically would reinforce stereotypes that often had little to do with how women or non-whites lived or what they valued. Elites also accounted for only a small (albeit powerful) minority of the population: If one wishes to understand Latin American societies in the past, it is necessary to take into account the lives and views of the majority. Even when read critically, elite versions of interethnic and gender relations typically make women, indigenous peoples, or Afro-Latin Americans appear *lifeless*—as if they never set goals, acted on behalf of their own interests, or experienced the full range of human emotions.

When researching poor indigenous and Afro-Latin American populations, historians also face the challenge of studying peoples who were mostly illiterate. Nineteenth-century political turmoil disrupted administrative functions, and money for bureaucratic salaries was in short supply, making documentation on everyday life hard to find. Even available cases make analysis of non-whites' viewpoints difficult, because statesmen rarely labeled individuals according to their ethnic identities in state records. These challenges make researching and writing history from below exceptionally difficult for the nineteenth century. However, since the 1980s several historians have been conducting research in underexplored local government archives, or developing new questions to scrutinize seemingly gender- or race-neutral sources, in order to find the lives and voices of women, indigenous peoples, and Afro-Latin Americans. They have unearthed crucial information about how less-powerful people both experienced and influenced major economic, social, and political changes in the nineteenth century.

Elite and subaltern experiences of economic, political, and social change were often quite different. For example, in Section II it was apparent that only wealthier white and *mestizo* men enjoyed expanding rights under new republican governments, whereas women, the poor, and non-Europeans gained little. One also finds that elites and commoners experienced economic change quite differently: The early nineteenth century was a period of economic and political crisis for most elites, but for many indigenous peasants and humble artisans it was a period of relative stability. Most large estates were contracting rather than expanding in the early nineteenth century, making peasants' access to land fairly secure.

The relative weakness of large estates also increased peasants' opportunities to sell food and goods in local markets, and artisans benefited from high protective tariffs that were common in the period. In contrast, late nineteenth-century economic recovery often benefited elites but devastated peasants and artisans. Economic growth led to reduced tariffs and a flood of manufactured goods with which artisans could not compete, and large-estate expansion typically came at the expense of peasant communities. Subaltern women often suffered even more than their male counterparts, given that they experienced both economic and gender domination at the hands of employers.

Although women were excluded from formal political participation, many of them were concerned with political matters. Some middle-class and elite women agitated for better education, greater respect for their roles as mothers, and rights to work outside the home. Some sought the vote, but the drive for female suffrage did not begin in earnest until the twentieth century. Instead, most middle- and upper-class women activists in nineteenth-century Latin America embraced, rather than rejected, state-sanctioned gender ideologies. However, they reinterpreted these gender norms in order to expand women's and girls' rights to study and work before they married and to protect their interests after marriage. Middle-class and elite women activists sometimes tried to address economic problems that their poorer sisters experienced, running charities or classes for working-class women as a means of helping poor women to improve their conditions. As a rule, however, poor and non-white women had little to do with early women's movements and were more likely to engage with the state through participation in court cases or rebellions alongside their male peers.

Peasants, especially peasant men who fought in wars, often developed a sense of nationalism. As Javier Marión's chapter in Section I suggested, rural combatants typically expected their governments to respect and reward their commitments to and sacrifices for the nation. Peasants who adopted *liberal* or nationalist ideas, however, often understood these concepts differently from elites. For example, unlike *liberal* elites, peasants did not consider individualism and communalism to be mutually exclusive categories. Instead, the extent to which peasants embraced either individual or communal rights depended on the issue being raised: They might value the right of individual adult males to have a say in government, while simultaneously protecting communal land rights. By and large, peasants sought respect and input in political affairs at the local level, wider voting rights, and lower taxes.[1]

Indigenous peoples also struggled against the state in this period. In the densely populated peasant regions, these conflicts usually took the form of rebellions that lasted no longer than a few days or weeks. However, full-fledged wars sometimes occurred, particularly in frontier regions. Crow explores late nineteenth-century struggles between the Chilean government and the indigenous people known as the *Mapuche* through the memoir of a *Mapuche* man, Pascual Coña. Coña's life story shows that not all indigenous peoples sought incorporation into the dominant culture. It also reveals flaws in official government histories that downplayed state violence *and* in revisionist histories that viewed the *Mapuche* as only innocent victims.

As important as peasant nationalisms and struggles with the state were, most encounters between less-powerful peoples and the state centered on the battles and negotiations of everyday life, and it is on these more ordinary encounters that other chapters in this section focus. Both Christiansen's and Haworth's chapters show how men and women were adept at "invoking the state's support" (as Christiansen terms it) in order to advance their interests in interpersonal conflicts. Christiansen offers excerpts of criminal trials in which poor people used the courts to mediate family discord,

---

[1] Florencia Mallon, *Peasant and Nation: The Making of Postcolonial Mexico and Peru* (Berkeley: University of California Press, 1995); Peter Guardino, "Barbarism or Republican Law? Guerrero's Peasants and National Politics, 1820–1846," *Hispanic American Historical Review* 75, no. 2 (1995): 185–213.

Above is a photograph of an indigenous soldier and his wife, taken in Peru in 1868. Indigenous peasants were actively involved in several Peruvian military struggles, the most dramatic being the War of the Pacific (1879–1884) that was fought between Chile and Peru. Historian Florencia Mallon has shown that peasants in some communities set up guerrilla forces to defend their home regions from the Chilean armies, building on a long history of peasant participation in military engagements. How does this image compare or contrast with elite descriptions of indigenous peasants that appear in Section II, or in O'Connor's chapter in this section?

The husband's and wife's clothing are also interesting in this image. The husband is in full military uniform, symbolizing his contribution to the nation. The wife is in civilian dress made up mostly of European peasant clothing adopted by indigenous peoples; the only fully Andean elements were her braids and carrying cloth. Her blouse, open in this photograph, would likely be buttoned under normal circumstances. How do these aspects of dress differentiate "Indian identity" and character according to gender? Do you think that the photographer might have staged this photograph in order to exoticize the woman?

Source: Courtesy of the Library of Congress.

whereas Haworth explores one young woman's quest to have the state intervene to allow her to marry a man against her guardians' will. The young woman in question hailed from the town's elite, reminding readers that "subaltern" does not always mean "poor." O'Connor's chapter focuses on court proceedings involving cases of indigenous domestic violence and murder, allowing readers to explore ways that indigenous life and gender relations were, in practice, much different than elite stereotypes suggested. In all three of these chapters, the document excerpts offer examples about how family and gender issues structured both everyday life and extraordinary events.

The chapters in this section function on three levels. First, they offer evidence of how less-powerful peoples engaged with government policies and state officials. Second, they provide a glimpse of what it meant for the majority to live, struggle, and even love in nineteenth-century Latin America. Third, they offer examples of how professional historians go about finding and making sense of the lives of less-powerful peoples in the Latin American past. Although the limitations placed on women, the poor, and non-whites in nineteenth-century Latin America were significant, these chapters recall something that Linda Gordon, a historian of the United States, once wrote: "To be less powerful is not to be powerless, or even to lose all the time."[2] Employing information in these chapters on all three functional levels will enable readers to experience the joys and challenges historians encounter when they look at history "from the bottom up."

---

[2]Linda Gordon, "What's New in Women's History," in *Feminist Studies, Critical Studies,* ed. Teresa de Lauretis (Bloomington: Indiana University Press, 1986), 24.

Chapter 10

Invoking the State's Support: Estranged Spouses, In-laws, and Justices of the Peace in Peru

Tanja Christiansen, Independent Scholar

Peru

In the trial transcripts included in this chapter, we meet a motley crowd of small-town citizens and villagers. The documents through which they speak to us are taken from the archives of the local justice of the peace and the provincial criminal court in Celendín and Cajamarca, two provinces in northern highland Peru. In them, we read about husbands' and wives' complaints against each other and how slander affected both single and married men and women. Women openly asserted their perceived right to opt out of abusive marriages, only to be faced with elite judges laying down the law. Faced with verbal or physical abuse, peasant women and men defended their names and retaliated against their enemies. Though they rarely won their suits, plaintiffs who brought their marital problems and vendettas before the court created lasting records that make subaltern voices come alive for modern-day readers.

Celendín was an isolated agricultural region with a much less-pronounced Indian presence than other parts of Peru. By the late nineteenth century, most litigants would have been *mestizos* or acculturated Indians; none required an interpreter. They were wealthy enough to leave their work on their land for a day to file a complaint before the justice of the peace and pay for the required stamped paper, but poor enough to come to blows and file a suit if a neighbor carelessly allowed her pig to chew a hat to pieces. Despite its isolation and high altitude (8,596 feet), Celendín was a fertile agricultural area consisting of a patchwork of large *haciendas* and independent small-holdings of various sizes. The majority of Peru's population lived in places like Celendín: remote and isolated, and imperfectly controlled and managed by the Peruvian state, whose representatives were few and often pursued their own agendas. The glimpses we catch of common people's behavior and interaction with local officials are, therefore, illustrative of lower-class Peruvians and Latin Americans across the board.

Nineteenth-century Peruvian law reflected elite understandings of gender roles and gave men extensive authority over their wives. Although paternalistic, this logic granted women control over the domestic sphere: The male "represents the family in its dealing with the world, while the wife is in charge of administering all domestic business."[3] Legislators regarded marital harmony as a prerequisite for social stability and argued that ensuring clear lines of command was important in order to minimize marital discord. Until 1918 in Peru, marriage was defined in accordance with the Catholic Church's provisions and could not, in theory, be dissolved. Annulment was a complex and costly procedure that only urban elites could afford. A legal alternative was to file for the separation of bed and board; however, as these documents show, this, too, was usually blocked by local judges who feared marital breakup as a harbinger of social unrest.

By the late nineteenth century, reputation and honor complemented and sometimes even replaced notions of race as the organizing principles for social worth. In 1877, jurist Francisco García Calderón commented that "reputation and honor are more highly valued and desired than riches, because they win society's esteem."[4] Insults were particularly harmful to women, ruining their marriage prospects or resulting in spousal abandonment. Wives could not themselves press criminal charges for slander unless specifically authorized to do so by their husbands, but fathers and even nephews stepped into the breach on behalf of female relatives. If convicted, slanderers were fined or sentenced—occasionally to prison sentences of several years. Another possible outcome was a public apology from the defendant. However, as the documents show, judges were not sympathetic to assertive women.

Several of the cases included here were settled before the justice of the peace in a matter of days, producing only one or two pages; others made it all the way to the judge of the first circuit in Cajamarca. Most disputes left behind only brief historical records, and many suits were discontinued for no apparent reason. Possibly the litigants reached an agreement out of court or, more likely, ran out of resources to pursue the matter further. Perhaps the file was "misplaced" following a well-placed bribe to a court official. In any case, there is no information on how the fascinating stories continued. The documents are full of both informative details and tantalizing holes. What happened after the judge passed sentence? Were his orders to keep the peace followed? Why is the trial documentation incomplete? Who—if anybody—was telling the truth in this trial? And what did plaintiffs and defendants look like: were they white, *mestizo*, or Indian? Readers can only guess—and maybe, in wondering, come to understand a little more about the lives of ordinary people in the Latin American past who sought with

---

[3]Francisco García Calderón, *Diccionario de la legislación peruana* (Lima: Líbreria Laroqe, 1879), 565.

[4]Ibid., 242.

aplomb, if rarely success, to defend their independence and autonomy before court officials.

Questions to Consider:

1. How did elite views of marriage, apparent in judges' comments, compare and contrast with how husbands and wives described what they wanted from their marriages?
2. How did women use a wide array of family members to help them in times of need, and how did the courts look upon any assistance these women received?

3. How did women and men try to demonstrate that they had honor, and how was honor connected to marriage?
4. What clues can you find in the documents about whether conflicts were either one-time events or part of long-standing vendettas or marital conflicts? Do the documents suggest that going to court was either a typical or an unusual response to conflict? How does this affect the way we read the documents?
5. What challenges do we historians face when using these sources? What makes these sources interesting and valuable?

Francisca Cotrina vs. Eugenio Chávez: Filing for Alimony[5]

To His Honor, the Judge of the First Circuit

I am Francisca Cotrina, the legitimate wife of Eugenio Chávez of this neighborhood. I appear before you to state that my husband left me more than a year ago, for no other reason than his desire to live at his own pleasure and give himself up to womanizing. Out of modesty and respect for this court, I will not mention any names. My husband has treated me improperly, and not in accordance with the respect owed a spouse, whom he should grant the appreciation that is her due. Your Honor, Judge of the First Circuit, what little time that I have spent in the company of my husband has been a sacrifice for me. I have not had a single day of peace. Wishing to avoid any pernicious consequences, so that my husband should not be able to hold anything against my reputation or honor, I have returned to my mother's home, care and authority. All I beg for is that my said husband provide maintenance for our under-age son Santiago, as I am a poor woman and do not have the means to support him. For this reason [I beg that] justice may be done [and the court stipulate an appropriate alimony sum].

I therefore beg that having presented myself to the court, you will have the grace to

ordain in this matter. I swear that I act on the best of intentions.

Celendín, 9 September 1864. [Signed:] For my sister, the petitioner, Carlos Cotrina

In Celendín at two o'clock of the afternoon on 20 September of 1864, Eugenio Chávez and his spouse Francisca Cotrina appeared before the court [having been ordered there for the purpose of reconciliation by the judge], with their mediator Don Agustín Matute.

After they had stated their accusations regarding their respective faults in the past, and there being no merit at all in continuing any type of legal action between the spouses, and even less in continuing their lives separately from one another, as this causes an uproar to society and gravely offends the state of matrimony, the mediator proposed all possible means of a reconciliation so that the spouses' marital life be resumed in an orderly and peaceful manner.

As they were open to reason, the Judge ordered that they confine to oblivion and cover with a cloud all the small faults and domestic annoyances the two had experienced.

Furthermore, he ordered that Eugenio Chávez, once he had been re-united with his wife Francisca Cotrina, and she with her husband, love each other, remain faithful, assist each other and conscientiously provide for the subsistence and education of their child;

[5]*Source:* Archivo Departamental de Cajamarca, Corte Superior de Justicia, Jueces de paz 1, legajo 1, 9 September 1864.

that neither of them has the right to oppose themselves capriciously and stubbornly to God's will, who has joined them in matrimony.

Therefore, if they should separate from each other again, transgressing both the divine will and the natural order (as well as social mores) and disobeying the authorities, they will be prosecuted and punished harshly with the laws appropriate for those who are recalcitrant and lead a life of pleasure and corruption. Eugenio Chávez shall, without loss of time, return to his home to live in it together with his wife and child – well away from the parents of either spouse, as well as any brothers- and sisters-in-law, who wish to meddle in their marriage.

If they do not have an appropriate house [far from the interference of their respective in-laws] available, they should move to any house that is at a sufficient distance from the in-laws.

María Jesús Gil vs. Apolinar Rodríguez and Evangelista Chávez Following Assault[6]

In Celendín, at noon on 5 September of 1864, María Jesús Gil, about 24 years of age, single, of the village of Huashmin, a woman who dedicates herself to womanly duties and adheres to the Catholic faith, appeared in person and stated that first Evangelista Chávez and then Apolinar Rodríguez, had beaten her on Friday morning, following certain prior events that had taken place involving the former's wife regarding an agreement they had had. Having been shown the black-and-blue marks and bruises, the judge ordered that the accused [Evangelista Chávez and Apolinar Rodríguez] be presented to the court. [As she was illiterate] the constable Inocente Días signed for the plaintiff, witnessing the aforesaid.

[Signed: illegible signature] for María Jesús Gil - José Yno Sente Días sss[7]

In Celendín at two o'clock of the afternoon, on 9 September of 1864, the plaintiff María Jesús Gil and her sister Petrona Gil appeared before this court, as well as the defendants Evangelista Chávez and Apolinar Rodríguez. Following some questioning into the facts of the matter, it emerged that the injuries inflicted on the two women could be seen with the bare eye, as the plaintiff's left hand remains injured. [It emerged that] following certain exchanges with Chávez's wife, Chávez had hit her with his very own [illegible], to the extent that they threw stones at him, and that Apolinar Rodríguez, who is their uncle, tried to restrain them by grabbing their hair.

Nobody has the right to mete out justice on their own; it is impossible to tolerate or accept this sort of misbehavior. Both Chávez and Rodríguez have confessed to the facts. María Jesús Gil should not have caused such unpleasant scenes with her inappropriate and noisy complaints just because of the damage caused to a hat of hers by a local beast, which bit her hat into pieces; this fact is a result of her own carelessness, for which the animal's owner cannot be held accountable.

For all these reasons, the judge imposed on Evangelista Chávez a sentence of two days in jail, and a sentence of 24 hours on Apolinar Rodríguez, and compensation for the hat. In future the litigants should observe better behavior, and seek to restrain their habitually provocative tongues and their habit of putting violent hands on anyone. The writ was concluded, and signed by the plaintiff, by Evangelista Chávez, by Don Manuel Días Arana and by Apolinar Rodríguez, Don Buenaventura Pereyra.

Witnessed [Signed: illegible signature]

For María Jesus and Petrona Gil [Signed: illegible signature]

[Signed:] for Evangelista Chávez - Manuel Diaz Arana

[Signed:] for Apolinar Rodríguez - Buenaventura Pereyra

[Signed:] Toribio Amayo

---

[6]*Source:* Archivo Departamental de Cajamarca, Corte Superior de Justicia, Jueces de paz, legajo 1, 9 September 1864.

[7]This is the signature as it appeared in the document. This is likely the same person as 'Inocente Dias' whose name appears in another document in this chapter. The signature was made with a shaky hand, reminding readers that there were many different levels of literacy, and that name spellings—and some other words—were often still not standardized in nineteenth-century Latin America.

Bacilia Pinedo Files a Complaint Alleging that Her Husband Has Evicted Her[8]

In Celendín, at one o'clock of the afternoon of 17 September of 1864, Bacilia Pinedo appeared before this court. To judge from her appearance she is about 30 years of age, born in and of this [provincial] capital, married and engaged in womanly occupations, and as she was very poor and without the funds to pay a lawyer, she filed a spoken complaint against her wedded husband Nicolás Cochay, of this same neighborhood, asserting that he had evicted her from their marital home, for no reason other than his brutal manners. He has maltreated her throughout their marriage, as was noted in the period of the late justice of the peace Don Angeles Velásquez. Unable to bear any longer all the ill-use she has been suffering, and having been kicked out rudely by her husband, despite the fact that she has three small children, and is unable to support herself as a result of her poor health, having given birth with ill results a few days ago[9], she informed the court of all this. The judge ordered the defendant to appear. Having been called by the constable, the defendant was informed of his wife's accusation. He stated that she had a habit of leaving and moving house at her pleasure, and that everything he had been accused of was untrue.

Having heard the accusations, the judge ordered that the two spouses resume their marital life in their home immediately, in order to look after their children, care for each other, on the understanding that the wife is the one who looks after and manages everything within the home, while the husband is the family's head, and is obliged to attend to anything, and carry out whatever external business may be necessary in order to feed his entire family and educate his children; the wife being his life-long companion and mistress of her husband's house, and that she is in no sense a negligible servant of his, and that in the event of the couple recurring with similar uproar and scandalous antagonisms for no reason other than capriciousness and minor misunderstandings or divisive gossip spread by the general enemy of marriage, the one who is adjudicated guilty shall be punished in an exemplary fashion, and the writ was concluded.

They signed; the constable Inocente Días, who was present together with the judge, signed for the wife, witnessed. [Signed:] Ceija [end of document]

[8]*Source:* Archivo Departamental de Cajamarca, Corte Superior de Justicia, Jueces de paz, legajo 1, 17 September 1864.
[9]Child mortality was high, and a reading of wills in the region shows that some women lost as many as half their children.

Marcos Silva of the Village of Malcate, Province of Celendín, Accusing His Father-in-Law, Toribio Cachay, of Leading His Wife, Doña María Antonia Cachay, Away from Her Duties[10]

Marcos Silva of Malcate in this province, legitimate husband of María Antonio Cachay; I appear before Your Honor and proclaim the following: as I cannot remain indifferent to the improper behavior of my father-in-law Toribio Chachay, who leads my aforesaid wife astray and takes her to wherever he wants, abandoning me.

[10]*Source:* Archivo Departamental de Cajamarca, Corte Superior de Justicia, Causas criminales, legajo 1, 25 August 1864.

My friendly suggestions [to him to change his behavior] have had no effect whatsoever. Instead, he capriciously unsteadies her. At the moment he has had her with him for six days, without informing me as to the reason for this behavior – all this in spite of the fact that they have been warned by the justice of the peace Don Leandro Pereira that these misdemeanors will be punished severely.

They have been censured by the legal authorities on two occasions. This obliges me to address myself to Your Honor to accept my complaint, so that you order the seducer to cease his activities. As a married woman, my wife has manifest commitments, allowing her husband to enjoy her services, instead of having her separated from me for no reason at all.

My father-in-law should be made to feel the punishment he deserves for his behavior, and which could lead to terrible consequences. I am therefore seeking a remedy to this all-consuming evil.

I therefore beg you that you, heeding what I have set forth, make use of the measures at your disposal so that my father-in-law present my wife to the court and explain his reasons for acting in this manner, as the current situation is intolerable. I formally swear that I do not act from malice. Celendín, 25 August 1864. [Signed: unpracticed signature] Marcos Silva

Your Honor, judge of the first circuit, Marcos Silva, of Aciento de Malcate, legitimate husband of María Antonia Cachay in the suit regarding her father Toribio Cachay's disturbance and vile *seducción*,[11] wronging María Antonia Cachay's husband, whom

she should care for and attend to, before Your Honor, I present this report, to state: that following my petition revealing my father-in-law's devious conduct resulting in the separation of a married woman from the side of her husband for no reason that could provoke this at all, this was presented to the court in the hope that Your Honor would order an act of conciliation.

I therefore present myself and beg Your Honor that you will attend to my [suffering] and put an end to the [suffering] to which my father-in-law subjects me by stubbornly seducing his daughter so that she remains in his company, abandoning her spouse whenever she wants, despite my previous protests in the presence of the Justice of the Peace Don Leandro Pereira.

The aforementioned cannot but [protest] against this treacherous neglect of his person caused by the interference of her father. In the presence of the above-mentioned judge, he was instructed that he did not have the right to lead his daughter astray and separate her from her husband, who has been left forlorn, without any person there to care for me in my illnesses, and assist me in my daily [care].

This seducción – the result of wrongful advice – only brings with it confusion into a family, leading to disorder which may produce pernicious consequences.

Therefore, rather than presenting my sufferings in person and in speaking, I communicate through this letter, indicating that my father-in-law, such as he claims to be [the rest of this file is missing].

---

[11]The term *seducción* did not, in this case, refer to sexual activities. Rather, it meant that a dependent was led (or lured) away from his or her rightful duties to a master or superior. Husbands would use the term against wives who served someone other than them, because it was an insult to their patriarchal powers and rights. Large estate owners also used the term *seducción* when relating how other estate owners lured peons away from their employ with promises of better wages or labor conditions.

José Quevedo and Don Valerio Chávez, of the Neighborhood of Celendín, in Litigation with Doña Clara Pita Regarding Assault on María Chávez, the Former's Wife[12]

With complete disregard for the authorities, Doña Clara Pita of my neighborhood, has with little honor suggestive of more [illegible] yesterday [illegible] at about 2 p.m. blemished the reputation and conduct

of my wife, to the extent of calling her a whore, thief [. . .]. Out of concern for my own honor, knowing full well that the honor of man is worth more than his own life, I therefore legally challenge the defendant to prove the accusations of theft and adultery against my wife. Meanwhile, my wife shall be placed under restraint or arrested until she has been

---

[12]*Source:* Archivo Departamental de Cajamarca, Corte Superior de Justicia, Causas Criminales, legajo 6, 13 November 1863.

proven innocent – otherwise I will separate from her with immediate effect.[13]

[Signed:] José Quevedo

[Excerpt of document presented by Valerio Chávez, father of María Chávez:] [Clara Pita has insulted my daughter] and called her a whore and a thief, and claimed that her conduct is offensive, all this in the presence of her husband. With his wife accused of such heinous crimes, her husband immediately left her. This separation continues until the present – having heard his consort's honor attacked so audaciously he no doubt believed that Doña Clara Pita was fully informed of the [alleged] adultery and crimes of my aforementioned daughter. [My daughter and her husband were officially reconciled on 14 November,] however, the judge's order has remained illusory, and without effect (for which I do not know the reasons), resulting in the continued separation of my above-mentioned daughter from her husband. As a father, desirous of my daughter's happiness and prosperity in her marriage, I have done my best to persuade my son-in-law to resume relations with his wife. But as he is not in any sense of the word satisfied of his wife's conduct, he continues separated from her. Therefore, seeing the damage caused by the injuries uttered by Doña Clara Pita, I make use of the authority granted me by the law as father, and file civil and criminal charges against this woman, so that you may order the witnesses to be examined to prove all the above. [Signed:] Valerio Chávez

[After months of litigation, Clara Pita was absolved due to lack of evidence. The rest of the text is not included here. There is no information on how María Chávez or her marriage fared.]

Suggested Sources:

Trials similar to (and including) those listed here are analyzed in Tanja Christiansen, *Disobedience, Slander, Seduction and Assault. Women and Men in*

Cajamarca, Peru, 1862–1900 (Austin: University of Texas Press, 2004). An examination of bar owners, artisans, and the like in the southern town of Arequipa who defended their reputations and honor can be found in Sarah C. Chambers, *From Subjects to Citizens. Honor, Gender, and Politics in Arequipa, Peru, 1780–1854* (University Park: Pennsylvania State University Press, 1999). For an insightful study of how women and men in urban Lima used civil and ecclesiastical courts to help them negotiate (and sometimes escape) difficult marriages, read Christine Hünefeldt's, *Liberalism in the Bedroom. Quarrelling Spouses in Nineteenth-Century Lima* (University Park: Pennsylvania State University Press, 2000). Hünefeldt also includes a chapter on matrimonial alliances and conflicts in her book on slaves and slaves' struggle for manumission in Peru in *Paying the Price of Freedom. Family and Labor among Lima's Slaves, 1800–1854* (Berkeley: University of California Press, 1994). An excellent overview of Latin American gender historiography is Sueann Caulfield's "The History of Gender in the Historiography of Latin America," *Hispanic American Historical Review*, 81, nos. 3–4 (August-November 2000): 449–490. More recent studies comparing elite and lower-class perspectives on gender roles and honor can be found in Sueann Caulfield, Sarah C. Chambers, and Lara Putnam, eds., *Honor, Status and Law in Modern Latin America* (Durham, NC: Duke University Press, 2005); and (on the colonial period) Lyman L. Johnson and Sonya Lipsett-Rivera, eds., *The Faces of Honor: Sex, Shame and Violence in Colonial Latin America* (Albuquerque: University of New Mexico Press, 1998). For information on gender and *hacienda* life in Cajamarca, see Carmen Diana Deere, *Household and Class Relations: Peasants and Landlords in Northern Peru* (Berkeley: University of California Press, 1990).

There are few primary documents available to the general public describing women's lives in nineteenth-century Peru, but Clorinda Matto de Turner's novel *Torn from the Nest* (New York: Oxford University Press, 1998), written in Spanish in 1889, is an elite woman's attempt at describing

---

[13]Peruvian law stated that any wife accused of a sexual misdemeanor should be placed under arrest in the home of a "decent" family until the matter had been investigated. This was in order to prevent her from sinning any further while the matter was being investigated. Such an "arrest" was a necessary preliminary action for a suit for separation of board and bed.

gender roles in the southern Peruvian highlands. French-Peruvian feminist Flora Tristán described her own experience of Peru as an illegitimate child. See Flora Tristán, *Utopian Feminist: Her Travel Diaries and Personal Crusade* (Bloomington: Indiana University Press, 1993). For another travel account including some pages on Cajamarca and Celendín, read Heinrich Witt, *Diario y observaciones sobre el Perú, 1824–1890* (Lima: Oficina de Asuntos Culturales, COFIDE, 1987).

Chapter 11

The Death of Francisco Bravo: Marriage, Violence, and Indians in Nineteenth-Century Ecuador

Erin E. O'Connor, Bridgewater State College

On February 25, 1870, indigenous peasants from the small village of Tigsán, Ecuador, reported to the local authorities that they had discovered Francisco Bravo's lifeless body in a hollow under the Pisillíg Bridge. Bravo had apparently been placed there after being beaten to death. Authorities suspected that Bravo's wife, Manuela Tenemasa, and her alleged lover, José Ñaula, had committed the crime. The ensuing murder investigation generated over seventy folios,[1] recording various eyewitness accounts, expert reports, statements from the accused, lawyers' arguments, and communications over court proceedings, with the majority of detailed evidence and testimony in the case appearing in the first ten folios. This lengthy criminal case provides readers with a great deal of evidence, not only about the crime committed, but also about everyday life in an Ecuadorian indigenous peasant community. It is, in particular, a fruitful case for exploring how gender relations functioned among indigenous peasants.

This chapter presents excerpts from Francisco Bravo's murder trial in order to allow readers to explore for themselves the nuances of life, work, and family among Ecuadorian peasants. It juxtaposes this case with a short excerpt from a domestic violence case against another indigenous man, Asencio López, in which elites used gender stereotypes to identify Ecuador's indigenous peoples as backwards and barbaric. Together, the cases highlight the centrality of gender to inter- and intraethnic relations. Reading the two court records together also highlights differences between elite claims and indigenous realities, and the cases remind readers that they cannot always take elites' views as truth. Importantly, the cases expose elite prejudice without presenting indigenous life and customs as completely good or simple. Instead, indigenous peoples appear more realistically, as having both strengths and shortcomings.

The criminal cases excerpted here took place in the central highland province of Chimborazo, home to one of the largest indigenous populations in Ecuador. In the nineteenth and early twentieth centuries, many of the indigenous peoples of Chimborazo lived as *conciertos* (debt peons) on large estates, but there were also peasant communities where indigenous peoples farmed their own subsistence plots of land. The Bravo trial shows that the line between peasants and estates was often blurred, because many of the peasants in the case made references to connections they had to a nearby *hacienda*. Finally, if scrutinized closely, the myriad information offered in criminal cases from this province conveys a great deal about indigenous peoples' lives in central highland Ecuador.

It is unlikely that indigenous peoples thought much about the state as they went through their daily lives, just as people living in the United States today do not necessarily think about the role of government in their everyday lives as they work, learn, love, and play. Yet, the backdrop of Indian-state relations is important for understanding the human relationships and encounters with state officials that one observes in these criminal proceedings. In the 1870s, Ecuador's central-highland indigenous peoples struggled with the after-effects of the abolition of *tribute* and with the expansion of large estates. Abolishing *tribute* theoretically equalized all Ecuadorians before the law in theory and put an end to one of indigenous peasants' worst economic burdens; in practice it often increased rather than relieved indigenous economic strife. Peasants lost communal land rights, local indigenous governments, and exemptions from other taxes that they had enjoyed under the *tribute* system.[2] At the same time, the expansion of large estates made subsistence difficult for many indigenous peasants in the Ecuadorian highlands, who often found it necessary to work either seasonally or permanently on large estates. This crisis occurred under the leadership of Gabriel García Moreno, who dominated Ecuadorian politics from 1860 to 1875. García Moreno merged social *conservatism* with economic progress (associated with a strong export economy) in order to initiate Ecuador's first meaningful state formation project. Garcian Indian policies changed dramatically over time: For the first eight to nine years of his rule, García Moreno maintained many of the privileges Indians had enjoyed under the *tribute* system. From 1869 to 1875, however, he turned away from protective policies, and Indian-state relations were left largely in the hands of local authorities, who almost always supported elite interests in interethnic conflicts.

Ecuadorian statesmen sought to rationalize Indians' ongoing marginalization and poverty by pointing to supposedly inherent indigenous characteristics rather than to elites' actions. The first

---

[1] Two-sided sheets of paper.

[2] For further discussion masculinity in Latin American nations, see Dym on citizenship in Central America (Chapter 6), and O'Connor on marriage and nation (Chapter 8).

document excerpts, taken from the domestic violence case against Asencio López, show that Ecuadorian statesmen adhered to similar racial ideas as those espoused by Argentine Domingo Faustino Sarmiento in Chapter 6. However, the López case also reveals that Ecuadorian state officials used gender ideologies to reinforce their arguments about Indians' so-called barbarism.

The documents presented here reveal the centrality of gender, especially marriage, to both Indian-state relations and to the everyday functioning of indigenous communities. Both state officials and indigenous peasants used ideas about men's and women's proper social roles to uphold power inequalities, and their gender ideologies overlapped in many ways. For example, state laws and indigenous customs alike identified women with the home and asserted that men had the right to expect obedience from their wives. Yet, indigenous and state-sanctioned patriarchies were not exactly the same. Read carefully, the document excerpts in this chapter offer evidence not only of how elite stereotypes failed to capture the complexity of indigenous gender relations, but also of how state officials and indigenous peoples adhered to distinct notions about men's and women's proper roles in society.

Questions to Consider:

1. How did lawyers in the case against Asencio López manipulate gender ideas to try to prove that Indians were barbaric? How do these views compare with Sarmiento's assertions about civilization and barbarism?
2. How does evidence from Francisco Bravo's murder trial undermine, or at least complicate, the elite views expressed in the trial against Asencio López?
3. How did Manuela Tenemasa and her peers describe her life and actions? Given how indigenous peoples portrayed Tenemasa, were you surprised by the sentence in the case? What do these discrepancies seem to suggest about elite versus indigenous gender ideologies?
4. Social historians often use criminal records not only to explore crimes themselves, but also to better understand everyday life among poor peoples in the past. What clues do you have in the Francisco Bravo trial that can help you to piece together a picture of what life was like among indigenous peasants in nineteenth-century Ecuador?

Supreme Court Trial against Asencio López for Domestic Violence[3]

Excerpts of Defense Attorney Alejandro Rivadeneira's Explanation of Why His Client Should Receive a Reduced/Lenient Sentence

[Because of] López's coarseness [rural character]; coarseness which is congenital, with very few exceptions, to the indigenous class to which he belongs . . . there is a deep-seated custom between the poor Indians, in which a wife requires a dozen monthly

blows from her husband as a token of his affection for her: a peculiar way to show love!; but . . . when a husband smashes in his wife's head, when he beats her, he is driven by love, rather than by hate and vengeance. . . .

Malice is proportional to the cognizance one has regarding the nature of the action . . . an Indian who knows little about the nature of the actions which he executes, knows even less when his intellectual faculties are weakened through the deplorable use of alcoholic beverages . . . Truly, it is a sad thing that such men and customs exist . . . but the tribunals of justice must take things as they find them; measuring

---

[3]*Source:* Archivo Nacional de la Historia, Quito: Criminales: December 19, 1874.

the intensity of malice by the intelligence of the delinquent, by the customs which justify certain actions, by the gravity of the crime, which should at least influence the extent of the punishment.

Excerpts of Prosecutor Elias Laso's Demand for the Harshest Possible Sentence for López

The judge should use all means at his disposal to contain the savage custom which unfortunately exists among our lower orders . . . of mistreating wives without taking into account the consideration that a man should have for a woman, not only because of religious or family obligations, but also because it is characteristic of the rational mind. In a Catholic society which . . . elevates marriage as a sacrament; in a free republic born in the century of enlightenment and . . . which guarantees individual rights to all within its territory . . . it is not impertinent to invoke the offended natural rights and request that you weigh heavily these offenses which deface the customs of a faithful people, renowned through other qualities for their gentle character.

[López was found guilty and sentenced to two years' imprisonment, the maximum penalty for domestic violence. This was unusual: men of all races who were accused of domestic violence were often set free on grounds of insufficient evidence.]

This photograph of indigenous men and women in Chimborazo province was published in Blair Niles's 1923 travel account of time spent in Ecuador. The caption reads "Reeling Home from Market." How might this caption have influenced readers' interpretation of the photograph? How did this image and caption reinforce the ideas about Indians that lawyers presented in the first document excerpt? Consider how this compares and contrasts with what you learn about daily life in indigenous villages in the second document excerpt. Based on information from the murder trial transcripts, what alternate caption or interpretation might you suggest?

Source: Blair Niles, *Casual Wanderings in Ecuador.* New York: The Century Company, 1923, p. 116.

Superior Court Trial Following the Murder of Francisco Bravo[4]

Francisco Abendaño *Teniente parroquial*[5] and Vice commissary etc.

On this day the 25th of the present month, this authority has been informed by Matias Bravo that Francisco Bravo has been found dead in a hollow of the Pisíllig Bridge, and it appears to the informant that the death was caused by another hand. Suspicion falls upon José Ñaula, lover of Manuela Tenemasa, legitimate wife of the aforesaid deceased Francisco Bravo. [. . .]

Immediately afterward, the Señor Teniente entrusted with the proceedings in this case stopped at the parish jail where José Ñaula is being held for his presumed guilt in the present homicide. He is being questioned in order to reveal the truth . . . [about] the following questions: The first was regarding his given name and surname, and his domicile, to which he answered that his name was José Ñaula of this local community in the *anejo*[6] of Pisillig, and of majority age. The second question was if he knew the deceased Francisco Bravo, and if he was his enemy or rival, and if he had information on the cause, date, and hour of his death. He answered that the deceased, Francisco Bravo, is a neighbor and the legitimate husband of Manuela Tenemasa. He says that since their childhood he and [Bravo] had a civil and friendly relationship, but that after Bravo got married, he became extremely jealous to the point of ending the friendship . . . He also responded that he has not lived with the woman as her husband suspected . . . With respect to the death of Bravo he responded: that he knows nothing about the death of Francisco Bravo . . . [W]hen asked about Thursday during the day and the early morning of Friday, in what house or houses he found himself and with which persons and conversations he had with them, and other particulars, he answered: that on Thursday he ended the day in the company of Juan Guaraca, Fortunato Buñay, Francisco Paca, Tomas Lema and Luis Cajilema, all commissioned with watching over donkeys for the *hacienda* of Moyocancha, and at around one in the afternoon they left for the house of the widow Curivilla, of the deceased Magdaleno Caguana, where they entered and participated . . . [bottom of the page illegible] . . . drinking some barley *chicha* . . . as a result of which all of them became drunk. At six or later in the afternoon he returned home on his own where he passed the night in the company of his mother, Matea Pilaminga, and his brothers Pablo and Mateo Ñaula, all of them together in their home. When he arrived at his house, he encountered Manuela Tenemasa talking with his aforementioned younger brothers, with the purpose of asking for cow's milk. After quite a while his mother Matea Pilaminga arrived from the anejo of Guailla, and when she entered, the said Tenemasa widow of Bravo, hid behind the door and furtively exited for the street when night came, and left the exponent to sleep. On Friday, until the time when the alcaldes knocked on his door, he remained in his house. Moreover he declares that the expressed Tenemasa told him that she slept at her mother María [Nilori's] house that night. He says that this is the truth which he affirms and ratifies. He does not sign because he does not know how, and expresses that he is of majority age.

Immediately afterward the Señor Teniente entrusted with the proceedings took the statement of Manuela Tenemasa, the presumed accomplice in the crime under investigation, as much for being the wife of the deceased, as for being the public and notorious concubine of the suspect. In virtue and without insisting on an oath, he put the following questions to her: the first regarding her name and surname, marital status, and domicile. She answered that [she] is Manuela Tenemasa, legitimate wife of Francisco Bravo, her home in this place in the anejo of Pisíllig. To the second question regarding the

---

[4]*Source:* Archivo Nacional de la Historia, Riobamba: Criminales: February 25, 1870.

[5]The *Teniente Parroquial,* also referred to in these documents as *Señor Teniente,* was the local political authority or lieutenant.

[6]An *anejo* was an indigenous community in which peasants, although they had their own land, were also connected and beholden to the owner of a nearby large estate. In this case, members of the anejo of Pisillig often worked for the owners of the *hacienda* Moyocancha.

nature of her marriage and her familiarity with José Ñaula, she answered: that her marriage had been in a bad state as a consequence of the illicit relationship that she had with José Ñaula . . . and as [Ñaula] was not her husband, she had to go about with him in secret to remote places. Since they were concerned about her husband's jealousy, she demanded of Ñaula that the relationship be restrained, and she had lived with her husband until his death. To the third question regarding the reason that she was absent from her house on the day of the twenty fifth of the current month, she answered: that on that day her husband had left the house for the fiesta that was being celebrated on the *hacienda* Moyocancha grande,[7] she left for her parents' sheep farm. When she arrived at her parents' house at about three in the afternoon, her grandmother Juana Chicaisa informed her that her husband was returning from the festivities and was moving past the slope of land belonging to Vicente Chicaisa, and he was apparently drunk. Upon hearing this news, she stayed in [her parents'] house without returning to her husband for fear that he would beat her. She passed the night in the company of her mother, María Nilori, and did not leave to go anywhere [until] the next day, Friday, [when] the Alcaldes Juan Guaraca, Mariano and Manuel Padia [? page ripped] [arrived] around twelve and told her that her husband's dead body had been found in a hollow near her house. Having said this she and the Alcaldes went to said hollow, where she saw her husband's body hobbled, his mouth open, with the same clothes as the day before . . . in his belt a knife with a white handle, and at his neck half a strip of cloth, and the other half in a clump of straw, the condition of the cadaver showing without a doubt that he had died from hanging . . . She says that what is stated here is the truth which is affirmed and ratified, being of majority age and not signing because she doesn't know how.

Immediately after the Señor Teniente in the case called upon the *indígena*[8] Pablo Ñaula, who is over fourteen years of age, and less than twenty; therefore Señor Silvestre Beltran was assigned as his curator . . .

[H]aving been informed of the previous documents of the proceedings, he says: that on Thursday the twenty fourth of this month at about five in the afternoon he had secured some pigs that he was pasturing in the countryside for his mother, Matea Pilamunga. As he returned to the house, he overheard his older brother, José Ñaula, fighting with the *indígena* Francisco Bravo but could not understand what they were saying. At this time Manuela Tenemasa appeared, saying the following phrase to Ñaula, animated with fury: "Let's kill him."

She repeated these words various times with grave tenacity. The witness entered the room in order to put down a bundle of straw, at which point his brother José Ñaula closed the door and fastened it forcefully, and then José Ñaula, Francisco Bravo, and Manuela Tenemasa disappeared without anyone seeing where they went, as a consequence of the day being very foggy. The witness passed the night inside, in the company of the young child Francisco Ñaula, who is about three years old. The next morning Carmen Villa came to the house to borrow a pot, and before she arrived the witness saw through a crack in the door that his brother, José Ñaula, was sleeping on the kitchen floor. [His brother] got up and headed toward the witness, and informed him that he [the witness] had seen nothing and did not know about him [the accused] conversing with anyone, saying that he would hit him if he said anything. Thus he was silent and did not talk of what happened with his sister-in-law Carmen Villa . . . This he claims through the medium of his curator to be the truth . . . and ratifies it, expressing that he is of fourteen years of age, and has not failed to tell the truth because he is the brother of the accused. [. . .]

In the civil parish of Ti[g]sán on the twenty eighth of February of 1870. The Señor Teniente of the case calls upon the *indígena* Antonia Guaman, a married woman, as a witness, who . . . said: That on the day of Thursday the twenty fourth of this month, the witness passed in front of the house of the indicated José Ñaula, going in the direction of her house, and that she saw the deceased Francisco Bravo pass through the door of the aforementioned Ñaula. She then heard his voice, saying to Ñaula that he hand over his [Bravo's] wife, . . . [and stated] that wherever he went so his wife should be, and that he

---

[7]Estate owners often used celebrations on their estates to reinforce socioeconomic ties with workers.

[8]Indigenous person.

hand over his wife . . . The next day she learned that the aforementioned Bravo had been found dead. [She asserts] that all she has said is true . . . and did not sign because she does not know how to read or write.

On the same date the Señor Teniente called as a witness the *indígena* Jacoba Guaraca, a married woman, who . . . said: That on the day of Thursday which corresponded with the twenty fourth of the current month at about five in the afternoon, the witness went to fetch water and passed by Francisco Bravo, who was heading for José Ñaula's house, and that after entering that house, [Bravo] left it in a state. The next day she learned that the said Francisco Bravo had been found dead. She also declares that it was publicly and notoriously known that for many years José Ñaula had lived publicly in concubinage with Manuela Tenemasa, the legitimate wife of Francisco Bravo. She gives her oath that she has told the truth and . . . she did not sign because she says that she does not know how.

Immediately thereafter the Señor Teniente called upon the *indígena* Manuela Guamán as a witness, a woman sixteen years old, because of which she was provided with Señor José Balladares as a curator . . . [and] she said: that on the day of Thursday the twenty fourth of the current month, at about five in the afternoon, she left to get parents' donkey from the pasture when she saw Francisco Bravo. Shortly thereafter she heard the alarming voice of the said Francisco Bravo without being able to understand what he said, because he was far away from her; moreover she did not see José Ñaula . . . On the next day she learned of Francisco Bravo's death when it became widely known in the anejo of Pisíllig. [She asserts] that she does not know anything other than that which she has expressed above. This she says is true . . . [and] her curator signing for her because she said that she did not know how.

[March 1, 1870] The court has received notice from José María Arias, who is in charge of the public jail, that the accused José Ñaula has confessed the truth about the crime with which he is accused. The Señor Teniente and we the clerks of the court went to the prison in order to receive the new declaration [in the] investigation . . . [and Ñaula] said: That on Thursday [February 24th] . . . he encountered Manuela Tenemasa, the legitimate wife of the

deceased Francisco Bravo, who was in his house waiting for him when he returned . . . [After] Tenemasa left, he waited a while and then followed behind her. He encountered the aforesaid Tenemasa in the middle of the road near her parent's house, fighting with her husband, the deceased Bravo. When he arrived on horseback, [Tenemasa] was holding and twisting the scarf that [Bravo] wore around his neck. Bravo then saw him and said "with what motive did you bring my wife to your house? I am going to complain at the judge's office." To which [Ñaula] replied that "you always go to [inform] to the judges, when I have given you no reason, because I have not called on your wife" . . . and he threw the stirrup at Bravo with all his might and hit him in the stomach so that he fell to the ground. [Bravo then] spoke incoherently due to being startled by the incident, and because he was extremely inebriated. When the man fell to the ground his wife threw herself on him and sat on his chest and stomach, and taking the handkerchief that he wore strangled him to death. Seeing him dead, the woman told the deponent "since this misfortune falls upon both of us, we should hide the body [in the mess by Bravo's own house] so that the judges think that he hanged himself." And with that she untied [illegible—the handkerchief around his neck?] . . . and [the deponent] brought the cadaver to said hollow leaving the woman at the scene of the crime. He placed the cadaver as if hanging, supported by a clump of straw, and returned to his house. The woman left for her parents' house, and the next day they were both brought in by the alcaldes mentioned before. The hour in which the crime was committed was about six in the afternoon. This he says is the truth . . . and he did not sign because he does not know how . . .

The deponent Ñaula afterward added to the previous statement: that he believes and assures that it was not possible that [Bravo] died of the blow [from Ñaula] because he was still alive and able to talk, therefore note that the woman killed him by strangling him with a kerchief. At the time of the fight the witness Jacova Guaraca was present, but she left before the act was committed. This he swears is the truth.

Continuing, the Señor Teniente . . . [brought] Manuela Tenemasa before him in the same manner as before, who said: that in her first declaration she hid the truth. On the date in question, Thursday the twenty-fourth at about six in the afternoon she was in José Ñaula's house, where she had been waiting for him since very early to receive two pieces of cloth that he had in his possession. At that time he arrived mounted on a horse, and seeing her he did not want to [let her go] until his mother Matea Pilam[u]nga arrived at her house and said to her son Ñaula "with what motive did a married woman come to my house?" And she ordered [Tenemasa] to leave. The declarant arranged with Ñaula that he would take her to her house, and on the road she encountered her husband, Francisco Bravo, who was drunk and returning from the fiestas of Moyocancha. He grabbed her and began to mistreat her, and at this time Ñaula arrived mounted on a horse. Because [Bravo] was mistreating his wife . . . Ñaula, agitating the horse, gave [Bravo] a blow in the stomach which threw him to the ground, and then he took out the stirrup and hit him one more time in the stomach . . . [When] he said that [Bravo] was still alive, she went to her husband and took the scarf that he had on, and twisted it until he died. Then Ñaula said that since they had done this terrible deed they should put him to the side of his [own] house so that the judges would think that he had died from hanging . . . and then Ñaula went back to his house and she went to her parents' house until the next day when they were brought before the alcaldes. And Jacova Guaraca was there at the beginning of the fight, but then left for her house. She says that this declaration is true and does not sign because she says that she doesn't know how . . . she further she declares that Ñaula was very drunk from the drinks he had consumed that day.

[*José Ñaula was found guilty of homicide and sentenced to death, while Manuela Tenemasa was found guilty as his accomplice and sentenced to confinement in a charity hospital for six years and eight months. Ñaula's defense lawyer tried on two occasions to get the verdict changed to an acquittal, but he failed both times.*]

Suggested Sources:

Published primary sources providing *indigenous* perspectives are not available. However, one can consult travel accounts and novels for top-down views of Indians in nineteenth-century Latin America, though it is imperative to be on the look-out for elite biases when reading them. See, for example, United States diplomat Friedrich Hassaurek's *Four Years among the Ecuadorians* (Cincinnati, OH: Robert Clarke, 1892 [1867]) offers interesting discussions of all aspects of Ecuadorian society, including indigenous peoples. Other interesting foreign travel accounts of the Ecuadorian landscape and society are: Blair Niles, *Casual Wanderings in Ecuador* (New York: The Century Co., 1923); and James Orton, *The Andes and the Amazon* (New York: Harper & Brothers, 1870). Jorge Icaza offers a more sympathetic account, though still from an elite viewpoint in his indigenist novel *The Villagers (Huasipungo),* trans. Bernard Dulsey (Carbondale, IL: Southern Illinois University Press, 1964 [1934]).

Secondary sources on indigenous peoples and the nation state in nineteenth-century Ecuador are few, but it is a growing field. Among available sources are: Erin O'Connor, *Gender, Indian, Nation: The Contradictions of Making Ecuador, 1830–1925* (Tucson: The University of Arizona Press, 2007); Mark Van Aken, "The Lingering Death of Indian *Tribute* in Ecuador," *Hispanic American Historical Review* 6, no. 3 (1981): 429–459; Derek Williams, "Indian Servitude and Popular Liberalism: The Making and Unmaking of Ecuador's Anti-Landlord State, 1845–1868," *Hispanic American Historical Review* 83, no. 4 (2003): 697–733. For an excellent essay that discusses similar issues in Bolivia, see Rossana Barragan, "The 'Spirit' of Bolivian Law: Citizenship, Patriarchy, and Infamy," in *Honor, Status, and Law in Modern Latin America,* ed. Sueann Caulfield, Sarah C. Chambers, and Lara Putnam (Durham, NC: Duke University Press, 2005), 66–86. For an interesting synthesis on race and nation in the nineteenth-century Andes, see Brook Larson, *Trials of Nation Making: Liberalism, Race, and Ethnicity in the Andes, 1810–1910* (New York: Cambridge University Press, 2004).

Chapter 12

Minors, Marriage, and the State: "*Habilitación de edad*" in Nineteenth-Century Mexico

Daniel S. Haworth, *University of Houston-Clear Lake*

For nineteen-year-old Petra Fernández, the situation had become desperate in early 1854. At that time, she was unmarried and an orphan. Lacking grandparents or other extended family to take her in, Petra had grown up under the care of a guardian in her hometown of Celaya, Guanajuato. She had been quarreling with her male guardian, Antonio Leiva, for weeks over the fact that she wanted to marry Cayetano Olmedo, the son of a prosperous family who was the local administrator of the state tobacco monopoly. His position entailed overseeing the distribution of tobacco products and collecting the excise tax levied on them. His proposal of marriage offered Petra an escape from insecurity: She was a minor, a year away from legal adulthood for an orphan, and she was subject to the authority of her guardian, Antonio Leiva. Even though Cayetano's widowed mother approved the match, law and custom required the couple to obtain Leiva's consent, too. This, Leiva refused to give, for he intended Petra to marry one of his sons, or so she confided to the local priest. In response, Petra appealed to the governor, Gen. Francisco Pacheco, to grant her an *habilitación de edad* and thereby legally declare her an emancipated adult, freeing her to marry as she wished.

This conflict over marriage choice played out in a setting broadly representative of nineteenth-century Mexican life. Located in south-central Guanajuato, 150 miles northwest of Mexico City, Celaya thrived as a center of business and administration in the Bajío, a broad swath of prime agricultural land, the most productive in Mexico, encompassing half of Guanajuato and parts of two neighboring states. Celaya in 1854 was home to approximately 37,000 full-time residents.[1] The town and its surrounding hinterland—dotted with hamlets, small farms, and *haciendas*—made up a social and commercial unit, meaning that Petra inhabited a world that was neither completely urban nor rural, but a mixture of both. She moved within a corporatist social environment wherein the groups to which one belonged defined one's public identity at least as much as one's individual attributes. Membership in such networks served as a crucial hedge against insecurity, but also it ensured that individual actions were subject to community scrutiny and could be fodder for gossip. This was especially true if one moved among Celaya's leading families, as did Petra. She was by no means privileged in other ways, though. Being an orphan and a woman in a patriarchal society left her doubly exposed to masculine whim.

Law and tradition alike upheld the idea that a man should enjoy more expansive rights than a woman. For example, the legal concept of *patria potestad* granted the father—or in his absence, the senior adult male in the household—supreme authority in family affairs. By that same token, *patria potestad* defined the woman as subordinate, first to the father, then, if she married, to her husband. So overarching was *patria potestad* that it applied even to widows, circumscribing the limited autonomy they accrued upon the death of their husbands. However, as Petra's case demonstrates, a father's authority was nonetheless subject to regulation.

Petra sought to take advantage of laws designed to curb abuses of patriarchal power. In her letter to the governor, she contended that her case complied with Laws 9 and 18, in Book X, Title II, of the *Novísima Recopilación* [New Compilation], a compendium of edicts from the thirteenth to the early nineteenth centuries used throughout the Spanish Empire at the time of Mexican independence, and apparently valid in Mexico in 1854. Law 9 prohibited parents and guardians from forcing a minor to marry against his or her will. Law 18 allowed a young woman who lacked surviving parents or grandparents to marry without the consent of her guardian upon reaching the age of twenty. Yet all might be lost if Petra waited another year. In that time, Leiva might hastily marry her off to one of his sons, or Cayetano might give up in the face of Leiva's intransigence and withdraw his proposal. Her hope, therefore, rested on a clause in Law 18 that empowered minors, regardless of age, to seek habilitación de edad from government officials.[2]

---

[1] Datos para la memoria, que se ha de presentar a la 16 Legislatura del Estado en Enero de 1852.
Noticia de las poblaciones que en el Estado de Guanajuato, cuentan de cuarto mil habitantes arriba, Guanajuato, 1852, Archivo Histórico del Estado de Guanajuato, Fondo Secretaría de Gobierno, Sección Secretaría de Gobierno [hereafter AHEG/Secretaría], box 248, folder 1.

[2] The *Novísima Recopilación* is reproduced in its entirety in *Códigos antiguos de España: Colección completa de todos los códigos de España, desde El Fuero Juzgo hasta La Novísima Recopilación*, vol. 2 (Madrid: n.p., 1885). For Book X, Title II, Laws 9 and 18, see vol. 2, 1714–1715, 1717. Colonial laws remained in effect in Mexico long after independence.

These measures and others like them, in no way eliminated patriarchy; rather, they modified its expression. They also determined the options available to Petra in confronting Leiva's opposition. Seeking habilitación de edad forced her to appeal to a male official to override the prerogative of the man who was her legal guardian. Hence her effort proceeded within the social and institutional boundaries that patriarchy created.

Government being an exclusively male domain, male voices dominated the case. The exception to this pattern came in the carefully worded petition that opened the document set. In the petition, Petra wrote directly to the governor. Otherwise the circumstances of the case were recounted in correspondence between the governor, three other officials, and a priest, all men. Governor Pacheco initiated a formal inquiry with instructions to Celaya's two justices of the peace and the parish priest to report on the matter. Their assessments were collected and reviewed by the legal affairs division of the governor's office, the head of which added his own recommendation. The entire file was then submitted to the governor for final consideration. Included here is a letter written to the governor on Petra's behalf by an older male acquaintance, perhaps a friend of her deceased parents or of Cayetano's family. Antonio Leiva's perspective emerges forcefully from the priest's report. Cayetano, by contrast, never speaks directly. Rather, he appears as the subject of earnest discussion. His reputation in the eyes of the community was one of the criteria that officials used to assess the merits of Petra's request. Otherwise, he had no say in the matter.

Petra's quest amounted to a benign expression of the individual's subordination to state power, one of the many ways ordinary people experienced their inclusion in the evolving political entity known as Mexico. In doing so she, like women throughout nineteenth-century Latin America, derived agency from adapting to changes wrought by the collapse of colonial rule. Among the most significant was the fact that independence led Latin Americans—women as well as men—to explore the meaning of freedom. For women, this generally, though not always, involved private action, as opposed to the public debate among male politicians of the period.[3] So it was with Petra. Though she acted within the traditional structure of patriarchal authority, resorted to a body of colonial law to justify her appeal, and would be bound by whatever ruling the governor might make, she nevertheless claimed her right as an individual to determine her future.

Questions to Consider:

1. What were the various factors that led to Petra's success? Which of these proved to be most decisive to the outcome of her case, and why?
2. Why did government officials take Petra's case so seriously? What might the governor have hoped to achieve by approving her request?
3. How did Cayetano's social status and wealth affect this case? What does this show about how and why marriage and class reinforced each other in provincial towns in nineteenth-century Mexico?
4. What does evidence in this case suggest about men's and women's differential experiences of adulthood—when it began, and what it involved—in nineteenth-century Mexico?

---

[3]Isser Woloch, ed., *Revolution and the Meanings of Freedom in the Nineteenth Century* (Stanford, CA: Stanford University Press, 1996); for another example of a women exploring the meaning of freedom through private action, see Sarah Chambers, "Republican Friendship: Manuela Sánchez Writes Women into the Nation, 1835–1856," *Hispanic American Historical Review* 81, no. 2 (May 2001): 226–257; for a contrasting example, see James E. Sanders, "A 'Mob of Women' Confront Post-Colonial Republican Politics: How Class, Race, and Partisan Ideology Affected Gendered Political Space in Nineteenth-Century Southwest Colombia," *Journal of Women's History* 20, no. 1 (Spring 2008): 63–89.

Documents Pertaining to Petra Fernández's Petition for *Habilitación de Edad*[4]

Your Excellency,

María Petra Fernández, resident of Celaya and an orphaned minor of nineteen years of age to which the accompanying baptismal register attests, in light of your Excellency's well known willingness to hear this appeal . . . does formally declare: that Cayetano Olmedo, the *Administrador de Rentas*[5] for this city, sought permission to marry me from Mr. Antonio Leiva. He being my guardian, his consent is required by law in the absence of my parents and grandparents, yet Mr. Leiva refused and opposes the marriage without reason, in my opinion, given that Mr. Olmedo is widely known among the population as an honorable man of means, one who derives from his position the necessary resources to uphold his matrimonial responsibilities and comply with the corresponding obligations.

Given these facts, with no judge willing to strike down Mr. Leiva's resistance, and having exhausted all other appropriate means, I must now respectfully resort to your Excellency as I do, so that in view of the irrational and illogical resistance of my guardian, I request, in conformity with Title II, Book X, laws 9 and 18, of the New Compilation, the consent I have thus far been denied, and the concession of the license[6] that is indispensable for my marriage to Mr. Olmedo.

In these terms: entering a hopefully adequate plea as sustained by all the reasons that to it pertain, I implore you to decree as I have asked, this being just.

Celaya, January 4, 1854

Petra Fernández[7]

Justice Section
Confidential

María Petra Fernández, resident of Celaya, has appealed to this government for recognition of her majority in order to marry Mr. Cayetano Olmedo, also of Celaya, to which her guardian Mr. Antonio Leiva is opposed. This Government desires to proceed in the present case with all due circumspection. [Therefore] you should report whatever you may suspect or know regarding the relative merit of the proposed matrimony; that is, whether you fear a disastrous outcome, or the contrary, or if the resistance manifested by the young woman's guardian is reasonable or purely capricious, and all else you deem necessary to illustrate the substance of the case. In that the wisdom of the resolution to this matter will depend on the nature of your report, I recommend that you proceed with the utmost conscientiousness.

God and Liberty,

Guanajuato, January 19, 1854

Francisco Pacheco

Copy of the communication sent to the First and Second Justices of the Peace and the parish priest of Celaya.

[Office of the] Secretariat of Government

Guanajuato, February 21, 1854

Mexican Republic
Department of Guanajuato
First Justice of the Peace of Celaya

Most Excellent Sir,

Because I know Mr. Cayetano Olmedo so well I can respond to your respectable note of the

---

[4]*Source:* For Petra's case file, see Maria Petra Fernandez solicita habilitación de edad para contraer matrimonio sin consentimiento de su tutor, con Cayetano Olmedo, [Celaya,] Guanajuato, 1854, Archivo Historico del Estado de Guanajuato, Fondo Secretaría de Gobierno [hereafter AHEG/Secretaría], Sección Secretaría de Gobierno, box 277, exp. 1.

[5]The term "renta" refers to the proceeds from the sale of a good, exclusively reserved for the government, in this case tobacco.

[6]That is, official recognition of Petra's legal majority.

[7]Petra signed the petition. In the body of the petition, the handwriting differs from that of her signature. Most likely, she dictated her statement to a notary (*escribano*).

nineteenth of the present month in regards to the suitability of his proposed marriage with Miss María Petra Fernández. [Mr. Olmedo] is a young man of good conduct, who by virtue of his character obtained recognition of his majority from the previous state legislature in order to administer his assets, as per Decree Number 209 of May 26, 1851. Moreover, he presently serves as the Administrador del Tabaco, from which he earns a living sufficient to sustain his family and responsibilities. In light of such qualifications I judge that no ill will come of the marriage in question. . . .

God and Liberty,

Celaya, January 26 1854.

José María Ramírez

Mexican Republic
Department of Guanajuato
Second Justice of the Peace

Most Excellent Sir,

I write in response to your official note of the nineteenth of this month in which you request that I inform you as to the suitability of the marriage between Mr. Cayetano Olmedo and Miss María Petra Fernández. In my opinion and that of the sensible persons of this city with whom I have consulted on this matter, I consider it suitable to the happiness of both parties for the same reasons set forth by the First Justice of the Peace, and that I find no legal justification for the opposition manifested by Mr. Antonio Leiva, the conservator of the aforementioned girl.

God and Liberty,

Celaya, January 26, 1854

Joaquín Galvan

Report submitted to his Excellency the Governor of the State, produced by the parish priest of Celaya in favor of recognizing the majority of the orphan girl Miss María Petra Fernández.

Confidential

Most Excellent Sir,

. . . For some time, Governor, Mr. Cayetano Olmedo's intention to marry Miss Fernández

has been spoken of in Celaya and not withstanding the diversity of opinion for and against the suitability of this marriage, I personally view the matrimony to be opportune inasmuch as my immediate contact with the each party's family has given me the resources to analyze the underlying rationale of various matters related to the present case.

Here recorded, your Excellency, are Mr. Antonio Leiva's arguments against the suitability of the joining of the Administrador Mr. Cayetano Omedo with the girl Miss María Petra Fernández.

1) Mr. Cayetano Olmedo is an inexperienced youngster, with little regard among the population, lacking in dedication to his work, and in aptitude for his official duties.

2) Mr. Cayetano Olmedo possesses no other resources to support a family than what he earns as the Administrador del Tabaco, and as there may be reason to suspect that the state government may sooner or later reassume administration of the tobacco monopoly, leaving local functionaries unemployed, and deprive Olmedo of his post, this will lead to his family's ruin.

3) Mr. Cayetano Olmedo, assuming he retains his job, cannot easily earn from it enough to support his own family and that of his mother Mrs. Clara . . .

4) Mr. Cayetano Olmedo only wishes to marry in order to free himself of the maternal yoke via the independence legally conferred to him as a husband.

5) The young woman Miss Petra Fernández is lazy and unversed in the management of a home, nor does she know how to sew, knit, cook, etc., etc., and other such skills necessary to the management of a home.

6) The love that the two share will not last and will cause them regret.

All of the above, General, Mr. Antonio Leiva expressed to me when we met to discuss the matter of his steadfast refusal, [after] Mr. Cayetano Olmedo and his mother Mrs. Clara commissioned me to approach him on their behalf. As Mr. Leiva's objections do not prescribe justice or wisdom, and to the contrary threaten to give reign to a transcendental caprice, I redoubled my efforts so that either he would consent or give me more solid reasons for his opposition. But all was in vain. In compliance with my parochial duties and in honor of your instructions of the seventeenth of this month, I reproduce for you the arguments I marshaled against his position, so that as the judge in this case, you may decide . . .

A detailed refutation of objections one and two follows, both mirroring and expanding upon the assessments set forth by the justices of the peace. The refutation to the second objection concludes with a demonstration of the couple's ability to survive even if, as Leiva thought probable, Cayetano were to be deprived of his position.

. . . I conclude by saying to your Excellency, that Mrs. Clara Olmedo has confessed to me of having more than ten thousand pesos,[8] which, if well managed, will free Miss Fernández from hunger and all the other ills Mr. Leiva predicts.

Additionally, more than two years ago Mrs. Regina Fernández, Petra's sister, married a clerk who earns fifteen pesos per month, and Mr. Leiva raised no objection, nor any fear that the girl would starve, such as he now places before us.

It is good, your Excellency, to inveigh against deceptions, so that they might not be rendered cheaply or easily. I therefore wish to ask Mr. Leiva which of the two sisters will be better placed? Ms. Regina in having married the clerk, Mr. Echeverria? Or Miss Petra, whom Mr. Olmedo has chosen? The house of Echeverría, your Excellency, has no name in Celaya, and though unknown for any other reason than its almost proverbial misery, that

family has earned Mr. Leiva's sympathy; while the house of Olmedo, which by virtue of its modest well being, its exquisite dealings with others, its moral reputation, [and], your Excellency should note, its extensive relations with the leading families of the community— the Linares, the Villaseñor, the Caballero, the González, the Herrera, the Arizmendi, the Rábago, the Maldonado, the Concha, etc., etc., etc.—nevertheless fails to merit Mr. Leiva's trust. Is this just, your Excellency? Is this behavior becoming of a guardian? To the contrary, should not Mr. Leiva bless the marriage that offers his charge the unexpected opportunity to associate herself with a family of the Olmedo's category? . . . [In fact,] the young woman Fernández, General, is on the verge of abject misery, and the pressure of the case obligates me to confess to your Excellency that *I myself have helped her to buy shoes . . .*[9]

[*In response to Leiva's third objection, in which he claims that Olmedo's income is insufficient to support his wife and mother*] there is no doubt that this concern does not apply to Mr. Cayetano Olmedo. On his own account and without borrowing money, he has effectively managed his finances. Any misfortune he might suffer will in no way compromise the interest of any guarantor, and likewise, should he lose his job, his assets, free of any lien, will sustain him and his family.

What is more, Mr. Leiva speaks of two families doubling Mr. Olmedo's costs; but his allegation is unfounded in light of the fact that neither Mr. Olmedo nor his mother have ever thought to separate from one another should he marry, precisely so as not to multiply expenses of children, attending to the home, daily activities, etc., etc. Thus Mr. Leiva's argument in this instance cannot be substantiated in one way or another. . . .

The tenor of the fourth objection is [hence] of the most gratuitous sort. One should not think ill of those who have

[8]At this time, 1 peso equaled 1 United States dollar; 1,000 pesos was sufficient for a family of four to live comfortably for a year. Cayetano's mother evidently possessed a fortune. Michael P. Costeloe, *The Central Republic in Mexico, 1835–1846 : Hombres De Bien in the Age of Santa Anna* (New York: Cambridge University Press, 1993), 20.

[9]Emphasis is reproduced from the original document.

otherwise always conducted themselves honorably, but [what Mr. Leiva alleges about Cayetano's desire to free himself of his mother] is impossible. It being the case that Cayetano manages his mother's reported assets [he depends on her all the more].[10] Were they to be at odds with one another, his mother might be obliged to retract her promises to him [i.e., she might refuse to continue combining her resources with his], and he, unprotected, would have trouble obtaining another guarantor because of the scandal created by his ingratitude. Mr. Olmedo has the greatest interest in remaining at his mother's side, for in his new condition, he needs her more than ever.

The fifth objection should not be commented upon by a priest in the presence of the supreme authority of the State. I would fear to undertake such commentary, for I cannot speak to this incrimination of the young woman Fernández; and if I could, I would surely waste your Excellency's time with the refutation of small matters.

The sixth objection sheds light on the capriciousness of Mr. Leiva's refusal to permit the marriage of his charge and Mr. Cayetano Olmedo. In adhering to his position, Mr. Leiva implies that every man and woman in the universe should not marry for fear of future regret and the extinction of conjugal love. Few indeed are those who share this doctrine, and should Mr. Leiva attract disciples, then he would make more than four commentators on the Bible[11] sweat for upholding the mandate given in the book of Genesis to *grow and multiply*.

However sufficient I may regard what I have written to convincing your Excellency, I cite particular reasons that assist me in arguing in favor of the marriage Mr. Olmedo and Miss Fernández, and achieving finally official recognition of the young woman's legal majority.

1) So as to be close to Mr. Olmedo, this girl has resisted living with her brother-in-law at the Mendoza *hacienda*, and for most of the year has remained in the house in Celaya, visited only her older sister, who lives [nearby], for Petra fears being carried off or seduced (which is more probable), should she lose her case.

2) Her older sister is about to be married.[12]

3) The Olmedo family values Petra, and is equally in favor of Cayetano's desire to marry her.

4) This girl would have difficulty finding a husband of equal quality.

5) Petra informs me that Mr. Leiva has cursed at her, with the objective being to make her desist, and she has lost his respect.

6) Mr. Leiva's intent (as Petra has told me in confidence), is to force her to marry one of his sons.

7) Petra tells me that her married sister [Regina] mistreats her.

8) Should Petra lose her case, it will be difficult for either her or Mr. Olmedo to break off their relationship, and a scandal will surely result.

9) As this girl lacks patrimony and will eventually lose her youthful attractiveness, she will not easily find another suitor of Mr. Olmedo's category as she grows older.

10) The wisest people in town believe "that the young woman should be regarded as very happy with Olmedo having chosen her."

---

[10]It was common practice among elite families for sons to administer the assets of their widowed mothers. That depended on the mother's consent, however. Widows enjoyed special legal status. They could control their personal property, whereas married women did so only to a limited degree. Furthermore, upon the death of Cayetano's father, his assets would have been divided between his children and his wife. Hence, Cayetano and his mother were financially interdependent.

[11]This appears to be an allusion to the epistolary chapters of the New Testament.

---

[12]The reference here is to a second, unnamed older sister. The priest cites the fact of her impending marriage to reinforce his point that Leiva's opposition to Petra marrying Cayetano is without merit considering that he has raised no objection to either of her sisters marrying.

11) In being married, Olmedo will better attend to his affairs, so he will lose no time in their courtship and less still in attention to the obligations of the matrimonial state. His mother shares my feelings on this matter.

. . . I believe, in virtue of Olmedo's irremediable desire [for Petra] . . . ; in virtue of the ongoing distraction this case has caused him to the detriment of his obligations, which threatens to erode his position in the community; in virtue of the mounting expenses that in a state of passion, he like every young man invests in finery, dances, secret gifts, etc., etc.; and very particularly, in virtue of the expressed motives of the young woman Miss Petra Fernández; that your Excellency will use at his discretion the faculty that the law concedes him to grant what she requests . . .

Celaya, January 26, 1854

Antonio Casalot

Secretariat of the Government of Guanajuato
Justice Section

Dear Sir,

In light of the reports submitted by the First and Second Justices of the Peace of Celaya, and of the parish priest of same, regarding the suitability of the proposed marriage of Mr. Cayetano Olmedo, resident of that city, with Miss Petra Fernández, also of Celaya; and considering as well the motives which the conservator of Miss Fernández expressed to the aforementioned priest, which are insufficient to deny the young woman's request, I am of the opinion, assuming you agree, that the necessary permission should be conceded to the aforementioned Miss Fernández so that she may marry.

Guanajuato, February 22, 1854

Feliciano Segovia

Government of Guanajuato

22 February 1854

Accordingly, the requested permission is conceded, which will be communicated to the necessary authorities.

Pacheco

Suggested Sources:

For analysis of changes and continuities in nineteenth-century Mexican gender norms, see Julia Tuñon, "Mexican Women in the Nineteenth Century: Idols of Bronze or Inspiration of the Home?" in *Women in Mexico: A Past Unveiled*, trans. Alan Hynds (Austin: University of Texas Press, Institute for Latin American Studies, 1999). On women's legal status, see Silivia Marina Arrom, *The Women of Mexico City, 1790–1857* (Stanford, CA: Stanford University Press, 1985); and Carmen Diana Deere and Magdalena León, "Liberalism and Married Women's Property Rights in Nineteenth-Century Latin America," *Hispanic American Historical Review* 85, no. 4 (November 2005): 627–678. As Petra's case shows, women were not simply the passive subjects of decisions enacted by male officials. This applied even to women in confinement, as discussed in Lee M. Penyak, "Safe Harbors and Compulsory Custody: *Casas de Depósito* in Mexico, 1750–1865," *Hispanic American Historical Review* 79, no. 1 (February 1999): 83–99.

A variety of sources shed light on the broader context of women's lives in nineteenth-century Mexico. Mexican novelists took their society and its customs as their subject. Manuel Payno's *Los bandidos de Rio Frio* has been translated into English. Manuel Payno, *The Bandits from Río Frío: A Naturalistic and Humorous Novel of Customs, Crimes, and Horrors*, trans. Alan Fluckey (1891; repr., Tucson, AZ: Wheatmark, 2007). Women from a variety of backgrounds are prominently featured in accounts by foreign visitors, though the reader must be cautious to recognize occasional bias in the visitor's perceptions. See Frances Calderón de la Barca's memoir of her time in Mexico as a diplomat's wife in *Life in Mexico* (1843; repr., Whitefish, MT: Kessinger, 2004). The German naturalist Carl Sartorious recorded his encounters with ordinary women he met while making his way inland from the port of Veracruz and in Mexico City; see *Mexico about 1850*, ill. Johann Moritz Rugendas (1858; repr., Stuttgart: Brockhaus, 1961). Foreign photographers visiting Mexico documented the lives of its people. Images by Francois Aubert, Claude-Jóseph-Désiré Charnay, and Louis Falconnet, in "A Nation Emerges: Sixty-Five Years of Photography in Mexico," J. Paul Getty Library Digitized Library Collections, http://www.getty.edu/research/conducting_research/digitized_collections/mexico/hml/photographers/index.html (accessed June 28, 2007). Finally, Argentine filmmaker María Luisa Bemberg et al. offer a visually accurate recreation of nineteenth-century life in *Camila*, which recounts the story of Camila O'Gorman, the daughter of a government minister in 1840s Argentina, who caused a scandal by eloping with a priest (1984; Buenos Aires: Cinemateca/Condor Media, 2002).

Chapter 13

Memories of Mapuche Rebellion and Subjugation in Southern Chile

Joanna Crow, *University of Bristol*

Chile

The *Mapuche* (often called Araucanians) are renowned for their heroic and successful resistance against the Spanish conquistadors. The Spanish state was forced to acknowledge *Mapuche* independence after numerous bloody battles and the death of the royal governor of Chile, Pedro de Valdivia, in 1554. They maintained their independence throughout the colonial period and during the first decades of republican rule. Pascual Coña was a *Mapuche cacique* (community leader or chief) from Puerto Saavedra in southern Chile. He was born in the late 1840s or the early 1850s, when the *Mapuche* were still an autonomous people, and died in 1927, just over 50 years after they and their territory were finally incorporated into the Chilean state. In line with the dominant discourses of "progress and modernization," and in a manner akin to that of its Argentine neighbors (Domingo Faustino Sarmiento, the author of *Facundo*, spent a great deal of time in Chile), the Chilean state sought to "civilize" the "barbaric" *Mapuche*. Pascual Coña's memoirs simultaneously challenged and helped to perpetuate such discourses. Alternately humorous and tragic, the memoirs provide a unique insight into *Mapuche* culture and society and show that *Mapuche* people had an important role to play in the changes that took place in Chile during the late nineteenth and early twentieth centuries.

The document that follows is one chapter from these memoirs. Before he died in October 1927, Coña recounted his life story to a Capuchin missionary, Father Ernesto Wilhelm of Moesbach, who transcribed it in Mapuzungun (the native language of the *Mapuche*) and then translated it into Spanish. Now deemed a classic source by *Mapuche* and non-*Mapuche* academics alike, it was initially published in a journal in the 1920s and 1930s. It first appeared as a complete work in 1930 with the title *Life and Customs of the Araucanian Indians in the Second Half of the Nineteenth Century* (*Autobiography of the Indian Pascual Coña*); Moesback was named as the author.[1]

In the opening lines of the book, Coña conveyed a certain pessimism about the future of his people, lamenting that they were forgetting their history, losing their traditions and language as they became more "Chileanized." The original prologue emphasized the values of his autobiography for capturing the culture and customs of a people who were supposedly on the verge of extinction. Chilean elites viewed the *Mapuche* as an inferior people, destined to disappear in "modern" Chile, while other "whiter"

and "fitter" races flourished (political elites in Chile, as in other Latin American countries, were greatly influenced by theories of *Social Darwinism* and scientific racism). Today, in contrast, the testimony—republished with a bilingual title, sold in high street bookshops, promoted by major institutions such as the Biblioteca Nacional (National Library), and reviewed in mainstream newspapers—is used to affirm the survival of *Mapuche* culture, and to demonstrate this people's ability to produce their own histories and resist assimilation into the dominant Chilean culture.

Coña's testimony provides a wealth of information about the agricultural practices, social organization, domestic life, housing, marriage customs, and gender relations of *Mapuche* society in the late nineteenth and early twentieth centuries. It also offers an illuminating account of the way in which *Mapuche* people negotiated with missionaries, particularly the Capuchins. What provides the reader with most food-for-thought, however, is Coña's version of the state's colonization of *Mapuche* territory (1860s–1880s).

According to the 2002 census, almost 700,000 of Chile's 15 million people self-identify as *Mapuche*; they are the most numerous, visible, and vocal of Chile's indigenous peoples. The *Mapuche* were originally from the southern regions and they still make up a large proportion of the rural population in the south, but, as a result of the process of mass urbanization that began in the 1930s, they also live in many other parts of Chile. Indeed, more than 50 percent of the *Mapuche* live in the capital city Santiago. Regardless of where they live today, however, many *Mapuche* still think of the southern regions, particularly rural Araucanía, as their homeland.

The excerpt that follows narrates the events of the last major *Mapuche* uprising against the Chilean state in 1881. Chilean governments have tended to depict the military invasion and conquest of *Mapuche* territory—the state's response to the rebellion—as a peaceful and unproblematic event. In his opening speech to congress in 1883, President Domingo Santa María congratulated Chileans for this "happy occurrence," which had apparently been achieved without inflicting any harm on *Mapuche* people.

---

[1]Moesbach claimed authorship of Coña's story, thereby relegating the *Mapuche* leader to the role of informer. He transcribed and translated Coña's words and was surely in a position to influence the story that finally appeared in print. A reprint of the book, published in 1973, renamed Coña as the author; all subsequent editions have followed suit, but they also acknowledge Moesbach's mediating role.

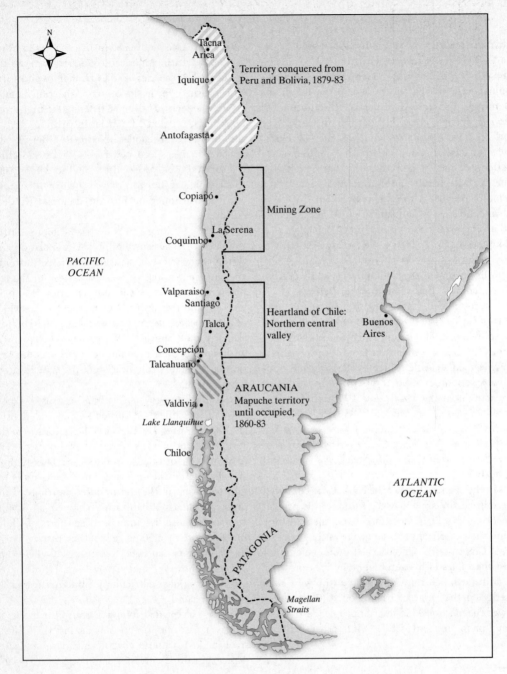

Conquest of the *Mapuche* was a crucial part of the process of national consolidation. Note the location of *Mapuche* territory between Concepción and Valdivia on the map. How and why did the existence of an independent *Mapuche* territory stand in the way of Chilean national unity? Why might this territory have been even more problematic once the Chilean state gained control over the northern desert region (from Arica down to Antofagasta) from Peru and Bolivia during the War of the Pacific (1879–1884)?

Source: Leslie Bethell, (ed.), *Chile since Independence*, p.5, 1993, Cambridge University Press.

Indeed, he claimed that they had given themselves up willingly once they knew they could trust in the "civilizing" protection afforded by Chilean law. Many prominent historians, such as Sergio Villalobos (who won the National Prize for History in 1992), support this view of events, outlining the campaigns in rather mechanical terms (which forts were established when and where) and sidelining the bloodshed and suffering involved. Since the 1980s, a counterhistory has emerged to challenge the official interpretation, underscoring the violent nature of the occupations; the atrocities committed by the Chilean army; and the brave, but ultimately unsuccessful, resistance mounted by *Mapuche* communities. José Bengoa, for example, claimed that the "great insurrection" of 1881 was forever etched in the historical memory of this people. As narrated by Bengoa, the government's response to this rebellion was not pacification but instead extermination.

Pascual Coña's testimony helps to complicate these clear-cut oppositional views of history, offering a fascinating insight into his and other *Mapuche* experiences (as he saw it) of Chilean occupation. Pascual Coña did not join the rebellion. He, like Pascual Painemilla, sided with the Chilean forces. Many of the other *Mapuche* leaders who appear in the text, such as Neculmán, Colihuinca, Quilempán, Painén, and Painecur, initially supported the uprising, but they took on a variety of different roles that sometimes changed as events unravelled. Coña's testimony introduces the reader to several Chileans, who were either members of the army or so-called negotiators sent by state authorities to meet and talk with *Mapuche* leaders.

Coña's narrative of events helps to elucidate some of the key themes of this section, particularly indigenous historical agency: Coña was an active participant in national political developments and in the production of a history about these developments. His firsthand account illuminates the variety of *Mapuche* experiences of Chilean colonization and details their pragmatic responses to the uprisings and subsequent military intervention, showing how they developed multiple strategies for survival. It documents their suffering but also reinforces their ability to adapt to changing circumstances. Overall, it indicates just how complex the relationship was between the *Mapuche* and the Chilean state.

Questions to Consider:

1. How did Coña tell the story of the 1881 rebellion? Can you find ways that his indigenous identity influenced his narrative and manner of relaying events?
2. How did Coña describe the rebellion? How does his version of events help to complicate the standard narratives outlined in the chapter introduction?
3. What image(s) did Coña present of *Mapuche* people?
4. What were relationships like in his narrative between the *Mapuche* and representatives of the Chilean state, or military? The *Mapuche* and the Church? Different *Mapuche* groups with each other?

Pascual Coña, "The Rebellion of 1881"[2]

1)
1. The *Mapuche* people of old hated foreigners. They used to say: "We've got nothing to do with these strange people; they're of a different race." Sometimes the leaders who lived near these *huincas* would attack them; they fought and lost, and thus their hatred towards them increased.[3] As a result of this great aversion towards the huincas, indigenous people throughout the region began to plot against them. The first step was

---

[2]*Source:* Father Ernesto Wilhelm de Moesbach, *Vida y costumbres de los indígenas araucanos en la segunda mitad del siglo XIX* (Santiago: Imprenta Cervantes, 1930); pp. 270–287.

---

[3]*Huinca* meant foreigner, often traitorous, thieving foreigner.

taken by the Pehuenche (Argentine) leaders in a message to the *Mapuche* leader Neculmán in Boroa, Chile, which instructed him to prepare for war, as they were doing in Argentina. They also sent a knotted rope indicating when the general uprising would take place.[4]

2. When the messenger from the indigenous people of Argentina arrived he said: "I have been sent by Chaihueque, Namuncura, Foyel and Ancatrir; they told me to "go and see the noble chiefs in Chile." Hence, my being here. On behalf of my leader I say to you, Chilean chiefs, the following: "We still have the issue of these huincas; we are going to rise up against them. The indigenous people of Argentina will finish them off, and we want you to do the same with yours, we want you to attack as well; together we will launch a war against them." They also told me to "take these knots, and get them to agree, because the huincas are hateful." This is the message they gave me, said the messenger to Neculmán.

3. Neculmán thanked him for the message and immediately enlisted a messenger to spread the word to his subordinates. [He said] "Tomorrow we shall hold a meeting; a messenger has arrived from the Mapuche chiefs in Argentina, so tomorrow we will meet." The messenger then went off to pass on the news. [. . .]

    [*When leaders met the next day, they all agreed to rise up against the Chileans, after which Neculmán sent notice of the uprising to all the other* Mapuche *leaders.*]

4. Pascual Painemilla of Rauquenhue and Pascual Paillalef of Alma were not informed. They supported the huincas; for that reason many wanted them dead. Everybody who had received the message untied a knot each day. On

the last day, they called all the main leaders to get together. When the meetings had taken place – it was a time of famine, the wheat had already ripened[5] – certain Chileans discovered what was going on. Five men were sent to advise the *Mapuche* against the rebellion. They were Vicente Jaramillo (who was in charge), Blas Morales, Domingo Lagos, Domingo Alonso and Pascual Trintray (who was indigenous). They went to speak to Colihuinca.[6]

5. When Marimán, who had just concluded his meeting, found out about the arrival of this group, he ordered some of his men to bring them to him. While the group was sleeping the night at Colihuinca's place they were surprised, taken prisoner and carried off. Marimán and his band were so pleased: "We've captured the bulls (victims), today we will celebrate a nguillatún," they said. People say these Chileans were tied up and had their hearts ripped out while still alive. The *Mapuche* offered the hearts up to their Gods (in return for their requests) and dipped their spears in the blood of these men. In this way those Chileans who tried to prevent the rebellion met their deaths.

2)

1. Once they had carried out the mass meetings everywhere, we also became aware that a great uprising was about to take place. So Painemilla and I went to the army headquarters in Puerto Saavedra. There was a young lady Elvira Navarrete there, employed as a telegraphist. We visited her with the intention of cheering her up, so that she wouldn't be frightened about the rebellion, but she got very scared and started crying. Painemilla was accompanied by some of his men who were armed with spears. To enliven the

---

[4]The word used in Spanish was *nudos*, meaning "knots," which I have translated as "knotted rope," as it was often rope that was used. Very basically, it was used as a way of communicating—indigenous peoples would send messages to one another using such techniques, often referencing a date or a period of time. Possibly, the *Mapuche* learned this from the Incas who sent messages in a similar way.

[5]Moesbach noted here that "It was 1 November 1881."
[6]To restate: Vicente Jaramillo, Blas Morales, Domingo Lagos and Domingo Alonso were all Chileans; they were sent, on the part of the Chilean authorities, to advise the *Mapuche* not to rebel. Pascual Trintay also went with this group, but he was an indigenous man working with the Chilean authorities. Colihuinca was one of the *Mapuche* leaders who had agreed to join in the *Mapuche* rebellion.

young lady they carried out war exercises: that just scared her more, though, and the more scared she was the more she cried. Her mother said to her: "Don't be afraid; these are not enemies, they are protecting us," but she didn't believe her and got even more upset.

2. At that moment[7] a young man called Hualmén arrived, out of breath, from Ruca-trara and said: "I bring you bad news: disaster is near; those huincas sent to speak to the rebel leaders were all killed." We then left the young lady and came back. Father Constancio had already left for Toltén; the mission was without a priest. Chief Mozo of Boroa had taken him, telling him about the enemy's plans; he was thus saved.[8]

3. The next morning Calfupán, the main leader of Colileufu, held his meeting. He brought together warriors from Colileufu, Deume and Trahuatrahua. [. . .]

4. I was not going to go to the meeting, but in the end I went to find out what was going on. I left my wife with a *Mapuche* family, in spite of the fact that women had nothing to fear from the uprising. Half way there I met a *Mapuche* who was on his way back from the gathering. I said to him: "I don't know what's going on," to which he replied "It is all a terrible mess, the meeting has finished. Don't go; soldiers have arrived from Toltén, for that reason every-one has returned. Over there, on the beach near the sea, there are many Chileans with weapons, Painemilla is with them; they're on their way to Toltén with the soldiers."

5. After hearing this I ran to the beach and saw them there; a great number of Chileans were walking together with six soldiers. Painemilla was amongst them; he must have seen me because he beckoned to me with a white hanker-chief. As soon as I understood his sig-nal I ran to join them, I became part of the

convoy and we marched along the whole length of the beach. Above on the cliffs was Pedro Painén, together with his men, all of whom were armed with spears; they had come from the meeting. At the southern limit of Puauchu they stopped. "It looks like they want to cut us off and attack," the soldier in charge said. He immediately got his soldiers in line; we followed behind. But Painén's group did not approach to attack us, they just watched us closely. We protected ourselves against them and passed by; we didn't do anything.

6. Later I discovered that Painén and Quilem-pán had made a pact together: "If the rebel-lion fails and the rebel leaders don't reach Toltén we'll say: we know nothing, we were not involved." But if it succeeded and the rebels had taken Toltén, they wanted to follow and join them to help in the joyful rebellion. We then carried on to Toltén. We were caught out by the rain and hence ar-rived in Toltén soaked through to the skin. At dawn we continued the journey. From the other side they came to ferry us across in a boat; we passed through and arrived in Toltén where we stayed for five days.

7. During our stay in Toltén, Painemilla received a message from Calfupán, which stated the following: "So, you have saved yourselves; the uprising took place, they must almost have caught you, but now they have retreated. The leaders of the rebellion, Colihuinca, Painecur, Huichal and Carmona, demanded I join them: they pleaded 'we are going to attack Toltén, you have to help us.' I refused. I said to them: 'if you want to be defeated, do so alone, even if you do think you can beat the soldiers. They have many weapons, so I don't dare.'" These words scared the leaders of the rebellion and they turned back.

8. The messenger also told us "When the rebels reached Boca-Budi, Painecur of Pichihueque killed the Chilean José María López." His brother Martín López suffered the same fate. The two of them had been crossing the river in a canoe with some women, so the rebels came at them from both sides of the river, jumped

---

[7]Moesbach added a note that the date was 1 November.
[8]Moesbach noted: "Father Constancio left in the afternoon of 1 November, before Huelmén arrived. He had decided not to go, trusting in the many benefits he had brought to the *Mapuche*, but chief Mozo convinced him he would pointlessly lose his life."

into the canoe and killed them. They didn't kill the women though; I found out afterwards that they fled to Toltén.

9. Calfupán's men chased the rebel leaders as they were retreating. The latter were even more intimidated by this and tried desperately to get away. Calfupán's men enjoyed seeing them so fearful and continued to hunt them down; they managed to grab a couple of their horses, they killed one person and took five *Mapuche* people prisoner. These five captives were taken to Toltén, they were from Mañiu; they were later released.

10. The uprising was thus quashed; they hadn't even managed to get as far as Toltén. The rebel leaders returned to their rucas and rested. We had only been in Toltén five days. What the rebels did in other regions I do not know, so cannot say. All I heard, later, was that in Nehuentúe, on the other side of the River Cautín, a Chilean called Severino Ibáñez was killed.

3)

1. We'd only been at home two days when a message from Painemilla arrived saying "You must come, we are meeting in Toltén." "Tomorrow, we have to leave again," the messenger said. We returned to Toltén by horse and we found Painemilla rounding up a large number of men: he was doing it on the orders of Governor Pascual López of Toltén. The gathering took place on the north side of the River Toltén. People from Queule arrived; residents of Toltén crossed the river, and many of us also turned up. Painemilla got all of these people together, obeying the orders of the Governor, who had put him in charge of the counter-attack against the rebel leaders.

2. I don't know the exact number but there must have been hundreds of us, all armed with spears, as well as ten Chileans with fire arms; I also had a rifle. Eventually we set off to exact revenge upon the *Mapuche* rebels. We climbed along the north bank of the River Toltén, passed through Peñehue and arrived

in Puculón. There we waited and met up with other groups; all the groups met there in the plains of Puculón. Once everyone was gathered together, we walked across the great mountain that you find there and came out in a place called Puqueno, where we met up with still more men and rested for a while.

3. While we were there an indigenous man, who had taken part in the rebellion, came up to us to ask for forgiveness. The Chilean Juan Peña quickly pronounced that "this despicable Indian attacked us in Peñehue." If I remember correctly, he said the Indian had killed his mother and also taken many of her things. "I will kill him," he said; he took the *Mapuche* to one side, got out his shotgun and pulled the trigger, but it didn't fire. Then he asked to borrow the rifle of another Chilean Juan Aburto. He lent it to him and Juan Peña pulled the trigger, shooting the man in the head. He fell to the ground and died almost instantaneously.

4. Chief Painequeu also came to give himself up. Juan Peña once again said "this person has invaded Peñehue; I'll kill him too," but this time Painemilla would not permit it and so Painequeu escaped death. Consequently, Painequeu pledged his help and support, and Painemilla accepted. We restarted the march and arrived in Liuco, where Painequeu lived. We stayed there the night and rested. The next morning Painequeu and his son brought more people to fight against their co-nationals.[9,10]

5. We saddled up and managed to reach the ridge of Cudico near Mañiu. There we got together a great herd of sheep, perhaps one thousand of them; you couldn't hear yourself speak for all their bleating. We rested and killed a couple of the sheep so that the people fighting

---

[9]Moesbach added a note here stating: "Thus was lost the ancient morale of the Araucanian people, who had defended their independence for three centuries."
[10]The use of the term "co-nationals" (*co-nacionales* in Spanish) is interesting—it suggests that the *Mapuche* thought of themselves as a "nation" during the late nineteenth century.

could eat meat; we had a feast and then bedded down for the night.

6. The next day our men went off in search of more animals. Meanwhile some indigenous people came up to ask for forgiveness (for rebelling); another two were brought to us having been taken captive. Again on this occasion Juan Peña repeated his accusation: "These two men also invaded Peñehue; I have no option but to kill them." He grabbed the two men, who begged Painemilla to save them, but he was having none of it.[11] So, the Chileans took them up the mountain and killed them. We didn't hear their screams.

7. That afternoon we prepared the horses and returned to Liuco, where we had camped before. We took many sheep and cattle with us. When we got there we stayed the night. The following day our people went off to another region to look for livestock. On one mountain we found a herd of sheep with a sheep dog, well hidden on a cliff, but they had all died of starvation. We went past, further up the mountain, where we found many fugitives, women and a few men. These tried to escape into the forest. The women stayed but screamed in fear, thinking that we were going to kill them. They weren't killed; they just had to give up the silver jewelry and other ornaments that they carried with them. One group of men took care of this task, the other rounded up the cows and mares found there.

8. Afterwards we returned to our camp in Liuco. The booty was given to Painemilla, but only half, the other half the men hid for themselves; they did not give everything back. Painemilla had amassed much silver – he filled up a bag and put it away safely. The next day we set off for Quilco. There we met Pelquimán, Neculmán's son. He was leading a large group of men (replacing his father), and all were armed with spears ready to attack the *Mapuche* rebels.

9. As Neculmán had not succeeded in his plan to defeat the Chileans in Toltén, he sent a message to Imperial, using Pancho Jaramillo to communicate his request. Via this messenger he said to the Governor "I have not taken part in the rebellion, so please do not blame me, my Governor. If you so wish, I am ready to help in the reprisals against the leaders that ordered the rebellion." The Governor acceded and replied to Neculmán "Yes, do that; I want to believe that you are not to blame. Punish all those leaders and their men, and do not get involved in any other conspiracies." Having received this reply, Neculmán got his men ready and put Pelquimán (who had led the uprising) in charge of them. [. . .]

10. We returned to our place of rest in Liuco. Calfuqueu of Mañiu approached with his men and gave himself up. He brought silver adornments for Painemilla, as payment for his safety and their reconciliation; he was well received. Painemilla ordered us to "come and shake hands with this good chief." And we shook his right hand. Calfuqueu looked relieved. Painemilla reprimanded him: "Do not do such a thing again; if ever there is another rebellion as absurd as this, do not take part." Painequeu made his promise and all of his men also submitted to Painemilla. They then left.

11. Then came along a man who brought a small paper note sent by General Urrutia. I read it and it contained the following order: "Painemilla, put an end to this conflict! If you continue fighting with these people, I will have you killed." As soon as Painemilla found out, he brought the fighting to an end. Immediately we got on our horses and rounded up all the cattle and livestock; there were 600 cattle and at least 1000 sheep. We took them to Mañiu and we drove them into the meadows (Puerto Saavedra).

12. It was there that the Governor received the animals stolen during the fighting. He had come there from Toltén with his soldiers. Other animals were also handed over to him. When we arrived, the meadow was full of cattle; Pascual Paillalef had rounded them up

---

[11]We do not know why Painemilla refused to step in to save the two *Mapuche* men; possibly he felt they deserved to be shot because of their involvement in the rebellion, or he may simply have wanted to appear strong and resolute in front of the Chilean Juan Peña.

during other expeditions. The poor *Mapuche* no longer owned anything, not even their houses; they had all been reduced to ash; they were left in a really dismal state. And with this the conflict came to an end. We returned to our homeland Rauquenhue without having to move again, we lived in complete tranquillity; there were no more incidents. Although we did hear that the Chileans in other regions refused to stop bothering and inciting the unfortunate *Mapuche*.

13. People say that Huichal, Colihuinca and Juanito Millahuinca all met with the Governor to make peace. They brought saddlebags full of silver objects, so they say. But the Governor took the silver goods and had these leaders chained up. A few days later they were released from prison, taken to Boca-Budi and shot. That is what I heard had happened and it must have been true because these leaders were the most guilty, especially Colihuinca who had given up the five Chileans to those who ripped out their hearts, over there on the other side of Carahue. Marimán, who had killed those gentlemen, escaped and went into hiding. When the amnesty for the *Mapuche* was enacted, Marimán was also included. He subsequently came out of his hiding place, went on several recreational trips and boasted of his friendly relations with the authorities.

14. I also heard that in Nehuentúe, on the other side of the River Cautín, there was a Chilean named Patricio Rojas. This monster arrested *Mapuche* people, and locked them inside a ruca. He then set fire to the ruca and watched the indigenous people die in the flames. Such was the story of the conflict – the rebellion and its aftermath – in the coastal region. For the *Mapuche*, things went from bad to worse. While they had taken few goods from the Chileans, some of the latter had greatly enriched themselves, thanks to the animals stolen from the *Mapuche*.

Suggested Sources:

Though primary sources by the *Mapuche* are difficult to obtain, particularly in English, *Mapuche* poets have received national and international critical acclaim. Cecilia Vicuña has written a useful introduction to the work of four *Mapuche* writers, and John Bierhorst has translated it into English. See Cecilia Vicuña, ed., *Ul: Four Mapuche Poets*, trans. John Bierhorst (Pittsburgh, PA: Latin American Literary Review Press, 1998). Some of the poetry evokes the violence of the colonial period and the occupation campaigns of the late nineteenth century. The best overview of Chilean history since independence is Simon Collier and William Sater, *A History of Chile, 1808–2002* (Cambridge: Cambridge University Press, 2004). The authors make a brief reference to the Chilean state's occupation of *Mapuche* territory. Stephen Lewis shows how dominant images of the *Mapuche* have evolved since the colonial period. See Stephen Lewis, "Myth and the History of Chile's Araucanians," *Radical History Review* 58 (Winter 1994). In his collection of essays, Ariel Dorfman recently reflected on the paradoxical nature of such images. See Ariel Dorfman, "Who Are the Real Barbarians? Memory and the Fate of Latin America," in *Other Septembers, Many Americas: Selected Provocations, 1980–2004* (London: Pluto Press, 2004). A useful although dated introduction to *Mapuche* culture and society is Louis Faron, *The Mapuche Indians of Chile* (New York: Rhinehart and Winston, 1968). Florencia Mallon provides an insightful comparison of the place of indigenous peoples in the national narratives of Chile, Mexico, and Peru. See Florencia Mallon, "Decoding the Parchments of the Latin American Nation-State: Peru, Mexico and Chile in Comparative Perspective" in *Studies in the Formation of the Nation-State in Latin America*, ed. James Dunkerley (London: Institute of Latin American Studies, 2002).

Section IV

Changing Notions of Race, Gender, and Nation, ca. 1900–1950

Beginning around 1900, many Latin American nations turned away—at least rhetorically—from late nineteenth-century aims to Europeanize their nations as a means of advancing national progress. Simultaneously, United States intervention in the Cuban Independence War in 1898 (a.k.a. the "Spanish-American War") marked its rising influence in Latin American politics. Meanwhile, European powers, distracted by world wars and anticolonial movements, were on the decline in the region. Finally, the early twentieth century was an era of modernization in Latin American politics and the economies. Depending on one's viewpoint, these changes either promised or threatened to alter social and economic relations that had shaped individual and group identities and options for centuries.

One particularly important change concerned Latin American political and intellectual elites' views of race relations. Although nineteenth-century elites had attempted to emulate European nations, large populations of indigenous or Afro-Latin American peoples frustrated their endeavors. By contrast, early twentieth-century politicians and intellectuals seemed to rediscover subaltern peoples living among them, and they imagined positive contributions that women and non-whites might make to their nations. Elites' formal pride in cultural and racial diversity denoted a shift in Latin American nationalisms that is often referred to as either the "cult of *mestizaje*" (cultural intermixing), or "*racial democracy*." Regardless of the terminology used, these trends marked a new formal relationship between subalterns and the state. Latin American nations were, theoretically, becoming more inclusive.

Changes in Latin American nationalisms occurred in conjunction with other political and socioeconomic transformations. In Cuba and Mexico, new nationalisms coincided with revolutionary warfare. True social revolutions are rare events in which peoples from all walks of life, all cultural backgrounds, and all regions of a colony or nation rise up to overthrow a ruling regime, with coalitions forming among groups of people (often of different classes or races) who would not normally see each other as political allies. Once the ruling regime is overthrown, however, revolutions descend into civil war, with one faction ultimately taking over political power. Revolutionary outcome is just as important as revolutionary warfare—to be a true social revolution, one must find evidence of significant and enduring political, social, and (often) economic change. In Mexico, this transformation directly followed the revolutionary conflict. In Cuba, however, the Independence War (1895–1898) appeared to have all of the trappings of revolutionary upheaval—but due to a variety of factors (including United States intervention), revolutionary changes did not occur until after Castro's attack on the Batista government in the late 1950s.

The new ruling elite transformed the relationship between formerly marginalized individuals

This photograph, taken in February 1959, shows Fidel Castro and a group of his followers standing in front of the statue of Martí in Matanzas, Cuba. Castro himself stands atop a female liberty figure that has broken the chains of tyranny that had once bound her. Castro often used Martí's rhetoric in his speeches as he rose to power in Cuba. What message do you think did he intend to send by straddling this statue? Look closely at the photograph. To what extent does the image of the guerrilla fighters build on the symbolism of the statue, and to what extent are they juxtaposed?

Source: Courtesy of the Library of Congress.

and the state, typically with both positive and negative results.

Some of the chapters in this section examine sociopolitical changes that accompanied revolutionary upheaval in Cuba and Mexico. The chapter on "Raceless Nationalism" presents essays by José Martí, Cuba's most famous independence

hero, whose ideas about race and national identity moved Cubans from all walks of life to rise up against the Spanish colonial regime. Martí's ideas later inspired Fidel Castro in his struggle against the Batista government in the 1950s and as he established his own power in the early 1960s. In Mexico, peoples from different regions, classes, races, and genders came together in 1910 to overthrow dictator Porfirio Díaz (r. 1876–1911), a struggle that resulted in multifaceted civil wars until almost 1920. The chapter "Peasants, Gender, and the Mexican Revolutionary Conflict" in this section examines what it meant to live through these civil wars from the perspectives of a peasant man and woman. Once the Mexican revolutionary war was over, the process of revolutionary state building embraced *indigenismo*, in which scholars and politicians celebrated the glories of the indigenous past and proclaimed that they would redeem and strengthen indigenous peoples and cultures in the present. O'Hara's chapter focuses on how national and racial ideas developed over the course of revolutionary conflict and state building through examination of a lesser-known group of indigenous peoples, the *Tarahumara* of northern Mexico.

Historical documents often reveal the limits of new racial and citizenship ideas. Foote, for example, presents writings by an Italian missionary, Antonio Metalli, who wanted to incorporate the Cayapa, a coastal indigenous population, into the Ecuadorian nation in the early twentieth century. His emphasis on the Cayapas' potential for civilization and citizenship stood in contrast with his discussions of supposed Afro-Ecuadorian barbarism as it was reported to him by Cayapa informants. Foote's chapter reveals tensions that could emerge between indigenous and African-descended populations in this era, as well as the ongoing racism that underpinned new ideas about citizenship and nationhood. For Brazil, Otovo's documents from a school where young women learned scientific methods of child-rearing, uncover that it was mainly white elite Brazilian women who benefited from this education. Although it was poor, non-white Brazilian women

whose babies faced the greatest challenges for survival, physicians and health advocates did not afford any participatory role for these women in the formulation of ideas about mothering or public health policies.

Some twentieth-century developments created new opportunities for subaltern groups, whereas other transformations brought new challenges, problems, and insecurities to the poorest and most marginalized members of society. Less-powerful peoples often experienced positive and negative impacts simultaneously. For example, peoples of indigenous and African descent enjoyed a more positive formal status within their nations, which provided a basis on which they could make demands of the state. At the same time, they continued to face deeply embedded racism in their everyday lived experiences. Middle-class and elite women gained some new rights and greater respect for their contributions—mainly as mothers—to the nation, but women's political status in Latin America changed only slowly and unevenly. Poor, non-white women were least likely to benefit in any meaningful way from the new ideas about race, gender, citizenship, and nationhood that were emerging.

Though limited and contradictory, the intellectual and political changes apparent in this section marked an important transition in Latin American history. Rather than looking to the colonial past or to Europe, elites began to look to the future and to take pride in the cultural complexity of their nations. Their new ideas about race, gender, and nation may not have always changed the everyday lives of subaltern peoples, but they opened the possibility for successful grassroots organization that would later begin to challenge sociopolitical hierarchies in a more meaningful way.

Chapter 14

José Martí Promotes "Raceless Nationalism" in Cuba

Erin E. O'Connor, Bridgewater State College

Cuban patriot José Martí spent many years in exile in the United States due to his involvement in various plots against Spanish rule, and he died on the battlefield in 1895 just as the final push in the struggle for Cuban independence began. Despite the fact that Martí did not participate directly in determining the outcome of independence, he ranks among the most famous figures in Cuban history. More than a century after his death, Martí's essays on Cuban independence and identity are still reproduced in many countries and languages. Moreover, Cuban politicians from all points on the political spectrum, and from the independence period through the current day, have consistently called on Martí's rhetoric to justify their agendas. What makes Martí such a compelling figure in Latin American history? Certainly, he was a fine and passionate writer, but his fame results from more than that: Martí was one of the first, and best known, of men who turned away from nineteenth-century attempts to strengthen Latin American nations through Europeanization. Instead of bemoaning the presence of indigenous and African peoples within his nation, Martí officially celebrated racial diversity and inclusiveness both in Cuba and in Latin America more generally. Though his claims about Cuba did not match reality, they marked an important ideological shift that influenced interethnic negotiations in Latin America for much of the twentieth century. Excerpts from Martí's writings, therefore, allow one to grasp important changes—and continuities—in Latin American nationalist thought in the early to middle twentieth century.

Martí formed his discourses on *Cubanidad* (Cuban identity) and race during the long struggle for independence from Spain. The first Cuban independence struggle, fought from 1868 to 1878, failed due to deeply embedded class and race divisions, leaving the planter class divided over the question of whether to abolish slavery. Abolition came, under Spanish rule, in 1886, at the same time that world market prices for sugar dropped precipitously. The Cuban economy declined suddenly and dramatically, and even middle-class families struggled to make ends meet. Newly freed Afro-Cubans who lacked work on plantations migrated to cities, where they quickly became an urban underclass drawn to crime and prostitution out of desperation. Meanwhile, peoples of all classes and racial backgrounds found independence increasingly appealing, though for very different reasons. Plantation owners wanted little, if any, socioeconomic change, proposing merely a shift from colonial to national rule. Middle classes were mainly concerned with rule of law and moderate reforms. The poor—most of whom were Afro-Cuban—sought a national government that would address problems of wages, prices, land tenure, and racism in Cuban society. Despite the potential for a widespread popular uprising in Cuba, differing race, class, and political agendas made it difficult to forge a unified front against Spanish rule. Martí's rhetoric played an important role in fostering a sense of unity in Cuba both during and after the wars for independence. Historian Lillian Guerra noted that leaders from very different racial and ideological backgrounds manipulated Martí's ideas for their own purposes as they struggled to determine which group's vision would shape the new government.[1] Excerpts from Martí's statements about race clarify why his rhetoric was at once unifying and divisive.

José Martí's ideas were tailored to the times in which he lived, and they reflected his political commitments. Martí joined the first Cuban independence movement as a youth, and he was exiled to Spain at the age of 17, where he earned a law degree. After traveling to Mexico, Guatemala, and Venezuela, he returned to Cuba for a few years under amnesty in 1878, but he was forced to leave again in 1881. From that time until his return to Cuba in 1895, Martí lived in New York City, where he established the pro-independence newspaper *Patria* and used essays and poetry to draw elite Cubans to the independence cause. Yet his ideas also filtered down and appealed to poorer Afro-Cubans, helping the independence struggle to become a multiclass, multiracial cause—albeit one that maintained significant class and racial tensions. His death in 1895 during one of the first skirmishes of the war for independence made him a martyr figure whose writings became even more influential over time.

Martí was one of several Latin American intellectuals to envision new forms of national and regional pride between 1890 and 1940. In Mexico, for example, José Vasconcelos published *La Raza Cósmica* (The Cosmic Race) in 1925, in which he identified Mexico as a prime location where the four different races (European, indigenous, African, and Asian) were blending together to form a new and

---

[1]Lillian Guerra, *The Myth of José Martí: Conflicting Nationalisms in Early Twentieth-Century Cuba* (Chapel Hill: University of North Carolina Press, 2005).

superior fifth race—the "Cosmic Race." In particular, Vasconcelos contrasted the positive impact of miscegenation in Mexico with the negative results of racial exclusivity in the United States. Similarly, Brazilian sociologist and politician Gilberto Freyre wrote extensively on the benefits of racial mixing in Brazilian history and identity, and he is to this day identified as the "Father of *Racial Democracy* Theory." Freyre argued that one major result of racial intermixing in Brazil was that non-whites faced no legal barriers to advancement; therefore, true democracy existed among the different races in the nation. Like other early twentieth-century nationalists, Freyre drew a distinction between Brazilian racial harmony with the racial discord he had observed in the United States.

Though they came from different backgrounds and made different kinds of arguments, all of these men contributed to a new sense of pride in Latin American identity and cultural diversity. In some cases, as with Martí and Vasconcelos, intellectual nationalists sought to reach an audience that included men of different racial backgrounds. Freyre, however, wrote for exclusively elite audiences. Many of these men developed their ideas by living for a period in the United States, where they witnessed firsthand the bad as well as good features of this emerging world power. Perhaps ironically, these ideas of *racial democracy* often reinforced rather than weakened racial inequalities. Although intellectuals used their theories of *racial democracy* and racial harmony to assert that Afro-Latin Americans or indigenous peoples faced no obstacles to socio-political mobility, racism persisted in social and government practices. Though there were few overt segregation laws such as those found in the United States before the Civil Rights movement, Latin American racism was subtle but widespread. If, for example, Afro-Cubans or Afro-Brazilians tried to address racial inequalities, government officials (often white elites) accused them of acting in a racist manner by trying to create racial divides where none had previously existed!

Despite their considerable limitations, Latin American notions of *racial democracy* were more inclusive than racial theories in the United States and Europe at the time, and they offered Afro-Latin Americans some opportunities for participation in their nations. Moreover, although elites manipulated *racial democracy* theories to buttress existing racial hierarchies, the ideas also kept them from being able to pass overtly racist policies or laws. Finally, Afro-Latin Americans employed these new ideologies to advance their own interests, such as when they created multiracial labor organizations.[2] In short, *racial democracy* theories defy simplistic generalization, and their impact on Latin American societies was both considerable and complex.

Questions to Consider:

1. Why do you think Martí's assertions about race won over Afro-Cuban support the Cuban independence movement? What might Afro-Cubans have expected from independence based on Martí's writings?

2. What parts of Martí's writings might have concerned Euro-Cuban elites the most? What might have appealed to them the most?

3. Assess the various claims and statements that Martí made about race in these documents. Was he asserting racial equality? Why or why not?

4. What was the role of *manliness* in these writings? What does that tell us about the relationship between gender and nationalism in Cuba?

5. How do the views of race presented in this chapter compare with ideas presented in other chapters in this section? What do your conclusions tell you about how and why Latin American national identities and race relations were changing by the early twentieth century?

---

[2]See, for example, Alejandro de la Fuente, "Myths of Racial Democracy: Cuba, 1900–1912," *Latin American Research Review* 34, no. 3 (1999): 39–73.

José Martí on Race and Nation

"Our America"[3]

The prideful villager thinks his hometown contains the whole world, and as long as he can stay on as mayor or humiliate the rival who stole his sweetheart or watch his nest egg accumulating in its strongbox he believes the universe to be in good order, unaware of the giants in seven-league boots who can crush him underfoot or the battling comets in the heavens that go through the air devouring the sleeping worlds. Whatever is left of that sleepy hometown in America must awaken. These are not times for going to bed in a sleeping cap, but rather, like Juan de Castellanos's[4] men, with our weapons for a pillow, weapons of the mind, which vanquish all others. Trenches of ideas are worth more than trenches of stone.

A cloud of ideas is a thing no armored prow can smash through. A vital idea set ablaze before the world at the right moment can, like the mystic banner of the last judgment, stop a fleet of battleships. Hometowns that are still strangers to one another must hurry to become acquainted, like men who are about to do battle together. Those who shake their fists at each other like jealous brothers quarreling over a piece of land or the owner of a small house who envies the man with a better one must join hands and interlace them until their two hands are as one. Those who, shielded by a criminal tradition, mutilate, with swords smeared in the same blood that flows through their own veins, the land of a conquered brother whose punishment far exceeds his crimes, must return that land to their brother if they do not wish to be known as a nation of plunderers. The honorable man does not collect his debts of honor in money, at so much per slap. We can no longer be a nation of fluttering leaves, spending our lives in the air, our treetop crowned in flowers, humming or creaking, caressed by the caprices of sunlight or thrashed and felled by tempests. The trees must form ranks to block the seven-league giant! It is the hour of reckoning and of marching in unison, and we must move in lines as compact as the veins of silver that lie at the roots of the Andes.

Only runts whose growth was stunted will lack the necessary valor, for those who have no faith in their land are like men born prematurely. Having no valor themselves, they deny that other men do. Their puny arms, with bracelets and painted nails, the arms of Madrid or of Paris, cannot manage the lofty tree and so they say the tree cannot be climbed. We must load up the ships with these termites who gnaw away at the core of the *patria* that has nurtured them; if they are Parisians or Madrileños then let them stroll to the Prado by lamplight or go to Tortoni's for an ice. These sons of carpenters who are ashamed that their father was a carpenter! These men born in America who are ashamed of the mother that raised them because she wears and Indian apron, these delinquents who disown their sick mother and leave her alone in her sickbed! Which one is truly a man, he who stays with his mother to nurse her through her illness, or he who forces her to work somewhere out of sight, and lives off her sustenance in corrupted lands, with a worm for his insignia, cursing the bosom that bore him, sporting a sign that says "traitor" on the back of his paper dress-coat? These sons of our America, which must save herself through her Indians, and which is going from less to more, who desert her and take up arms in the armies of North America, which drowns its own Indians in blood and is going from more to less! These delicate creatures who are men but do not want to do men's work! Did Washington, who made that land for them, go and live with the English during the years when he saw the English marching against his own land? These *incroyables* who drag their honor across foreign soil, like the *incroyables* of the French Revolution, dancing, smacking their lips, and deliberately slurring their words!

And in what *patria* can a man take greater pride than in our long-suffering republics of America, erected among mute masses of Indians upon the bloodied arms of no more than a hundred apostles, to the sound of the book doing battle against the monk's tall candle? Never before have such advanced

---

[3]*Source:* From *José Martí: Selected Writings*, introduction by Roberto Gonzalez Echevarria, edited by Esther Allen, translated by Esther Allen, copyright © 2002 by Esther Allen. Used by permission of Viking Penguin, a division of Penguin Group (USA) Inc.
[4]Castellanos was a sixteenth-century Spanish poet and chronicler of the conquest of New Granada (present-day Colombia).

and consolidated nations been created from such disparate factors in less historical time. The haughty man thinks that because he wields a quick pen or a vivid phrase the earth was made to be his pedestal, and accuses his native republic of irredeemable incompetence because its virgin jungles do not continually provide him with the means of going about the world a famous plutocrat, driving Persian ponies and spilling champagne. The incapacity lies not in the emerging country, which demands forms that are appropriate to it and a grandeur that is useful, but in the leaders who try to rule unique nations, of a singular and violent composition, with laws inherited from four centuries of free practice in the United States and nineteen centuries of monarchy in France. A gaucho's pony cannot be stopped in mid bolt by one of Alexander Hamilton's laws. The sluggish blood of the Indian race cannot be quickened by a phrase from Sieyès.[5] To govern well, one must attend closely to the reality of the place that is governed. In America, the good ruler does not need to know how the German or Frenchman governed, but what elements his own country is composed of and how he can marshal them so as to reach, by means and institutions born from the country itself, the desirable state in which every man knows himself and is active, and all men enjoy the abundance that nature, for the good of all, has bestowed on the country they make fruitful by their labor and defend with their lives. The government must be born from the country. The spirit of government must be the spirit of the country. The form of the government must be in harmony with the country's natural constitution. The government is no more than an equilibrium among the country's natural elements.

In America the natural man has triumphed over the imported book. Natural men have triumphed over an artificial intelligentsia. The native *mestizo* has triumphed over the alien, pure-blooded criollo. The battle is not between civilization and barbarity[6], but between false erudition and nature. The natural man

is good, and esteems and rewards a superior intelligence as long as that intelligence does not use his submission against him or offend him by ignoring him—for that the natural man deems unforgivable, and he is prepared to use force to regain the respect of anyone who wounds his sensibilities or harms his interests. The tyrants of America have come to power by acquiescing to these scorned natural elements and have fallen as soon as they betrayed them. The republics have purged the former tyrannies of their inability to know the true elements of the country, derive the form of government from them, and govern along with them. *Governor*, in a new country, means *Creator*.

In countries composed of educated and uneducated sectors, the uneducated will govern by their habit of attacking and resolving their doubts with their fists, unless the educated learn the art of governing. The uneducated masses are lazy and timid about matters of the intellect and want to be well-governed, but if the government injures them they shake it off and govern themselves. How can our governors emerge from the universities when there is not a university in America that teaches the most basic element of the art of governing, which is the analysis of all that is unique to the peoples of America? Our youth go out into the world wearing Yankee- or French-colored glasses and aspire to rule by guesswork in a country they do not know. Those unacquainted with the rudiments of politics should not be allowed to embark on a career in politics. The literary prizes must not go to the best ode, but to the best study of the political factors in the student's country. In the newspapers, lecture halls, and academies, the study of the country's real factors must be carried forward. Simply knowing those factors without blindfolds or circumlocutions is enough—for anyone who deliberately or unknowingly sets aside a part of the truth will ultimately fail because of the truth he was lacking, which expands when neglected and brings down whatever is built without it. Solving the problem after knowing its elements is easier than solving it without knowing them. The natural man, strong and indignant, comes and overthrows the authority that is accumulated from books because it is not administered in keeping with the manifest needs of the country. To know is to solve.

---

[5]Sieyès was a leading figure in the French Revolution.
[6]Martí referred here to nineteenth-century notions about civilization and barbarism like those that Sarmiento espoused (see Chapter 5 of this Volume).

To know the country and govern it in accordance with that knowledge is the only way of freeing it from tyranny. The European university must yield to the American university. The history of America from the Incas to the present must be taught in its smallest detail, even if the Greek Archons go untaught. Our own Greece is preferable to the Greece that is not ours; we need it more. Statesmen who arise from the nation must replace statesmen who are alien to it. Let the world be grafted onto our republics, but we must be the trunk. And let the vanquished pedant hold his tongue, for there is no *patria* in which a man can take greater pride than in our long-suffering American republics.

Our feet upon a rosary, our heads white, and our bodies a motley of Indian and *criollo* we boldly entered the community of nations. Bering the standard of the Virgin, we went out to conquer our liberty. A priest, a few lieutenants, and a woman built a republic in Mexico upon the shoulders of the Indians.[7] A Spanish cleric, under cover of his priestly cape, taught French liberty to a handful of magnificent students who chose a Spanish general to lead Central America against Spain. Still accustomed to monarchy, and with the sun on their chests, the Venezuelans in the north and the Argentines in the south set out to construct nations. When the two heroes clashed and the continent was about to be rocked, one of them, and not the lesser one, turned back.[8] But heroism is less glorious in peacetime than in war, and thus rarer, and it is easier for a man to die with honor than to think in an orderly way. Exalted and unanimous sentiments are more readily governed than the diverging, arrogant, alien, and ambitious ideas that emerge when the battle is over. The powers that were swept up in the epic struggle, along with the feline wariness of the species and the sheer weight of reality, undermined the edifice that had raised the

flags of nations sustained by wise governance in the colonial practice of reason and freedom over the crude and singular regions of our *mestizo* America with its towns of bare legs and Parisian dress-coats. The colonial hierarchy resisted the republic's democracy, and the capital city, wearing its elegant cravat, left the countryside, in its horsehide boots, waiting at the door; the redeemers born from books did not understand that a revolution that had triumphed when the soul of the earth was unleashed by a savior's voice had to govern with the soul of the earth and not against it or without it. And for all these reasons, America began enduring and still endures the weary task of reconciling the discordant and hostile elements it inherited from its perverse, despotic colonizer with the imported forms and ideas that have, in their lack of local reality, delayed the advent of a logical form of government. The continent, deformed by three centuries of a rule that denied man the right to exercise his reason, embarked—overlooking or refusing to listen to the ignorant masses that had helped it redeem itself—upon a government based on reason, the reason of all directed toward the things that are of concern to all, and not the university-taught reason of the few imposed upon the rustic reason of others. The problem of independence was not the change in form, but the change in spirit.

Common cause had to be made with the oppressed in order to consolidate a system that was opposed to the interests and governmental habits of the oppressors. The tiger, frightened away by the flash of gunfire, creeps back in the night to find his prey. He will die with flames shooting from his eyes, his claws unsheathed, but now his step is inaudible for he comes on velvet paws. When the prey awakens, the tiger is upon him. The colony lives on in the republic, but our America is saving itself from its grave blunders—the arrogance of capital cities, the blind triumph of the scorned *campesinos*, the excessive importation of foreign ideas and formulas, the wicked and impolitic disdain for the native race—through the superior virtue, confirmed by necessary bloodshed, of the republic that struggles against the colony. The tiger waits behind every tree, crouches in every corner. He will die, his claws unsheathed, flames shooting from his eyes.

---

[7]This "priest" is a reference to Miguel Hidalgo y Costilla, the priest who led Mexico's first independence movement (see Chapter 1).

[8]This reference is to the meeting of Simón Bolívar and José de San Martín in Guayaquil (Ecuador) during the wars for South American independence. San Martín arrived from Argentina, Bolívar from Peru; both men claimed the right to liberate Peru from Spanish rule, but in the end San Martín left Peru to Bolívar.

But "these countries will be saved," in the words of Argentine Rivadavia,[9] who erred on the side of urbanity during crude times; the machete is ill-suited to a silken scabbard, nor can the spear be abandoned in a country won by the spear, for it becomes enraged and stands in the doorway of Iturbide's Congress[10] demanding that "the fair-skinned man be made emperor." These countries will be saved because, with the genius of moderation that now seems, by nature's serene harmony, to prevail in the continent of light, and the influence of the critical reading that has, in Europe, replaced the fumbling ideas about phalansteries in which the previous generation was steeped, the real man is being born to America, in these real times.

What a vision we were [in the nineteenth century]: the chest of an athlete, the hands of a dandy, and the forehead of a child. We were a whole fancy dress ball, in English trousers, a Parisian waistcoat, a North American overcoat, and a Spanish bullfighter's cap. The Indian circled about us, mute, and went to the mountaintop to christen his children. The black, pursued from afar, alone and unknown, sang his heart's music in the night, between waves and wild beasts. The *campesinos*, the men of the land, the creators, rose up in blind indignation against the disdainful city, their own creation. We wore epaulets and judge's robes, in countries that came into the world wearing rope sandals and Indian headbands. The wise thing would have been to pair, with charitable hearts and the audacity of our founders, the Indian headband and the judicial robe, to undam the Indian, make a place for the able black, and tailor liberty to the bodies of those who rose up and triumphed in its name. What we had was the judge, the general, the man of letters, and the cleric. Our angelic youth, as if struggling from the arms of an octopus, cast their heads into the heavens and fell

back with sterile glory, crowned with clouds. The natural people, driven by instinct, blind with triumph, overwhelmed their gilded rulers. No Yankee or European book could furnish the key to the Hispanoamerican enigma. So the people tried hatred instead, and our countries amounted to less and less each year. Weary of useless hatred, of the struggle of book against sword, reason against the monk's taper, city against countryside, the impossible empire of the quarreling urban castes against the tempestuous or inert natural nation, we are beginning, almost unknowingly, to try to love. The nations arise and salute one another. "What are we like?" they ask, and begin telling each other what they are like. When a problem arises in Cojimar they no longer seek the solution in Danzig. The frock-coats are still French, but the thinking begins to be American. The young men of America are rolling up their sleeves and plunging their hands into the dough, making it rise with the leavening of their sweat. They understand that there is too much imitation, and that salvation lies in creating. *Create* is this generation's password. Make wine from plantains; it may be sour, but it is our wine! It is now understood that a country's form of government must adapt to its natural elements, that absolute ideas, in order not to collapse over an error of form, must be expressed in relative forms; that liberty, in order to be viable, must be sincere and full, that if the republic does not open its arms to all and include all in its progress, it dies. The tiger inside came in through the gap, and so will the tiger outside. The general holds the cavalry's speed to the pace of the infantry, for if he leaves the infantry far behind, the enemy will surround the cavalry. Politics is strategy. Nations must continually criticize themselves, for criticism is health, but with a single heart and a single mind. Lower yourselves to the unfortunate and raise them up in your arms! Let the heart's fires unfreeze all that is motionless in America, and let the country's natural blood surge and throb through its veins! Standing tall, the workmen's eyes full of joy, the new men of America are saluting each other from one country to another. Natural statesmen are emerging from the direct study of nature; they read in order to apply what they read, not to copy it. Economists are studying problems at their origins.

---

[9]Bernardino Rivadavia was the first president of the Argentina; he was also one of the men who defended the colony of La Plata from British invasion in 1807.

[10]Agustín Iturbide was a military leader who initially fought in the Spanish forces against the Hidalgo insurrection, but he later joined the independence forces. This reference is to a conservative proclamation that Iturbide forced the Mexican Congress to adopt in 1822.

Orators are becoming more temperate. Dramatists are putting native characters onstage. Academies are discussing practical subjects. Poetry is snipping off its wild, Zorilla-esque[11] mane and hanging up its gaudy waistcoat on the glorious tree. Prose, polished and gleaming, is replete with ideas. The rulers of Indian republics are learning Indian languages.

America is saving herself from all her dangers. Over some republics the octopus sleeps still, but by the law of equilibrium, other republics are running into the sea to recover the lost centuries with mad and sublime swiftness. Others, forgetting that Juárez[12] traveled in a coach drawn by mules, hitch their coach to the wind and take a soap bubble for a coachman— and poisonous luxury, enemy of liberty, corrupts the frivolous and opens the door to foreigners. The virile character of others is being perfected by the epic spirit of a threatened independence. And others, in rapacious wars against their neighbors, are nurturing an unruly soldier caste that may devour them. But our America may also face another danger, which comes not from within but from the different origins, methods, and interests of the continent's two factions. The hour is near when she will be approached by an enterprising and forceful nation that will demand intimate relations with her, though it does not know her and disdains her. And virile nations self-made by the rifle and the law love other virile nations, and love only them. The hour of unbridled passion and ambition from which North America may escape by the ascendancy of the purest element in its blood—or into which its vengeful and sordid masses, its tradition of conquest, and the self-interest of a cunning leader could plunge it—is not yet so close, even to the most apprehensive eye, that there is no time for it to be confronted and averted by the manifestation of a discreet and unswerving pride, for its dignity, as a republic, in the eyes of watchful nations of the Universe, places upon North America a brake that our America must not remove by puerile provocation, ostentatious arrogance, or practical

discord. Therefore the urgent duty of our America is to show herself as she is, one soul and intent, rapidly overcoming the crushing weight of her past and stained only by the fertile blood shed by hands that do battle against ruins and by veins that were punctured by our former masters. The disdain of the formidable neighbor who does not know her is our America's greatest danger, and it is urgent—for the day of the visit is near—that her neighbor come to know her, and quickly, so that he will not disdain her. But when he knows her, he will remove his hands from her in respect. One must have faith in the best in man and distrust the worst. One must give the best every opportunity, so that the worst will be laid bare and overcome. If not, the worst will prevail. Nations should have one special pillory for those who incite them to futile hatreds, and another for those who do not tell them the truth until it is too late.

There is no racial hatred because there are no races. Sickly, lamp-lit minds string together and rewarm the library-shelf races that the honest traveler and the cordial observer seek in vain in the justice of nature, where the universal identity of man leaps forth in victorious love and turbulent appetite. The soul, equal and eternal, emanates from bodies that are diverse in form and color. Anyone who promotes and disseminates opposition or hatred among races is committing a sin against humanity. But within that jumble of peoples which lives in close proximity to our peoples, certain peculiar and dynamic characteristics are condensed—ideas and habits of expansion, acquisition, vanity and greed— that could, in a period of internal disorder or precipitation of a people's cumulative character, cease to be latent national preoccupations and become a serious threat to the neighboring, isolated and weak lands that the strong country declares to be perishable and inferior. To think is to serve. We must not, out of a villager's antipathy, impute some lethal congenital wickedness to the continent's light-skinned nation simply because it does not speak our language or share our view of what home life should be or resemble us in its political failings, which are different from ours, or because it does not think highly of quick-tempered, swarthy men or look with charity, from its still uncertain eminence, upon those less favored by history who, in heroic stages, are climbing the road that republics

---

[11]Zorilla (1817–1893) was a Spanish poet, whom Martí did not admire.
[12]A famous classical *liberal* Benito Juárez was born a Zapotec Indian and served as president of Mexico from 1857–1863.

LE MONDE ILLUSTRÉ

GONZALO DE QUESADA, SECRÉTAIRE GÉNÉRAL. — JOSÉ MARTI, DÉLÉGUÉ GÉNÉRAL. — JUAN GUALBERTO GOMEZ, CHEF DES INSURGÉS, A MATANZAS.

Cuban independence leaders Gonzalo de Quesada (1868–1915), Jose Martí (1853–95), and Juan Gualberto Gómez (1854–1933). The illustration is an engraving from 'Le Monde Illustre', 16th March 1895. How do these portraits reinforce points that Martí made in the excerpts in this chapter about the role of race in Cuban identity and nationalism? What do these portraits suggest about issues of class in the leadership of the independence movement?

Source: The photo of the image was provided from the Bridgeman Art Library International.

travel. But neither should we seek to conceal the obvious facts of the problem, which can, for the peace of the centuries, be resolved by timely study and the urgent, wordless union of the continental soul. For the unanimous hymn is already ringing forth, and the present generation is bearing industrious America along the road sanctioned by our sublime forefathers. From the Rio Bravo to the Straits of Magellan, the Great Cemi,[13] seated on a condor's back, has scattered the seeds of the new America across the romantic nations of the continent and the suffering islands of the sea!

El Partido Liberal (Mexico City), January 20, 1891

"My Race"[14]

"Racist" is becoming a confusing word, and it must be clarified. NO man has any special rights because he belongs to one race or another: say "man" and all rights have been stated. The black man, as a black man, is not inferior or superior to any other man; the white man who says "my race" is being redundant, and the black man who says "my race" is also redundant. Anything that divides men from each other, that separates them, that singles them out, or hems them in, is a sin against humanity. What sensible white man thinks he should be proud of being white, and what do blacks think of a white man who is proud of being white and believes he has special rights because he is? What must whites think of a black man who grows conceited about his color? To insist upon the racial divisions and racial differences of a people naturally divided is to obstruct both individual and public happiness, which lies in greater closeness among the elements that must live in common. It is true that in the black man there is no original sin or virus that makes him incapable of developing his whole soul as a man, and this truth must be spoken and demonstrated, because the injustice of

---

[13]A spirit worshipped by the Taino peoples of the Caribbean.
[14]*Source:* From José Martí: *Selected Writings*, introduction by Roberto Gonzalez Echevarria, edited by Esther Allen, translated by Esther

this world is great, as is the ignorance that passes for wisdom, and there are still those who believe in good faith that the black man is incapable of the intelligence and feelings of the white man. And what does it matter if this truth, this defense of nature, is called racism, because it is no more than natural respect, the voice that clamors from a man's bosom for the life and the peace of the nation. To state that the condition of slavery does not indicate any inferiority in the enslaved race—for white Gauls with blue eyes and golden hair were sold as slaves with letters around their necks in the markets of Rome—is good racism, because it is pure justice and helps the ignorant white shed his prejudices. But that is the limit of just racism, which is the right of the black man to maintain and demonstrate that his color does not deprive him of any of the capacities and rights of the human race.

And what right does the white racist, who believes his race has superior rights, have to complain of the black racist, who also believes that his race has special traits? What right does the black racist who sees a special character in his race have to complain of the white racist? The white man who, by reason of his race, believes himself superior to the black man acknowledges the idea of race and thus authorizes and provokes the black racist. The black man who trumpets his race—when what he is perhaps trumpeting instead is only the spiritual identity of all races—authorizes and provokes the white racist. Peace demands the shared rights of nature; differing rights go against nature and are the enemies of peace. The white who isolates himself isolates the Negro. The Negro who isolates himself drives the white to isolate himself.

In Cuba there is no fear whatsoever of a race war. "Man" means more than white, more than mulato, more than Negro. "Cuban" means more than white, more than mulato, more than Negro. On the battlefields, the souls of whites and blacks who died for Cuba have risen together through the air. In that daily life of defense, loyalty, brotherhood, and shrewdness, there was always a black man at the side of every white. Blacks, like whites, can be grouped according to their character—timid or brave, self-abnegating or egotistical—into the diverse parties of mankind. Political parties are aggregates of concerns, aspirations, interests, and characters. An

essential likeness is sought and found beyond all differences of detail, and what is fundamental in analogous characters merges in parties, even if their incidental characteristics or motives differ. In short, it is the similarity of character—a source of unity far superior to the internal relations of the varying colors of men—that commands and prevails in the formation of parties. An affinity of character is more powerful than an affinity of color. Blacks, distributed among the diverse or hostile specialties of the human spirit, will never want or be able to band together against whites, who are distributed among the same specialties. Blacks are too tired of slavery to enter voluntarily into the slavery of color. Men of pomp and self-interest, black and white, will be on one side, and generous and impartial men will be on the other. True men, black or white, will treat each other with loyalty and tenderness, taking pleasure in merit and pride in anyone, black or white, who honors the land where we were born. The word "racist" will be gone from the lips of the blacks who use it today in good faith, once they understand that that word is the only apparently valid argument—valid among sincere, apprehensive men—for denying the Negro the fullness of his rights as a man. The white racist and the Negro racist will be equally guilty of being racists. Many whites have already forgotten their color, and many blacks have, too. Together they work, black and white, for the cultivation of the mind, the dissemination of virtue, and the triumph of creative work and sublime charity.

There will never be a race war in Cuba. The Republic cannot retreat and the Republic, from the extraordinary day of the emancipation of blacks in Cuba and from its first independent constitution of April 10 in Guámiro, never spoke of whites or blacks. The rights already conceded out of pure cunning by the Spanish government, and which have become habitual even before the Island's independence, can no longer be denied now, either by the Spaniard, who will maintain them as long as he draws breath in Cuba—in order to continue dividing Cuban blacks from Cuban whites—or by the independent nation, which will not, in liberty, be able to deny the rights that the Spaniard recognized in servitude.

As for the rest, each individual will be free within the sacred confines of his home. Merit, the clear and continual manifestation of culture and inexorable trade will end by uniting all men. There is much greatness in Cuba, in blacks and in whites.

April 16, 1893

Suggested Sources:

An excellent collection of José Martí's writings the collection from which these documents were taken: José Martí, *Selected Writings*, trans. Esther Allen (New York: Penguin Classics, 2002). Brazil was also a prominent location in which ideas about raceless nationalism developed. Those interested in these concepts should also consult some of Gilberto Freyre's famous works: *The Masters and the Slaves: A Study in the Development of Brazilian Civilization*, 2nd. English-language ed., trans. Samuel Putnam (New York: Alfred A. Knopf, 1970), and *New World in the Tropics: The Culture of Modern Brazil* (New York: Alfred A. Knopf, 1959). Also see *The Mansions and the Shanties: The Making of Modern Brazil* (Berkeley: University of California Press, 1986 [1963]). Brazilian Novelist Jorge Amado (1912–2001) wrestled with these same themes, most notably in his 1969 *Tent of Miracles*, trans. Barbara Shelby (New York: Knopf, 1971). Nelson Pereira dos Santos produced a film in 1978 titled "Tent of Miracles" based on Amado's reflections. One can also find similar claims about race and democracy in Mexico; see José Vasconcelos, *The Cosmic Race/La raza cosmica* (Baltimore: Johns Hopkins University Press, 1989).

Excellent secondary sources on Cuba include: Alejandro de la Fuente, "Myths of Racial Democracy: Cuba, 1900–1912," *Latin American Research Review*, Vol. 34, No. 3 (1999), pp. 39–73, and his book, *A Nation for All: Race, Inequality, and Politics in Twentieth-Century Cuba* (Chapel Hill: University of North Carolina Press, 2001). Also see Lillian Guerra, *The Myth of José Martí: Conflicting Nationalisms in Early Twentieth-Century Cuba* (Chapel Hill: University of North Carolina Press, 2005); and Ada Ferrer, *Insurgent Cuba: Race, Nation and Revolution, 1868–1898* (Chapel Hill: University of North Carolina Press, 1999). For readers interested in the relationship between the United States and Cuba, see Louis A Pérez, Jr., *On Becoming Cuban: Identity, Nationality, and Culture* (New York: The Ecco Press/Harper Collins, 1999).

Chapter 15

We Must Civilize Our Cayapa Indians: Father Antonio Metalli's Assessment of Race and Gender in Coastal Ecuador

Nicola Foote, Florida Gulf Coast University

This chapter examines an Italian missionary's ideas about the behavior of the Cayapa Indians of coastal Ecuador he had been sent to evangelize and the Afro-Ecuadorian peasants who shared their territory. Historians writing about race in Ecuador—following the lead of the nation builders whose policies they have traced—have typically focused on highland and Amazonian indigenous groups. Yet there are also important Afro-Ecuadorian and coastal indigenous populations whose experiences of and contributions to the formation of Ecuador's racial hierarchies were distinct from those communities most often considered. The province of Esmeraldas is central to understanding this alternative history. Located on the coastal border with Colombia and dominated by dense tropical forest and mountainous terrain, until the 1950s Esmeraldas was almost entirely cut off from the Andean capital of Quito and the main port of Guayaquil. This geographic isolation meant that during the colonial era it was subject to little penetration by the Spanish, and this, combined with strong coastal currents that led to multiple shipwrecks of passing slavers, made the province a haven for runaway slaves. The maroons formed relations with the local indigenous populations and established an autonomous polity that successfully resisted the Spanish Crown until the eighteenth century. However, although cooperation with indigenous groups was central to the survival of first-generation maroons, and marital alliances and miscegenation quickly took place, intercommunity relations were often tense. Blacks and *mulatos* often sought to exploit indigenous labor for economic profit, while the groups often came into conflict over land. Thus cultural, economic, and religious interaction between black and indigenous groups, and isolation from Hispanic society, continued into the national period.

The 1895 Liberal Revolution marked a major shift in Ecuadorian politics. The *liberal* regime sought to expand the power of the state and integrate the country more firmly into the global economy. It sought modernity through such means as the integration of national territory via railway and road-building projects, the formation of national banks and a national currency, and the establishment of national military service. It also explicitly projected a more inclusionary vision of citizenship in which Indians were understood to be an important part of the nation who had the potential to become full citizens at some undetermined point in the future. Indigenous people were central to *liberal* goals for several reasons. Firstly, Indians represented

almost half of the population. The *Social Darwinist* ideas about race that had been dominant in the nineteenth century, and which held that the economic success of a country depended on the racial composition of its population, were still an important influence in Ecuador. However, they were adapted by *liberal* elites, who argued that Indians could become useful and successful citizens if they were able to transform their cultural and economic behavior in line with white-*mestizo* norms. This transformation was to be achieved through state policy in fields such as education, health care, and sanitation. There were also pragmatic reasons for such ideas—highland Indians in particular were perceived to be under the control of the *conservative* landholding elite and the Catholic Church; the two main rivals to the *liberals* who themselves were drawn mainly from the coastal bourgeoisie. In order to achieve *liberal* economic goals such as the creation of a mobile labor force, the realities of Indian lives—such as dependence on the *haciendas*—needed to change.

A major problem for the *liberal* state was that it simply did not have enough revenue to pursue its goals. Rather than investing in infrastructure and resource development themselves, they invited foreign companies to exploit natural resources. For the provision of education and health care, *liberal* statesmen often turned to foreign missionaries despite the regime's ostensible anticlericalism. United States Protestant groups who brought connotations of North American capitalism and progress were favored. However, these preferred to settle among highland indigenous groups, and so at the same moment that the *liberal* government was stripping the Catholic Church of its property in the highlands and expelling the Jesuits, other Catholic orders were invited to work with lowland Indians. When it came to nomadic groups such as the Cayapa in Esmeraldas, *liberals* viewed evangelization—with its focus on the adoption of "Christian" behavior as well as beliefs—as a key agent of cultural transformation.

Afro-Ecuadorians were not included in this new vision of a future expanded citizen base, and they continued to be ignored and marginalized both by the state and its proxies despite the centrality of black soldiers from Esmeraldas to *liberal* military success. The exclusion of Afro-Ecuadorians underlines the limits of the ideals of the *raceless democracy* projected by intellectuals such as Martí and Freyre: While the limits of national inclusion *were* being renegotiated, some groups were still labeled as unfit for membership in the nation.

It is in this context that one must locate the series of articles considered here, which were published in a weekly series in the Esmeraldas newspaper *El Bien Social* by the Italian missionary Father Antonio Metalli. The articles sought to emphasize the importance of evangelizing the Cayapa Indians as an integral part of the wider project of turning them into citizens. Gender was at the heart of Metalli's characterization of Indian life. In the first few articles, which cannot be reprinted here for reasons of space, he railed against customs such as polygyny, female infanticide, and the gendered division of labor. He equated Cayapa seminakedness with barbarity and ran a clothing drive to have elite women donate skirts, trousers, and dresses to give to the Cayapa. The later entries, replicated here, focused on the relationship between the Cayapa and Afro-Ecuadorians and offer readers a rare and striking insight into the relationships between marginalized groups. The articles were clearly aimed at local elites, who, like most coastal elites in this period, were largely *liberal* and anticlerical. Metalli's goal was to convince them that his evangelizing mission was central to the *liberal* project and to persuade them to support his endeavors both politically and fiscally. The newspaper's support of his endeavor—to the point of giving him

prime weekly print space—reflected its conviction regarding the need to transform and integrate the local indigenous population as well as its ambivalence about the Afro-Ecuadorian population. The case study was an important one because it underlined the complexities and contradictions in the more racially inclusive forms of nationalism that the Ecuadorian *liberal* state claimed to advocate. It also shows the limits of the new racial and citizenship ideas discussed in this section. The ideals of *mestizaje* included some but excluded others, and it often set those identified as "inside" the boundaries of the new nation against those who were "outside."

Questions to Consider:

1. How did Metalli describe the Cayapa? How did he describe Afro-Esmeraldans? How and why did he use gender ideas to express his views of these two cultures?
2. Based on the information in these documents, what do you think Father Metalli was actually trying to achieve with his work in Esmeraldas?
3. To what extent were economic, political, and religious relationships between Afro-Ecuadorians and Cayapa mediated through women?
4. What sense can we get from the documents about how the Cayapa viewed the missionaries and the Ecuadorian state?

Father Antonio Metalli on Civilizing the Cayapa[1]

(March 9th) We have proved with evidence in our last correspondence, that the unhappy Cayapa are beings capable of advancement and perfectly able to educate themselves, above all the adolescents and the children, whose intelligence has still not been contaminated by the excessive use of liquor and the chewing of tobacco which dulls the adults. . . . The most expeditious way

to civilize our Indians is to hand over the Cayapa tribes to Catholic missionaries, of some foreign order. The success of the Salesians in civilizing the cannibalistic Indians of Patagonia can be seen as a model, where the Indians have so improved under the direction of the Salesians to the extent that they can manage machines and engineering for trains and railways that cross the desert. . . . President Leonidas Plaza[2] has

---

[1]*Source:* Father Antonio Metalli, from a weekly series of articles appearing in the Esmeraldan newspaper, *El Bien Social,* between January and June 1902.

[2]*Liberal* president of Ecuador from 1902 to 1906 and 1912 to 1916.

the opportunity to make himself immortal in the annals of Ecuadorian history and in the hearts of all his compatriots; and later the beneficiaries of his generosity would surely erect a monument in gratitude.

(March 23rd) We must not abandon the idea of installing schools for boys and girls in the province, which if they were run by teachers of irreproachable conduct, and under our immediate inspection, would give optimum results. Our Indians would not reject the schools, I am sure of this, because I have spent four years preparing them. An example can be seen in the *cacique* Antonio Añapa, an Indian who is still young and who has traveled a lot, and who has visited Quito and almost all the towns of the coast. In 1896 he went to Guayaquil accompanied by his wife and niece, and he always lamented to people there the state of backwardness of his people. With the aim of obtaining, through this *cacique*, facilities to drive the Indians to the route of civilization, we proposed to the tribes that the other governors would be under the orders of Añapa, and, with not very much work . . . our proposal was accepted, and in August 1900 Antonio Añapa assumed supreme mandate with the title of "Governor General of the Cayapa Tribes." Through the control that he exercised we were able to build four more houses of worship in San Miguel, two more in Sapayo, and a house of government in Punto Venado, which all had a significant positive effect on the distribution of our material. With a little bit of patience we could introduce some radical reforms suppressing the barbarous customs that so degrade our Indians. The most important of these reforms, and that which most exercises the Indians themselves, is the establishment of schools for Indian children of both sexes. To achieve this it was necessary to pay special attention to Añapa's niece, and this permitted us direct access to all the caciques since she was a Cayapa princess. We have recorded here the conversation we had with her about these issues:

Añapa: Do you know Guayaquil?
Metalli: Yes, we have worked there for many years.
Añapa: Do you like the city?
Metalli: Yes, very much, we have a devoted congregation there.
Añapa: Are you *liberal* or *conservative*?

Metalli: We are *liberal*, in order to lavish such goods as we can on the Cayapa.
Añapa: I am *liberal*, for this reason I asked of you. I like Guayaquil and the Guyaquileños very much. These forests bore me and I cannot look at the Indians . . . they are common and drunk. . . . I hope to marry a Guayaquileño.[3] I have seen that the women of Guayaquil look beautiful, my husband will teach me how to read and write, as well as how to speak, and I have the best Spanish among the Cayapa – isn't that true father?
Metalli: It is indeed. Would you like it if the Cayapa learned how to read and write?
Añapa: If I were governor, I would see to it that all my people learned. We Indians are bestial because we don't know anything.
Metalli: I will work in setting up schools for the Cayapa, and if I meet a Guayaquileño who wants to marry a good and lively Cayapa woman I will look for you.

We also present the speech we made to the assembled Cayapa and the reply that we received from the Governor General Añapa.

Speech to Cayapa: Children!! The government of Ecuador desire that you sow much rice, cacao, plantains and sugar cane along both banks of the river, from end to end, making thus decreed the ownership of every Cayapa. It also desires that you no longer give faith to the witches; it is God that you must fear, and it is he who will punish your failings, and if it is necessary we will lend you every aid to defend your land and property. The government also desires that you accept teachers for your children, and wishes to oblige the parents to send their children to school.

Reply from Governor General Añapa.

I tell your government that I, Governor General Añapa, and all my people, very much desire to sow all our lands, but that sowing will not work for us, but rather will maintain the thieving blacks and *mulatos*

---

[3] A man from Guayaquil, the main port city in Ecuador.

who . . . rob our bananas and plantains, our rubber, all our work, and are scaring my people with their sorcery. I tell your government that we accept teachers, but here in Punto Venado. I will give them a house and plenty of food, but I ask that the government pay them because we Indians do not have money.

(4 May) There is one other important obstacle to the civilization of the Cayapa, which is the strange emigration of *mulatos* and blacks, which both now and in the past has occurred without any legal authorization. By the art of sorcery and witchcraft these blacks have seated themselves in Cayapa lands, obliging the Indians to move by brute force. Not only do they take possession, they also rob them of the products of their scarce work — rubber, tagua, plantains, bananas, domesticated animals, even canoes, and then disappear from Ecuadorian territory afterwards. They are generally idle, and maybe keep a badly constructed ranch which serves them as a pretext to live in bad faith from the work of our Indians. These are not exaggerations — we receive daily complaints from our Indians, and we have witnessed more than once the robberies, extortions, pretensions and threats of this dangerous band of immigrants. To give an example: at the fall of evening one day not too long ago more than 20 blacks and *mulatos* penetrated the furthest settlement of San Miguel de los Cayapas, armed with shotguns and machetes. Without asking for lodging, they took by assault the living quarters of the Indians, demanding to eat as if it was their own home. We observed all this from the mission house which dominates the little village, but we could not resist such an assault against the unhappy race. . . . We implored them in the name of god, and in the sacred character of the priest to lay down their arms. Lay down arms . . . ? They resisted with threatening movement that made evident such *mulatos* were not moved by holy interventions.

(May 11th) On another occasion we had to snatch from the arms of a gigantic *mulato* a young Indian girl. The *mulato* was goring at her breasts, pulling her along the ground — with such fine perversions! We were called to attention by the screams emitted by the poor Indian girl. We have heard that it is not uncommon for the *mulatos* to force themselves on the poor Indian women. . . . In Sapayo, at our indication, the Cayapa made the government house in the style of our dwellings, that is, with walls and fences, and nails to sustain the walls. One afternoon while we were met together in the living room of said house, around 70 Indians, among them men, children and women, and according to their custom, sitting against the walls, because the Indian very rarely uses chairs, a certain badly intentioned *mulato*, climbed up the ladder and struck a hard blow against the main wall, this collapsed and children, women and men fell onto the patio, there were considerable injuries and one poor Indian woman who was located in an interesting state almost died. . . . Another day two blacks arrived in San Miguel, bringing a well-fattened pig, selling it at two reales a pound, and Patere, one of the Indians told us that the pig was his own, that the black had stolen it and was now selling it for a profit. We pressured him to make this fact known to the watchman of the village of Telembí, Señor Rozo, who answered that it was true that the black had robbed said Indian. Last year we found the Indians of Punta Venado had just finished all their supplies, and so that they didn't leave the settlement so quickly, we bought a pig to give to them. We were dividing said pig into rations when a black presented himself to us, charging the right to pilfer in the name of Señor Leopoldo Paredes, the municipal tax collector. . . . The poor Indians! Reports that we received from people who merit complete credit, and that at times are cooperators with our mission, such as Dr. Guillermo A. Ross, Eustorgio Campos, Reinaldo Batioja, Bruno Prado, and others broke our hearts . . . but didn't frighten us. We heard that during the eight months of our absence the witches whom we mentioned in our second collaboration had devastated, totally devastated, the vineyard of our evangelical efforts. The witches also gave missions to the Indians, propagating among them superstitions that they had left behind them grudgingly. These upstarts, fearful of losing their vile characteristics, knowing that we would soon arrive to continue catechizing the Indians, and bringing them clothes to cover their nudity, have known to infuse them with fear, making them believe that our zeal is a ruse, a game, and that they should leave the Cayapa capital of Punta Venado, encouraging them to go back into the forest, and not pay any attention to our call. The witches also count on an old black woman, who scoffs that we are the Devil sent to distract them. Today this miserable black woman has made them believe, our poor children, that the clothes that we bring them have the magic power to convert the Cayapas who have the disgrace to wear them into tigers. We have also been informed that the witches are vaccinating the Indians against this possibility, charging them two sucres for each vaccination. Who is to say what fluid these heartless people will use? . . . We have reported about what occurred to the mayor of Tola, and made clear that his presence is very necessary, and that he must begin legal proceedings . . . We are hoping for the compliance of the mayor, Don Alejandrino Batioja in deploying all his energies on this, and that in accordance with the law, punishment will befall these propagators of magic. If by misfortune we can't do anything to obtain the authority of La Tola, with the weight of His good will, we will go into the forests with the benediction of God, to find our poor Cayapa children. We are still accompanied by two Cayapa boys who can help us with this – Luis Dario Tello, our scribe and catechist, who is no more than 15, and born in La Tola, and Juan Sandoya, our cook, who is 14, and a native of Zamborondón. . . . The Indians have still not buried the memory of the horrible murders witnessed in the Cayapa forests, perpetrated by *mulatos* against a large Indian family. Surprised in the late hours of the night, seven unfortunate Indians fell under sharpened machetes. They still have not buried the tracks of such horrible butchery; in past days the unhappy Indian Rosa has been wandering the streets of Esmeraldas, the sole survivor of this unfortunate family, with her right arm also severed at the trunk. . . . I must reiterate my hopes for the Cayapa – that they can peacefully dedicate themselves to agriculture. We will start them off by showing them how to sow the extremely fertile lands that they possess with rubber, cacao, rice and plantains, and they will be able to produce a surplus of more than one million sucres per year.

(May 18th) After much wrangling, we [missionaries] were allowed to meet with the Cayapa government, through the intermediary of the two young boys, but the first interview they granted with us

was very cold, and none of the governors broke their silence. We hugged them with paternal affection and shared out cigars, but we received almost no response. We realized that the Indians totally lacked trust in us, and that they viewed the mission as something very mysterious. We asked our sons why they maintained this silence with us, and what it meant. The governor of San Miguel, an Indian of Herculean proportions who seemed to be nearing 70 years of age, replied that they had been advised that we were coming with clothes that our government had given us in order to cheat and swindle the Cayapa. He was backed up by the Governor of Sapallo who insisted that "no-one is going to lie to or deceive me, they would run into my people immediately." The governor-general of the Cayapa confirmed that they had been assured by a *mulato* that the clothing we had brought was to turn them all into soldiers, to take away their children, and turn Punto Venado into a government post. We understand that the *mulatos* have successfully penetrated the imagination of our Indians, and convinced them that the government wants to nationalize the tribes, and drag them from their beloved Punto Venado. . . . This is the bad luck that has been prophesied by the fortune tellers and witches, this is the propaganda, the conflict that we have in these forests, the imaginary songs of foreign blacks and *mulatos* that live from theft, fraud and swindle in Ecuadorian territory. We tried to assure them that our intentions were good, and that we had been ill-advised by vileminded people, and that the current government had no interest in Punta Venado, and desired only that all the Indians enjoy their land peacefully, and that we would give them guarantees so that the *mulatos* would not continue to persecute them, and that the clothes we brought them from Guayaquil and Esmeraldas were simply a gift.

(June 1st) The Governor of Sapallo interrupted us, and told us to tell the Governor of Esmeraldas that the *mulatos* had done them many wrongs, and to tell the mayor to get the *mulatos* out of this region. We left assuring them that Padre Antonio was always a friend of the Cayapa. . . . The Mayor of La Tola, Don Alejandrino Batioja, has put all his energies into the persecution of witches. He related to us that he had captured one of the most famous,

Cipriano Hernandez Castrellón, a native of Colombia who is in prison in La Tola, and who will most probably be taken to Esmeraldas for his trial. He is the same witch that we made relations with in our first collaborations, who entered San Miguel when we abandoned the settlement last year. He tried to hide in Bobón, but the escort saw him and tied him up. Most of the witches remain hidden, the other exception is the black Alejandrino Mina, who abducted the Indian Innocencia, and . . . who has fallen into the hands of justice. . . . If the first authority of La Tola continues to drive himself rigorously against the enemies of the civilizing work which we have begun, he will be rewarded with the applause of his compatriots, and he will be well-merited by the government.

Suggested Sources:

There are few English-language secondary sources that deal directly with the themes and period addressed here. Most studies that deal with the history of Cayapa and Afro-Esmeraldans as individual groups are by anthropologists John V. Murra, "The Cayapa and the Colorado," in *The Handbook of South American Indians,* vol. 4 (Washington, DC: Smithsonian Institution, 1948); and Norman Whitten, *Black Frontiersmen: Afro-Hispanic Culture of Ecuador and Colombia* (Prospect Heights, IL: Waveland Press, 1985), both of which are classics that still have much validity and insight. Another good article, examining how highland indigenous groups imagine blacks and blackness is Rachel Corr and Norman Whitten, "Imagery of 'Blackness' in Indigenous Myth, Discourse and Ritual," in *Representations of Blackness and the*

Performance of Identities, ed. Jean Rahier (Westport, CT: Greenwood Press, 1999). For those interested in the racial and political dynamics of early twentieth-century evangelism, Alvin Goffin's book, *The Rise of Protestant Evangelism in Ecuador, 1895–1990* (Gainesville: University of Florida Press, 1994) provides a fascinating and detailed case study of Protestant missions. Nicola Foote, "Race, State and Nation in Early Twentieth Century Ecuador," *Nations and Nationalism* 12, no. 2 (2006): 261–278, provides an overview of differing *liberal* policies toward black and indigenous groups, using Esmeraldas as a primary case study.

In terms of primary sources, the best English-language sources for the study of early twentieth-century race relations in Esmeraldas come from travelers and social scientists. S. A. Barrett, *The Cayapa Indians of Ecuador* (New York: Museum of the American Indian, 1925) details Cayapa customs and practices and also reflects on the efforts at evangelization. A very useful traveler's account is United States musicologist Isador Lhevinne's, *The Enchanted Jungle* (New York: Coward-McCann, 1933). Another academic work from this period is Carlos Manuel Larrea, *Geographical Notes on Esmeraldas, Northwestern Ecuador* (New York: American Geographical Society, 1924). It is more concerned with physical than cultural geography but does provide some brief reflections on both groups discussed here. Literary sources represent a wonderful window into black and indigenous realities in Esmeraldas, and perhaps the most useful is Adalberto Ortiz's *Juyungo: A Classic Afro-Hispanic Novel* (Washington, DC: Three Continents Press, 1982 [1943]), which charts the conflicted life of a troubled *mulato* as he struggles to deal with the economic and political changes wrought by the increased presence of the state.

Chapter 16

Peasants, Gender, and the Mexican Revolutionary Conflict

Erin E. O'Connor, Bridgewater State College

lthough peasants have been at the heart of most social revolutions, it is far easier to obtain information about the actions and aspirations of middle- and upper-class revolutionary leaders than it is to find out about the lives and views of humble rank-and-file soldiers. This chapter introduces readers to the revolutionary wars that raged in Mexico from 1910 to 1917 through the eyes of a peasant couple who told their life stories to anthropologist Oscar Lewis in the 1940s and 1950s.[1] *Pedro*

---

[1]These names were pseudonyms. Lewis, like most anthropologists, changed the names of his informants in order to protect their identities. Lewis also interviewed one of Pedro and Esperanza's sons.

Martínez: A Mexican Peasant and His Family has been classic reading on the Mexican Revolution since its publication in 1964, because it offers a rare glimpse into the lives and views of poor, rural peoples who—although they did not lead the armies or the governments that followed the civil war—made the Mexican Revolution happen. In particular, these testimonies allow readers to compare and contrast peasant men's and women's revolutionary experiences.

The Mexican Revolution began when Francisco Madero, a large landowner from the northern Mexican state of Coahuila, challenged *liberal* dictator Porfirio Díaz (r. 1876–1911) for the Mexican presidency in 1910. Madero's candidacy gave new hope to many Mexicans who, for various reasons, wanted to see the Díaz era come to an end. When the votes were tallied, however, Díaz was declared the winner even though Madero almost certainly won more legitimate votes. Madero fled to the United States, where he drew up the "Plan of San Luís Potosí," proclaiming the presidential elections illegitimate and calling on Mexicans to rise up against the Porfirian government. Mexico's rural and urban poor responded in droves to the call to arms. Unlike Madero, who sought only moderate reforms, the poor in his armies wanted to put an end to nineteenth-century *liberal* policies that had exploited and impoverished them.

Political instability and violent upheaval continued, and by the time Madero fled Mexico City in 1913 (only to be assassinated on his way into exile), many different revolutionary factions vied with each other for control of the nation. Some leaders were profoundly *conservative* and sought the return of elite rule; others were moderate reformists who focused mainly on political change; yet others espoused radical land and labor reforms. One of the most famous military leaders of the Mexican Revolution was Emiliano Zapata, a *mestizo* peasant from the state of Morelos whose "land to the tiller" policy gave him a massive following among the poor in central Mexico. In northern Mexico, poor railroad and livestock estate workers rallied under Francisco "Pancho" Villa, a former cattle rustler who promised land redistribution and improved wages for workers. Popular as they were, neither of these men could garner the elite or foreign support necessary to win the contest for control of the Mexican state. Instead, moderate Venustiano Carranza and his "Constitutionalists" defeated other revolutionary factions in 1917 and began the process of building the Mexican revolutionary state. By this time, however, Mexico's poor men and women had made it clear that political stability would remain elusive until at least some of their demands were met. Eventually, peasant demands for justice resulted in massive land redistribution under President Lázaro Cárdenas in the 1930s, and by 1940 the revolutionary state-building process was complete.

Pedro Martínez's life symbolized how the revolution changed Mexico and Mexicans. Born to a poor indigenous family, Pedro was an illiterate estate worker when the revolution broke out. By the time that Lewis interviewed him in the 1940s, Pedro self-identified as a *mestizo*, converted from Catholicism to Seventh-Day Adventism, learned to read and write, and participated in local politics. Yet his family remained poor, and he was distraught that the national government was turning away from the social reforms of the 1930s.

Esperanza's descriptions of the revolution—and indeed her life story in the book more generally—are much shorter than Pedro's. In order to assess this adequately, one must consider how an anthropological work such as *Pedro Martínez* was produced. Although Oscar Lewis was genuinely fond of Pedro Martínez, they were far from equals, and the power discrepancies between Lewis and Esperanza were even greater. Mexican peasant gender norms, combined with the considerable inequalities between a United States scholar and a female peasant, led Esperanza to describe her life much more briefly than her husband did. Yet if Lewis failed to bridge the power gap as successfully with Esperanza as he did with Pedro, at least he listened to her. Most mid-century anthropologists did not interview peasant women at all, assuming that their views were the same as peasant men's. As excerpts here show, this was not always true.

Esperanza Martínez offers readers an example of how the Mexican Revolution affected noncombatant women. There were, however, many poor indigenous and *mestiza* women who were "camp followers," traveling with armies that their husbands, or fathers, or brothers joined. They cooked food for the soldiers,

This photograph features Valentina Ramírez in 1913, who fought with Carranza's forces. Do you ordinarily think of "revolution" as including female combatants? Why or why not? How does this photograph contrast with Pedro and Esperanza's descriptions of the revolution?

Source: Courtesy of Centro de Estudios de Historia de Mexico, Mexico City, Condumex.

mended clothes, and tended to the wounded.[2] Though often disdained by male military leaders, camp followers provided critical support that kept armies moving and helped ordinary soldiers maintain morale. When their male comrades fell in battle, many women picked up weapons and joined in the fighting. These women combatants, known as *soldaderas,* fought in all the revolutionary armies, but because most were from the ranks of the poor, their numbers were particularly high in Zapata's and Villa's armies. Zapata recognized *soldaderas'* value and allowed women to rise to the rank of captain in

his armies (but no higher). Villa, however, claimed that women weakened his forces by distracting his men—even though his armies could not have survived without women's various war contributions.[3]

Once the revolutionary war ended, women's contributions to the revolution disappeared from historical memory until the 1960s and 1970s, when new interest in women's history accompanied second-wave feminist movements in the United States and Latin America. Even decades later, scholars are still working to piece together the story of the Mexican Revolution "from below." Pedro and Esperanza's accounts still have much to teach readers about this monumental event in Mexican history.

Questions to Consider:

1. Try doing a two-tiered writing assessment to evaluate the document excerpts. First, read Pedro's account and then stop to answer the question: What did the revolution mean to Mexican peasants? Read Esperanza Martínez's version *after* writing about Pedro. Once you are done, use her account to describe what the revolution meant to peasants. How can you make sense of the different answers you get to this question in these two accounts?

2. How and why were Pedro and Esperanza concerned with their reputations as a "good man" or a "good woman" when they recalled their experiences of revolution? Why do you think they made their family obligations prominent in their descriptions?

3. Can you identify questionable or contradictory details in Pedro and Esperanza's accounts? What do these discrepancies teach us about how to analyze oral histories?

4. How does evidence in this chapter compare and contrast with O'Hara's chapter on *Tarahumara* Indians and the Mexican Revolution? How do these two chapters expand your understanding of "who makes history happen"?

---

[2]Camp followers were not a new phenomenon with the Mexican revolution. See Elizabeth Salas, *Soldaderas in the Mexican Military: Myth and History* (Austin: University of Texas Press, 1990), which discusses women and war before the revolution in Chapter 2. For South America, see Evelyn Cherpak, "The Participation of Women in the Independence Movement in Gran Colombia, 1780–1830," in *Latin American Women: Historical Perspectives,* ed. Asunción Lavrin (Westport, CT: Greenwood Press, 1978), 219–234.

[3]Elizabeth Salas, "The Soldadera in the Mexican Revolution: War and Men's Illusions," in *Women of the Mexican Countryside, 1850–1990,* ed. Heather Fowler-Salamini and Mary Kay Vaughan (Tucson: University of Arizona Press, 1994).

Pedro and Esperanza Martínez Describe Living through the Mexican Revolution[4]

Pedro's Story

[In Zapata's army,] we knew what we were fighting for—Land, Water, Forests, and Justice. That was all in the plan. It was for this reason that I became a Revolutionary. It was for a cause! Many joined just to get rich, to steal whatever they could. Their sons are rich now, because the fathers robbed. When a plaza was captured, they would sack the houses and give half the loot to their officers. But others were true revolutionaries and joined to help Zapata.

In my judgment, what Zapata was fighting for was just. Porfirio's government took everything away from us. Everything went to the rich, the *hacendados*[5], those with the power were the masters, and we had nothing. We were their servants because we could not plant or make use of any lands that did not belong to the *hacienda*. So they had us subjugated. We were completely enslaved by the hacendados. That is what Zapata fought to set right.

I joined the Revolutionary ranks because of the martial law in Morelos, declared by Carranza. If they found you sitting in your house, they would shoot you. If they found you walking, they would shoot you. That was what they called martial law. There was *no* law! Naturally, when I saw this, I said to myself, "Rather than have them kill me sitting, standing or walking, I'd better get out of here." And so I went to war along with the *Zapatistas*. [. . .]

[*Pedro then described what it was like to fight in the revolution*]

. . . We entered a place, a little cornfield in a valley, where the fighting was very bad. The *Zapatistas* were on one hill and the *carrancistas* [members of Carranza's forces] were on another and we were in the middle, fighting hand to hand with other *carrancistas*.

The two armies got all mixed up, there in San Gregorio. There was a tremendous hail of bullets and the dead piled up like stones in a *milpa* [cornfield]. The man just next to me fell. We were together but the bullet hit him. At five o'clock a bullet got the captain who had been blaspheming the day before. In the dark we didn't know who was a *Zapatista* and who was a *carrancista* because even the *carrancistas* didn't have uniforms then; we were all dressed just as we were, like peasants. We didn't even know whom to shoot at. The *Zapatistas* on the hill above us shouted, "Don't shoot below because they are our men!" The *carrancistas* on the other hill also yelled, "Don't shoot because they're ours!" They stopped fighting; only the ones in the middle fought each other with the butts of their rifles and with knives. *Caray!* I will always remember that fight.

All I did was try to defend myself. They gave us a password to say. When anyone asked "Who lives?" the answer was "Azteca!" or "Tlayacapán!" But then the other side also had a password, "Carranza!" If you gave the wrong answer, you were killed right off. The one who didn't answer at all didn't die. So I didn't answer. "Who lives?" I didn't say anything. Even if they put a bullet in me, I didn't answer. That's how I saved myself. We were being chased, and I met up with someone. "Who are you?" I said. He answered by yelling to me, "Catch the man next to you! He's a *zapatista*!" So I shot him instead. I stopped him but who knows if I killed him? In all my fighting, I never saw with my own eyes whether or not I killed anyone. [. . .]

[*As the fighting continued, Pedro gradually made his way to the village of Azteca where Esperanza was still living with their children.*]

When I arrived [in Azteca], I found my wife dying of hunger. She was still living in my house. We were practically newlyweds then; we had three children but one had died and we were left with only two.

But now I began to give her money and to provide food. I was earning money, with my gun, as a *Zapatista* in the army, and we also found food in the abandoned milpas. One day I went to the fields to bring squash to eat. I went with another man and we saw something in the sky. What did we know about

---

[4]*Source:* Oscar Lewis, *Pedro Martínez: A Mexican Peasant and His Family* (New York: Random House, 1964), 89–91, 92–94, 99, 101–102, 107–108, 112, 115–116. Reprinted by permission of Harold Ober Associates Incorporated. Copyright © 1964 by Oscar Lewis.

[5]*Hacendados* were owners of large estates. During the Díaz era (often called the "Porfiriato" after the dictator's first name), these estates expanded, frequently at the expense of the local peasantry.

airplanes then! We hid between the stalks and were afraid. What thing was up there? The plane spotted some rebel lines marching near Yautepec and dropped two big bombs. How we were frightened!

A few days later the government troops entered Azteca and things were very bad. The *carrancistas* finally drove us out. This time I took my wife and children with me.

We still kept fighting. I would leave my wife in a nearby village and would go to join the battle. We had many combats over here near Santa María, and still more over toward Yautepec. Marino Solís, the general from my village, was in charge at that time. It was my colonel, Leobardo Galván, who joined us up with General Marino. Sometimes we were ahead and sometimes the *carrancistas* were. There were heavy losses, men and horses too. Fleeing all the time! Yes, sir, to the south. After they drove us out of Santa María, we went to Tejalpa. After a few days in Tejalpa, we went on to Jiltepec. One week in Jiltepec and then to San Vicente, where we hung around for a month. [. . .]

Meanwhile, Zapata followed the lines to Yautepec and went as far as Tizapán. He had cannons and machine guns but he lost them all. That was the last big battle of the war, there in Tizapán, in 1916.

That's where I finally had it. The battle was something awful! The shooting was tremendous! It was a completely bloody battle, three days and three nights. But I took it for only one day and then I left. I quit the army and left for Jojutla, without a *centavo* in my pocket. I said to myself, "It's time now I got back to my wife, to my little children. I'm getting out!"

That's why I left the army, for my wife. How I loved my wife! I didn't leave because I was afraid to fight but because of my wife, who had to find food for herself and the children. I said to myself, "No, my family comes first and they are starving. Now I'm leaving!" I saw that the situation was hopeless and that I would be killed and they would perish. [. . .]

I was on the way back from Guerrero[6] when the news of Zapata's death came. Mmmm! It hurt me as much as if my own father had died! I was a *Zapatista*

down to the marrow of my bones. I had a lot of faith in Zapata's promises, a lot of faith. I did indeed! I was one of the real *Zapatistas*! I felt very bad, but there I was on my way back from Guerrero. I believed the news. Yes, I believed it right away. [. . .]

Esperanza's Story

I was not afraid when the Revolution began because I didn't know what it was like. After I saw what it was, I was very much afraid. I saw how the federal troops would catch the men and kill them. They carried off animals, mules, chickens, clothes. The women who came with the soldiers were the ones who took away everything.

The government soldiers, and the rebel soldiers too, violated the young girls and married women. They came every night and the women would give great shrieks when they were taken away. Afterward, at daybreak, the women would be back in their houses. They wouldn't tell what happened to them and I didn't ask because then people would say, "Why do you want to know? If you want to know, let them take you out tonight!"

For greater safety, we would sleep in the *corral* [where the animals were kept]. Our house was very exposed because the street is one of the main entrances to the village and the soldiers would pass that way. Pedro took us to a relative's house further into the village. There the soldiers never entered. The *Zapatistas* were well liked in the village, because although it is true they sometimes carried off young girls, they left the majority of women in peace. And after all, everyone knew what kind of girls they took. The ones who liked that sort of thing!

Sometimes the *Zapatistas* would come down to the village and send someone from house to house to ask for *tortillas*.[7] At other times, the government

---

[6]Pedro had described working as a plowman in Guerrero for three years, where he lived with his wife, and with their children—all but one of whom died.

[7]The soldiers here were demanding considerable labor from the village women. For centuries, and indeed until the 1940s—later in some areas—*campesina* women made tortillas by hand every day. This process took hours because it began with hand-grinding corn, then shaping and cooking each tortilla. Poor women did this work daily, as tortillas would go stale by the next day. For more information on the making—and meaning—of tortillas in Mexico, see Jeffrey Pilcher, *Que Vivan Los Tamales! Food and the Making of Mexican Identity* (Albuquerque: University of New Mexico Press, 1998).

troops did the same thing. We always gave them whatever they asked for. After all, what else could we do? But the government men were the ones who behaved the worst and did us the most harm.

One time the government called all the women together in the village plaza. I was in bed. My baby had been born a month before. Sick as I was, they made me get up and go. When they had us all there, they told us to go and grind corn and make tortillas for the soldiers and then come to sleep with them that night. We ground the corn and delivered the tortillas and went off into the hills to sleep. Sleep with the soldiers! Not for anything would we have stayed for that! [. . .]

There was no work here anymore and Pedro had nothing to do. There was no way to earn money for food. But I didn't want him to go as a *Zapatista*. I would say to him, "Even if we don't eat, Pedro." He would answer, "What are we going to live on? If one works, the government grabs him and kills him." That's why when someone cried, "here comes the government!" Pedro would take his *sarape* [blanket] and make for the hills.

One day Pedro appeared, carrying his rifle. He told me, "Well, I've done it. I've joined up." He had become a *zapatista* because they offered to give him food. I got very angry but he said at least he would have something to eat and furthermore they would pay him. Then he told me he would have to go to Mexico City with the rebels and he promised to send me money.

He went with the *Zapatistas* and left me without a centavo. There I was with nothing and I had two children to support, the girl of two years and the boy of two months. Also, I had in my care Pedro's cousin who was about eight years old. I cried in anguish because I didn't know what to do.

My brother was angry with Pedro. He said Pedro was lazy and didn't want to work. Pedro had planted corn seed but he didn't want to go to the hills to take care of it. My brother said, "Just as soon as he returns I'll tell him to take back his children and I will support you."

I would leave Pedro's little cousin to rock the baby and go to my brother's house to grind corn. I made the tortillas in my brother's house and then I would go running back to see about the children. My sister-in-law would let me have six or seven tortillas. I wouldn't eat until after I had divided it with the children.

That way the time went by, eating only a few tortillas a day. I had some china plates and I went to sell them. They would give me a handful of corn for each plate. I sold my grinding stone for three *pesos*, but at that time corn cost one peso and half a *cuartillo* so the money lasted no time at all.

My brother became angrier with Pedro. "When he comes back give him his children, and you come here." I would say, "How can I leave him? I don't know where he is but he has gone to get money."

At last Pedro sent me sixty pesos with Pablo Fuentes. But where to buy corn? No one in the village would sell any. A neighbor woman told me to go to Yautepec where they had corn. We went together early the next morning. I had an infant in my arms and so did she. On the road we met the government troops marching to Azteca, but they didn't harm us.

We reached Yautepec and went to the house of an aunt of mine. She said to us, "Ah, my little ones, what have you come here for? Why did it occur to you there would be corn here? Here there is nothing."

The next day we returned to Azteca without a single grain of corn. I continued living all alone in my house. My neighbor, seeing me alone, began to talk to me of love. He would say things . . . that I should sleep with him and he would help me get food. I told him, "You are old enough for me to respect you as a father and you should stop saying such things to me." Then he asked me not to tell Pedro, but I said I was going to.

I never did tell Pedro, to avoid a fight and also because he might think that maybe out of necessity I had paid attention to that old man. And why start bad feeling with one's neighbors? I did tell my brother, though. He said, "Don't pay any attention to him. He is an old man. I will talk to him. He thinks because we are alone we don't know how to behave ourselves."

It was a dreadful time. We suffered a lot. I no longer had clothing and wore a soldier's khaki shirt. For Pedro I had to make a shirt of some heavy unbleached muslin.

Then Pedro got sick and I had a very hard time. I had to sell everything I owned, a few turkey hens and another grinding stone. When we get sick we always have to sell everything.

Suggested Sources:

Pedro Martínez was one of many of Oscar Lewis's publications on Mexican society. Readers who find his work interesting might also consult *Five Families: Mexican Case Studies in the Culture of Poverty* (New York: Basic Books, 1975), and *The Children of Sanchez* (New York: Vintage Press, 1979). Readers interested in placing the revolution within the course of Mexican history should consult Gilbert M. Joseph and Timothy J. Henderson, eds., *The Mexico Reader: History, Culture, Politics* (Durham, NC: Duke University Press, 2002). The Mexican Revolution and its impact on the rural poor also captured the imagination of writers and film makers. See, for example, Mariano Azuela's classic novel *The Underdogs*, trans. E. Munguía (New York: Signet, 1996 [1915]). Azuela, a novelist who joined Villa's forces, captures his own disillusionment with the revolutionary process in this story of upheaval and corruption. For a testimonial novel on women in the revolution, see Elena Poniatowska's *Here's to You, Jesusa!*, trans. Deanna Heikkinen (New York: Penguin, 2001 [1969]). Poniatowska based her novel on actual interviews with a woman who participated in the revolution but ended her life in poverty and solitude; the writer also worked with Lewis as one of his assistants. For a film that captures a Hollywood take on the Mexican Revolution, which readers might want to compare and contrast with the actual historical events and problems, see Dir. Elia Kazan's *Viva Zapata!* (Los Angeles: Twentieth Century Fox Film Corporation, original release, 1952). Those interested in newly available documentary footage on Villa's faction of the revolution should see *Los rollos perdidos de Pancho Villa/The Lost Reels of Pancho Villa* (New York: SubCine, 2003).

Secondary sources on the Mexican Revolution, even in English, are too numerous to list here, but an excellent broad-based discussion of the period is Alan Knight, *The Mexican Revolution*, 2 vols. (Cambridge: Cambridge University Press, 1986). A classic, and still important, study of Zapata's role in the Mexican Revolution is John Womack, *Zapata and the Mexican Revolution* (New York: Knopf, 1969). John Tutino's *From Insurrection to Revolution in Mexico: Social Bases of Agrarian Violence, 1750–1940* (Princeton, NJ: Princeton University Press, 1986) is a sweeping monograph that explores over a century of socioeconomic tensions in Mexico in order to explain why the countryside exploded in widespread violence in the 1910s. Elizabeth Salas wrote the now-classic study of women in the Mexican Revolution in her *Soldaderas in the Mexican Military: Myth and History* (Austin: University of Texas Press, 1990). Readers interested in understanding rural women's experiences of Mexican history more generally should consult essays in Heather Fowler-Salamini and Mary Kay Vaughan, eds., *Women of the Mexican Countryside, 1850–1990* (Tucson: University of Arizona Press, 1994). For the long struggle for women's rights, with a particularly strong emphasis on middle-class feminism, see Shirlene Soto, *Emergence of the Modern Mexican Woman: Her Part in the Revolution and Struggle for Equality* (Denver, CO: Arden Press, 1990).

Chapter 17

"Bettering the Tarahumara Race": *Indigenismo* in Mexico, 1906–1945

Julia Cummings O'Hara, Xavier University

This chapter presents excerpts of four different documents from early twentieth-century Mexico: a controversial piece of legislation, a unique boarding-school charter, a study commissioned by the president himself, and a children's public-school textbook. Together, these documents illustrate how political and cultural elites in Mexico viewed the nation's indigenous people both before and after the revolution that began in 1910. Mexico is a pluralistic society; along with Spanish, dozens of indigenous languages are spoken, and a wide variety of regional and local cultures coexist within the nation. Before the revolution, however, many Mexicans perceived this pluralism as a problem to overcome. During the regime of Porfirio Díaz (1876–1911), many *liberal* elites embraced the tenets of an intellectual trend now known as *scientific racism*. Generated by European pseudoscientists and philosophers such as Herbert Spencer, scientific racism sought to categorize the world's peoples into inferior and superior races. These thinkers concluded that individuals of the so-called Caucasian race were destined to dominate African, Asian, and indigenous peoples, just as racially heterogeneous nations such as Mexico were destined to be dominated by the supposedly "white" nations of northern and western Europe and the United States. Scientific racism provided Porfirian elites with a way to explain and justify indigenous peoples' marginalization within the nation.

Following the revolutionary conflict of 1910–1920, a new generation of leaders publicly rejected anything associated with Porfirian Mexico, especially ideas that were rooted in nineteenth-century scientific racism. During the 1920s, with the influential philosopher José Vasconcelos serving as Secretary of Education, the revolutionary state aimed to incorporate the country's indigenous peoples into the national body politic through an array of economic, linguistic, and cultural programs, and to inculcate in them a modern, secular spirit of national identity.

One of the most contentious questions for historians of Mexico is whether the story of the revolution is one of deep and lasting change or one of surprising continuities between pre- and postrevolutionary Mexico. The excerpted documents provide an opportunity to explore this question by charting the relationship of the Mexican state to the *Tarahumara* Indians between 1906 and 1945. The *Tarahumara* inhabit the Sierra Madre Occidental Mountains of the northern state of Chihuahua. The site of numerous peasant uprisings and the frequent refuge of the legendary Pancho Villa, this is a region steeped in revolutionary mythology. The *Tarahumara*, however, have a more enigmatic past. During the colonial period, the unforgiving landscape of the Sierra Madre proved challenging to the early Jesuit missionaries who sought to convert the *Tarahumara*

Diego Rivera's mural *Harsh Treatment of Indian Laborers by Their European Master* in the Palacio de Cortés (Cuernavaca), Mexico. This mural, like many others of the revolutionary state-building era in Mexico, depicted the cruelties of class-race repression and exploitation preceding the outbreak of the revolution. The murals also often suggested, either directly or indirectly, that the new revolutionary state was resolving these problems. How do the themes and suggestions of a mural like this compare and contrast with documents presented in this chapter?

Source: The Granger Collection, New York.

to Christianity. Accustomed to living in highly mobile, sparsely populated, and autonomous communities, the *Tarahumara* fiercely resisted congregation into missions. Many Jesuits perished trying to quell the frequent *Tarahumara* uprisings during the seventeenth century, and in the eighteenth century, the mission population dwindled. When the Spanish colonial state expelled the Jesuit order in 1767, Franciscan missionaries inherited many of the Jesuits' properties and maintained the missions until the mid-nineteenth century.

From 1850 to 1910, *liberalism* and industrialization effectively redrew the demographic, economic, and cultural map of the Sierra. The discovery of mining resources, the construction of the railroad, and the development of a thriving timber industry all brought an influx of nonindigenous Mexicans into the region. Porfirian land-tenure reforms further threatened the integrity of *Tarahumara* communities by collapsing long-standing racial boundaries and dramatically eroding the *Tarahumaras'* access to land. *Tarahumaras* acted to defend their communities through peaceful political protest, legal challenges, armed uprisings, and even by serving in the Mexican army to help secure Mexico's northern frontier. And, although historians still have much to learn about how the *Tarahumara* contributed to the 1910 revolution, it is certain that many resisted their marginalization by joining Villa and other revolutionaries. The *Tarahumaras'* long history of both resistance and cooperation made them vital participants in the public debates that were so central to the political life of the developing Mexican nation.

The first excerpt comes from the "Law for the Betterment of the *Tarahumara* Race," passed in 1906 by the state legislature of Chihuahua, calling for the formation of a Central Indigenous Protection Committee to establish and oversee special agricultural colonies for the *Tarahumara*. The outbreak of the revolution prevented the law's full implementation; the only provision implemented was the creation of a *Tarahumara* agricultural colony in what is now the bustling town of Creel. Still, the law serves as a fascinating starting point for assessing the impact that the revolution had on the *Tarahumaras'* relationship with the state.

The second excerpt presents the goals of the Casa del Estudiante *Indígena* (Home for Indigenous Students), a government-run boarding school in Mexico City created in 1924 for indigenous boys from throughout Mexico. This school's history exemplifies the development of *indigenismo*, an important revolutionary ideology in which Mexican elites symbolically embraced indigenous cultures. *Indigenistas* considered themselves friends of the Indian and were eager to preserve the archaeological remains of Mexico's Aztec past; they also publicly questioned the usefulness of race as a meaningful social category. The Casa del Estudiante Indígena was founded as an official effort by indigenistas to prove that the indigenous "races" of Mexico were

capable of being educated on par with nonindigenous Mexicans and of taking full advantage of the benefits of Mexican citizenship. Because of the *Tarahumaras'* long history of marginalization, school administrators believed they represented a valuable example of the kind of transformation that could be made by students at the school. But whether *indigenismo* also produced a deep commitment to social justice for living, breathing Indians remains an open question.

The third excerpt, from a Department of Labor survey of the *Tarahumaras'* Sierra Madre region commissioned by President Lázaro Cárdenas in 1936, reflects a shift in indigenista ideas and policies. Many indigenistas now concluded that economic and material inequality among "Indian," "*mestizo*," and "white" Mexicans—not racial degeneration—was the primary cause of indigenous oppression. The 1936 survey sought to regulate when and how whites and Indians should mix, legitimating certain arenas of interaction while discouraging (or even outlawing) others.

The final excerpt in this chapter contains two short selections from a bilingual (*Tarahumara-Spanish*) textbook intended for an audience of *Tarahumara* public-school children. Produced in 1945 by the National Campaign against Illiteracy, this textbook and others like it aimed to reach bilingual indigenous children, teaching them to read in both their native languages and in Spanish. The text sought to appeal to students by including themes familiar to rural and indigenous youth and by employing an informal and conversational style, often using first-person narrative from the point of view of an indigenous child. Although the teachers who used these texts in their classrooms were often indigenous education *promotores* (facilitators) and rural teachers, the authors of the texts were Department of Public Education employees. Thus, although the stories read as first-person narratives, one must remember that these texts present us with the voices of nonindigenous teachers and administrators rather than the views of the *Tarahumara* themselves.

The excerpts in this chapter explore both the opportunities and the continuing challenges that indigenous Mexicans such as the *Tarahumara* confronted when efforts at nation building collided with questions about racial, economic, and social inequality. Although *indigenismo* and the expansion of public education presented subaltern Mexicans with new avenues for mobility and status, the excerpts that follow hint at the unfinished nature of Mexico's social and cultural revolution.

Questions to Consider:

1. How did the various authors of these excerpts seem to define the boundaries between the racial categories of "Indian," "white," and "*mestizo*"? What changes do you see over time, particularly regarding the impact of the 1910 revolution on how these categories were defined?

2. What did the authors of these excerpts suggest about the different roles that indigenous and nonindigenous people were expected to play in resolving the "Indian problem" in Mexico?

3. Based on the document evidence provided, how would you describe the relationship between Indians and the nation in Mexico between 1910 and 1945? To what extent was *indigenismo* inclusive of the Indians themselves?

4. What comparisons and contrasts can you make between Mexican *indigenismo* and the ideas about race and national identity expressed by José Martí in Chapter 14?

Law for the Betterment of the Tarahumara Race (1906)[1]

November 3, 1906

The Twenty-Fifth Constitutional Congress of the State of Chihuahua has decreed the following:

Law for the Betterment and Culture of the *Tarahumara* Race

ARTICLE ONE: In the capital of this state, a commission shall be created that is dedicated to addressing all that pertains to the culture, conservation, instruction, and improvement of the *Tarahumara* race. This assembly shall be named the Central Indigenous Protection Committee and it shall be comprised of at least five proprietary members and five supplemental members, who shall be named and removed freely by the Executive of the state . . .

ARTICLE FOUR: The Central Committee shall have the following authorities and obligations:

  I. To promote all that is advantageous to the civilization of the Indians, their social

improvement, their education, the administration of their property, the care of their colonies; and, to acquire the protection that the Federal and State Government and society ought to impart to the *Tarahumara* tribe.

  II. To ensure that the demarcation and partition of all *ejidos* belonging to *Tarahumara pueblos* are accomplished with due expediency and under the most just and liberal conditions.

  III. To congregate the Indians, whether in established *pueblos* or in *pueblos* that shall be established in the future, and endow them with lands, farm implements, and, when necessary for them to begin to enjoy civilized and domestic life, giving rewards to those who do congregate in *pueblos* or colonies.

  IV. To take care that sufficient quantities of maize, bean, potato, and other seeds that can be cultivated on their lands are annually distributed to individuals of the *Tarahumara* race, along with young fruit trees, principally apple, so that they might cultivate them and take advantage of their produce.

---

[1] *Source:* Enrique C. Creel, "Exposicion de motivos que presento el Ejecutivo del Estado sobre la civilizacion y mejoramiento de la Raza Tarahumara y Ley expedida acerca del asunto por la Legislatura" (Chihuahua: Imprenta del Gobierno del Estado de Chihuahua, 1906).

V. To regulate the internal regimen of the *Tarahumara* colonies so as to preserve order, morality, fine customs, and love of work, and endeavor to establish in [these colonies] the type of industry that most suits the inclinations, habits, and aptitudes of the inhabitants.

VI. To promote the establishment of rural schools where indigenous children are given an elementary education and taught to cultivate plants and trees appropriate for sustenance, the care of domestic animals, some manual industries, and all that may inculcate in them a love of the land and be a legitimate source of income.

VII. To inspire the community's philanthropy, especially donations of clothing and amusing objects that will awaken in the Indians feelings of affection and gratitude toward the white race.

VIII. To achieve, through persuasion, the Indians' voluntary release of their sons or daughters, in order to send them to schools in the state capital and the district head-towns, ensuring a sufficient number of white families to receive the *Tarahumara* children and have them at their side, whether out of philanthropy or because of payment, but always treating them with kindness, teaching them gentle habits, and instructing them in the moral principles that contribute to the improvement of their condition.

IX. To uphold, as a principal objective of their work, the goal of not contradicting the Indians in their religious ideas, games, dances, festivals, and diversions or in their intimate and deeply rooted customs; but to procure the gradual, tenacious, and constant evolution of the race until bringing [the *Tarahumara*] to civilization by surrounding [them] with the benefits enjoyed by cultured people, so that in this way the Indians come to be good citizens and to contribute with their labor to the progress of the Mexican Family.

X. To improve the situation of those Indians who do send their children to school, who show proof of attaining and propagating alcohol temperance, and who demonstrate themselves to be lovers of a well-mannered and civilized lifestyle, by augmenting their landholdings and also increasing the number of their tools and the quality of cows, sheep, and goats which shall be given to them at the appropriate time of each year . . .

ARTICLE SIXTEEN: The Executive of the State is authorized to revise, clarify, and amend the present law.

Goals of the Casa del Estudiante Indígena (1924)[2]

Preface

The Federal Secretary of Public Education hereby establishes and supports "The Home for Indigenous Students" in conjunction with the program instituted to intensify its efforts toward to the education of the rural masses, thereby training them for the free and conscious exercise of their natural, social, and political rights and responsibilities.

Recruitment

The following requisites and conditions are to be taken into account for the selection of the Indians who shall enroll in the "Home for Indigenous Students:"

1. That they be male Indians who, during the period of their enrollment, are between 14 and 18 years of age, regardless of their grade level. Fifteen- and

---

[2]*Source:* Secretary of Public Education of Mexico, *Home for Indigenous Students: Sixteen Months of Work on a Collective Psychological Experiment with Indians* (February, 1926-June, 1927).

sixteen-year-olds are preferred, as well as those who have completed first and second grade in a rural school, but in the event that none with the latter qualification can be found, those without any academic experience may enroll.

2. That they offer the necessary characteristics of intelligence, physical vigor, and health so that they are not frustrated during their time at the Home.

3. That they be natives of districts with dense indigenous populations.

4. That they regularly reside outside of medium or large population centers.

5. That they speak and understand with relative perfection the indigenous language of their region of origin.

6. That the Home exclude those Indians able to become incorporated into the Mexican social community without relying on official aid, as well as those who are already being incorporated through the help of private entities.

7. That at least two Indians from the same region, who speak the same language, come to the Home, except in those cases in which the fixed quota is only one.

8. That each presumptive indigenous enrollee arrive with three filled-out questionnaires that refer to 1) personal background 2) family background 3) reports on the socio-economic life of the region of which he is a native.

Cultural and Social Incorporation

The [Home for Indigenous Students] has the fundamental objective of eliminating the evolutionary distance that disconnects the Indians from the present era, of transforming their mentality, tendencies, and customs, in order to add them to civilized, modern life and incorporate them integrally within the Mexican social community. To that effect, the Home shall surround its members with the best material conditions made possible by the budget (dormitory, meals, hygiene, clothing, entertainment, and other primary necessities), it shall make them participants in the basic culture, shall impart to them knowledge of manual, agricultural, and industrial skills, and, in sum, it shall give them an integral education that shall convert them

into progressive entities on their own behalf, but *through no motive shall it keep them isolated*, forming a separate socio-educational group; on the contrary, it shall act such that the indigenous youth feel vigorously that they are members of the great national family; it shall make them study, work, play, stroll the streets, etc., in proximity with *creoles* and *mestizos*; that they breathe, struggle, triumph, suffer or endure in contact with them, which will provoke nexuses of material and moral interest, currents of reciprocal intelligence, aspirations and basic common goals, so that tomorrow they can influence and be influenced, consciously, for the benefit of Mexican cohesion and unity.

Racial Solidarity

Another of the essential goals of this establishment consists of initiating the unity and spiritual fusion of the diverse indigenous families that populate the National Territory, to bring—through the indigenous students—a mutual understanding, sincere friendship, enduring cordiality, school camaraderie, and esprit de corps; in sum, it seeks indigenous racial solidarity and strives for each Indian who has been sheltered here to return to his native soil, continue considering all Indians to be his racial brethren, inviting their participation in that which he has learned and, animating them toward social action that will enlighten and enrich them, be a new element who works for the emancipation of the rural masses.

Human Solidarity

It must be noted that we are not trying to encourage any kind of ethnic exclusivity, much less to provoke racial animosity, as such a goal would fundamentally jeopardize the social and cultural incorporation of the Indian that is so sought as one of the factors that must become a predominant part of the definitive formation of the national soul. We celebrate the past, present, and future potential of the indigenous masses, but at the same time, the mutual dependence of all men, and in particular all Mexicans, must be affirmed. The Institution will keep alive the concept of culture as part of the common intellectual heritage, not as a benefit to be used selfishly but rather as a treasure that has been entrusted, to be administered with honor and in

congruence with collective interests; it is ardently desired that each one tether his wellbeing to that of the rest and take inspiration in the noble longings of coordination, cooperation, and fraternity.

Department of Labor Recommendations for Resolving the Varied Problems of the *Tarahumara* (1936)[3]

The delegation from the Department of Labor finds it necessary to call the following recommendations to the attention of President Lázaro Cárdenas, with the goal of resolving the varied problems of the *Tarahumara* race.

Education

1. Entrust the Tónachic boarding school to the indigenous teacher Ignacio León and allow him to develop his proposed plan for colonies.
2. Increase the boarding schools' service personnel, given that the work is overwhelming for the *Tarahumara* girls who have to make enormous quantities of tortillas.
3. Provide each boarding school with a good motor or a boiler in order to provide steam baths.
4. Provide the boarding schools with washing machines, given the prevalence of lice left behind after parents visit their children.
5. Provide the boarding schools with *nixtamal*[4] mills.
6. Send various craftsmen to improve the system used for the manufacture of sarapes and organize this industry.
7. Establish a musical instrument-manufacturing industry (violins and guitars).
8. Send married teachers to the region and give them better training, especially in the material organization of the school and the home.

9. Create in each indigenous settlement a Teachers' House which serves as a model home for the community and at the same time allows the teachers to live as civilized people.
10. Provide the teachers with the help necessary to serve their students a daily meal.
11. Raise the salaries of Josefina Carrasco, a teacher from Choguita, and María Orpinel (the widow Bustillos), from Aboreáchic, due to the dedication and care with which they educate "their *inditos*." Each Saturday, Mrs. Orpinel brings five or six indigenous children to Rocheáchic, where she feeds them alongside her own children, using money from her own salary.[5]
12. An honorarium for Patricio Járis and Ignacio León, from Norogachic and Tónachic, respectively; both have spent their own salaries, the first to build a school that cost 800.00, and the second to start a colony.[6] [. . .]

---

[5]This recommendation recognizes the role that nonindigenous people, especially local school teachers, were expected to play in the state's effort to educate Tarahumara children. The word "indito," or "little Indian," here seems to describe indigenous children, but it should be noted that it was also frequently used—quite condescendingly—to refer to indigenous adults. Choguita, Aboreáchic, and Rocheáchic are the names of local villages.

[6]Patricio Járis and Ignacio León, both *Tarahumaras*, were graduates of the Home for Indigenous Students in Mexico City. One of the primary goals of the home was to send trained indigenous professionals back to their home regions to become teachers and community leaders. This recommendation seems to be an effort to acknowledge these two highly respected indigenous leaders for their efforts and to compensate them for their generous monetary contribution of 800 pesos toward a new school and colony. The colonies were a kind of supervised settlement for indigenous graduates of local government-run boarding schools.

---

[3]*Source:* Department of Labor Recommendations for Resolving the Varied Problems of the Tarahumara Race from *The Tarahumara Race: Investigation Carried Out by the Department of Labor (1936)*.
[4]Nixtamal refers to corn cooked in lime to make tortillas; in the mid twentieth century, the term was often used to reference mechanized mills that would do this, instead of women spending hours grinding corn by hand.

Agriculture

1. Found *Tarahumara* colonies in Babícora and San José de Alburquerque [*sic*], installing Mennonite farmers as directors or managers.[7]
2. Revise the land distributions carried out in the Conchos basin that have only benefited the capitalists. Introduce an indigenous population of twenty-five percent into this region.[8]

Indian Department

1. Establishment of storehouses in Norogachi, Tónachi, and Rocheáchic for the purchase and sale of Indians' seeds, cattle, and merchandise.
2. Initiation of consumers' cooperatives.
3. Annual celebrations of Indigenous Conventions in the *Tarahumara* region.

---

[7]Beginning in 1922, Mexico accepted numerous Canadian-born Mennonites, who established agricultural colonies in central Chihuahua, outside the present-day city of Cuauhtémoc in the foothills of the Sierra Madre Occidental. The Mennonites were perceived as capable and industrious farmers who could provide stability to this tumultuous and sparsely populated region. That the Mexican government would sell large tracts of land to a foreign religious group only two years after the revolution ended is one of the many ironies of Mexico's postrevolution history. Today, the Mennonite population in Chihuahua is estimated to be at least 50,000.
[8]The Chonchos River basin, one of northern Mexico's most fertile agricultural regions, had originally been inhabited by Tarahumaras. This recommendation speaks to the Cárdenas administration's efforts to carry out a land reform program aimed at restoring ancestral lands to communities that had experienced dispossession during the nineteenth century, and especially during the Porfiriato.

Department of Labor

1. Designation of a resident Labor Inspector in the Upper *Tarahumara* region, with periodic visits to the Lower *Tarahumara* region.
2. Organization of integrated labor unions, which is to say, unions of Indians and *mestizos*.
3. Said inspector ought to be in constant communication with indigenous leaders.

Agrarian Department

1. Close all definitive files related to the distribution [*dotación*] of land to indigenous settlements.
2. Send one or more agronomists with the goal of possibly orienting the Indians toward new cultivations, especially pastures. [. . .]

Health Department

1. Send one or more sanitation brigades with specialists in dentistry.
2. Move the sanitation outpost in Batopilas [a sparsely populated village of non-indigenous people] to the indigenous population center of Norogachic.
3. Send at least one health worker to Tónachic, Chonguita [*sic*] and Rocheáchic.
4. Start a campaign among Indians and *mestizos* alike to research and cure venereal diseases.

Selections from a Bilingual *Tarahumara*-Spanish Textbook (1945)[9]

My Village

I was born here and I want to stay here, because I really love my village. My village is quiet, it is where I have my house and live happily. I do not want to complain about it, but I wish our houses were more comfortable and pretty, that we had streets and a park with a gazebo. Queta and Quirino went to the city and they say it is very

---

[9]*Source:* Tarahumara Collection pamphlet section, *Somos Tarahumaras*, pg. 115 by José Hernández Labastida and Francisco Javier Alvarez, 1945. Used with permission of University of Texas at El Paso Library Special Collections Department, MS219.

pretty and it has some streets between two and five kilometers long. Why can't my village be better? If we all want it to be, it will.

We are *Tarahumaras*

We are *Tarahumaras*. We live in the Sierra Madre mountains of Chihuahua. We love these lands, which we inherited from our grandparents and which watched us being born. We are poor and ignorant of many things, because for many years we have been forgotten. We do not have good houses because we do not know how to make them. Many of us live in misery because we have been dispossessed of our best lands and the few that remain have been worn out. But the day of our betterment has finally come. The Government brings us justice. It has founded schools and missions, sent representatives to defend us; it recovers our lands and teaches us how better to work them. We will learn Spanish in order to communicate with all people. Our children will inherit a better life, for the honor of our State and the Fatherland.

Suggested Sources:

Readers interested in changing notions of race in Latin American history should consult Richard Graham, *The Idea of Race in Latin America, 1870–1940* (Austin: University of Texas Press, 1990). For sources on the impact of the revolution on Indian-state relations in Mexico, see Alexander Dawson, *Indian and Nation in Revolutionary Mexico* (Tucson: University of Arizona Press, 2004); Stephen E. Lewis, "The Nation, Education, and the 'Indian Problem' in Mexico, 1920–1940," in *The Eagle and the Virgin: Nation and Cultural Revolution in Mexico, 1920–1940*, ed. Mary Kay Vaughan and Stephen E. Lewis (Durham, NC: Duke University Press, 2006). Sources on the *Tarahumara* are less extensive, but two

relevant sources are: Julia Cummings O'Hara, " 'In Search of Souls, in Search of Indians': Religion and the 'Indian Problem' in Northern Mexico," in *Race, Nation, and Religion in the Americas*, ed. Henry Goldschmidt and Elizabeth McAlister (New York: Oxford University Press, 2004); W. Dirk Raat and George R. Janecek. *Mexico's Sierra Tarahumara: A Photohistory of the People of the Edge* (Norman and London: University of Oklahoma Press, 1996).

Among the most famous primary sources on *indigenismo* in Mexico is José Vasconcelos, *The Cosmic Race: A Bilingual Edition*, trans. Didier T. Jaén (Baltimore: The Johns Hopkins University Press, 1997). Also see Jeff Biggers' memoir, *In the Sierra Madre* (Champaign: University of Illinois Press, 2006), where he describes the year he spent among the *Tarahumara* in northern Mexico. For a 1930s anthropological account of travel and life among the *Tarahumara*, see Robert Zingg, *Behind the Mexican Mountains*, ed. Howard Campbell, John Peterson, and David Carmichael (Austin: University of Texas Press, 2001).

For a fascinating primary source, watch *The Forgotten Village*, dir. and prod. Herbert Kline, 67 min. (Eureka, CA: Pan-American Films, Inc., 1941 [2005]), DVD. Written by John Steinbeck, it is a documentary-style film that explores the conflict between the state's vision of progress and a rural Mexican village's culture and traditions. For a melodramatic love story set in the early twentieth century about a daughter of a prostitute, watch *María Candelaria*, dir. Emilio Fernández, 102 min. (San Diego: Grupo Nuevo Imagen, 1944 [2007]), DVD. Also see *La pasión de María Elena/ The Passion of María Elena*, prod. Mercedes Moncada Rodríguez and Javier Morón Tejero, dir. Mercedes Moncada Rodríguez, 76 min. (Chango Films, dist. First Run/Icarus Films, Brooklyn, NY, 2003), videocassette.

Chapter 18

Rescuing the Sacred Mission of Motherhood: Brazil's Campaign for Healthy Babies and Educated Mothers

Okezi T. Otovo, University of Vermont

The two graduation speeches from the Brazilian Puericulture School in this chapter illustrate the social complexities of the maternal and child health movement of the early twentieth century. The *Escola de Puericultura* (the Puericulture School) in Salvador, Bahia, was the first of its kind in Brazil; young ladies of high society took classes there in scientific child-rearing, or *puericultura,* based on medical theories first promoted by nineteenth-century French obstetricians such as Dr. Adolphe Pinard. Professional training at the school entailed four months of coursework, including both theory and applied knowledge as students practiced their skills on the babies enrolled in the school's free daycare for working mothers. Students were also required to spend a significant portion of the course assisting at the Catholic orphanage of the *Santa Casa de Misericórdia.* Through a combination of instruction in hygiene, anatomy, development, and feeding with practical experiences and observations, school officials expected that their carefully guided scientific approach to infant and child hygiene would help reduce the high mortality rates among children under two years of age. To emphasize this expectation, Dr. Álvaro Pontes Bahia, president of the Bahian League against Infant Mortality, typically took the floor and gave a speech at the school's biannual graduation ceremonies, congratulating the newest graduates and encouraging them to maximize their training.

Public concern over maternity and infant mortality was not new in Bahia. In the late nineteenth century, Bahian physicians at the medical school had begun to decry the nation's high infant mortality rates as a sign that Brazil continued to lag behind more advanced and industrialized countries. The situation of the state of Bahia seemed particularly dire at the turn of the century, following the 1888 abolition of slavery and the 1889 establishment of the Republic. While southern Brazil benefited from a booming coffee economy and extensive European immigration, industrialization, and urbanization, the sugar-producing northeast had already lost much of its national importance and influence. The state of Bahia had an overwhelmingly black and brown population, experienced widespread rural unrest, and failed to attract European immigrants due to its struggling economy. With little chance of "whitening" its population through immigration and miscegenation as southern Brazilian elites anticipated, Bahian intellectuals and policy makers attempted to cure Bahians' supposed backwardness through scientific population reform.

Like their counterparts across Latin America, Brazilian intellectuals of the early twentieth century turned away from explicitly racist explanations for the nation's economic and political challenges and focused instead on resolvable public health problems such as disease and infant mortality. Bahian physicians remained at the forefront of progressive ideologies of the integration of science into public health policy and were clearly influenced by the growing science of *eugenics. Eugenics* was a worldwide movement aimed at social improvement through the control or manipulation of reproduction. Whereas United States and European eugenics movements were often explicitly racist and repressive, Latin American proponents of *eugenics* generally attempted to intervene in the lives of their fellow citizens during their reproductive years and influence how people made choices about health, marriage, birthing, and child-rearing. Even in Latin America, however, racial and class ideas influenced whom *eugenics* proponents targeted for their interventions. Puericulture was one expression of this type of campaign.

As the puericulture movement grew, local physicians in Bahia founded several preventive child health care clinics for poor families, and the state government established its own public initiatives, attending to the health needs of thousands of children. This development marked a significant rupture from the previous state practice of generally leaving children's health concerns to religious orders. By the 1930s, every child was a public concern—in theory—as the state apparatus extended its reach to focus on health rather than illness.

In 1938, under Dr. Bahia's leadership, the Bahian League against Infant Mortality founded the Raymundo Pereira de Magalhães Puericulture School based on the principle that female education was the key to the prevention of infant mortality. Physicians and nurses taught a series of courses to young women and even primary school girls on the latest, scientifically proven methods for taking care of children, hoping that their young students would later avoid the parenting mistakes that physicians attributed to be the cause of the majority of childhood deaths. School leaders further hoped that their influence would reach far beyond the walls of the classroom, expecting graduates to advocate use of their newly acquired techniques not only within their own families but also among poor women. Often graduates of the Puericulture School became visiting nurses, canvassing poor neighborhoods, inspecting the homes of pregnant women and new mothers, and instructing those mothers in the latest tenets of scientific child-rearing. Graduates organized women's assistance associations, sponsoring free pediatric clinics, free daycares, and maternal soup kitchens. They hosted and attended bazaars and galas to raise money for maternal causes.

By the 1930s and 1940s, a significant community of Brazilian physicians, scientists, politicians, and cultural figures became concerned with the quality and quantity of the population and advocated for direct social interventions that could promote a national regeneration. Maternal and child health programs gained even greater public attention under the *Estado Novo* of President Getúlio Vargas[1] as he promoted a number of new laws and national programs aimed at aiding working men and women and their children such as setting a minimum wage, protecting child laborers, and providing subsidies for poor families. Although Vargas disregarded many of these programs in practice, Bahian reformists widely regarded him as a champion of child health and welfare and an advocate for programs to assist poor mothers.

Poor black women were particularly implicated in this reform movement due to the high mortality rates of poor children and their role as the primary caregivers for children of all classes. Black women's social position had changed little since abolition: Most continued to work as domestic servants, and the modern concern over children's health ensured that their family lives would continue to be open to outsiders' supervision. Though poor women were the focus, the infant hygiene campaign needed female allies from other sectors as well, frontline advocates for science in the home who could offer their social tutelage to poorer women. These wealthy,

educated female advocates received professional certification at the Puericulture School.

The following two documents are speeches given at the closing ceremonies of the Puericulture School in the 1940s. In the first, the president of the Bahian League against Infant Mortality, Dr. Álvaro Pontes Bahia, congratulated the graduates. In the second speech, student Ms. Leticia Fernanda Sigueira Trigueiros spoke on behalf of the graduates, summarizing their experiences in the course and expressing their appreciation to their teachers. Trigueiros was one of fourteen young women receiving certificates in puericulture that day; she spoke eloquently on the role of mothers in a changing society. In keeping with their commitment to social action, the graduates invited Mrs. Maria Esolina Pinheiro—affectionately called the class "godmother"—to be the guest speaker for their class. Pinheiro was a prominent social worker, child advocate, and educator who best represented the responsibility of society women to champion the cause of children, particularly those born to so-called "uneducated" mothers. As Trigueiros delivered her speech in November of 1941, her audience included families of the graduates, prominent members of society, media representatives, local politicians, and even Isaías Alves, Secretary of Education and Health for the State of Bahia.

The documents in this chapter demonstrate changing concepts of gender and nationalism in early twentieth-century Brazil, particularly concerning the pursuit of national, scientific progress through "proper motherhood." Modern society encouraged a participatory role for middle- and upper-class women as mothers of the nation, and assuming responsibility for public health created a new relationship between ordinary citizens and their state. Race was no longer the primary arena for discussing social problems. As the wealthiest sectors of Brazilian society modernized and debated twentieth-century nationalism, however, the vision of the "other" Brazil was never far from the minds of intellectuals and reformers. Abolition and the promulgation of new ideas about "raceless nationalism" did not eliminate the close correlation of race and social position or the tendency of the wealthy to see the darker, poorer classes as the primary impediments to national progress.

---

[1]President Vargas established an authoritarian government termed the *Estado Novo* (1937–1945) with the explicit goals of promoting deep and lasting economic and social reforms.

Questions to Consider:

1. How did the authors connect women's "sacred mission" as mothers to larger issues of Brazilian society? What role did they think women should have in solving social problems?
2. How did both speakers discuss the issue of modernity versus tradition—Brazil's past and its future? What evidence can you find in the documents that they were ambiguous as well as excited about the modern family and women's role in it?
3. Based on the readings, how was mothering related to class in 1940s Bahia? Do you get a sense that the authors envisioned divergent roles for different classes of mothers?
4. Afro-Brazilians made up the demographic majority, and the overwhelming majority of the poor, yet neither Dr. Bahia nor Trigueiros ever mentioned race when discussing mothers' contributions to Brazil's future. Thinking back to the introduction to the chapter on "Raceless Nationalism," why do you think race was not discussed?

Álvaro Pontes Bahia, Closing Speech, Graduation Ceremony – *Escola de Puericultura* (circa 1940)[2]

. . . [I]t is just that upon celebrating one more diploma ceremony for students that completed the intermediate course, [we celebrate] the joy of young women whose efforts and dedication is united with the satisfaction of the instructors of this institution. This satisfaction is not only for one more victory, but also for the incentive and applause that such a useful and laudatory initiative brings to Bahian society, represented by this select audience. [. . .]

Certainly, you are convinced today that I do not exaggerate when I declare that teaching puericulture must be the foundation of the campaign in favor of children's health and welfare. No one doubts that "the more children are valued, the more maternal education must be valued." All agree that puericulture education should be ample and obligatory for future mothers, following the incisive opinion of the great Pinard. That is that "young women should learn to care for children as well as they learn to read and to count." Learning technical notions about how to watch over the health of the child is not a waste of your time; first you accumulate wealth that will pay compensatory

interest when you are mothers of families. But puericulture education should not be seen only from the angle of preparation of future mothers. Along with an education oriented to the sacred mission which nature exhorted of woman – maternity, puericulture education also seeks to awaken in her an interest in the social aspects of childhood assistance. Pay close attention that you are not only future mothers of families: you are also puericulture experts. That is to say, you are guardians of the health and welfare of children.

From this day, you take on this new obligation to the society and the nation. The diploma that you have earned grants you the condition of agents in this legion of self-sacrificers whose motto is to work for the child. And you take on the duty, at times both gentle and severe, to propagate that which you have learned, to combat routine, to sweep away misconceptions and abuses, to educate – in sum, to cooperate in the elevation of the Fatherland and to serve humanity. Hopefully, your hearts are truly animated with apostolic inspiration for the well-being of children. You can do and inspire so much. The protection of children is without a doubt the singularly propitious terrain for female activities. This is because innate reserves of maternal sentiments reside in the hearts of women and appear, as if by enchantment, before the suffering of a child – to the point when the sweet miracle of transformation

---

[2]*Source:* From the archives of the Liga Álvaro Bahia contra a Mortalidade Infantil, Hospital Martagão Gesteira in Salvador, Bahia, Brazil. O.T. Otovo obtained permission to use the photo in her scholarly works.

This photograph shows the 1943 Puericulture School graduating class. How did these women dress, groom, and pose themselves for the ceremony? How does their appearance in the photograph reflect the ideas evident in the document excerpts about women's proper social roles and behavior?

Source: From the archives of the Liga Álvaro Bahia contra a Mortalidade Infantil, Hospital Martagão Gesteira in Salvador, Bahia, Brazil. Photograph courtesy of Okezi T. Otovo.

into true mothers occurs, awakened and overjoyed with affection for someone else's little ones as for the children of their own love. [This] assures an incontestable superiority [over men] in eagerness to support children.

Over the course of these four months, you witnessed the daily unfolding of the most moving scenes: of children who experienced hunger and suffered all manner of discomforts or were victims of lack of culture – as misery and ignorance are partners in the destruction of thousands and thousands of lives of tender and innocent children; of others who have never known one day of joy or happiness—nor have the right to be children because they were abandoned in orphanages or raised aimlessly, the great majority illegitimate, socially anonymous. Of others still, small ones suffering from serious illnesses who were brought across great distances to outpatient clinics, feverish, exposed to sun and rain because no hospital bed exists in this city for children of this age. Single

mothers who seek to alleviate themselves of their children in order to live [who find] no support in the law and [are] victims of the injustices of men. These children, in a lamentable social paradox, rather than being an enchantment become an impediment to their mothers' existence. Or other women who, abandoned by their partners of many years, struggle, surrounded by all manner of deprivations and misery, only to ensure scarce sustenance for their disheveled and undernourished children – victims of the collective injustice and indifference of men that still have not come to understand the preeminence that the protection of childhood should occupy.

Dear friends and goddaughters. It is worth emphasizing the fact that no formal pledge is pronounced upon receiving the diploma that this School confers. However, we all are certain that you will pledge yourselves not to diminish your enthusiasm and interest for the cause of the child. You know the duty and responsibility that falls

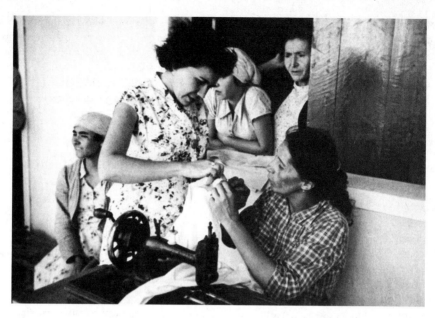

In this photograph (year unknown), a female home economics advisor assists a Brazilian woman working at a sewing machine on the porch of her new home in Mimosinho. A few other family members look on nearby. How does this photograph reflect the assumptions about gender, class, and domesticity that one encounters in the Puericulture School speeches in this chapter?

Source: UN/DPI PHOTO/United Nations.

upon you to cooperate in the campaign for the Brazilian child. You are familiar with the so-called "Rights of the Child" in detail, as well as the "Children's Charter:" the Rights from the famous Geneva conference and the other promulgated in one of the memorable meetings at the White House.[3] You are informed of the disadvantageous situation our country finds itself within the ranking of nations, particularly for infant mortality, and that one can estimate the prosperity and culture of a people through these mortality coefficients is not an unknown concept to you. You are thoroughly familiar with the remedies used to combat this social ill, so compromising to our

claims as civilized people – especially the role of educative measures. And finally, you are aware of how valuable your condition as guardians of the health and welfare of children can be.

Closing this meeting, from which I will take a pleasant memory, I am certain that I need not exhort you to cultivate your enthusiasm in favor of the child. I am certain that you will dedicate a little of your time and your efforts to the unfortunate children whenever you can. And the proof of this is the elegant and generous party where you were the first to rush to aid the appeal formulated by the Bahian League against Infant Mortality . . . giving support for the idea of a patrimonial fund, capable of amplifying the radius of their activities in benefit of children.

It does not matter that you may imagine your contribution to be modest. This is just at face value. At base, it is magnificent. Take notice that it is a seed. Small are the seeds from which majestic

---

[3]Here Dr. Bahia was making reference to the "Geneva Declaration of the Rights of the Child" adopted by the League of Nations on September 26, 1924; and President Hoover's "Children's Charter" part of the 1930 White House Conference on Child Health and Protection.

trees grow. Your captivating offering, that so moves and encourages us, is a good seed from which the work we aspire to will blossom and develop well into the future. We could not have wished that the sowing of this field, ploughed by kindness, were more auspicious and spoke better to

the hearts of those who promoted the idea. The leaders of the League against Infant Mortality and in particular the teaching corps of the Puericulture School applaud your gesture and gratefully kiss your generous and noble hands.

Be happy, dear goddaughters!

Leticia Trigueiros, Graduation Speech, *Escola de Puericultura* (November 24, 1941)[4]

Most Excellent Mr. Secretary of Education and Health, Most Excellent Mr. Director of this School, Dear Professors, Most Excellent Mrs. Maria Esolina Pinheiro, Ladies, Gentlemen, and Colleagues:

Today, more than ever, we see the evidence of the problems concerning Maternity and Childhood and the evolution of human society, paired with incessant social transformation, that effect the mater cell of Christian society which is the family. A problem whose solution is infinitely difficult due to its complexity.

Without a doubt resulting from the demands and imperatives of modern life, the woman who until yesterday was only the companion of a man, the soul of the home, became the collaborator, if not the competitor in almost all sectors of human activity. Dislocating her energies and her spirit for needs and cares very diverse from those that constituted, since the oldest times, her reason for being: the noble and supreme end – to generate and to educate.

To generate is to create; it is to form the physical being, the exterior. To educate is to form the interior being, to awaken the sensibilities, the reason, the intelligence and the character.

It is within the home, the heart of the family, where this miracle blossoms because the home cannot be substituted.

However, it saddens us to say that we feel everyday that the home loses its sense of being a home. . . .

The vertigo of the century, the pursuit of pleasure, of enjoyment, this wave that impregnates the modern generation with lightness and futility rolls over this life tarnishing all that it has that is dignified and truly noble.

With that characteristic capriciousness, this wave irreverently invades respectable areas. It disturbs, confuses, disorganizes, and destroys.

The . . . institution of the family was not immune to the malevolent action of this creator of chaos. This undesirable introduction exposed the family to the most serious dangers.

One thinker said that in some ways we are witnessing a "civilization in transition." Nothing could be more exact. And the disorder that produces this transition results, without a doubt, from the false understanding of woman in modern society. In spite of her unique capacity, she cannot attend with efficiency to such heterogeneous needs such as those of the home and specialized work, activities that transfer her from her orbit – the family.

And as the home is the more complex of the two, the one which requires the greater expense of energy, we see her sacrificing herself for this diffusion of activities.

By this we do not mean to say that a woman should excuse herself from work outside the home when needed as a source of income and whose absence would disrupt the equilibrium of the family budget. No, women adapt so well to productive labor directed towards social work. [This work adapts] not just to her capacity, inferior to men only in regards to uninterrupted work, but also to her sensibilities—to her physical make-up. All unanimously recognize

[4]*Source:* "Untitled speech" given by Leticia to the graduates of the Escola de Puericultura. Taken from the archives of the Liga Álvaro Bahia Contra a Mortalidade Infantil; Salvador, Bahia, Brazil. Published: *Estado da Bahia,* 25 November 1941.

the natural tendency that women have toward social works. So much so that Paul Strauss stated, "Social Service should be practiced preferably through female assistants, expressions of devotion, tenderness, and ingenuity."

The objective of the modern woman then would be the mastery of the professions for which she is most apt. Professions that do not complicate—on the contrary that facilitate—her activities in the home which constitute her primordial concern.

In this course that we have just finished and that we will greatly miss, after four months of collaboration and sharing of ideas, we not only learned to care for children and to perfect and cultivate the maternal instinct. No. One aspect of life was revealed to us that had until now gone entirely unnoticed—the damages resulting from the ignorance that exists among our poor classes. This ignorance can be seen from the lack of awareness of the most elementary notions of hygiene to the use of primitive treatments – the survival of illusions and superstitions.

And we learned, therefore, that the goal of this course was much more extensive than we had supposed at the beginning. It was more than a course on scientific disclosure, on the principles of Puericulture. They did not only teach us the necessities for having strong and educated children based on the principle that "education begins in the cradle." It went beyond this to instill in each one of us the desire to "serve," to make life a little better for those who have nothing and dare not hope for anything. [. . .]

. . . The generation that preceded us dreamed of political reform. Social evolution was on everyone's lips and in everyone's minds. They clamored, with loud shouts, for reforms. With disordered desire, they agitated to the restless masses.

And our ideology is that nothing is feasible without the education of the masses. Our generation had the merit to perceive that this education is a slow process; it requires time and clear understanding of the problem of educating and instructing the most disfavored classes so that they will occupy their place in society, not through strikes and disorder, but by recognizing their value. Infant hygiene and prenatal clinics, hospitals and dispensaries are not worth anything if we do not have a population capable of utilizing and enjoying their benefits. It is this work

that is required of women in our day. And of all these problems that require solutions, that of childhood which goes hand in hand with maternity is certainly the most important, as these are one in the same.

We must by all means maintain the classic binominal – mother and child. Remembering always that "every child that is removed from maternal intimacy has his life put at risk."

Every woman carries within her, in a latent state, the ability to form characters, to shape personalities, to generate a being that will be the continuation of her ideas, a being to whom she can communicate her own qualities. How else can one explain the love that girls have for dolls if not the appearance of the maternal instinct? And this tendency, despite the futile upbringing and the greed for pleasures that the majority of our young women receive, has not changed until today. We still find this love for "the child" sung and celebrated by all poets everywhere. [. . .]

No longer is it simply the customary tenderness for children that women feel, the maternal instinct—which though beautiful, true, and verifiable, is not enough in itself for the wellbeing of children. Children will certainly benefit from a maternal heart, but they will not be protected from the illnesses that are horrendously transmitted particularly in the first year of life, thereby increasing infant mortality which is so elevated among us.

Being a mother is not simply conceiving and giving birth. A true mother is she who makes of her child, the completion, the perfect complement of her being to whom she provides physical and spiritual sustenance.

It is she who knows her child best, not only due to being in intimate conviviality with him but also the almost supernatural power to decipher, through just babbles and gestures, the blossoming of sentiments, of desires, of the total complexity of a being in formation. And later she will know how to console him in the small and great disappointments of life.

As Pasteur stated, "two sentiments strike me when I come close to a child, one is tenderness for the present, [and] the other is respect for who he may become one day."

The present and the future of the child are in your hands. He will be your guardian angel, preparing you to receive him, not only with your maternal love, but also to raise him eugenically, thereby avoiding future pain and anguish.

God created woman to be a mother. It is necessary therefore that the sex labeled fragile be equipped with total fortitude so that she can perform this great mission of which she is responsible.

Dear Colleagues:

Let me express my gratitude for your gesture of confidence, giving me the honor that so touched me of being the voice of your thoughts and your elation in the expression of today's ceremony.

Your thoughts, which are mine as well, that the results of this learning would not end today, [but would continue through] the exchange of ideas and the healthy spirit of collaboration.

To the distinguished teaching staff of this school, a group representing the real values of our land, we express our most profound gratitude, along with our admiration that is as immense as it is justified.

To the spirit of our beloved godmother – all the sensibilities of our affection.

And to the eminent educator and illustrious Secretary of the State, Dr. Isaías Alves de Almeida – in homage of our respect and admiration.

Suggested Sources:

The early twentieth century brought new ideas about political and social *liberalism* that opened up new possibilities for women's political and economic activities. See Susan Besse, *Restructuring Patriarchy: The Modernization of Gender Inequality in Brazil, 1914–1940* (Chapel Hill: University of North Carolina Press, 1996). Even so, traditional ideas about patriarchy and social class continued to structure family life. For the example of Bahia, see Dain Borges, *The Family in Bahia, Brazil 1870–1945* (Stanford, CA: Stanford University Press, 1992). For the classic broad study of eugenics in Latin America, see Nancy Leys Stepan, "*The Hour of Eugenics": Race, Gender, and Nation in Latin America* (Ithaca, NY: Cornell University Press, 1996). Among other important works on the topic are: Julyan Peard, *Race, Place, and Medicine: The Idea of the Tropics in Nineteenth-Century Brazil* (Durham, NC: Duke University Press, 2000); Donna Guy, "The Pan

American Child Congresses, 1916 to 1942: Pan Americanism, Child Reform, and the Welfare State in Latin America," *Journal of Family History* 23, no. 3 (1988): 272–291; Irene Rizzini, "The Child-Saving Movement in Brazil: Ideology in the Late Nineteenth and Early Twentieth Centuries," in *Minor Omissions: Children in Latin American History and Society,* ed. Tobias Hecht (Madison: University of Wisconsin Press, 2002), 165–180; James E. Wadsworth and Tamera L. Marko, "Children of the Pátria: Representations of Childhood and Welfare State Ideologies at the 1922 Rio de Janeiro International Centennial Exposition," *The Americas* 58, no. 1 (July 2001): 65–90. Ideological changes did not bring revolutionary social change, especially for poor women. See Barbara Weinstein, "Unskilled Worker, Skilled Housewife: Constructing the Working-Class Woman in São Paulo, Brazil," in *The Gendered Worlds of Latin American Women Workers: From Household and Factory to the Union Hall and Ballot Box,* ed. John D. French and Daniel James (Durham, NC: Duke University Press, 1997), 72–99. Despite new forms of assistance, poverty continued to have a profound effect on mothers' survival strategies throughout the twentieth century as analyzed by Nancy Scheper-Hughes in *Death without Weeping: The Violence of Everyday Life in Brazil* (Berkeley: University of California Press, 1992).

For one of the most famous academic accounts of family life that reveals as much about the dominant perspectives of their times as the worlds it sought to describe, see sociologist Gilberto Freyre's *The Masters and the Slaves: A Study in the Development of Brazilian Civilization* (New York: A. A. Knopf, 1946). Ruth Landes documented her research experiences in Bahia, Brazil, in the 1940s as she investigated the gendered dynamics of traditional Afro-Brazilian religion and was often surprised that race and gender dynamics defied her expectations. See Ruth Landes, *The City of Women* (New York: McMillan, 1947). Diaries can be an excellent source of information about both family life and broader race, class, and gender issues. See Helena Morley, *The Diary of "Helena Morley,"* trans. Elizabeth Bishop (New York: Farrar, Straus and Cudahy, 1957); and Carolina Maria de Jesus, *Child of the Dark: The Diary of Carolina Maria de Jesus,* trans. David St. Clair (New York: Mentor/Penguin, 1963).

Section V

Gender and Struggles with Conformity in the Twentieth Century

Ecuador, 1929
Brazil, 1932
Uruguay, 1932
Cuba, 1934
El Salvador, 1939
Dominican Republic, 1942
Panama, 1945
Guatemala, 1945
Venezuela, 1947
Argentina, 1947
Chile, 1949
Costa Rica, 1949
Haiti, 1950
Bolivia, 1952
Mexico, 1953
Honduras, 1955
Nicaragua, 1955
Peru, 1955
Colombia, 1957
Paraguay, 1961

From 1930 to 1980, many Latin American women began entering political and economic spheres in unprecedented numbers. From 1929 to 1961, Latin American countries gradually granted women the right to vote in national elections, providing them a new means of making their ideas and demands heard. Women's concerns, however, varied considerably according to their class, race, and religious or political beliefs. Whereas some feminists advocated equal rights with men, more conservative women rarely challenged the gender status quo. Meanwhile, because of industrialization, many women entered the formal wage labor force for the first time. Although both suffrage rights and wage labor changed women's lives in important ways, long-standing and restrictive gender norms remained largely intact and continued to limit women's social, economic, and political opportunities.

Suffrage had a mixed impact on Latin American women, particularly when one takes issues of class and race into account. Though the years in which women won the right to vote in national elections varied widely, most Latin American countries granted this right around the middle of the century, as the chart above makes clear.

Governments sometimes granted voting rights to women in conjunction with class and race reforms. In Bolivia, for example, women won the right to vote in 1952, the same year that the *Movimiento Nacionalista Revolucionario* (Nationalist Revolutionary Movement, or MNR) came into power, promising reforms to increasingly frustrated—and organized—women, leftists, and indigenous peoples. In other nations, however, the extension of political rights was uneven. In Mexico, men across class and race lines secured the vote with the passage of the 1917 constitution that resulted from the Mexican Revolution. Women, however, did not gain the right to vote in national elections until 1953, following decades of feminist struggle. The gender and class-race contrasts are also noteworthy in Ecuador, where the government granted literate women the right to vote in 1929. However, the literacy requirement disenfranchised the majority of Ecuadorians, who were mostly of indigenous or African descent, until it was dropped in 1979. Such policies divided women along class-race lines and poor non-whites along gender lines, reinforcing the political dominance of white male elites despite the expansion of formal political rights. Moreover, granting women the right to vote did not necessarily mean that central government officials were interested in challenging long-standing gender stereotypes. Some male legislators, in fact, had supported female suffrage believing that women would support traditional values, including gender norms, when they voted.

Mid-twentieth-century economic changes also had a contradictory impact on women. Many Latin American nations—notably Argentina, Brazil, and Mexico—experienced significant industrial and urban growth in this period. Traditional gender norms remained intact with industrialization, even though female wage laborers accounted for a significant percentage of the factory workforce and many women were active members (sometimes leaders) in unions. In particular, state officials and industrial elites found ways to *modernize* patriarchy in order to meet their changing objectives with the expansion of the female wage labor force. Politicians often feared that women's movement out of the home would threaten the patriarchal social order, whereas industry owners focused on finding the cheapest possible labor. The solution these groups often proposed to both problems was to define women as unskilled workers who supplemented family income but who ideally belonged in the home. This was not necessarily true, because many working-class women earned the majority of their families' income. Affirming women's supposedly inherent domesticity, despite their

new economic roles, reinforced men's authority over women and justified paying women workers low wages.[1]

Chapters in this section present a variety of women's responses to the modernization of gender norms. The chapter on Eva Perón explores how she often reinforced traditional gender norms even though she herself was a prominent political figure. Susan Besse's chapter on Brazilian anarchist feminist Maria Lacerda de Moura shows that some women rejected long-standing gender stereotypes and double standards.

The last two chapters in the section explore how race, class, and gender intersected to influence women's lives and views. In Cuba, Castro declared that the revolution would liberate women from traditional gender restrictions. Yet interviews conducted by Margaret Randall in the 1970s show that the revolution had, at best, a mixed impact on Cuban women. The section closes with an excerpt from the life story of Domitila Barrios de Chungara, a Bolivian tin miner's wife who worked ardently to secure better working conditions and pay for miners and better living conditions for miners' families. Barrios de Chungara's assessment of gender versus class concerns, as expressed in her observations on an international meeting on women's issues, stands in contrast with Lacerda de Moura's critique of gender norms. Juxtaposed, these two chapters remind readers that there was no single form of "women's protest."

The chapters in this section allow readers to explore different, and often conflicting, meanings of womanhood in Latin America in the middle of the twentieth century. Considered together, they show that it is impossible to categorize this era as either liberating or restrictive for women, because it was both at once. Latin American

---

[1]For an excellent discussion of this process in Brazil, see Barbara Weinstein, "Unskilled Worker, Skilled Housewife: Constructing the Working-Class Woman in São Paulo, Brazil," in *The Gendered Worlds of Latin American Women Workers*, ed. John D. French and Daniel James (Durham, NC: Duke University Press, 1997), 72–99.

In countries such as Argentina, Chile, and Peru, groups of mothers organized to demand the return of their (adult) children who were abducted by their authoritarian governments. In Argentina, for example, approximately 30,000 citizens disappeared under military rule from 1976 to 1982. Government officials claimed to be waging a war against communist subversives who threatened the nation's economic recovery, traditional ways of life, and Catholicism. Although early victims were often leftists or labor organizers, many of the disappeared had no ties to subversive activities. Protest was virtually impossible: Speaking out typically led one to become the next disappeared victim. The Mothers of the Disappeared emerged as one of the only protest groups that could (mostly) survive in this atmosphere. Having failed to locate their children through legal channels, a small group of women began marching around the main square in Buenos Aires in 1976, silently carrying photos of their children. In a short time, their numbers grew to the thousands. The Mothers' protests brought international attention to the atrocities of the so-called Dirty War being waged in Argentina, playing a role in the ultimate demise of the military regime. Look closely at the illustration: How did these women use motherhood symbols to make a political statement? How did their protests problematize the idea that "home" and "politics" are separate categories?

Source: Peter Visscher © Dorling Kindersley Media Library.

women acted on these contradictions in a variety of ways, because their problems, aspirations, and agendas were as diverse as their lived experiences. Rather than try to rectify contradictions like these, it is more fruitful to engage in historical inquiry that explores how and why these paradoxes and initiatives developed, and what their legacy has been.

Chapter 19

Maria Lacerda de Moura Advocates Women's Self-Realization through Free Love and Conscientious Maternity

Susan K. Besse, City College, CUNY

M aria Lacerda de Moura (1887–1945)— Brazilian school teacher, radical feminist, anarchist, and writer—eventually rejected family, religion, and *patria* [fatherland]. She even lost faith in education, which she concluded served only to "conserve the fossil of a reactionary past in the dominion of priests, kings, demagogic democrats, the military, and riches."[2] Only by abandoning prejudice, dogma, and tradition, she argued, could women regain dignity and put their intelligence at the service of their own conscience rather than at the service of men. Her alienation from male-defined projects of national progress, political revolution, and religiously conceptualized moral regeneration led her to advocate free love and *conscientious maternity*.[3]

Born in a small town in the rural state of Minas Gerais, Maria Lacerda initially did what was expected of her; she attended normal (teacher-training) school, married at seventeen, and for ten years "led the life that every recently married [middle-class] woman leads:—embroidering, sewing, painting decorations for the house, playing the piano, going for walks, chatting purposelessly, sleeping well and eating better, reading novels, and enjoying relatively good health."[4] Still childless after eight years of marriage, she adopted a four-year-old nephew in 1912. However, by her late twenties, she dedicated herself to serious study and eventually abandoned her family in favor of writing, teaching, and political activism. In 1921, she moved to the city of São Paulo, Brazil's epicenter of tumultuous urbanization, industrialization, and modernization.[5]

Fabulous profits of the region's booming coffee economy had attracted a large influx of European immigrants who swelled the ranks of the city's industrial proletariat. Female and male workers led waves of strikes during the 1910s and 1920s that were met by brutal police repression. The year 1922 marked the founding of the Brazilian Communist Party and the *Brazilian Federation for the Progress of Women*, as well as the first of two major barracks revolts of junior military officers who articulated the desire of middle-class sectors for honest government and social legislation. In the same year, São Paulo's modernist avant-garde organized Modern Art Week; their call for national artistic innovation found its most radical expression in the "Antropofagia Movement," which advocated a ritual, symbolic "devouring" of European values in order to wipe out patriarchal and capitalist society with its rigid social and psychological boundaries.

Stepping into the midst of this social and intellectual ferment, Maria Lacerda experienced a profound change of consciousness. She proudly identified with "the discontented, the disinherited, and the righteous,"[6] and embarked on a search for "isms" that would satisfy her intellectually and could bring about an end to all forms of exploitation. But after years of struggle, she found no lasting community of support nor any political party or "ism" with which she could identify. She had no patience with male-dominated leftist movements, whose radicalism stopped short of critiquing women's subordination. Nor did she feel affinity for Brazil's *liberal* feminists. She broke with the Brazilian Federation for the Progress of Women over its timidity in critiquing women's subordination within the family, its silence on issues of divorce and sexual freedom, and its failure to address seriously issues of central concern to the female proletariat. Nor did she fit in the world of the modernist avant-garde. Moralistic and doctrinaire, not only did she fail to appreciate these artists' irreverent sense of humor, but she expressed contempt for what she regarded as their decadent salons, their frivolous *chic* wardrobes, and their hypocritical embrace of the proletariat while accepting the patronage of the city's coffee aristocracy.

Between 1918 and 1934 Maria Lacerda published more than seventy articles and thirteen books (some of which sold out several editions). However, after 1935, she ceased publishing, retreated into mysticism, and lived out the final years of her life in solitude on an island.[7] Tired, disillusioned, and

---

[2]Maria Lacerda de Moura, *Amai e . . . não vos multipliques* (Rio de Janeiro: Civilização Brasileira, 1932), 35.

[3]By "conscientious maternity," Maria Lacerda de Moura meant maternity that is desired, freely chosen, and the product of genuine love. She believed that conscientious maternity could best be realized outside the bonds of legal marriage.

[4]Maria Lacerda de Moura, *A mulher é uma degenerada?* 3rd ed. (Rio de Janeiro: Civilização Brasileira, 1932), 25.

[5]The only comprehensive study of the life and work of Maria Lacerda de Moura is Míriam Lifchitz Moreira Leite, *Outra face do feminismo: Maria Lacerda de Moura* (São Paulo: Editora Ática, 1984).

[6]Maria Lacerda de Moura, *A mulher,* 138.

[7]The timing of Maria Lacerda's withdrawal from society may have been related to political conflicts in Brazil. In 1935, President Getúlio Vargas banned leftist parties, crushed a leftist uprising, and arrested and jailed thousands of dissidents. This paved the way for him to dissolve Congress in 1938, to assume dictatorial power under a new constitution, to impose press censorship, and to use legislation and the tax code to actively discourage female wage labor.

embittered by the obstacles she had encountered in fighting for change, Maria Lacerda protested: "all women who have achieved self-realization have been either single, widowed, divorced, or badly regarded by their entire family [and society]."[8] "Thus the affliction and the tragedy with which the superior woman fights, alone, heroic, struggling against the current. . . . The tragedy of precursors!"[9]

Indeed, Maria Lacerda de Moura was not alone in her attempt to be true to herself while participating in the larger social struggles of Brazil and the world. In *Plotting Women: Gender and Representation in Mexico*, Jean Franco explores the frustrated attempts of several artists (Frida Kahlo, Antonieta Rivas Mercado, Elena Garro, and Rosario Castellanos) to "plot women as protagonists" into the "master narrative" of Mexican nationalism of the early twentieth century. Ultimately, Franco concludes, these brilliant women who challenged the dominant male paradigms fought lonely struggles. "Without power to change the [male master narrative], they resorted to subterfuge, digression, disguise, or deathly interruption [suicide]."[10]

A few of the other well-known Latin American women of this time whose unorthodox views and lives made them targets of social disapproval and hostile attacks were Brazilian writer/artist/political activist Patrícia Galvão, Puerto Rican factory worker/political activist Luisa Capetillo, Puerto Rican poet Julia de Burgos, Argentinean poet Alfonsina Storni, Colombian political activist María Cano, and Peruvian political activist/poet Magda Portal. Perceived as threatening the order, good customs, and morality of the nation, and rarely understood even by their few supporters, these women—along with many others who are less well known or forgotten—suffered rejection and isolation that stunted their lives and their work.

The following passages come from *Amai e . . . não vos multipliques* [Love and . . . do not reproduce, 1933], a collection of articles previously published in the newspaper *O Combate*. In this ninth of her thirteen books, Maria Lacerda developed her analysis of the nature of women's oppression, extended her attack on the institutions of legal marriage and the family, and elaborated her ideals of free love and conscientious maternity. Like Argentinean and Chilean feminist anarchists of the previous generation,[11] Maria Lacerda de Moura was uncompromisingly hostile to the authority of religion, the state, and the patriarchal family. However, she (like them) offered little practical advice on how to realize the ideals of free love and conscientious maternity, avoided the issue of abortion, failed to call on men to share responsibility for housework and childcare, and interpreted "true" or "pure" love as being first of the mind, second of the emotions, and only thirdly sexual.

Maria Lacerda de Moura articulated a radical viewpoint that very few of her peers were willing or able to act on. The narrowness of the Brazilian market provided only small numbers of women with the economic independence or social status to change profoundly their lifestyle and consciousness. Nevertheless, the fact that her numerous books sold so well suggests that many urban middle-class women probably shared her critique of the sexual double standard and were searching for ways to redefine women's roles and subjectivities within Brazil's rapidly modernizing society.

Questions to Consider:

1. Why did Maria Lacerda de Moura frequently refer to women "slaves" in her writing? Do you find this characterization of women to be useful or misleading? Why?
2. Maria Lacerda de Moura attacked male leftists for their hypocrisy, pointing out that their families were "very bourgeois." The leftists she attacked countered that it was her writings that reflected a "bourgeois mentality." What

[8]Maria Lacerda de Moura, *Religião do amor e da belleza*, 2nd ed. (São Paulo: Editôra "O Pensamento," 1929), 88.

[9]Maria Lacerda de Moura, *Amai*, 190.

[10]Jean Franco, *Plotting Women: Gender and Representation in Mexico* (New York: Columbia University Press, 1989), xxiii.

[11]Maxine Molyneux, "No God! No Boss! No Husband! Anarchist Feminism in Nineteenth Century Argentina," *Latin American Perspectives* 13, no. 1 (1986); and Asunción Lavrin, *Women, Feminism, and Social Change in Argentina, Chile, and Uruguay, 1890–1940* (Lincoln,: University of Nebraska Press, 1995), 129–133.

were the grounds for and the validity of these contrasting points of view?

3. Maria Lacerda attacked bourgeois feminists on the grounds that their efforts to secure legal equality for women, including enfranchisement, ignored women's most important need to be the owner of her own body. How might feminists have responded to her writings?

4. How did Maria Lacerda de Moura define "free love"? How might women's material

circumstances have made "free love" seem threatening, impractical, and/or otherwise unappealing?

5. Why did Maria Lacerda de Moura consider legal marriage to be "immoral"? What for her was a "moral" choice? How did her conservative opponents define "morality" and "immorality" in terms of family relationships? Can one say that one side or the other is "immoral"?

On the Nature of Women's Oppression[12]

The eternally tutored [woman], twice enslaved, in the name of claiming her rights, in the name of female emancipation, in the name of so many causes, of so many idols—fatherland, family, society, religion, morality, good customs, civil and political rights, feminism, communism, fascism, and everything else ending in *ism*, revolutions and barricades—continues to be the same slave, an instrument skillfully manipulated by men for sectarian, economic, religious, political or social ends. [. . .]

Within all [leftist political parties], with the most varied labels, I know those that are interested in nothing but their own liberty and the triumph of their party, without the least concern for women, [being] totally ignorant of her rights and her needs. They are libertarians and their legal family is very bourgeois.

Laborites, syndicalists, fathers of whatever religions, revolutionary or clerical priests, socialists, demagogues and feminists, the so-called free press, political parties, adherents of feminist benevolence, everyone, absolutely everyone seeks to stifle the true inner necessity of the woman. All suffocate her highest aspirations in the chaos of competition among political parties or of all-absorbing material progress, in the insane activity of modern life—for this civilization of procurement of flesh and of consciences. [. . .]

Until today, which was the party or program that presented a solution for the problem of female happiness?

Who remembered to liberate the woman? [. . .]

The most progressive men, those who preach emancipation and liberty for women . . . of others— are like cave men when their own wives decide to put into practice their libertarian theories.

In reality, instead of emancipating herself with [the progress of] civilization and economic emancipation, the woman is enslaved by multiple other factors. [. . .]

Discovering the woman, man or rather society convinced itself that this discovery was going to be extremely profitable. [Society] has established itself as procurer and gigolo and pimp and proprietor: either it exploits female flesh or it exploits female labor or it exploits female sensibility or it exploits female intelligence and guile. Nothing escapes.

Everything is prostitution, outside or inside of marriage.

Rent of just one [woman] for a lifetime or rent of various for a certain time. Rent of the body, rent of labor, rent of knowledge.

The woman lives '*at the service*' of social procurement.

The woman becomes the accomplice of other tyrannies, she is rounded up for another kind of domestication—servility to other dogmas, to the dogmas of parties, of sects, of patriotism, of the resolute fist of athletic competitions[13], of piety in the form of religion or charity.

---

[12]*Source:* Maria Lacerda de Moura, *Amai e . . . não vos multipliques* (Rio de Janeiro: Civilização Brasileira, 1932), pp. 15, 48–53, 60–61.

[13]This is a literal translation. The author scorned competitive sports.

Under the pretext of feminist demands, her reason closes yet again, and the woman positively moves away from the true problem—the human problem, the right to life as an animal on the zoological ladder, the individual claim to oneself, the right to be owner of one's own body, of one's will, of one's desires, of free expression—to live life in all the plenitude of its latent possibilities, to learn to be free and to free oneself from the personal chains of inferior and dominating instincts, fossilized in the subconscious, to rise to yearnings to be something more than an instrument of voluptuousness and of exploitation, to climb one degree higher toward individuality—through the liberty to live according to one's own heart and to think with one's own mind.

As long as the woman lets herself be led by others, by the ingenuity or the malice of parties, programs, votes, charity, duties—idols of the home, society, privileges, conventions:—fatherland, family, religion, the "what will people say?"—she will be the eternally exploited by social destiny, by

human imbecility, by the moralizing procurement of the family and of legality. [. . .]

How distant we are from ourselves!

Doubly a slave; the millennial tutee of man, instrument of voluptuousness or exploitation, servant to the idols of honor, parties, programs—she is the queen of the home, she is the goddess, she is the saint, she is the redeeming angel of all of humanity—in the language of Julio Dantas—the old dandy of this [normative] literature that poisons and corrupts and spoils and puts to sleep and kills the latent energies and delicate intuition of the true feminine nature. [. . .]

I think that the woman has the right to do even all the nonsense that the man does. [. . .] If [men] vote, she can vote too, if they get drunk, if they poison themselves and their offspring with morphine or cocaine, if they prostitute themselves in politics—for what reason do they seek to impede the virtuous wife from amusing herself with *chic* extramarital affairs or with elegant vices such as politics, for example?

The Bourgeois Family[14]

The "social mission" of the woman, her domesticated servility, her slavish loyalty, leads her to subject herself unconsciously to laws, to bow her head to the "incontestable" masculine superiority in all regards, to cultivate her own ignorance, to give birth to children until she exhausts herself and to deliver them stupidly to the *Patria* which, in turn, will offer them as cannon fodder—in order to overfill the coffers of all the Caesars of power and of the dollar.

[Women's social mission] leads her to subject herself to her husband—"head of the couple," because the woman can only be head of the gramophone.

Rights?

Only duties, and nor can she merit anything more as the "queen and goddess and saint of the sacred home."

The family is the legal buttress of private property. [. . .]

The dissolution of customs is a product of the family, just as prostitution is a defense of the family. [. . .]

Ignorance and feminine servility are deliberately cultivated in order that the institution of the family is defended and protected at all cost.

The basis of the family is female slavery, is the criminal preconception of the woman as private property of the man.

Family means: servility, ignorance, slavery, exploitation of the woman. [. . .]

Within the contradictions of bourgeois-capitalist morality, [. . .] everything is done to satisfy the bestial pleasure of the strongest. There exists a police to maintain order and to curb disorder, to curb theft and to watch out for social well being, and [. . .] at the same time to safeguard the morality and good customs of the sacrosanct institution of the bourgeois family. [. . .]

Prostitution is necessary, bourgeois sociologists declare; it is the safeguard of the family and society. But morality and good customs are constrained by

[14]*Source:* Maria Lacerda de Moura, *Amai e . . . não vos multipliques* (Rio de Janeiro: Civilização Brasileira, 1932 pp. 66–69, 81, 83, 86–88, 94, 98–99, 138, 143, 151.

persecuting and regulating prostitution! In our Latin countries, the cult of the hymen, hymenolatry[15] is the cause of barbarous crimes, of tremendous injustices, and moral sadism, of incommensurable misfortunes. [. . .]

According to the code of this moralism, a virgin who gives herself to a man has no option but suicide if she is abandoned. Within this morality, the young woman is *dishonored, lost, ruined* and has to carry the weight of all these attributes that seek to make the human creature useless for life. [. . .] Never did human cruelty sink so low as when it declared that the woman must guard her virginity in order to deliver it to her "husband" on a previously determined day. [. . .]

Strange morality, strange customs: if a young man is a "seducer," a coward, if he conquered through deceit, with promises [of marriage] that he was certain ahead of time never to fulfill, if he "abused," if he refused to "protect" the "seduced"—how is it that the family and society require that the deceived young woman go to live with this same protector and proprietor for her whole life? [. . .]

Hymenolatry of civilized Christians. / Profoundly ridiculous. / [. . .] Miserable morality of colonels, of cowards, of idiots. / The man grows with his adventures, acquires prestige, fame, [and] glories, even and principally among women. / Within the narrow and evil conception of this morality of hypocrites and pimps, morality of masters and slaves, the same act practiced by two individuals of different sexes has the opposite meaning; the woman degrades herself, becomes immoral, is irremediably lost, if she does not find a man to give her the title of *wife* in the presence of the law and social conventions. [. . .]

But the woman does not stop herself from cheating . . . Marriage is an open door for adultery. She lies, deceives, betrays. She makes use of deceit and hypocrisy—the sole arms she has at her disposal. [. . .]

Within the highest degree of Christian morality, the prostitute and the spinster are the two victims of the most sacred institution of the legal family. [. . .] Barbarous is the prejudice of virginity, of chastity forced on the female sex, chastity imposed by law and by society, as is barbarous prostitution that is "necessary" to protect the "purity" of the flesh of *jeunes filles*[16] (as if virgin flesh contained purity of conscience, purity of soul.) [. . .]

The spinster, [. . .] the famous reliquary of the honor of the family [. . .] is the most degraded and the most nonsensical—for the naiveté, the ignorance, and the foolishness with which she sacrifices herself unnecessarily, becoming the object of ridicule and mockery of the whole family for which she sacrificed herself, and of the whole society that imposes this sacrifice on she who does not have the courage to set herself free, consequently, [to be] anti-social. [. . .]

The woman has always been, and is still today, the object of purchase or sale, wronged, maltreated, insulted, despised, ridiculed by society, governed, administered, codified, policed by men, who allow their companion no other way of life but the legalized prostitution of a marriage of convenience or the prostitution [that is] clandestine or of the streets—also legalized by the State which regulates it *pour épater les bourgeois* . . . [17] [. . .]

There is no prostitution only when love is made divine in the joy of living integrally, when a woman chooses her companion freely and does not need his support to sustain herself, because she is not a social parasite [but] lives of her own work. [. . .]

Female consciousness must awake to the only emancipation possible for the woman [. . .]—the emancipation of the mind, of the interior *I* and of the senses to the liberty to dispose of oneself without asking permission from an owner and master and proprietor, inside or outside of legality. [. . .]

To emancipate oneself is to know oneself. To emancipate oneself is to realize oneself. To emancipate oneself is to place oneself outside laws and social conventions, to be as antisocial as possible—without paradox—to love one's fellow creature.

---

[15]Cult of virginity. See the following paragraphs.

[16]The author's use of the French words for "young women" mocks the pretentiousness of the Brazilian elite's identification with foreign culture and language.

[17]French for "to shock the bourgeoisie."

Free Love[18]

The solution to the social question lies in Love and in Conscientious Maternity. [. . .]

Now, to satisfy sexual necessities is not to fall into the extreme opposite, indulging oneself—as happens with the majority of the human species, transforming an organic function into repeated and multiplying acts of licentiousness or lasciviousness, without any control over the senses.

For the superior woman, the solution to the problem [of Love] is, in fact, complex [and] difficult, in the latin milieu of protectors and masters, knights, moralists, Pharisees, [and] monogamous Christians who exhibit the hypocritical comedy of unisexual civilization. [. . .]

If it is difficult among us, latins, [to find] a solution to the feminine problem, if the drama of female emancipation is bitter and inwardly tormenting, if the precursors [who] sacrifice themselves [are] cursed by a civilization of official procurement, it is not hopeless if we look at the problem in its true aspect which is the

individual prism, for there are individual men of great moral valor and admirable sensitivity who are searching for a solution for their own problem of passion, alarmed not to find the kind of female mind that completes and harmonizes with theirs. In the failure to meet one another, there is a near tragedy . . .

[These men] are rare: the man contents himself more easily. Nature makes men only to fertilize on the physical plane . . . and this exigency closes men's minds to appreciating the woman. [. . .] The exceptional man is almost a god.

This is always the basis of the tragedy of the sexes, the drama of being two: the woman loves with her heart, with her feelings. [. . .]

The whole object of education ought to be [. . .] sexual differentiation and psychological or spiritual approximation [of the sexes]—this would be a happy formula. [. . .]

[B]iologically, the woman [. . .] has the same possibilities to attain physical and mental evolution as the man—everything depends on practice and education—like the man has in a latent state all feminine capabilities—more delicate sensitivity, more lively intuition, etc. etc. [. . .] [M]entality has nothing to do with sex.

[18]Source: Maria Lacerda de Moura, *Amai e . . . não vos multipliques* (Rio de Janeiro: Civilização Brasileira, 1932 pp. 158–161, 199–200, 205, 207.

Conscientious Maternity[19]

I prefer [the children of Love] always [to be born] outside of the law: freer, more beautiful, more intelligent, more generous: it is natural selection.

The children of legal marriage that is not a union of love, excepting perhaps the first born, child of a small piece of illusion and curiosity, are generally, children of neglect, of chance, of dowry, of inheritance, of commerce in sum, children of boredom, of self-indulgence, of habit, or even of vice.

The superior woman, the conscientious modern woman, not the suffragist or the authoress of *chic*

salons, the academic *bashleu*[20] or the athletic champion, but the truly superior woman—no longer wants to be the "mother of slaves," and because of this, she is rebelling against the idea of the "master," of the legal proprietor.

She wants to be free and she wants her children to be free. Thus the necessity of learning to have the courage to register them as "children of unknown father"—if their father is not capable of conscientious paternity, and . . . perhaps it would be preferable not even to register them, not to make them citizens, servants of the State and fodder for cannons.

[19]Source: Maria Lacerda de Moura, *Amai e . . . não vos multipliques* (Rio de Janeiro: Civilização Brasileira, 1932 pp. 137, 165, 184–185.

[20]French word meaning "blue-stocking," a disparaging term that refers to elite women who have intellectual or literary interests.

This is the beginning of conscientious Matriarchy.

Thus will be born the children of Love, the children of a Maternity that is desired not imposed authoritatively and accepted servilely [. . .] without protest. [. . .]

It is through conscientious Maternity that the illuminated contours of a new life will be sketched; it will be the extinction of wars, of hunger, of the sinister social prejudices of all of the human species, it is the assault on crimes of passion, it is the abolition of prostitution and of the no less revolting crime of forced chastity for the single woman and of maternity imposed through ignorance on the married woman, it is the end of infanticide, it is the resolution to the question of the law of population. [. . .]

To be a mother in the physiological sense is very little for the woman. Physiological maternity is not always enough for her. Maternity of the spirit is far more transcendent. And in this sense, there are also men who are mothers.

Do not set dogma for individuals. If I had intense desires to be a mother, I know mothers, in considerable numbers, who never desired it. To designate a single path for the woman—maternity—is masculine authoritarianism founded in dogma and repeated servilely by the woman, for the sake of propriety.

In Praise of Individualism[21]

There is nothing except interior joy, individual happiness. We can only aspire to the moral progress of each individual considered as a single unit. [. . .]

[B]y defending her legitimate rights to liberty to love and to free and conscientious maternity, [the woman] makes herself divine, elevates herself to the height of her latent potential. [. . .]

Women's sexual liberty will be the supreme conquest that will completely remodel the old world.

Suggested Sources:

Modernization of the gender system within Brazil's rising urban-industrial society accommodated new opportunities for women while preserving the gender inequality thought necessary to guarantee the order and progress of Brazil's still hierarchical society. See Susan K. Besse, *Restructuring Patriarchy: The Modernization of Gender Inequality in Brazil, 1914–1940* (Chapel Hill: University of North Carolina Press, 1996). The life of Patrícia Galvão is especially revealing of both new opportunities and restrictions that women faced in this period. See

Susan K. Besse, "Pagu: Patrícia Galvão—Rebel," in *The Human Tradition in Latin America: The Twentieth Century*, ed. William H. Beezley and Judith Ewell (Wilmington, DE: Scholarly Resources, 1987), 103–117. The lonely struggles of several Mexican artists—Frida Kahlo, Antonieta Rivas Mercado, Elena Garro, and Rosario Castellanos—are powerfully revealing of female pioneers' frustrated attempts to "plot women as protagonists" into the male "master narrative" of early twentieth-century nations throughout Latin America. Refer to Jean Franco, *Plotting Women: Gender and Representation in Mexico* (New York: Columbia University Press, 1989), chaps. 5 and 6. Early twentieth-century Latin American feminist movements—both socialist and liberal—were key to shaping public debate and the reform of female education and employment, the legal status of wives and mothers, public health and reproductive rights, and suffrage. See Asunción Lavrin, *Women, Feminism, and Social Change in Argentina, Chile, and Uruguay, 1890–1940* (Lincoln: University of Nebraska Press, 1995). Twentieth-century Latin American feminism did not emerge in a vacuum; late nineteenth-century industrialization and urbanization—especially in Mexico, Brazil, and Argentina—gave rise to radical labor movements and anarchist feminist critiques of capitalist exploitation of women workers as well as of

---

[21]*Source:* Maria Lacerda de Moura, *Amai e . . . não vos multipliques* (Rio de Janeiro: Civilização Brasileira, 1932, pp. 162, 164–65.

religious and bourgeois morality. See Maxine Molyneux,"No God! No Boss! No Husband! Anarchist Feminism in Nineteenth Century Argentina," *Latin American Perspectives* 13, no. 1 (1986): 119–146.

The voices of only a few radical Latin American women of this period are available in English-language publications. A Puerto Rican tobacco factory worker, union organizer, and political activist published one of the earliest Latin American feminist treatises in 1911. While advocating socialist revolution, Capetillo argued that women's sexual freedom must be a political priority for the labor movement and central to any true radical agenda. See Luisa Capetillo, *A Nation of Women: An Early Feminist Speaks Out = Mi opinión sobre las libertades, derechos y deberes de la mujer*, ed. and intro. Félix V. Matos Rodríguez, trans. Alan West-Durán (Houston, TX: Arte Público Press, 2004).

Patrícia Galvão, a colorful and ultimately tragic figure of São Paulo's modernist avant-garde, self-published, anonymously, a powerful denunciation of the economic and sexual exploitation of women of the urban industrial working class. See Patrícia Galvão, *Industrial Park: A Proletarian Novel* [1933], trans. Elizabeth Jackson and K. David Jackson, afterword by K. David Jackson (Lincoln: University of Nebraska Press, 1993). Frida Kahlo, one of Mexico's leading painters and the wife of the famous muralist Diego Rivera, documented the last ten years of her turbulent life in a passionate, intimate, illustrated journal. A complete, full-color facsimile edition with translation and commentaries is available. See Frida Kahlo, *The Diary of Frida Kahlo: An Intimate Self Portrait*, intro. Carlos Fuentes, ed. Sarah M. Love (New York: Harry N. Abrams, 2005).

Chapter 20

❧

Eva Perón's Views on Women and Society in Argentina

Erin E. O'Connor, Bridgewater State College

Argentina

Few people in Latin American history are as well-known, or as controversial, as Eva Perón (1919–1952). She has been described as an angel and a whore, a feminist and an antifeminist, a powerful political player and a pawn within Peronism, a martyr and a self-centered self promoter. None of these extreme claims fits the historical data precisely, yet the myths surrounding this woman persist. Even during her lifetime, Eva Perón—or "Evita," as her supporters called her—was a compelling and controversial figure. Her early death from cancer in 1952 only magnified the stories and stereotypes surrounding her life, making it difficult to distinguish fact from fiction. Of course, Eva Perón herself fed many of these myths. This chapter allows readers to evaluate Eva Perón and her relationship to politics and women's rights issues using excerpts taken from one of her autobiographies.

María Eva Duarte was born to a humble family in a small town in Buenos Aires province on May 7, 1919. She was an illegitimate child born into a *casa chica* (secondary family) that her father kept, and her mother had to work to support her five children after their father died in 1925. Duarte left high school when she was sixteen and moved to Buenos Aires where, after many years of small jobs, she found steady work and a modicum of fame as a radio actress. In 1943, Duarte met and began a love affair with then Secretary of Labor Juan Perón. During their two-year romance, Eva Duarte was increasingly involved in Juan Perón's politics; she even maintained support for him when he was arrested in 1945. As a reward, Perón married her, and she was at his side when he campaigned for and won the presidency in 1946. "Evita" was a prominent first lady, making numerous appearances and speeches, and the public, especially the working classes, loved her. The elite, however, held her in disdain and questioned her morals because of her humble origins and acting career. Eva Perón often used elite disapproval to her political advantage, assuring workers that she shared in their struggle against the oligarchy.

Understanding Eva Perón's contributions to her husband's political success requires consideration of Argentine political and economic developments in the early to mid-twentieth century. Argentina had been a major producer of wheat, beef, and leather goods on the world market since the 1890s. The strong economy drew increasing numbers of European immigrants, who often clashed with the elite-run (and military-supported) government. These tensions increased in the 1930s when the Argentine government established *import substitution industrialization*.[1] From 1935 to 1945, the working class doubled in size, with a 62 percent increase in the female wage labor force. Workers were frustrated with wage controls and inflation, but they lacked strong leadership to confront the government successfully. At the same time, many of the owners of industry were foreign born and, therefore, excluded from political participation.

Colonel Juan Perón used Argentina's turbulent situation to his own advantage. A man of middle-class origins who used the military to establish a secure career, Perón participated in a 1943 military coup and was made secretary of the labor department. Although the appointment carried little real power, Perón realized that the frustrated and mostly native-born workers were a potentially powerful block of voter support. He made several concessions to the workers while Secretary of Labor, and he emerged as the "voice of the *descamisados*" (the shirtless ones, as he called Argentine workers). After the military government's failed attempts to arrest or discredit him in 1945, Perón won the presidency in 1946 (and reelection in 1952).

Peronist Argentina was a typical midcentury populist government.[2] Perón gained power through nationalist appeals to the popular sectors, and he presented himself as a paternal figure who intervened on behalf of the poor—but without alienating the industrial elite. He called upon the masses to help him gain the presidency so that he could continue to provide for and protect the poor from powerful elites and military authorities. His followers realized that they were feeding Perón's ambitions, but they believed that the benefits of populism outweighed the costs, particularly because constitutional procedures failed in the past to address their problems.

As president, Perón had to present himself as "father to Argentines," rather than focus on workers exclusively, especially if he wanted to maintain elite and military support. Still, workers remained his core support, and he could not appear to abandon them. Juan Perón turned to his wife, Eva, to take over as the voice of the *descamisados*. Eva Perón called on both her humble beginnings and her acting

---

[1]Import Substitution Industrialization (ISI) refers to the growth of light industry (consumer goods, such as appliances and clothing) to replace manufactured goods that had once been imported from industrialized western nations. This occurred in many non-western world regions, including Latin America, from 1930 to 1950.

[2]See Carlos de la Torre, *Populist Seduction in Latin America: The Ecuadorian Experience* (Athens: Ohio University Center for International Studies, 2000), xi–xii.

This photograph shows an automobile factory in the Peronist era with a portrait of Eva Perón in the background. What does the presence of the portrait in a factory workshop suggest about the importance of "Evita" to Perón's government?

Source: Z. Legacy. Corporate Digital Archive.

talents to fulfill this role. She held no government post, although she did establish the María Eva Duarte Perón Welfare Fund in 1947 to distribute collected funds to the needy. She was hugely popular with the poor, who looked on her as a caring mother figure. Argentine workers even nominated her as a vice-presidential running mate when Perón sought reelection in 1951; high military officials, however, refused to let a woman run on the ticket. Juan Perón submitted to their wishes.

Eva Perón's relationship to women's issues and rights was more complicated than her role as mother to the workers. She led the women's branch of the Peronist political party, and she also participated in the final push to win women the right to vote in national elections in 1947. The Peronist leadership made much of her involvement in the suffrage movement, suggesting that "Evita" had been a driving force behind getting women the vote. In truth, female suffrage resulted from decades of feminist agitation, and Eva Perón's advocacy came quite late in the process. In essence, Peronists attempted to usurp the feminist agenda, claiming its greatest achievements for the Peronist Party, and identifying Argentine feminist agendas as both ineffective and as contrary to the moral order.

Excerpts from one of Eva Perón's (ghost-written) autobiographies show that she had a multifaceted relationship with the cause of women's rights, and reading them can help one to avoid falling into the trap of oversimplifying this important and paradoxical figure in Argentine history. Although Eva Perón was unique in her ability to influence national politics in the 1940s and 1950s, she was caught in a web of gender, modernity, and tradition that was similar to the conflicts that many other Latin American women of her time faced. It is, therefore, no coincidence that one catches Eva Perón contradicting herself when discussing gender and nation in her autobiographical works.

Questions to Consider:

1. How and why did Eva Perón distinguish between "Eva" and "Evita"? What did she see as her purpose as "Evita"?

2. How did Eva Perón discuss the role of "woman" in society? What problems did she think faced Argentine women, and what solutions did she propose?

3. In what ways did Eva Perón contradict herself in this autobiographical discussion of her mission as "Evita"? What do you think these contradictions tell us about the relationship between Peronism and women?

4. What clues do you have in this excerpt about how and why Eva Perón played a critical role in the success of Peronism in the late 1940s and early 1950s?

5. Some scholars have referred to Eva Perón as a feminist, whereas others have claimed she was the polar opposite. Based on the excerpt that follows, where would you place her along the feminist/nonfeminist spectrum? How do you define feminism?

My Mission in Life[3]

Eva Perón and Evita

. . . I could have been the President's wife as others were.

It is a simple and agreeable job: appearing on holidays, receiving honors, getting dressed up according to protocol, which is almost the same as that which I did before, and I think rather well, in theater and film.

Regarding the oligarchy's hostility toward me, I can only smile.

And I ask myself: Why has the oligarchy rejected me?

For my humble origins? For my artistic profession?

But has anyone of that class ever paid attention to such things, in any part of the world, regarding the wife of a president?

Never was the oligarchy hostile to anyone who could be useful to them. Power and money have never had a bad record with a genuine member of the oligarchy.

The truth is something else: I, who have learned from Perón to walk less-trodden paths, did not want to continue with the old model of a president's wife.

Moreover, anyone who knows me even a little, not just now but from before as well, since I was a simple Argentine "girl," knows that I could never have taken part in the cold comedy of the oligarchs' salons.

I was not born for that. To the contrary, I always had in my soul a genuine repulsion for "that kind of theater."

Even more, I was not only the wife of the President of the Republic, but also the wife of the leader of the Argentine people.

Perón's double personality required a double personality of me: on the one hand, Eva Perón, the

[3]*Source:* Eva Perón, *La razón de mi vida* (Buenos Aires: Ediciones Peuser, 1951), pp. 86–89, 263–267, 273–287.

President's wife, whose job is simple and agreeable, a job of holidays, receiving honors, and going to gala functions; on the other hand, Evita, the wife of the Leader of a people, who have placed in him all their faith, all their hope, and all their love.

A few days a year, I play the role of Eva Perón; and in that role I think I do a little better each time, as it seems neither difficult nor disagreeable.

The vast majority of days, however, I am Evita, the bridge between the hopes of the people and Perón's fulfilling hands, the premier Peronist woman, and this does seem to me a difficult job, and one in which I am never totally content with myself.

I have no interest in talking about Eva Perón.

What she does already appears too often in the newspapers and magazines everywhere.

Instead, I am interested in talking about "Evita;" and not because I feel at all vain about this role, but because whoever understands "Evita" perhaps also grasps more easily her *descamisados,* the people themselves, who will never aggrandize themselves . . . they will never turn into an oligarchy, which is the worst thing that could happen to a Peronist!

Women and My Mission

. . . I never imagined that I would one day lead a women's movement in my country, and even less a political movement.

Circumstances opened this path to me.

Ah! But I do not stay in my comfortable role of Eva Perón. The path that opened before my eyes was the path that I took, if to walk it meant to help Perón's cause a little, which is the cause of the people . . .

I recognize that, above all else, I began working in the women's movement because Perón's cause required it.

It all began little by little.

When I realized, I was already presiding over a women's political movement . . . and, along the way, I had to accept the spiritual direction of the women of my Fatherland.

This forced me to meditate on women's problems. And more than think about them, I had to feel them and feel the light of the Doctrine with which Perón began to construct a New Argentina.

I remember the extreme tenderness of my friend and teacher, General Perón, as he showed me the infinite problems of the women in my Fatherland and in the world.

In these conversations I again observed the kindness of his nature.

Millions of men have, like him, encountered the increasingly acute problem of women's place in humanity in this anguished century, and I think that very few of them have stopped to penetrate it as deeply as Perón has.

He showed me in this, as in all other things, the path to follow.

The feminists of the world will say that to start a women's movement this way is not very womanly . . . to begin by recognizing the supremacy of a man!

However, I am not interested in their criticism.

Moreover, to recognize Perón's superiority is different.

Moreover . . . I have committed to writing the truth!

Passing from the Sublime to the Ridiculous

I confess that when I realized that I might be taking a "feminist" path, I was a little afraid.

What could I do, a humble woman of the people, where other women, better prepared than myself, had completely failed?

Submit to the ridiculous? Become one of the nucleus of women who resent both women and men, as had occurred with innumerable feminist leaders?

I was not an old maid, nor so ugly that I had to occupy such a post . . . that, generally in the world, since the English feminists until now, has belonged, almost exclusively, to women of this type . . . women whose first cause would be to be completely like men.

That is how they oriented their movements!

They seem to be overpowered with despair at not having been born men, more than by pride at being women.

They even thought that it was a disgrace to be women . . . resentful of those who did not want to stop being women, and resentful of men because they could not be like them. The "feminists," the vast majority of the world's feminists it seems to me, constituted a rare species of woman . . . one that did not seem much like a woman to me!

I did not feel much disposed to be like them.

One day the General [Perón] gave me the explanation that I needed.

"Can't you see that they are on the wrong path? They want to be men. It is as if in order to save the workers I had tried to make them into oligarchs. I would have been without workers. I think that would not have even improved the oligarchy at all. Don't you see that this class of 'feminists' denounces their womanhood? Some don't even wear makeup . . . because that, according to them, is particular to women. Don't you see that they want to be men? And if what the world needed was a women's political and social movement . . . how little would be gained for the world if women wanted to save themselves by imitating men! On our own, we men . . . have confused everything in such a way that that I do not know if it is possible to fix the world anew. Perhaps woman can save us on the condition that she does not imitate us."

I remember well that lesson from the General.

Never had his thinking seemed so clear and illuminating to me.

That was what I felt.

I felt that the women's movement in my country and in all the world had to carry out a sublime mission . . . and all that I knew of feminism seemed ridiculous to me. That is, led not by women but by those who aspired to be men, it ceased to be about women and was nothing! Feminism had passed from the sublime to the ridiculous.

And that is a step I shall try never to take!

The Home or the Factory?

Every day, thousands of women abandon the feminine sphere and begin to live like men.

They work almost like them. They prefer, like them, the street over the house. They are not resigned to be either mothers or wives.

They substitute for men everywhere.

Is this "feminism?" I think that it is more like the masculinization of our sex.

I ask myself if all this change has solved our problem.

But no. All the old ills continue and now new ones appear. Each day a greater number of young women are convinced that the worst job is to make a home.

And yet that is what we were born to do . . .

No profession in the world has less possibility for reward than our profession as women.

Even if we choose a good man . . . our home is never going to be what we dreamed about when we were single.

Within the doors of the home, the nation ends and other laws and rights begin . . . the law and rights of man . . . that many times is just a master and at times also . . . a dictator.

And there no one can intervene.

The mother of the family lacks any protections. She is the only worker in the world with no salary, guarantee of respect, or a limit to her workday, not even Sundays, or holidays, or any kind of rest, or compensation for wrongful dismissal, nor strikes of any kind . . .

I am not saying that it is always like this. I have no right to say anything, since my home is happy . . .

For that reason each day there are fewer women [willing] to make homes . . .

True homes, united and happy! And each day the world desperately needs more homes and, for that, more women disposed to fulfill completely their destiny and mission. For that reason the first concern of a women's movement that wants to improve women's lives . . . that does not aspire to change them into men, should be the home.

We were born to make homes. Not for the street. Common sense shows us the solution. We have to have in the home what we seek by going out into the street: our own small economic independence . . . that liberates us from turning into poor women without a horizon, without rights and without any hope!

An Idea

In reality, what happens with women is the same as what happens with men, families, and nations: as long as they are not economically independent, nobody gives them any rights . . .

If we do not find a solution to our dilemma, soon an inconceivable thing will come to pass in the world: only less capable women will accept the role of making a true home (not half a home or half a marriage) . . . those who do not find, outside of marriage and the home, another "economic" solution that allows them minimum rights.

A mother's rank in the family would therefore be reduced to a ridiculous level. They would say—and already are saying—that only silly women burn their bridges by marrying, creating a home, burdening themselves with children.

That must not happen in the world!

Moral values have broken down in these disastrous times: it will not be men who restore them to their ancient prestige . . . and nor will masculinized women. No. It will again be the mothers!

I don't know how to prove this, but I feel that it is an absolute truth.

But, how to reconcile all of these things?

For me it would be very simple and I do not know if it is too simple, or . . . impractical; although many times I have seen things which everyone thinks too simple turn out to be the key to success, the secret of victory.

To begin I think that each woman who gets married should be given a monthly salary from the day of her marriage.

A salary that pays all mothers in the nation and that comes from the income of all those who work in the nation, including the women.

No one could say that it was unjust to pay work that, even if one does not see it, requires the daily effort of millions and millions of women whose time, whose lives are spent in the monotonous but difficult task of cleaning the house, tending to the laundry, serving meals, raising children . . . , etc.

This salary could initially be half of the average national salary and thus a housewife, the mistress of the home, would have her own income free from her husband's control.

Later this basic salary could be increased with each child, even more in case of widowhood, losing it if she entered the workforce, in a word, all additions will be considered so long as the initial goals are respected.

I simply propose the idea. If it is workable, it will need to be given shape and converted into reality.

I know that for us, the women of my Fatherland, the problem is neither grave nor urgent.

For that reason I do not yet want to implement the idea. It would be better for everyone to think about it. When the right moment comes, the idea will be ripe.

The solution that I propose is so that the woman who makes a home does not feel inferior to the woman who earns her living in a factory or an office . . .

All this I reminds me a little of Perón's basic program in his struggle to liberate the workers.

He said that it was necessary to elevate the social culture, to dignify work and humanize capital.

I, always imitating him, say that to save a woman, and through her the home, it is necessary also to elevate feminine culture, to dignify her work and humanize her economy by giving her a certain minimal material independence.

Only thus can woman prepare herself to be a wife and mother as she prepares herself for dictation . . .

Thus will many women save themselves from delinquency and prostitution, which are the fruits of their economic enslavement . . .

I have had to create many institutes where children are cared for, wanting to sustain something that is unsustainable: the mother in the home. But I always dream of the day when it will not be necessary . . . when a woman is what she should be; queen and mistress of a dignified family, free of all pressing economic need . . .

A Great Absence

I believe that the women's movement organized as a force in each country and in the whole world should and could do a great good for all of humanity.

I do not know where I read once that in this world of ours, there is a great absence of love.

I, even though I may be plagiarizing a bit, would also say that the world actually suffers from a great absence: that of woman.

Everything, absolutely everything in the contemporary world, has been made according to men's wishes.

We women are absent from government.

We are absent from parliaments.

From international organizations.

We are in neither the Vatican nor the Kremlin.

Nor in the major imperialists states.

Nor in the "atomic energy commissions."

Nor in the large business consortiums.

Nor in masonry, nor in secret societies.

We are not in any of the great centers of world power.

And yet we have always been present in times of agony and in all the bitter times of humanity.

It seems as if our vocation were not to create but rather to sacrifice.

Our symbol should be the mother of Christ at the foot of the cross.

And yet our greatest mission is nothing other than to create.

I cannot understand, then, why we are not found in places where one tries to create man's happiness.

Do we not have the same common destiny as man? Should we not join together for the happiness of the family?

Perhaps by not inviting us to their grand social organizations man has failed and cannot make humanity happy . . .

That explains it: man does not have a *personal* interest in humanity as we women do.

For man, humanity is a social, economic, or political problem.

For us women, humanity is a problem of creation . . . because each woman and each man represent our pain and sacrifice.

Man accepts too easily the destruction of another man or woman, whether elderly or a child.

He does not know what it costs us to create them!

We women do!

For that reason, we women of the whole world, more than our creative vocation, have another to preserve life instinctively: the sublime vocation of peace . . .

When man gives us a place in decision making, the hour will have arrived in which to state our opinion, perhaps less from the head than from the heart.

But is it not our hearts that have suffered due to the errors of men's "brains?"

I do not scorn man or his intelligence, but if all around the world we had created happy homes together, why should we not be able to create a happy humanity together?

That should be our objective.

Nothing more than the right to create, alongside man, a better humanity.

Suggested Sources:

For an English-language translation of the book from which this chapter's selections were taken, see Eva Perón, *My Mission in Life*, trans. Ethel Cherry (New York: Vantage Press, 1953). For another ghost written autobiography, see Eva Perón, *Evita: In My Own Words*, ed. Joseph A. Page, trans. Laura Dail (New York: New Press, 2005). For a fascinating primary source on a woman who worked in the Argentine meatpacking industry, and who offers a different perspective on class and Peronism, that includes historical essays alongside personal testimony, see James French, ed., *Doña María's Story: Life, History, Memory, and Political Identity* (Durham, NC: Duke University Press, 2000). For one of the few documentaries to try to maintain a balanced evaluation of Eva Perón, see *Evita—the Documentary*, dir. Eduardo Montes-Bradley (Hallandale Beach, FL: Patagonia Film Group, 2007). It could be interesting, after finding out about the realities of Eva Perón's life and politics, to view the United States-produced feature film *Evita*, dir. Alan Parker (Los Angeles: Miramax, 1997) and starring Madonna.

The best biography of Eva Perón remains Nicholas Fraser and Marysa Navarro's *Evita: The Real Life of Eva Perón* (New York: W. W. Norton, 1996). For an examination of the relationships between workers and Peronism, see Daniel James, *Resistance and Integration: Peronism and the Argentine Working Class, 1946–1976* (Cambridge: Cambridge University Press, 1994). For a good collection of essays on Peronism, see James P. Brennan, ed., *Peronism and Argentina* (Wilmington, DE: SR Books, 1998). For those interested in the history of feminism and politics, an on the southern cone, including discussions of the drive for the vote in Argentina, is Asunción Lavrin, *Women, Feminism, and Social Change in Argentina, Chile, and Uruguay, 1890–1940* (Lincoln: University of Nebraska Press, 1995).

Chapter 21

A Revolution within the Revolution? Gender and Socialism in Cuba

Erin E. O'Connor, Bridgewater State College

How did ordinary people, and women in particular, experience the Cuban Revolution? In the early 1970s, a little more than a decade after Fidel Castro's 1959 victory over Fulgencio Batista, Margaret Randall interviewed fourteen women from different class and race backgrounds. By then, the communist party was in control of national politics, and new health care and educational systems were in place. Castro had established himself as the official head (*jefe máximo*)

of the Cuban government, but it was not yet clear that this would be a decades-long dictatorship (lasting until 2008). The Cuban leadership was still struggling in the 1970s to overcome Cuba's economic dependence on sugar exports, and social changes were advancing unevenly, including those that pertained to women's status in the newly socialist nation.

In the United States, Castro's revolution is best known for clashes with the United States government (The Bay of Pigs, the Missile Crisis), years of dictatorship and arbitrary arrests, Cuban émigrés seeking political freedom, and the United States economic blockade of Cuba. United States citizens' impressions of Castro and Cuba are shaped by a media, government, and émigré population that are intent on presenting the Cuban Revolution as a one-dimensional dictatorship. Historical evidence, however, suggests that the Cuban Revolution had a multifaceted impact on Cubans that included benefits as well as costs. It is undeniable that the Cuban government has a long record of arbitrary arrests and political censorship. But revolutionary leaders also committed themselves to providing all Cubans with adequate food, housing, and sanitation in order to put an end to hunger and improve their standard of living. Among the most famous of Cuban revolutionary achievements are universal, quality health care and education and government commitment to eradicating racial and gender inequalities.

In a speech before the Cuban Women's Federation in 1966, Fidel Castro proclaimed that the quest for gender equality was a "revolution within the revolution." He noted that Cuban women had lived, traditionally, under the burden of gender stereotypes that identified them with the home and motherhood, and which suggested that only men belonged in the public sphere of politics and the economy. Working-class women, he emphasized, suffered under the double burden of class and gender exploitation. Castro further claimed that women worked tirelessly to break free of pre-revolutionary gender stereotypes, and the revolution was committed to helping them meet their goals. He argued that only a socialist system could fully eradicate sexism and racism, because capitalist exploitation had created and bolstered gender inequalities.[1]

Castro put the power of law behind his promises. In 1963 and 1974, the government established and revised the "Maternity Law for Working Women," guaranteeing pregnant women free and adequate health care during and after their pregnancies. Maternity leave rights allowed for six weeks of paid leave before delivery and twelve weeks of paid leave after the birth of a child; women could take further unpaid leave and still be guaranteed their jobs when they decided to return to work.[2] The 1975 Family Code asserted that "both partners must care for the family they have created" and stated that both marriage partners had the right to practice a profession.[3] Government decrees even suggested that men should help with housework and encouraged the production and distribution of appliances to make housework easier. Daycare centers were established to ease mothers' transition into the workforce. In addition to reducing domestic burdens that kept women from entering the workforce, the new laws advocated a fundamental change in gender ideologies and relations.

The Castro regime did not advance women's rights simply out of an abstract commitment or altruistic ideal. The revolutionary government of the 1960s and 1970s needed women, including new mothers, to enter the workforce in unprecedented numbers in order to meet industrial and agricultural production goals. Moreover, Cuban women's political support was as important to the revolution as was men's, and addressing gender equalities was a

---

[1] Fidel Castro, "The Revolution within the Revolution," in *Women and the Cuban Revolution*, ed. Elizabeth Stone (New York: Pathfinder Press, 1981), 51–52.

[2] See "Law No. 1263: Maternity Law for Working Women," in Elizabeth Stone, 134–139. Consider how this compares with the United States Family and Medical Leave Act, which was not passed until 1993, and only requires employers to give women six weeks of maternity leave, which does not have to be paid.

[3] "Appendix B: The Family Code," in Elizabeth Stone, 146–147.

way of seeking this support. Yet, no government can legislate attitudes: Cuban women may have enjoyed new legal rights, but they still faced double standards that allowed men more sexual freedom than women and identified women with motherhood and housework.

United States journalist and activist Margaret Randall, who conducted the interviews presented in this chapter, published a plethora of books that bring Latin American women's voices to the English-speaking world.[4] Her works on Cuba and Nicaragua are particularly famous, as is her ardent and open belief that "socialism and feminism need each other."[5] Despite Randall's socialist perspective, her works are extremely useful for anyone interested in Latin American women and socialism. Randall did little to hide her commitments to socialism and feminism, making it relatively easy to evaluate this impact of her views on her work. She also often included her questions along with women's answers to them, so that readers can infer how her questions might have influenced the ways that women described their lives. Her forthrightness in this regard stands in stark contrast with the many journalists and scholars who, instead of presenting interviews as a series of questions and answers, paste answers together into a seamless narrative as if the interviewer had not taken part in shaping the answer through her or his questions. Perhaps most important, Randall captured the voices and views of women from a variety of backgrounds during moments of critical sociopolitical change. If her motives and aspirations were politically weighted,

her work is nonetheless rich with historical import for anyone interested in Latin American gender, politics, and society.

The excerpts that follow are from women of different ages and class-race backgrounds in Cuba. These women all spoke at a moment in Cuban history when the revolutionary government was still in the midst of trying to make its commitment to gender equality a reality. None of these fourteen women was or is famous, but their words teach one a great deal about what it meant to "live the Cuban Revolution." As with other chapters in this section, these Cuban women make it difficult to label the revolution's impact on gender relations as either successful or ineffective. Instead, they force twenty-first century readers to consider more deeply the achievements, costs, and limits of any government attempt to change deeply embedded social norms.

Questions to Consider:

1. To what extent did these women seem either to shed or uphold traditional gender norms?

2. What evidence do you find in these interviews about how age, race, and class background influenced women's views and experiences of the revolution?

3. What contradictions can you find in any of these women's statements about gender relations under revolutionary rule? What do such contradictions reveal about the revolution's impact on these women's lives?

4. Based on these interviews, would you say that the revolutionary government had mainly succeeded or failed in its proclaimed goal of putting an end to gender discrimination in Cuba at the time these interviews were conducted? Why?

5. How did Margaret Randall shape the tone and flow of these interviews? In what ways did she accept the women's assertions and views, rather than try to mold them to agree with her own perspective?

---

[4]In addition to her work on Cuba, Randall is also famous for *Sandino's Daughters: Testimonies of Nicaraguan Women in Struggle* (New Brunswick, NJ: Rutgers University Press, 1995); and *Sandino's Daughters Revisited: Feminism in Nicaragua* (New Brunswick, NJ: Rutgers University Press, 1994). Also see her book *Our Voices/Our Lives: Stories of Women from Central America and the Caribbean* (Monroe, ME: Common Courage Press, 1995).

[5]This phrase is, in fact, the title she gave to the introduction to her book *Women in Cuba: Twenty Years Later* (New York: Smyrna Press, 1981).

"Fourteen Cuban Women Speak"[6]

Here are the women:[7]

*Julia is twenty-six. She is married, a theater direc-
tor and lives in Havana where she is a member of the
CDR[8] and the Militia.*

*Josefina is a forty-one year old peasant woman,
married and with eight children. Of worker-peasant stock,
she has a fourth grade education and belongs to the
Federation of Cuban Women and the Militia. She lives in
a small village in the province of Havana, and both she
and her husband work in the nearby sugar refinery.*

*María is seventeen. Although she has an eighth
grade education, she works as a waitress because of a physical handicap. Her extraction is worker-peasant and she is
a member of the Communist Youth.*

*Olga is a twenty-four year old urologist. From a back-
ground of workers, she is a member of the Communist Youth.*

*Magda is thirty-nine and works in a city hospital.
She has an eighth grade education and is a member of the
Cuban Communist Party.*

*Miriam is forty, married with two children, works
in a factory and is a member of the Federation, the Militia, and the CDR. She has a sixth grade education.*

*Ana, a thirty-five year old nurse, is another member of
the Cuban Communist Party. Her origin is worker-peasant.*

*Carmen is a journalist for an important mass cir-
culation magazine. She is divorced, lives with her small
child, and is thirty-one years old. She also belongs to a
variety of revolutionary mass organizations.*

*A military woman, Yamila is also a member of the
Communist Party. She is twenty-eight, married with two
children, and has finished ninth grade.*

*Haydée holds an administrative position in a child
clinic. She is forty-seven, single, from a family of small
farmers, and has earned the distinction of "Advanced
Worker."*

*Gloria works in a grocery. She is thirty years old,
married to an ex-political prisoner, comes from a peasant
family and has a sixth-grade education. She doesn't belong
to any revolutionary groups.*

*Rosa works in a factory. She is twenty-three, single,
has a ninth-grade education and belongs to all the revolutionary organizations, including the Communist Youth.
Her background is peasant.*

*Idalia makes films. She is twenty-seven, married
and with two children and is a member of the Federation
of Cuban Women. At twenty-nine, she does intellectual
work in the book publishing industry. From a worker background, she is a member of all the revolutionary mass
organizations and the Communist Youth.*

These are the women, and this is what they say: [. . .]

*Olga, how did you first feel the Revolution in your life?
What changes did it mean for you?*

OLGA: Look when the revolution triumphed, I was
fourteen. I'd just started junior high school,
what we call basic secondary school. There I
met some members of the Socialist Youth
and with them I began to understand things
I'd never understood before. Then the first
real confrontation with reality I had was the
literacy campaign. When they announced
the campaign my father wasn't home; he
was involved in the rooting out of the bandits in the Escambray region. I asked my
mother if I could go and she said not without my father's permission, that that was
something he had to decide. My mother, because I was her only daughter, and we'd
never been separated and all that, she was
afraid to let me go. I wrote to my father and
he said I could go. I joined the brigades and
left with the first group the day before the
Bay of Pigs attack. I was at Varadero during
the attack, and that was an experience I'll
never forget. I always say that my real education was the literacy campaign, because of
being brought up the way I was. When the
Revolution triumphed I knew something
about the peasants here, how they lived and

---

[6]*Source:* From Margaret Randall, "Fourteen Cuba Women Speak:
from *Cuban Women Now,*" (originally published by Women's
Press, Toronto: 1974), 33–49.
[7]Randall's description of the women, and her questions to them,
appear in italics to set them apart from the women's responses.
[8]Comités de la Defensa de la Revolución (Revolutionary Defense
Committees).

all, but I never imagined what it was really like. That was a great experience for me: far from home, in another world, doing things I'd never done before, living and sharing with others and seeing the kind of work we needed to do here. [. . .]

Ana, did you always want to be a nurse?

ANA: In a school play, that must have been around the end of 1949, I played a nurse, and that was the beginning. [. . .] The school I wanted to go to was the Pelegrina Saldá, at the Calixto García Hospital. It was the best nursing school in those years, and where it was hardest to get into. That cost me long hours of tears and study, because I dreamed of something very hard to get. The first time I applied was terrible, that was the year they began measuring and weighing you. I weighed 163 pounds; they told me I couldn't hope to be a student. I had several things against me: the thing about the height and weight; the fact that I was a *mulato*; and I didn't have a recommendation, which was the most important part. For example, there were girls who came and said: Captain so and so sent me, or Lieutenant so and so, or such and such a senator, and I didn't have any recommendation at all. What saved me then was I started to cry; I cried and cried. [. . .]

During those three years of nursing school I got very good marks. When I was graduated I even won a head nurse's position because there was this American and I worked a lot in his pavilion. [. . .] They called me several times. The administrator interviewed me and then they made me wait. Until one of the women there called me over and told me: "Don't be a fool, they're not going to take you; people are talking about you being a *mulato* and the members of the clinic—those are the ones who keep it going—they're not going to take you, not because you're not a good nurse, but because you're a *mulato*!" I never went back.

Olga, how did you enter medical school?

OLGA: Imagine, before the triumph of the Revolution it wasn't easy for anyone to be a doctor; in general there were very few women who studied medicine. And today, if I remember right, there are more women in the school than men. Of course it was a social problem before.

Is this still a problem in any way, or has it been dealt with completely?

OLGA: Well, it's not completely wiped out; there's still the guy here and there who thinks women should be kept from certain jobs, but it's been wiped out to a great extent. And if conditions were better more women would be incorporated into all kinds of jobs.

What kinds of conditions are you referring to?

OLGA: The problems of kids and nurseries, because our development hasn't yet reached the point where we have enough nurseries, so that all mothers can have their children in nurseries.

So you think it's just a material question, or do you think there's still work to be done in terms of women's mentality?

OLGA: Well, there's still the mental thing, but I see more women interested in incorporating themselves into the labor force than I see men interested in women working. Men hold them back a lot of the time. Women's mentality has developed more than men's in that sense.

Haydée, what made you decide to go to work?

HAYDÉE: I started to work when I was twenty-five, because in my house there was this idea that women shouldn't work. We should busy ourselves with the things of the home, and wait for a man to come along and marry one of us, but never go to work. When I told my parents I wanted to work because I saw other women working, it was an insult for my parents.

Idalia, what does your work mean to you?

IDALIA: My work represents a way for me to realize myself intellectually and socially. I went to work because I felt my vocation was film making. I can work without abandoning my home, but I have to make a double effort that threatens my mental health. The Revolution should create better conditions, better laundry and ironing services, reorganize the distribution of foodstuffs, take more into consideration the problem of working women, and wage and ideological campaign against the traditional sexist mentality of men.

Berta, why did you start to work?

BERTA: Basically, because of the money. From the time I was fourteen I began looking for work. But listen to the kinds of jobs I found: once I was offered a job as a strike-breaker and I didn't want that, those were the strikes at the *Casa de los 3 Kilos*;[9] another time I got offered a job through Colonel Orlando Piedra and I didn't want that either. They were always offering you jobs in order to take advantage of you, because you were a young girl, who knows . . . And all that created problems with my father.

I got through school on prizes; remember, in the Institute, how you could get prizes to pay for your tuition? It was by subject—you had to study during the vacations—at the end of each course the best students got the prizes. Each prize was worth three pesos per subject; the tuition to the Institute was six pesos. So I was able to buy my tuition, and the most important

books, second hand, and since I didn't live very far away I came and went on foot.

JULIA: A desire to be socially useful was what motivated me to work, the will to be economically independent and the determination to realize myself fully.

Carmen, are there a lot of women in journalism today?

CARMEN: Oh, lots.

Was it the same before the Revolution?

CARMEN: No, not before, we were a tiny minority, a few old hags.

Do you think there's complete equality between men and women in this field now?

CARMEN: In terms of work? Sure.

In terms of work, I know, because the Revolution sees to that, but what about attitudes?

CARMEN: No, there's no discrimination. I myself have reported from an oil well; I've had to go down into a mine to interview miners, for example, at the Matahambre Mines. The miners were floored to see a woman down there. That was an experience I had as a reporter. They sent me to do this story of Matahambre that has a depth of I don't know how many thousands of feet and when they saw me down there, on the bottom level, they were really surprised because they said that was the first time they'd seen a woman down there. So I don't think so. No, here women journalists do all sorts of things.

Rosa, in your experiences here in productive work, what do you feel about the way men and women work?

ROSA: Well, as far as I've been able to see, up to now, the problem is that . . . look: men work when they're by themselves, of course there's always the exception; there are men who are lazy, alone or not, just like there

---

[9]Randall inserts a footnote here to note that *Casa de los 3 Kilos* was a kind of "5 & 10" store in Cuba before the revolution.

Fidel Castro during a visit to a school in Ciudad Libertad ("Liberty City"), Cuba, in 1964. In the 1960s, Castro enjoyed widespread support among the Cuban people for the numerous socioeconomic reforms his government enacted (the aura of support was further enhanced by the fact that his elite and middle-class opponents had mostly fled into exile). Note how many young women sought Castro's attention in this image. What seemed to be Castro's attitude toward them? Given your reading in this chapter, what hopes did Castro seem to embody for this generation of young women as they came of age? Once you have read through this text, return to this image and consider: How many of those hopes were met, and how many failed to materialize, a decade later?

Source: Corbis/Bettmann. Phyllis Collazo of New York Times/Redux Pictures.

are women who are that way; but men alone produce more than when they're working with women. I can prove it in our brigade. For instance, when we've had to plant cane at one end and we've carried it all the way down, happy as can be, and when we work with men, even when it's a little furrow or two: ah, no, no, no because if there's men then they should carry it! Nevertheless, when we work alone, there's never any problem at all.

GLORIA speaks: Before the revolution I was completely happy. My husband,

through his work, provided me with everything he could, within our limited way of life. I was very comfortable because he took care of everything in the house; he attended to his mother too and I didn't have to think about anything because he took care of everything. When he was arrested I felt so alone, so helpless, and I had to face all kinds of things, even my mother and father got sick. I didn't have anyone to look to, to turn to. I had to carry on and I thought if he'd have been at my side he'd have taken care of everything; I'd have someone to lean on, and it would have been different. When he was arrested I felt so alone, so sad, very sad in the sense that I had to do everything myself and I could and I did. But at the beginning I thought I couldn't. I can take care of myself in every way, but I would have liked, I'd like, well, I'd like it better if he was doing these things, because we women need the support of a man. We need to feel there's someone who thinks, who decides things for us, things that are difficult for us. That's a little bit of support you get from a man, that support so big, like the captain of a ship.

María, who was the maximum authority in your home?

MARÍA: My father.

Why?

MARÍA: Because, well, it was my mother's fault too. Because if my father worked nights my mama let us go to the movies but when he came home we had to be in bed. But she never tried to reason with him, and she let us go only behind his back.

Josefina, does your husband help you in the house?

JOSEFINA: Yeah, he helps me, let's say for instance there's times when I come from the mill at six, times at seven.

He's not prejudiced against helping you in the house?

JOSEFINA: Him? No, not on your life; he's a good man, poor thing.

He washes?

JOSEFINA: No, washing no, I do the wash.

Who cooks?

JOSEFINA: I do, no, no, I do everything.

What does he help with, then?

JOSEFINA: Well, he does some shopping, and sometimes when I'm late he cooks in the evening.

How do you get everything done in the house?

JOSEFINA: Oh, well, I'll show you how I get everything done. Come on back here so you can see. [She laughs] Where there's a will there's always a way. For instance that pile of clothes over there, I sprinkled that before I left for work today, and this one I leave for tomorrow. So I get up at five and by eleven everything's done and the kids off to school and everything.

María, do you think women's natural place is in the home with her children?

MARÍA: No, man, those are absurd ideas, because no one was born for anything in particular, but for what he or she wants to be. There are those who say that women are for the home and men are for the street; I don't agree with that. Women as well as men can work outside the home. Shopping, men can do that as well as women, and women, just because they work doesn't mean they can't do housework. And they can both clean house, for instance if the woman is sick I don't see why the man has to live in a dirty house, why can't he clean it himself.

Ana, who do you think has responsibility for the house?

ANA: Well, for example, I don't think it's my husband's responsibility to help me wash dirty clothes he brings home. I think that's my obligation, as his wife, to attend to his needs as well as carrying out all the other tasks of the Revolution. Aside from that, we women have a certain talent. When I'm tired I say so, and I sit down a bit; then he says: "I'll iron that shirt for you." You can do that, but never feeling it's his obligation. When we're both working in Havana and he comes home first, I think then it's his obligation to start things going until I get there. When I get home his responsibility ends. [. . .]

Haydée, do you think women can't do the work men do?

HAYDÉE: It's not what I think, but doctors themselves say there's a whole series of things, for example, hoeing, that adversely affects women's organisms.

Have you ever hoed?

HAYDÉE: We hoe every week, twice a week, and I've even been at it for a solid week at a time, hoeing morning and afternoon, and I haven't felt a thing. Of course you don't look all that feminine, but I don't think it really affects your health.

Josefina, do you think women are as strong as men?

JOSEFINA: Oh yeah, stronger sometimes. That's the truth. Look, I'm telling you, yesterday was some day at the mill! At home I washed like a mule, imagine, I heard the whistle at ten thirty and I was out on the road and my pants ripped, had to go back and change and get out on the road again to catch the bus. And when I get to the mill it's shut down since one a.m.! Heave wood, girl, to get that pressure back up! Together we got it up to a hundred and twenty. And that's the way it goes, when the mill stops, put on more wood, and when it ain't that, it's the scales. You see how it is. And let me tell you when the Federation got us to go to the mill there were fifteen of us women and the only one who stayed was me. They give me the hardest job, that the men don't even want. What

job do you think they gave me at the mill? The *trapiche,* girl, because this year they fixed it, but the year I started the *tonga* went like this here, and I had to grab the rod and pull it down.

Miriam, do you think there's a difference between men and women in terms of physical strength?

MIRIAM: Well, yes . . . I think women are weaker physically speaking, that's something we can't deny. But it's precisely because the work needs to be done and we don't yet have all the means necessary with which to do it, that we have to just go forward and do this kind of work.

So you think men are physically stronger, and women . . . ?

MIRIAM: . . . have a greater spirit of sacrifice. Well look, because here the woman isn't—well, I think that since women weren't used to working here, and we've all gone right out to work, we've gone out with a real spirit of sacrifice to really make this socialist revolution. It's because on the contrary we could have just sat at home and continued to be housewives, because work experience isn't what we had most of, because we were just housewives before. [. . .]

Magda, how do you feel about a young girl having sexual relations before she's married?

MAGDA: I don't think she should.

Why not?

MAGDA: Because I don't think so, because it's the principle of the thing; a woman should have sexual relations when she's married.

Miriam, do you think it's wrong for a couple to have sexual relations before they're married?

MIRIAM: I think it's fine. Sometimes I talk to my friends and I tell them I wish I were young again because everything that young people are doing is so fine, so clean; we've got so many prejudices. You've got such a good future, I'd like to begin again and be able to live the life you've got ahead of you. [. . .]

Rosa, what do you think of virginity?

ROSA: I think it's the biggest piece of garbage there is, and that's the truth; it's just a prejudice. I mean, it's just the product of the kind of upbringing we've had.

Do you think a different kind of education is needed, so that the next generation won't have those prejudices?

ROSA: I'm telling you, it's just my opinion, but I'm telling you that the day I have a daughter, my daughter's going to be free of those prejudices. I've suffered enough from that problem of prejudices. It's only in the last few years that my mentality has changed, and I'm old before my time from the number of prejudices I had suffered in my head. That has a lot to do with a woman's happiness!

Suggested Sources:

There are rich and varied readings on the Cuban Revolution, many of which include (or focus on) primary sources. For documents on women, Elizabeth Stone, ed. *Women and the Cuban Revolution* (New York: Pathfinder Press, 1981) is a marvelous collection that contains laws and speeches. Also see Margaret Randall's *Women in Cuba: Twenty Years Later* (New York: Smyrna Press, 1981). Oscar Lewis conducted interviews in Cuba that led to two classic volumes, both finished after his death. See Oscar Lewis, Ruth M. Lewis, and Susan M. Rigdon, *Four Women Living the Revolution: An Oral History of* *Contemporary Cuba*, and *Four Men Living the Revolution: An Oral History of Contemporary Cuba* (Chicago: University of Illinois Press, 1977). A collection of revolutionary documents focused on Cuban-United States relations is Julio García Luis, ed., *Cuban Revolution Reader: A Documentary History of 40 Key Moments in the Cuban Revolution* (New York: Ocean Press, 2001). For a longer view of Cuba in the twentieth century from the perspective of an Afro-Cuban woman, see María de los Reyes Castillo Bueno, *Reyita: The Life of a Black Cuban Woman in the Twentieth Century* (Durham, NC: Duke University Press, 2000).

There is an equally valuable collection of Cuban films. *Retrato de Teresa* (Portrait of Teresa), dir. Pastor Vega (New York: New Yorker Video, 1980), is a classic film that engages one in exploring the pressures that a married woman might feel in the "New Cuba" following the revolution. Director Tomás Gutierrez Alea has made several important films on Cuban society under the revolution, including *Hasta Cierto Punto* (Up to a Certain Point) (New York: New Yorker Video, 1983), which follows the life of a woman factory worker; and *Fresa y Chocolate* (Strawberry and Chocolate) (Burbank, CA: Miramax, 1995), exploring gay culture and identity in Cuba. His film *Memorias del Subdesarrollo* (Memories of Underdevelopment) (New York: New Yorker Video, 1968) also offers opportunities to observe and evaluate gender relations. Among documentaries addressing gender, see *Mariposas en el andamio* (Butterflies on the Scaffold) (New York, NY: Latin American Video Archives, 1996), on day-to-day life for gays and transvestites in a working-class Havana neighborhood, *Quién diablos es Julliette?* (Who the hell is Julliette?) (New York, NY: Kino on Video, 1997) about a teenage prostitute, and *Si me comprendieras* (If You Only Understood) (New York, NY: First Run/Icarus Films, 1998) in which several regular Cuban women describe their lives as they vie for a part in a film.

Chapter 22

A Bolivian Tin Miner's Wife Goes to the International Women's Tribunal in 1975

Erin E. O'Connor, Bridgewater State College

Domitila Barrios de Chungara (b. 1937) never worked in tin mines, but because both her father and husband did, mining shaped her existence. Her life revolved around tending to her family—first to her sisters, later to her seven children—and trying to run a household on a tin miner's meager wages, a task that led her to seek occasional work around the mine herself. She watched miners develop respiratory problems and saw their families lose everything when illness forced workers into early retirement. In 1963, she joined the House-wives Committee at the Siglo XX mine, where she became a leader among the housewives who fought to improve wages, work conditions, and housing at the mines. Though frequently persecuted and imprisoned, she was not dissuaded from seeking socioeconomic justice.

Barrios de Chungara's life experiences resulted from a contentious set of economic and political developments in twentieth-century Bolivia.[1] The rise of tin exports in the early 1900s coincided with intraelite struggles that manifest as clashes between *conservatives* and *liberals*. *Liberals* encouraged indigenous participation in these conflicts, identifying their *conservative* opponents as Indians' traditional oppressors. Once in power, however, *liberals* did little to advance indigenous interests, and instead many Indians lost land to owners of large estates under *liberal* rule. Tensions between Indians and large-estate landowners were made worse by economic crises in the 1920s and 1930s. Many indigenous peasants rebelled against landowners who usurped their farmlands, but the national government suppressed the uprisings. Those who lost land typically worked as debt peons on *haciendas* and were mainly concerned with wages, treatment, and work conditions. Finally, tin miners, who suffered greatly from fluctuations in the global economy, formed unions and protested to improve their pay and conditions. Though President Bautista Saavedra, an urban intellectual, initially welcomed unions and labor reforms, his government soon sided with elite groups against worker organizations and protests.

Adding another layer to the tensions between poor Bolivians and the state was the Chaco War (1932–1935) against Paraguay. The Bolivian government initiated this war over the territory of the Chaco Boreal, largely for its access to the River Paraguay (control of oil territories also a concern by the end of the war). Most of the troops were poor, rural Indians, whereas Bolivian whites made up the officer corps and *cholos* (peoples of mixed descent) served as sub-officials. Indigenous *campesinos* thus suffered the highest mortality rate in this war that ended in Bolivian defeat; their heightened class consciousness drew

This photograph shows Bolivian women working at the tin mines, rummaging through rocks to find tin. This was one of the few types of mine work open to women, who were marginalized based on both class and gender. Consider this picture after reading the document excerpt and consider: How does this photograph highlight Barrios de Chungara's main point about poor women and feminism?

Source: Super-Stock, Inc.

more Indians to leftist politics. Ultimately, the Chaco War left even middle-class Bolivians disillusioned and dissatisfied with the central government.

Economic problems, political fragmentation, regionalism, and class-race divides eventually came to a head in the early 1950s. In April of 1952 the "national revolution" of the *Movimiento Nacionalista Revolucionario* (Nationalist Revolutionary Movement, or MNR) promised to transform Bolivian society, politics, and economics. The MNR initially pursued land reform policies and nationalized resources, but the movement gradually turned from radical to moderately reformist to conservative. The 1960s saw the rise of populist military governments that claimed they would bring both relief and order. Then from 1971 to 1978 Hugo Banzer established conservative military rule that repressed popular organizations and allied itself more clearly with international corporate interests. For more than twenty-five years, promised reforms failed to address poor Bolivians' most dire problems, and each political shift strengthened the political power of military leaders who

[1]See Herbert S. Klein, *Bolivia: The Evolution of a Multi-Ethnic Society*, 2nd ed. (New York: Oxford University Press, 1992).

repressed grassroots activism in the name of order and stability. It was in this atmosphere of disillusionment and militarism that Domitila Barrios de Chungara became politically active.

Over the course of the 1970s, Barrios de Chungara went from being a poor tin miner's wife to an internationally renowned voice for her people. A Brazilian filmmaker met Barrios de Chungara while making a documentary film on the plight of Bolivian mining families and encouraged her to go to the International Women's Year Tribunal in 1975; the document excerpt in this chapter presents Barrios de Chungara's memory of the conference. Shortly thereafter, Brazilian journalist Moema Viezzer recorded Barrios de Chungara's life story in what is now a classic testimonial text. In the decades to follow, Barrios de Chungara has continued to devote her energies to fighting for social justice in Bolivia. She holds the global capitalist system responsible for the poverty and problems that the majority of Bolivians suffer, asserting that western owners of multinational corporations robbed Bolivians of their rightful wealth with the help of the Bolivian government. Barrios de Chungara's socialist views are typical of those found among leftists in poor regions of the world: She identifies both national class relations and international capitalist systems as the dual causes of her people's suffering.

Barrios de Chungara's life story of personal suffering and struggles for justice made her famous. *Testimonios*, or testimonial literature, were quite popular from the 1960s through the 1980s. In these books, individual women and men tell the story of their lives as a way of bearing witness to the atrocities beset upon their peoples, either by their own governments and elites or by international governments or businesses. Testimonial literature has given a voice to poor men and women and provided new and rich primary documents that explain Latin American societies and problems from their perspectives. Read carefully—because these sources are as subjective as any other primary documents—they provide a rich account of historical events and struggles for social justice.[2] In particular, many of these testimo-

nials highlight important ways that subaltern views differed substantially from middle-class or elite perspectives, as is evident in Barrios de Chungara's testimony. The excerpt offers her account of what it was like to travel from Bolivia to Mexico in order to participate in the International Women's Year Tribunal in 1975.

Barrios de Chungara's description of the Tribunal meetings reminds readers that the category of "woman" is shaped by class, race, and culture. Although deeply concerned with gender inequalities, Barrios de Chungara, like many poor women activists in Latin America, chose to engage in class-based activism rather than feminism (other women have associated mainly with ethnic-based activism). The following excerpt will help readers to explore the reasons behind such a choice, and to contemplate why class and race often determine how Latin American women make sense of the diverse problems they face in their everyday lives. Modernization, justice, and equality had very different meanings for a woman like Domitila Barrios de Chungara than they did for some of the other women in this section, and her proposed solutions differed accordingly. These divisions speak to the challenges that Latin American women from all backgrounds face as they try to improve not only their own lives, but the lives of their families and communities as well.

Questions to Consider:

1. What did Domitila Barrios de Chungara hope to achieve by going to the International Women's Tribunal?

2. How did her poverty and culture put her at a disadvantage during her trip?

3. How did Barrios de Chungara view the proposals she heard North American and elite Latin American feminists make? Why did she decide to speak up at the Tribunal meetings?

4. What do you think Barrios de Chungara valued the most, or learned the most, about her experiences at the Tribunal? Why?

5. What can you glean from this chapter about the challenges of trying to build an international women's movement? Do you have any ideas on how these challenges might be overcome?

---

[2]For a discussion of how and why some of these sources have become controversial, see the chapter on Rigoberta Menchú Tum in this volume.

At the International Women's Year Tribunal[3]

In 1974, a Brazilian movie director came to Bolivia, commissioned by the United Nations. She was traveling through Latin America, looking for women leaders, to find out their opinions about women's conditions and to learn how much and in what way they participate in bettering their situation.

With regard to Bolivia, she was very intrigued by the "housewives' front" which she'd heard about abroad and, also, she'd seen the women of Siglo XX acting in the movie *El Coraje del Pueblo* (The Courage of the People). So, after asking for permission from the government, she went into the mines. And she came to visit me. She liked what I said and she said it was important that everything I knew should be told to the rest of the world. She asked me if I could travel. I said I couldn't, that I didn't have money to even travel in my own country.

So she asked me if I'd agree to participate in a women's congress that was going to take place in Mexico, if she was able to get money for me. I had just found out that there was an International Women's Year.

Although I didn't really believe it much, I said yes, in that case I could go. But I thought it was just a promise like so many others and I didn't pay much attention to it.

When I got the telegram saying that I was invited by the United Nations, I was quite surprised and disconcerted. I called a meeting of the committee and all the *compañeras* agreed that it would be good for me to travel, along with one more *compañera*. But there wasn't enough for two of us to go. The next day I went before a meeting of union leaders and rank-and-file delegates and gave them my report and they agreed that I should participate in the event and they even helped me economically so that I could begin making the arrangements.

So with some other *compañeras* I went to La Paz[4] and we looked into the details, we got guarantees, and I stayed there alone to finish the arrangements.

Several days went by. It got to look like I wouldn't be able to make the trip because they didn't want to give me a travel permit.

And it turns out that some Siglo XX leaders arrived in La Paz and were surprised to see I hadn't left. So they went with me to the secretariat of the Ministry of the Interior. And they asked:

"What's happening with the *compañera*? Why isn't she in Mexico already? The International Women's Year Conference opens today. What's happened here? Is it or isn't it International Women's Year? Do our wives have the right to participate in this conference, or can only your wives go there?"

And they told me:

"Well, *compañera*, since they don't want to let you go, let's leave. Even though you have an invitation from the United Nations, they don't want to let you go to that conference. So we're going to complain to the United Nations. And not only that: we're going to have a work stoppage in protest. Come with us, *compañera*."

They were all set to take me out of the ministry when the guys there reacted:

"But . . . why didn't we start here in the first place! One moment, one moment, don't get so hot and bothered. If the lady has an invitation from the United Nations, we should have started there. Where's the invitation?"

The invitation! Every single day, at every turn, I was asked for the copy. And with the experience the miners have, they'd made lots of copies of it. So of course, one copy would get lost and I'd make another. And so on. And the original, well, the leaders themselves had it, because if the first copies got used up, they could make others.

I gave them one more copy; and after an hour, more or less, they gave me the documents. Everything was okay, everything was ready. The plane left the next day at nine in the morning.

When I was about to board the plane, a young lady from the Ministry of the Interior came over to me. I'd seen her there on various occasions, hanging onto her papers. She came over and said:

"Ay, señora! So, you got your pass? I'm so happy! You deserve it. I congratulate you! How I'd like to be in your shoes, so I could see Mexico! Congratulations!"

---

[3]*Source:* Domitila Barrios de Chungara (with Moema Viezzer), *Let Me Speak! Testimony of Domitila, a Woman of the Bolivian Mines*, trans. Victoria Ortiz, (New York: Monthly Review Press, 1978), 194–204.
[4]The capital of Bolivia.

But then, very mysterious, she went on:

"Ay, but señora, your return to the country depends a lot on what you say there. So it's not a question of talking about any old thing . . . you've got to think it out well. Above all, you've got to think of your children who you're leaving behind. I'm giving you good advice. Have a good time."

I thought about my responsibility as a mother and as a leader and so my role in Mexico seemed very difficult to me, thinking of what that young lady had said to me. I felt that I was between the Devil and the deep blue sea, as we say. But I was determined to carry out the mission the *compañeros* and *compañeras* had entrusted me with. [. . .]

In the hotel [in Mexico] I made friends with the Ecuadorian woman and went with her to the place where the Tribunal was being held. But I couldn't go till Monday. The sessions had already begun on Friday.

We went to a very big hall where there were four or five hundred women. The Ecuadorian said:

"Come on, *compañera*. Here's where they talk about the most important problems women have. So here's where we should make our voices heard."

There were no more seats. So we sat on some steps. We were very enthusiastic. We'd already missed a day of the Tribunal and we wanted to catch up, get up to date on what had been happening, find out what so many women were thinking, what they were saying about International Women's Year, what problems most concerned them.

It was my first experience and I imagined I'd hear things that would make me get ahead in life, in the struggle, in my work.

Well, at that moment a *gringa* went over to the microphone with her blond hair and with some things around her neck and her hands in her pockets, and she said to the assembly:

"I've asked for the microphone so that I can tell you about my experience. Men should give us a thousand and one medals because we, the prostitutes, have the courage to go to bed with so many men."

A lot of women shouted "Bravo!" and applauded.

Well, my friend and I left because there were hundreds of prostitutes talking about their problems. And we went into another room. There were lesbians. And there, also, their discussion was about how "they

feel happy and proud to love another woman . . . that they should fight for their rights . . ." Like that.

Those weren't my interests. And for me it was incomprehensible that so much money should be spent to discuss those things in the Tribunal. Because I'd left my *compañero* with the seven kids and him having to work in the mine every day. I'd left my country to let people know what my homeland's like, how it suffers, how in Bolivia the charter of the United Nations isn't upheld. I wanted to tell people all that and hear what they would say to me about other exploited countries and the other groups that have already liberated themselves. And to run into those other kinds of problems . . . I felt a bit lost. In other rooms, some of the women stood up and said: men are the enemy . . . men create wars, men create nuclear weapons, men beat women . . . and so what's the first battle to be carried out to get equal rights for women? First you have to declare war against men. If a man has ten mistresses, well, the woman should have ten lovers also. If a man spends all his money at the bar, partying, the women have to do the same thing. And when we've reached that level, then men and women can link arms and start struggling for the liberation of their country, to improve the living conditions in their country.

That was the mentality and the concern of several groups, and for me it was a really rude shock. We spoke very different languages, no? And that made it difficult to work in the Tribunal. Also, there was a lot of control over the microphone.

So a group of Latin American women got together and we changed all that. And we made our common problems known, what we thought women's progress was all about, how the majority of women live. We also said that for us the first and main task isn't to fight against our *compañeros*, but with them to change the system we live in for another, in which men and women will have the right to live, to work, to organize.

At first you couldn't really notice how much control there was in the Tribunal. But as the speeches and statements were made, things started to change. For example, the women who defended prostitution, birth control, and all those things, wanted to impose their ideas as the basic problems to be discussed in the Tribunal. For us they were real problems, but not the main ones. [. . .]

In one way or another, they tried to distract the Tribunal with problems that weren't basic. So we had to let the people know what was fundamental for us in all that. Personally, I spoke several times. Short speeches, because we could only use the microphone for two minutes.

The movie *La Doble Jornada* (The Double Work Day), filmed by the Brazilian *compañera* who invited me to the Tribunal, was also useful in orienting people who didn't have any idea of what the life of a peasant woman or a working woman is like in Latin America. In *La Doble Jornada* they show the women's lives, especially in relation to work. There you see how women live in the United States, in Mexico, in Argentina. There's a big contrast. But even more so when you see the part about Bolivia, because the *compañera* interviewed a worker in Las Lamas who was pregnant. She asked her: "Why aren't you taking it easy since you're expecting a baby?" The working woman said that she couldn't because she had to earn a living for her children and her husband too, because he's retired[5] and his pension is very small. "And the pension?" asked the Brazilian woman. Then the miner's wife explained that her husband had left the mine absolutely ruined physically and that all the money from the pension was spent trying to cure him. And that's why now she had to work, her children too, in order to support her husband.

Well, that was pretty strong stuff, and dramatic, no? And the *compañeras* at the Tribunal realized that I hadn't lied when I spoke about our situation.

When the movie was over, since I'd also been in it, they asked me to speak. So I said the situation was due to the fact that no government had bothered to create jobs for poor women. That the only work women do that's recognized is housework and, in any case, housework is done for free. Because, for example, they give me 14 pesos a month, in other words, two-thirds of a dollar a month, which is the family subsidy that's added to my husband's wage. What are 14 Bolivian pesos worth? With 14 Bolivian pesos you can buy two bottles of milk or half a box of tea . . .

That's why—I told them—you have to understand that we won't be able to find any solution to our problems as long as the capitalist system in which we live isn't changed.[6]

Many of those women said they'd only just begun to agree with me. Several of them wept.

The day the women spoke out against imperialism, I spoke too. And I said how we live totally dependent on foreigners for everything, how they impose what they want on us, economically as well as culturally.

In the Tribunal I learned a lot also. In the first place, I learned to value the wisdom of my people even more. There, everyone who went up to the microphone said: "I'm a professional person, I represent such and such an organization . . ." And bla-bla-bla, she gave her speech. "I'm a teacher," "I'm a lawyer," "I'm a journalist," said the others. And bla-bla-bla, they'd begin to give their opinion.

I worked up the courage to tell them about the problems that were being discussed there. Because that was my obligation. And I stated my ideas so that everyone in the world could hear us, through the Tribunal.

That led to my having a discussion with Betty Friedan, who is the great feminist leader in the United States. She and her group had proposed some points to amend the "World Plan of Action." But these were mainly feminist points and we didn't agree with them because they didn't touch on some problems that are basic for Latin American women.

Betty Friedan invited us to join them. She asked us to stop our "warlike activity" and said that we were being "manipulated by men," that "we only thought about politics," and that we'd completely ignored women's problems, "Like the Bolivian delegation does, for example," she said.

So I asked for the floor. But they wouldn't give it to me. And so I stood up and said:

"Please forgive me for turning this Tribunal into a marketplace. But I was mentioned and I have to defend myself. I was invited to the Tribunal to talk about women's rights and in the invitation they sent me there was also the document approved in the United Nations which is its charter, where women's right to participate, to organize, is recognized. And

---

[5]As an invalid. For the majority of miners, the invalid condition is caused by silicosis.

[6]Recall here that Barrios de Chungara's goal was a socialist system.

Bolivia signed that charter, but in reality it's only applied here to the bourgeoisie."

I went on speaking that way. And a lady, who was the president of the Mexican delegation, came up to me. She wanted to give me her own interpretation of the International Women's Year Tribunal slogan, which was "equality, development, and peace." She said:

"Let's speak about us, señora. We're women. Look, señora, forget the suffering of your people. For a moment, forget the massacres. We've talked enough about that. We've heard you enough. Let's talk about us . . . about you and me . . . well, about women."

So I said:

"All right, let's talk about the two of us. But if you'll let me, I'll begin. Señora, I've known you for a week. Every morning you show up in a different outfit and on the other hand, I don't. Every day you show up all made up and combed like someone who has time to spend in an elegant beauty parlor and who can spend money on that, and yet I don't. I see that each afternoon you have a chauffeur in a car waiting at the door of this place to take you home, and yet I don't. And in order to show up here like you do, I'm sure you live in a really elegant home, in an elegant neighborhood, no? And yet we miners' wives have a small house on loan to us, and when our husbands die or get sick or are fired from the company, we have ninety days to leave the house and then we're in the street.

"Now, señora, tell me: is your situation at all similar to mine? Is my situation at all similar to yours? So what equality are we going to speak of between the two of us? If you and I aren't alike, if you and I are so different? We can't, at this moment, be equal, even as women, don't you think?" [. . .]

In the end [two of the Mexican women] said to me:

"Well, you think you're so important. Get up here and speak."

So I went up and spoke. I made them see that they don't live in our world. I made them see that in Bolivia human rights aren't respected and they apply what we call "the law of the funnel": broad for some, narrow for others. That those ladies who got together to play canasta and applaud the government have full guarantees, full support. But women like us, housewives, who get organized to better our people, well,

they beat us up and persecute us. They couldn't see all those things. They couldn't see the suffering of my people, they couldn't see how our *compañeros* are vomiting their lungs bit by bit, in pools of blood. They didn't see how underfed our children are. And, of course, they didn't know, as we do, what it's like to get up at four in the morning and go to bed at eleven or twelve at night, just to be able to get all the housework done, because of the lousy conditions we live in.

"You," I said, "what can you possibly understand about all that? For you, the solution is fighting with men. And that's it. But for us it isn't that way, that isn't the basic situation."

When I finished saying all that, moved by the anger I felt, I left the platform. And many women came up to me, and at the exit from the hall, many were happy and said I should go back to the Tribunal and represent the Latin American women who were there.

I felt ashamed to think that I hadn't been able to evaluate the wisdom of the people well enough. Because, look: I, who hadn't studied in the university, or even gone to school, I, who wasn't a teacher or a professional or a lawyer or a professor, what had I done in the Tribunal? What I'd said was only what I'd heard my people say ever since I was little, my parents, my *compañeros*, the leaders, and I saw that the people's experience is the best schooling there is. What I learned from the people's life was the best teaching. And I wept to think: how great is my people!

We Latin American women issued a document about the way we see the role of women in underdeveloped countries, with everything we felt was important to say on that occasion. And the press published it.

Another thing that I got out of the Tribunal was meeting *compañeras* from other countries, especially the Bolivians, Argentines, Uruguayans, Chileans, who'd been in similar situations to those I'd experienced in prisons, jails, and all those problems. I learned a lot from them. I think I fulfilled the mission that the *compañeras* and *compañeros* from Siglo XX gave me. In the Tribunal we were with a lot of women from all over the world, and we made everyone who was represented there aware of my country.

It was also a great experience being with so many women and seeing how many, many people are dedicated to the struggle for the liberation of their oppressed peoples.

I also think it was important for me to see once again—and on that occasion in contact with more than five thousand women from all over—how the interests of the bourgeoisie really aren't our interests.

Suggested Sources:

Domitila Barrios de Chungara's life story is among the most famous testimonial literature for Latin America, and it is well worth reading in its entirety. For a source that explores the life of a market woman, see Hans Buechler and Judith Maria Buechler, *The World of Sofía Velasquez* (New York: Columbia University Press, 1996). The film that helped to bring attention to the Bolivian miners, including Barrios de Chungara, is *El coraje del pueblo,* dir. Jorge Sanjinés (RAI Radio Television Italiana, 1971).

There are some excellent studies of struggles for social justice in Bolivia. For a now-classic study,

see James Dunkerley, *Rebellion in the Veins: Political Struggle in Bolivia, 1952–1982* (New York: Verso, 1984). For a more recent and superb work, see Laura Gotkowitz, *A Revolution for Our Rights: Indigenous Struggles for Land and Justice in Bolivia, 1880–1952* (Durham, NC: Duke University Press, 2007). For a collection of essays on the topic, see Merilee S. Grindle and Pilar Domingo, eds., *Proclaiming the Revolution: Bolivia in Comparative Perspective* (Cambridge, MA: Harvard University Press, 2003). For more general background on Bolivian history, see Erick D. Langer, *Economic Change and Rural Resistance in Southern Bolivia, 1880–1930* (Stanford, CA: Stanford University Press, 1989). For a study of Andean culture, see Thomas Abercrombie, *Pathways of Memory and Power: Ethnography and History among an Andean People* (Madison: University of Wisconsin Press, 1998). For an interesting and important examination of public policy and social inequalities, see Ann Zulawski, *Unequal Cures: Public Health and Political Change in Bolivia, 1900–1950* (Durham, NC: Duke University Press, 2007).

Section VI

Foundations of Modern Indigenous Movements

Latin American Indian-state relations began undergoing changes in the 1960s, resulting by the 1990s in the formation of regional, national, and international indigenous rights organizations. Indigenous activism is one of the most powerful forms of social protest in contemporary Latin America and has reshaped national politics in Bolivia, Guatemala, and Ecuador. The chapters in this section use documents written about, for, or by indigenous peoples to help readers understand the evolution of Latin American indigenous movements. The section begins with state-generated legal changes in Chile and Paraguay and culminates with indigenous-based organizations seeking national and international economic, social, and political transformations.

Indigenous organization resulted in part from the diverse impacts of economic modernization in the mid- to late twentieth century. Industrial growth, the expansion of mining and oil industries, and infrastructural development all brought rural indigenous peoples into new forms of contact, and frequently conflict, with the modern world. These changes presented indigenous peoples with new problems, such as pesticide poisoning from treatment of export crops, or loss of land to export estates or mines. International development organizations also traveled to the Latin American countryside with the goals of increasing peasant production and keeping socialism from spreading among the poor. Though development agents did not always alleviate

indigenous peoples' main problems, interactions with international scholars and bureaucrats provided another eye-opening encounter with the wider world.

Also beginning in the 1960s, religious officials and educators often played key roles in transforming rural communities in ways that made later political actions possible. Many young urban teachers went to the countryside to battle illiteracy. Priests and nuns also arrived, following new initiatives from Rome to bring God's word and love to the humblest members of society. Living in the countryside often changed teachers' and religious officials' views of the work that they were called to do for the rural poor; instead of simply teaching *campesinos* to read or study the gospel, they often advocated socioeconomic and political changes. Samuel Ruíz described his assignment as bishop in Chiapas, Mexico, by stating that "I came to San Cristóbal to convert the poor ... but they ended up converting me."[1] Priests and nuns who embraced work with and for the poor were part of a movement known as *Liberation Theology*. Adherents of *Liberation Theology* believe that poverty, inequality, and oppression are problems that they, as Christians, must work to eradicate. They aspire to bring God's kingdom to earth and

---

[1] This quote appears in John Womack Jr., ed., *Rebellion in Chiapas: An Historical Reader* (New York: The New Press, 1999), 27.

201

struggle to achieve an era in which all individuals live in security and dignity.[2] Many Church officials and educators also played key roles in helping poor indigenous peoples organize and demand rights from their governments.

Western nations pressured Latin American government leaders to pass socioeconomic reforms and address human rights problems, sometimes making reforms a prerequisite for receiving financial assistance. Simultaneous international and grassroots demands sometimes led governments to enact economic or social reform laws that had important (albeit limited) impacts on indigenous peoples. René Harder-Horst's chapter, for example, traces the evolution of Paraguayan indigenous laws from the dictatorship of Alfredo Stroessner (r. 1954–1989) through the transition to democracy in the early 1990s. Both international and domestic criticisms of the dictatorship were crucial in the development of these laws, and the 1992 constitution's treatment of indigenous rights reflected these concerns.

Socialism also influenced Indian-state relations in many parts of Latin America. Joanna Crow's chapter presents the 1971 Indigenous Law, passed by the democratically elected socialist administration of Salvador Allende. Although Allende wanted to alleviate problems that the *Mapuche* faced, the law reveals the limits as well as the benefits of socialist support for indigenous communities. In Mexico, as the chapter on the modern *Zapatistas* shows, leftist guerrilla leader *Comandante* (Commander) Marcos sought to transform social as well as economic relations. The communiqué from March 1994 presented in this chapter focused on the combination of economic, cultural, and gender-based problems facing the poor, especially indigenous peoples in the region.

---

[2]Foundations of *Liberation Theology* also came from the Church hierarchy. Particularly important were Pope John XXIII's papal encyclical *Pacem in Terris* (Peace on Earth), and the Latin American Bishops' Conference in Medellín, Colombia, in 1968. *Pacem in Terris* can be accessed at: http://www.vatican.va/holy_father/john_xxiii/encyclicals/documents/hf_j-xxiii_enc_11041963_pacem_en.html. Documents resulting from the bishop's conference in Medellín are also available at http://www.shc.edu/theolibrary/resources/. (Both sources last accessed on March 13, 2009.)

Indigenous peoples were hardly passive recipients of changes. In many countries, grassroots indigenous organizations developed in response to the opportunities and problems resulting from economic and political modernization. Though each indigenous organization has its own particular history, many indigenous movements followed the same broad path. Indigenous peoples' political activities typically began at the local level in the 1960s and 1970s, followed by rising regional organization and activism in the 1970s and 1980s. By the 1990s, many indigenous activists began organizing nationally or internationally as a strategy to achieve economic and political change.

The rise of more active, and better organized, indigenous movements by the 1980s and 1990s was closely connected to the rise of *neoliberal* economic policies that were often devastating to indigenous communities. By the late 1980s, economic development models had failed; inflation rates soared and governments defaulted on loans. Powerful international economic institutions—most notably the World Bank (WB), the International Monetary Fund (IMF), and the Inter-American Development Bank (IADB)—pressured Latin American political leaders to embrace austerity policies now associated with *neoliberalism*. Neoliberalism called for free market economies to replace government ownership, subsidies, or protections for businesses. Banks, industries, utilities, and sometimes even educational or hospital facilities previously owned by the state were privatized. These changes, along with lowered protections on national industries, led to rising unemployment. Government services were also on the decline, further deepening the suffering and frustration of the poor.

Indigenous identity politics changed considerably over time. In the 1960s and 1970s, most indigenous activists identified as peasants and sought land redistribution and increased access to government resources. By the 1980s and 1990s, they emphasized their need for cultural dignity as well as economic changes. Consider the following document excerpt by the *Confederation of Indigenous Nationalities of Ecuador* (*CONAIE*), one of the earliest and most politically influential indigenous organizations to emerge in Latin America. The document is a list of demands that *CONAIE* leaders made of the Ecuadorian government following a protest in 1990 against *neoliberal* policies that devastated many in their communities.

CONAIE'S

Sixteen Demands[3]

1. Return of lands and territories taken from Indigenous communities, without costly legal fees.
2. Sufficient water for human consumption and irrigation in Indigenous communities, and a plan to prevent pollution of water supplies.
3. No municipal taxes on small properties owned by Indigenous farmers.
4. Long-term financing for bilingual education programs in the communities.
5. Creation of provincial and regional credit agencies to be controlled by *CONAIE*.
6. Forgiveness of all debts to government ministries and banks incurred by Indigenous communities.
7. Amendment of the first article of the constitution to proclaim Ecuador as a plurinational state.
8. Minimum two-year price freeze on all raw materials and manufactured goods used by the communities in agricultural production, and reasonable price increase on all agricultural goods sold by them, using free-market mechanisms.
9. Initiation and completion of all priority construction on basic infrastructure for Indigenous communities.
10. Unrestricted import and export privileges for Indigenous artisans and handicraft merchants.
11. Respect for the rights of children and greater government awareness of their current plight.
12. National support for Indigenous medicine.

---

[3]*Source:* For the full list of demands, see Les Field, "Ecuador's Pan-Indian Uprising," *NACLA Report on the Americas* 25, no. 3 (December 1991): 41. Thanks to Marc Becker for bringing the document to my attention.

Although economic demands remained central to indigenous movements, their leaders also argued strongly for *autonomy*. Indigenous organizations identify *autonomy* with both indigenous control of and sovereignty over traditional lands. Although most indigenous activists accept that they belong to a larger state structure, they call for the development of *plurinational* states that would officially recognize many different cultures, all of which would have an equal voice in the government—rather than having wealthy whites and *mestizos* to continue to dominate politics. Look closely at the *CONAIE* document: How were the activists' economic, political, and cultural demands interrelated? Readers should consider returning to this document after reading other sources in this section and consider how the 1990 *CONAIE* demands represent an intermediate stage between the top-down reforms in Crow and Harder Horst's chapters, and the later chapters on *Zapatistas* and international indigenous organizations.

Indigenous activists have often used new technologies to bring their local and regional concerns to a global audience. Both the chapter on the *Zapatistas* and Marc Becker's chapter on international indigenous alliances offer examples of indigenous activists using the Internet to reach a worldwide audience in order to pressure governments into changing policies toward indigenous peoples. Contemporary indigenous identities are simultaneously local and hemispheric. On the one hand, indigenous movements base themselves on cultural identities that are profoundly local, with customs, problems, and even languages differing from one region to another. On the other hand, indigenous activists have reclaimed the term "Indian" as a way of identifying common problems and goals shared among native peoples throughout the Americas. Becker's chapter, for example, presents declarations generated at international indigenous conferences based on participants' sense of shared problems, ways of life, and objectives as native peoples.

The political impact of indigenous movements is complex. Although in some countries (notably Ecuador and Bolivia) indigenous leaders have begun to wield significant national and international political power, ordinary indigenous men and women continue to grapple with poverty and racism in their daily lives. It is not yet clear what the long-term political impact of indigenous activism will be in Latin America, but certainly Indian-state relations have changed remarkably since independence. Indigenous peoples are making their voices heard more directly than ever before, and they are generating their own demands rather than waiting for whites or *mestizos* to solve their problems for them.

Chapter 23

Socialism and Indigenous Rights in Allende's Chile

Joanna Crow, University of Bristol

Chile

On May 19, 1971, Socialist president Salvador Allende presented a new Indigenous Law to the Chilean Congress. The proposed law was part of a broader shift toward a more democratic, inclusive discourse of Chilean nationhood. It officially recognized the country's ethnic diversity and, for the first time in Chilean history, indigenous identity was no longer confined to those who lived in an indigenous community or had access to communal lands. The Indigenous Law provided for the creation of new institutions such as the Indigenous Development Institute, the main objective of which was to promote the social, educational, and cultural development of indigenous peoples while taking into account their distinctive customs and traditions. It also included provisions to incorporate indigenous communities into the agrarian reform process and allow them greater access to education. In short, it presented indigenous people as key participants in and beneficiaries of Allende's revolutionary project.

Allende's Popular Unity government (a coalition of leftist parties) took power in December 1970. Allende rose to prominence in the Socialist Party during the 1930s, was elected to Congress in 1937, and served as Minister of Health between 1939 and 1940 (under the Popular Front government of Pedro Aguirre Cerda). He became a senator in 1945, and stood (unsuccessfully) as a presidential candidate three times before 1970. He proposed a radical reform program—including large-scale nationalization, the acceleration of agrarian reform, and the confiscation of property—but assured Chileans that this was to be accomplished through democratic channels. One of the problems besetting the "Chilean road to socialism" from the very beginning was that the Popular Unity only controlled one-third of the Senate and two-fifths of the Chamber of Deputies; the Right, which opposed most reforms against the economic interests of the elite, had the majority in both houses and became increasingly hostile. Allende also faced major problems within the Popular Unity: There was no consensus among the Left as to how far the reforms should go, nor how they should be implemented—some favored moderate measures pursued through legal means, whereas others demanded more drastic changes and advocated violence. Chilean society on the whole was polarized between Right and Left, and government supporters feared intervention from the United States, which, under the leadership of Nixon and Kissinger, sought to destabilize the Popular Unity administration as part of its war against communism.[4]

The Indigenous Law was one of the few major pieces of legislation that Allende managed to pass through Congress. It focused mainly on the *Mapuche*, the largest and most vocal of Chile's indigenous

peoples. In the early independence era the *Mapuche* were hailed as the founding fathers of the Chilean nation for successfully defending their homeland against the Spanish during the colonial period. However, by the mid-nineteenth century, Indian-state land disputes, and dominant racial discourses (see Chapter 5 on Sarmiento in Argentina and Chapter 13 regarding the nineteenth-century *Mapuche* Rebellion) led elites to stereotype the *Mapuche* as barbaric savages who threatened their nation-building project. At this point, the Chilean state began its colonization of *Mapuche* territory (1862–1883). One hundred years later many Chileans still considered the *Mapuche* primitive outsiders; Allende sought to challenge such racist imagery and redefine the place of the *Mapuche* in the Chilean nation.

In 1964, Allende signed the "Cautin Pact" with several leftist *Mapuche* organizations in Temuco. They pledged their support for his presidential campaign and, in return, he vowed to introduce important socioeconomic reforms to benefit *Mapuche* communities and respect their culture and religion. When he finally became president in 1970 (he lost the 1964 election to Christian Democrat leader Eduardo Frei Montalva), Allende was keen to show that he would live up to such promises. Shortly after his inauguration, he traveled to Temuco (the center of historic *Mapuche* territory) to preside over the closing of the Second National *Mapuche* Congress. During this congress *Mapuche* organizations drew up a set of proposals for a new indigenous law, many of which were incorporated into the final document that Allende presented to parliament in May 1971. Thus, *Mapuche* people were actively involved in the drafting of the law; their views were also brought in to the parliamentary debates about the law and they participated in the new institutions that the law created.

Indigenous Law 17.729 was finally enacted in June 1972, having undergone substantial modifications during its passage through Congress. Many politicians, particularly those on the Right, rejected calls to recognize Chile's ethnic diversity because they felt that this would threaten national unity and, indeed, national security: They were reluctant to grant special rights to certain sectors of society, on the basis that all Chileans were supposed to be equal,

---

[4]The meaning of "communism" and "socialism" in Allende's Chile (i.e., the exact nature of the reform program and the means through which it was to be carried out) is still much contested among scholars. For a concise account of this period, which draws on a useful array of primary and secondary sources, see Simon Collier and William Sater, *A History of Chile, 1808–1994* (Cambridge: Cambridge University Press, 1996), 330–358.

and they argued that any recognition of indigenous difference or *autonomy* would lead to the fragmentation of the Chilean state.

Less than a year after the enactment of the law, Allende's government was overthrown by a violent military coup. The new Junta of the Armed Forces, which had the support of the United States, declared that the Popular Unity had "engendered a blind, fratricidal struggle based on ideas alien to our national heritage" (i.e., socialism) and proclaimed that Chile's "very existence as an independent state [was] in danger." In 1974 Pinochet assumed sole power as president and his seventeen-year dictatorship reversed many of the Indigenous Law's most progressive measures, particularly concerning the defense of indigenous communal lands. Despite the modifications and short life span of the law, many *Mapuche* intellectuals and political activists have since hailed the Indigenous Law of 1972 as a major achievement and an important turning point in the relationship between the *Mapuche* and the Chilean state.

The document that follows is an extract of some of the main points from Allende's congressional address of 1971. The speech provides insight into the Chilean Left's attempts to include indigenous peoples as full-fledged members of the revolutionary nation. However, it also helps one to consider the limits of political programs that seek to absorb the so-called Indian question within the framework of class struggle.

Questions to Consider:

1. How did Allende describe indigenous peoples? In what ways did he seem to be including them in the Popular Unity government's revolutionary project?
2. What stereotypes of indigenous peoples did Allende challenge? What new stereotypes emerged?
3. How did Allende distinguish indigenous from nonindigenous *campesinos*?
4. Can you think of contradictions or potential problems that might result from this law, particularly with regard to agrarian reform?
5. To what extent did the Popular Unity's concern for indigenous rights transcend national boundaries and engage with debates taking place in Latin America more generally?

President Salvador Allende's Proposed Indigenous Law, 19 May (1971)[5]

It is with great satisfaction that I present to this house a draft law on indigenous peoples, which shows how determined the Popular Government is to keep its promises and to put an end to the shameful social injustice of Chilean society.

From the basic outline of our political program, one can see how much importance the Popular Unity places on the situation of the most marginalized sectors of our society. Together with the demands of the working classes and the peasants we also find those of a vast sector of society that has been, more than all others, forgotten and is undoubtedly the most authentic exponent of a system that has permitted

[5]*Source:* Mensaje de su Excelencia el Presidente de la República', *Diario de Sesiones de la Cámara de Diputados*, Sesión 39a, 19 de mayo 1971.

men to blindly exploit other men: indigenous people. The "indigenous" problem is a major concern for the Popular Government, as it should be for all Chileans. We said that we would defend the integrity and enlargement of indigenous communities, long since dispossessed of their lands, and that we would provide the necessary and technical assistance and credit so that they might have the same opportunities as the rest of the population.

We are aware that the problems faced by indigenous groups are distinct to those faced by the rest of the *campesinos* – hence why they need to be treated and dealt with by different procedures and systems – but neither legislators nor the average Chilean have always understood this fact, thus aggravating the situation further. Indigenous peoples have different values, just as they have different ways of behaving. Conscious that they have been the owners of their land for centuries, their attitude is that of someone who has been dispossessed of something that legally belongs to them, whereas for other peasants the acquisition of land constitutes a conquest. Indigenous peoples fight for the recuperation of their land, while other peasants demand the redistribution of the land to those that work it.

Thus, indigenous people are authentic small landowners, robbed of their land and crushed. In contrast, other peasants are essentially tenants, lease holders or share croppers. In their mutual relations there are often disagreements that lead to open confrontation, but this does not detract from the fact that the problem of Chilean peasants is at its very root the same for everyone.

This situation is not only relevant to Chile, but to many other Latin American countries that suffer from the indigenous problem. [. . .]

War and ignominy has scarred these peoples since the Conquest. A foreign system was imposed on them: their tribal autochthonous system was substituted for the European feudal system. Their lands were taken, their power destroyed, and they were subjected to nothing short of slavery.

As a result of these wars, the culture and social structure [of indigenous peoples] began to change. Land was shared out [among the Spanish] and Indians were enslaved to work this land; they thus became subjugated to another people, their culture became a subculture, integrated into a structure of conquest and colonization. Despite their heroic resistance and the centuries that it took to defeat Arauco,[6] domination and integration was eventually achieved, although this does not mean that the traits which allow us to identify indigenous peoples as those who live in the most backward, miserable and abject conditions have disappeared. Today, they constitute a social sector within the national structure, integrated through the loss of their land, the lack of resources, the imposition of an external legal system

and the general influence of the rest of society (which contributes to the acculturation process).

At the end of the nineteenth century, indigenous people mainly lived in the northern regions, the Frontier zone and the far south of our country. The position of indigenous groups has been steadily deteriorating, and it is a grave concern both in terms of their geographical reduction and their increasing pauperization. There are far fewer indigenous people in existence today [of any ethnic group]. [. . .]

The total indigenous population of Chile is approximately 800,000: a quarter resides in urban areas – mainly Santiago, Concepción and Temuco – and the rest live in rural areas, hence their importance regarding the agrarian situation. The main proportion of this rural sector is found in Arauco and Osorno (approximately 50%) and Cautín (approximately 25%), meaning that half of these provinces' population and almost two-thirds of their rural population is *Mapuche*. Between Bío-Bío and Osorno they own 596,000 hectares; that is 8% of the territory. In Cautin they own 343.306,04 hectares, or 20% of the territory.[7]

These statistics show how much the land-people ratio has changed during the century. While in the period 1884–1929 each person owned approximately 6.2 hectares, nowadays they own between 0.9 and 1.4 hectares. It is easy to see how such realities generate a circular process of pauperization. The lack of land obliges people to farm intensively, contravening all technical, conservation and land-use norms, which has exhausted the land and rendered it incapable of satisfying the most basic needs. The result is poverty, malnutrition, disease and the impossibility of incorporating oneself – in material terms – into the normal process of development experienced by the rest of the population. Indigenous peoples are left excluded from the education system, which further contributes to their pauperization. Those who – either flippantly or with spiteful selfishness – declare the *Mapuche* to be lazy, vice-ridden or bad farmers seem to forget how much impact these socioeconomic conditions have on the

---

[6]Arauco is a province of Chile, often referred to as Araucanía. This was historic *Mapuche* territory that remained independent during the colonial period and was only incorporated into the Chilean state in the late nineteenth century.

[7]One hectare is a unit of area equal to 10,000 square meters (or 2.471 acres).

people who suffer them. It thus becomes apparent that one of the requisites for putting an end to a process that will lead to the elimination of a whole people, if it is not rectified, is the significant increase of the amount of land available for each person.

Perhaps the three most influential factors in this destructive process are the *huinca's* [foreigner's, white man's] expropriation of indigenous lands, cheap Indian labor (also to the huinca's benefit) and the subjugation of Indian society to a foreign system. No analysis of the indigenous problem can separate the latter from the factors that influence it. All measures adopted, and therefore all new legislation, must take the general state of the country and the changes that its people have experienced into account, noting the variable nature of society as a whole. And particularly, we need to analyze the agrarian situation, given the important link that exists between agriculture and the livelihood of indigenous peoples.

Since ancient times, indigenous peoples have organized themselves as agricultural communities. On this point it is worth highlighting, as A. Lipschutz does, that "the different phases in indigenous history and indigenous legislation in this country coincide with that of the many other countries in Spanish America."[8] An affirmation which by itself – and especially if one acknowledges the intellectual merits of the author – both explains and confirms the immensity of the problem we are trying to solve on the Continent: the indigenous problem.[9] At its very heart originates the institution of the chief/boss, which is transformed into the lord . . . This community did not have individual property; common ownership was the

norm across the American Continent. The clan owned the land, not the individual, an important fact that undoubtedly helps to clarify many different aspects of the indigenous problem. This is why the draft law submitted for your approval today, recognizing that such a way of life is intrinsic [to indigenous people], not only respects but also favors the indigenous community, allowing for its real development, by establishing indigenous cooperatives for example. At the same time it encourages the development of all sectors that support change; it is also concerned with the organization of indigenous people – with establishing legal procedures to help speed up court cases in defense of indigenous communities' rights or an administrative institutional apparatus dedicated to indigenous affairs.

Such provisions will help the agrarian reform process run more efficiently, an agrarian reform which is – in its very essence – revolutionary. This in turn should help to perpetuate profound socioeconomic change, and a transformation of the old (underdeveloped) structures.

It is also necessary to clarify certain key concepts, because their ambiguity to date has caused many serious problems. Only an adequate definition of terms will allow us to avoid confusion and deal with the problem objectively. In our country people often draw on racial stereotypes when talking about the *Mapuche*, and by doing so have helped to legitimize the structures of domination. Many sectors of society favor the use of such stereotypes (which denigrate indigenous people) because they help to justify all the atrocities that have been committed. Paradoxically, however, when presenting themselves to the outside world, people tend to appropriate the positive traits associated with the Araucanian. Even the Spanish admired the Araucanian; indeed, he went so far as to dedicate a world-famous epic poem "La Araucana" to him.[10] But it is important to consider many other criteria [apart from race]: physical traits, the *Mapuche* as an ethnicity or a subculture, language, surname, self-identification, legal criteria or more practical (as opposed to conceptual) definition including those who have been born on a reservation or community.

---

[8]Alejandro Lipschutz was a biological scientist, originally of Lithuanian descent, who arrived in Chile during the 1920s. He became a Chilean national in 1930. Despite earning much of his income for his pursuits in biological science, he also became renowned for his anthropological and historical work, particularly his interest in indigenous histories. He was a member of the Communist Party and became actively involved in Allende's Popular Unity reform agenda—he helped to draft the Indigenous Law and he also advised the government on how to best incorporate *Mapuche* communities into the agrarian reform process.

[9]Such terminology can be misleading, mainly because it homogenizes Latin America's indigenous peoples, treating them as if they were all one and the same (and always had been). It also implies that the problem is caused by indigenous peoples, although in other incidences Allende specifically rejected this idea.

---

[10]Alonso de Ercilla, *La Araucana* [1569–1589] (Barcelona: Editorial Iberia, 1962).

The draft law expressly determines what is understood by each of the key terms that help us to understand the indigenous problem, and clears up the confusion and uncertainties of previous legislation, which caused many controversies (in most cases affecting the indigenous person more than anyone else).

That said, it is also very important to establish how far the changes will impact upon the socio-economic, cultural and political standing of indigenous peoples, prioritizing the measures relevant to their socio-economic situation. As noted by various studies an accumulative process of pauperization is underway; most land is concentrated in the hands of a few families, perpetuating the well-known state of affairs of our economy – ie., most of the wealth being owned by a small minority – which is the root cause of the most serious disturbances and injustices. In effect most *Mapuche* families own between 0.1 and 4 hectares of land. Moreover, as a direct consequence, *Mapuche* communities do not constitute a communal economic venture; rather, the cultivation and ownership of the land is individual and family based. The economic unit is – definitively – the family. This reality is of the utmost importance – the production itself, economic decisions and appropriation of the produce are all done at family level. As A. Carvajal has stated, "despite its collective legitimization [the land] is recognized and used by the members of the community, as family assets and it is passed on in these terms. In addition, they don't have an organization that collectively sanctions the activities of the community members. The discipline system is very weak and it requires external support (ie. legal) in order to work properly. And the community's level of communitarianism is highly variable: one notes a marked individualist tendency, characteristic of the small property owner.

[. . .] The dire situation and the highly explosive climate that accompanies it could have very dangerous consequences.[11] Indigenous people feel great insecurity and this further increases the risk [of conflict]: "even if legally the *Mapuche* have a collective link with the land, through the title deeds – we still insist – the form of ownership and farming are individual. Members of the reservation have the right to make use of the small plot of land allocated to them. They have inherited it and they have to leave it to their own children [when they die]. They have only very limited rights over this land: they can use it, rent it out under certain conditions or rent out part of it, but they cannot sell it without specific legal authorization. This form of land ownership is only legitimized through traditional consensus and, on many occasions, by use of force. In any case, the institutionalization of land access is carried out through different institutions to those created by dominant society – the legalization of *Mapuche* territorial property – which leads to great insecurity about land ownership." This intermingling of factors not only makes analysis and any diagnostics difficult; it also helps to breed disorder and violence.

It is therefore important to create and develop institutions that do not leave any room for doubts – regarding both their meaning or social purpose; [we need to] be able to improve [indigenous people's] technical and cultural training, acknowledging the harm that has been caused through their cultural marginalization. Their exploiters were well aware that indigenous people's lack of training and education assured their continued dominance. Only through education will they be able to make better (more rational) use of their lands and produce. They do not, as some have falsely claimed, reject new techniques; in fact it is the very reverse. Assistance/credit programs and other relevant measures will allow for their meaningful incorporation into the changes that are underway; it is not just empty rhetoric which only mocks their legitimate rights and demands. Nobody should be surprised by their aggression, which emerges as an almost necessary reaction to the oppression that they have suffered, sometimes tamely and lethargically. The aggression cannot be attributed to the role played by agitators; indigenous peoples have carried this explosive energy and rebellion within for a long time now.[12]

---

[11]By dire situation, Allende means the lack of land and resources, the fact that the land given to indigenous communities is often the least productive or fertile, and the individual farming of the land.

[12]See, for example, my chapter in this volume on the Chilean state's occupation of *Mapuche* territory in the late nineteenth century.

In consequence, this draft law places great emphasis on the organization of peasant cooperatives, which will play a highly important role in the development and liberation of indigenous peoples. I want to stress that in many countries this system has managed to improve the living conditions of the economically marginalized classes.[13] As we travel down the irreversible path towards to socialism, this important sector of society will become socially and economically organized according to clear objectives. [We need to] facilitate better access to goods, the means of production and markets that offer the best prices; to increase the control and quality of produce. [We need to] eliminate illegal and immoral practices in the processes of production and exchange or sale, and to increase savings, the basis of investment and capitalization, and the only way to overcome underdevelopment.

On the educational front, especially, we need to promote the training of the people in the cooperatives, both the leaders and the workers. We need to train leaders so that they not only have the enthusiasm but also the technical expertise, without losing sight of the importance of a comprehensive economic policy that aims to integrate our indigenous comrades with other sectors of production and encourage their maximum development. Only in this way will we ever be able to transform the system of land ownership.

In effect, the law establishes various practices, which not only control the functioning of the cooperatives but also defend them. Through them indigenous people will find the cohesion and real protection they have always lacked. Of course, these measures are not limited to increasing production; they will help to establish new ties of trust, understanding and cooperation that transcend all former resentments or frustrations. They promote profound change. At the same time they establish new procedures that not only simplify and speed up legal hearings (that have sometimes dragged on for years) but also allow one to gain a good knowledge of the situation in order to find the most just solution. Priority is given to substance rather mere formalities (which the well informed can manipulate) in order to defend the rights of indigenous people. On a practical level, the changes are very important given the tendency to misuse the testimony of witnesses, who were often ignorant or acted in bad faith, for all sorts of immoral purposes.[14] Now, [only] the testimony of those who know the facts best will be allowed, which will help to speed up proceedings. Similarly, we will eliminate the possibility of cover-ups and delays, which have always worked against those in the right.

Suggested Sources

Xavier Albó offers a useful summary of *Mapuche* political activism in Chile as part of a much broader study of "Andean People in the Twentieth Century," in F. Salomon and S. Schwarz (eds.), *The Cambridge History of Native Peoples of the Americas, Vol. III, Part II* (Cambridge: Cambridge University Press, 1999), 765–871. Florencia Mallon provides a detailed and insightful analysis of the relationship between one *Mapuche* community and the Chilean state during the twentieth century in *Courage Tastes of Blood: The Mapuche Community of Nicolás Ailío and the Chilean State, 1906–2001* (Durham, NC, and London: Duke University Press, 2005), which includes a chapter on the Allende regime and policy changes. Kyle Steen focuses on Popular Unity policy in *Agrarian Reform under Allende: Peasant Revolt in the South* (Albuquerque: University of New Mexico Press, 1977). Joanna Crow explores the competing ideas about indigenous and national identities that emerged during this period in "Debates about Ethnicity, Class and Nation in Allende's Chile (1970–1973)," *Bulletin of Latin American Research* 26, no. 3 (July 2007): 319–338.

James Cockcroft recently published some of Allende's public speeches in English translation in *Chile's Voice of Democracy: Salvador Allende Reader* (London: Ocean Press, 2000). The essay writer, novelist, and playwright, Ariel Dorfman, describes the

---

[13]Such claims can be contested; indeed, it could be argued that the cooperative system has failed in many countries.

[14]This might include witnesses trying to secure lands for themselves or their having been bribed to make a particular statement.

buildup to the military coup of 11 September 1973 and, in particular, the suffering of one *Mapuche* woman, who traveled to Santiago to denounce the abusive actions of military officials in the southern regions, in *Heading North, Looking South: A Bilingual Journey* (London: Hodder and Stoughton, 1998). Also useful is the English translation of Pablo Neruda's pro-Popular Unity collection of poems, *Incitación al nixonicidio y alabanza de la revolución chilena* [Incitement to Nixoncide and Praise for the Chilean Revolution] (Wever, IA: Quixote Press, 1980). See especially poems 42, 43, and 44, which evoke the heroic actions of sixteenth-century *Mapuche* warriors in order to defend and extol Chilean struggles against United States imperialism in the twentieth century.

Chapter 24

Indigenous Integration and Legal Changes in Paraguay

René Harder Horst, *Appalachian State University*

ar from being just dry words in a scroll or book collecting dust, laws are vibrant, evolving documents that are written, amended, and enacted with direct results for society. Legal documents reflect current political, social, and international climates and thus can help one better understand controversial events. Moreover, although governments at times try to use legislation to impress critics or may simply choose not to enforce inconvenient laws, people everywhere have pushed leaders to act on their laws, often with surprising results. This chapter engages these issues by following the evolution of legislation aimed at indigenous peoples during the Stroessner dictatorship (1954–1989), showing how the regime responded to various internal and international pressures. The chapter culminates with the 1992 constitution's treatment of indigenous rights, legislation that was an integral part of the democratization that Paraguay underwent following Stroessner's fall from power.

Alfred Stroessner, the son of an immigrant German brewer, first became president in 1954; to retain control of the presidency, he allied his Colorado Party with the Armed Forces and the upper classes. The ambitious leader remained in power for thirty-five years by using his party to monitor the population closely and eliminate opposition, modernizing the military, and tolerating corrupt business deals or construction projects that enriched his upper-class supporters. Despite his modernizing goals, Paraguay remained largely a rural nation, made up mostly of peasants living in poor conditions throughout the countryside. Among these peasants were seventeen indigenous tribes, the best known being the four *Guaraní* tribes that lived east of the Paraguay River.

Unlike some Andean indigenous peasants who were substantially integrated into national society at the expense of their individual cultural identities, the four Guaraní tribes had kept their independent identities by remaining in small isolated communities, supplementing their crops with forest resources, and limiting outside cultural influences. Throughout the colonial period, the Guaraní had interacted with the Europeans and, as the popular film *The Mission* shows, produced a peasantry with a mixed Spanish and native culture. Stroessner tried to change indigenous peoples to fit his view of modernity. The most frustrating feature of indigenous customs for the regime was their communal practices. Moreover, native people refused Catholic proselytism because of the legacy of conquest by force, and many had welcomed Protestant instruction as a way to distinguish themselves from surrounding Catholic *campesinos*. These practices aggravated the nationals, who despised the native people for their aloof, independent stance. Finally, the regime saw indigenous traits as backward obstacles to development and contrary to plans for national economic growth and political stability.

The first document in this chapter is the set of plans the regime made in 1958, when the dictator created an agency to settle the indigenous population in permanent locations and integrate them into the broader economy and national society. At the same time, the Stroessner regime created the new *Department of Indigenous Affairs (DAI)* and charged it with establishing greater state control over native

communities. Forcing cultural change is always difficult, however, and this was especially the case for a small agency such as the *DAI*, which lacked adequate resources or backing from other government departments. At the same time, there were many religious groups competing for influence within indigenous communities. The *DAI* carried out an initial count of the indigenous population, encouraged missionary activities, set up trading posts near communities to encourage natives to market their crops and become dependent on western goods, and explored ways for settlements to be more productive to national markets. These efforts were largely ineffective because the *DAI* was strapped for cash resources. Soon administrators of the small agency were completely frustrated.

In the process of trying to settle the indigenous peoples permanently, the regime also ran into additional problems, this time with the *Aché* people of eastern Paraguay. The Aché (pronounced a'shae) are a subgroup of the Guaraní who lived from hunting and gathering in a nomadic culture rather than from sedentary agriculture, as did the surrounding and much larger Avá, Mbyá, and Paï Tavyterã Guaraní tribes. Increasingly, members of the Aché were moved, sometimes by force, to work on agricultural estates, where they lived in abysmal and abusive conditions. In the winter of 1971, a German anthropologist named Mark Münzel arrived to study the Aché. The anthropologist noticed the deadly effects of initial contact, abuse, malnutrition, and death for the newly arrived Northern Aché. When Münzel denounced the abuses, the dictator expelled him from the country, following which the anthropologist logically accused the regime of trying to exterminate the Aché.

Foreign attention to Paraguayan human rights, and especially the indigenous situation, escalated over the next years, as the United States Congress and even the United Nations (UN) considered whether the regime had actually intended to eliminate Paraguay's indigenous people through purposeful genocide. In response to foreign scrutiny and eager to continue foreign aid, Stroessner's dictatorship revised the way it presented its plans for the native population. First, Stroessner closed the *DAI* in 1975 and replaced it with a new agency, the National Indigenous

Institute, the plans for which are presented in the second document excerpt in this chapter.

Institutional reorganization failed to persuade critics that the regime was concerned for the native population. In particular, the Carter administration (1977–1981), which focused on human rights abuses in Latin America, responded to the accusations of abuse by slashing United States assistance to Paraguay. In an attempt to recover foreign funding, Stroessner's generals scrambled to show that the regime was actually concerned about indigenous peoples and their living conditions.[1] Acting on advice from the UN, in 1981 the regime passed a new law that declared its revised goals for indigenous peoples of the nation (Law 904), which appears as the third document in this chapter. Law 904 promised to improve conditions for native peoples and settle them permanently, even repeatedly pledging to respect their indigenous cultures. This new legislation served to quiet the more serious opposition for several more years, but as the economy deteriorated and repression increased, indigenous rights again came to occupy a place in growing resistance against the dictatorship.

After opponents finally deposed the dictator in 1989, the next administration approved a new constitution to preserve the newly chosen democratic institutions. Allied with the Catholic Church, which in Paraguay had adopted a strong defense of human rights to counter the regime, indigenous peoples mobilized to ensure that the new administration would support their land rights and improve their conditions. After struggling for so long against a dictatorship bent on forcing them to disappear, indigenous peoples demanded that their fellow Paraguayans finally begin to respect indigenous rights. Native peoples secured allies among *nongovernmental organizations (NGOs)* and academics and opponents of the regime, contacted newspapers, and attracted enough attention to finally force their way into the national political process. Indigenous peoples in Paraguay were the only group to have an entire chapter of the 1992 constitution dedicated to their rights, excerpts of which appear as the last document in this chapter. Native delegates saw their inclusion as a definite legislative victory for the seventeen indigenous tribes.

The strong pan-indigenous organization and the alliances that indigenous peoples made in order to win inclusion in Paraguay's 1992 constitution shows that they were squarely situated within continent-wide trends in indigenous history. As in Indian-state relations elsewhere in Latin America, in Paraguay the situation during the last decade of the regime changed slowly in favor of the indigenous people as the dictatorship entered a crisis. Beginning in the mid-1970s, native people allied with other regime opponents and forged regional, national, and international indigenous rights organizations. As with indigenous movements in Ecuador, Guatemala, and Bolivia, native groups in Paraguay joined the opposition to the regime and forged a noteworthy form of social protest. In the space of a few decades, they shifted from being victims of economic and political modernization to agents of democratization.

Questions to Consider:

1. How and why did the Stroessner regime's goals for Paraguay's indigenous population change over the course of the dictatorship? Which of these changes appear to have been substantive, and which seem merely meant to appease critics?

2. Can you see clues in the documents to help explain how the Stroessner regime tried to use its social legislation for indigenous integration as a way to defend itself against international criticism mentioned in the chapter introduction?

3. How did the 1992 constitutional guarantees for indigenous peoples reflect recent political changes in Paraguay? Can you detect any lingering vestiges of policies from the Stroessner regime in the 1992 document?

4. Why might both indigenous peoples and the government have viewed the 1992 legislation as a victory in their long struggle?

---

[1]For a more extensive discussion on United States policies toward Paraguay during this period, see Frank Mora and Jerry Cooney, *Paraguay and the United States, Distant Allies* (Athens: University of Georgia Press, 2007), chap. 7, 193–230.

Creation of the Department of Indigenous Affairs (1958)[2]

Decree 1341, The Creation of the *Department of Indigenous Affairs,* Asunción, 8 November 1958

Given the need to adopt measures tending to gather the indigenous people scattered throughout the eastern and western regions of the republic in organized colonies, in order to avoid their extinction and adapt them to a sedentary way of life, and considering that Paraguay has assumed such responsibilities as a member state of the Inter-American *Indigenist* Institute;

That the studies conducted by the Ministries of National Defense and Education have proven the existence of an important autochthonous population that finds itself in an defenseless and helpless state; and it being impossible to postpone the need to adopt measures to direct them towards their reintegration into civilized national life,

The President of the Republic of Paraguay decrees:

Article 1: Be created the *Department of Indigenous Affairs,* dependent on the Ministry of National Defense and destined to centralize *indigenist* activities within the republic.

Article 2: The *Department of Indigenous Affairs* will unite the elements it judges necessary to formulate a specifically *indigenist* legislation.

Signed: Alfredo Stroessner; Marcial Samaniego, J. Bernardino Gorostiaga

Department of National Defense

---

[2]*Source:* The Archive of the Department of Indigenous Affairs, DAI, is located in the agency's library at their offices, 745 Don Bosco Street, Asunción, Paraguay.

Creation of the National Indigenous Institute, INDI (1975)[3]

Ministry of National Defense, Decree No. 18,365, 20 October 1975;

Considering:

That the *Department of Indigenous Affairs* has completed various studies and accumulated experience in the field of national *indigenismo,* but that it has become necessary to create a new structure according to current times, in which the national government is concerned for the integral improvement of all the ethnic groups in the country, and especially indigenous [*autóctono*-autochthonous] ones;

That the groups of national indigenous people have shown interest in their development by way of effective cooperation that contributes to raise their living standards and their integration into the dynamics of national society;[4]

The diverse Interamerican *Indigenist* Congresses recommend the creation of National *Indigenist*

Institutes in whose programs for advances indigenous people should participate, on equal footing, with the different government agencies, scientific centers and universities in perfect coordination;

That the National *Indigenist* Congress realized in our Capital, in August 1959, resolved to recommend the organization of a National *Indigenist* Council;

That in this time of peace that the Republic enjoys, it is feasible to coordinate the efforts of different state, independent and private organizations that until now have worked independently. A superior organization would [direct these organizations and] take charge of the planning and execution of development programs for the different indigenous groups of the country, nevertheless respecting their cultures;

Therefore, the President of the Republic of Paraguay Decrees:

Art. 1: That a National Indigenous Institute (INDI) be created and have the goal of encouraging the integral development of the different indigenous communities of the country as well as their effective integration into national society, while nevertheless respecting their cultures.

---

[3]*Source:* Ministry of National Defense, Decree No. 18,365, 20 October 1975.

[4]In fact, what indigenous people had actually requested was better treatment and land ownership, not further integration into national society.

Art. 2: The INDI shall be constituted by a council presided by the Minister of National Defense and integrated by the ministers of Interior, Public Health, Social Welfare, Labor and Justice, Education and Religion, the Ministry of Rural Welfare and member of the National Armed Forces.

Art. 3: The INDI shall create commissions necessary for the better fulfillment of its goals, composed by member of public and private organizations.

Art. 4: The INDI shall organize in the capital . . . a National Office under the direction of an Executive Director designated by the INDI Council . . . to prepare plans and programs for submission to the Council, so as to execute the same.

Art. 5: The INDI shall organize Regional Offices in the Interior of the Republic according to its needs, and with the same goals as indicated in the previous article, which shall be directed by and executive designated by the INDI Council

at the suggestion of the Director of the National Office.

Art. 7: The INDI may request public offices to waive customs fees in order to import materials necessary to carry out its goals.

Art. 8: The INDI correspondence shall be free of postal and telephone fees . . .

Art. 9: All national, departmental, military, police and judicial posts shall cooperate with the INDI for the smooth fulfillment of its work.

Art. 10: The INDI is authorized to create its own regulations.

Art. 11: The Ministry of National Defense shall include in its budget the expenses necessary to face the expenses incurred by this institution.

Art. 12: Be it registered, publicized, communicated and made aware.

Signed: President Alfred Stroessner, Minister of Defense Marcial Samaniego, General Auditor of War Ruben Ossorio.

Law No. 904 *Statute of Indigenous Communities* (1981)[5]

The Congress of the Paraguayan Nation Decrees with Force of Law:

Section 1. General Principles.

Chapter 1

Art. 1: This Law has as its object the social and cultural preservation of the indigenous communities, the defense of their heritage and traditions, the improvement of their economic conditions, their effective participation in the process of national development and their access to a judicial system that will guarantee them ownership of the land and other productive resources in equal rights to those of other citizens.

Art. 2: To the effects of this law it will be understood as indigenous community the group of extended families, clan or groups of clans, with their own culture and system of authority who speak an autochthonous language and share a common

habitat. Indigenous tribe *{parcialidad}* will be understood as a group of two or more communities with similar characteristics that identify themselves under a similar denomination.

Art. 3: Respect for traditional ways of organization will not prevent indigenous communities from voluntarily, and by exercising their right to self-determination, adopting other forms of organization established by law that should permit their integration into national society.

Art. 4: In no case shall the use of force or coercion be allowed as a way to promote the integration of indigenous communities into the national collectivity, nor as [part of] measures tending to assimilation that does not consider the interests and feelings of the very indigenous people.

Art. 5: The Indigenous communities may regulate their lives together through tribal norms as long as they are not incompatible with public order.

Art. 6: In legal matters that involve indigenous people, judges will keep in mind with tribal

[5]*Source:* Law No. 904 Statute of Indigenous Communities, 1981.

rights, being required to solicit established directives from the Paraguayan Indigenous Institute and other specialists in the matter. The benefit of the doubt shall favor the indigenous person with attention to their culture and tribal norms.

Art. 7: The State recognizes the legal existence of the indigenous communities, and will grant them legal status according to the dispositions of this law.

Art. 9: A request of legal recognition will be presented by community leaders, including the following information:

a. name of the community; list of the families and members, including ages, gender and marital status.

b. geographic location of the community if it is permanent, or with locations frequented by them if it is not, and

c. name of the community leaders and reasons for their authority.

Art. 10: The Institute, within a term not longer than thirty days shall request recognition of legal community status from the Executive Power by way of the Ministry of National Defense.

Art. 11: The Institute shall register the Decree that recognizes the legal status of an Indigenous Community in the National Registry of Indigenous Communities and shall send an authentic copy to the interested parties.

Art. 12: The leaders shall exercise legal representation of their community. The naming of leaders shall be communicated to the Institute, which shall recognize it within thirty days from the date on which said communication took place and shall inscribe it in the National Registry of Indigenous Communities.

Art. 13: If the community revokes the nomination of its leaders, it shall proceed regarding the new leaders with the dictates of the preceding article.

Art. 32: The duties of the INDI include the following:

a. establish and apply programs and policies;

b. coordinate, control, inspect and evaluate all indigenist activities in the public and private sector;

c. give scientific, technical, legal, administrative and economic assistance to indigenous communities, by itself or in coordination with other institutions and request assistance from national and foreign entities;

d. levy censuses of the indigenous population in coordination with indigenous and *indigenista* entities;

e. realize, promote and regulate studies of indigenous people and to propagate information about them, with the agreement of the INDI and the community;

f. adhere to the principles, resolutions and recommendations of international indigenist organizations, that coincide with the goals of this present legislation, and promote, in their place, the adherence of these to the objectives of the INDI;

g. support indigenous requests and accusations to state and private entities;

h. study and propose norms for matters of Civil Registration, Military Service, education, penal responsibility, identity documentation for indigenous people and assure their fulfillment;

i. maintain relations with national and international indigenist entities, evaluating their fulfillment of treaties on the subject;

j. promote the technical and professional development of indigenous people, especially for farming, forestry and crafts work, to train and prepare them for the organization and administration of their communities; and

k. realize other activities that relate to the goals of the INDI . . .

Section Four

Chapter 1 On General and Transitory Arrangements

Art. 65: The public and private institutions should grant active participation to the INDI when preparing plans and programs for indigenist matters.

Art. 66: Landowners on whose lands there are indigenous settlements, are required to notify the INDI within ninety days of the declaration of this law.

Art. 67: Within one year from the date of the promulgation of this law, the private entities that have purchased lands for indigenous settlements shall have transferred them to the communities for whom they were purchased.

Art. 70: The INDI shall by itself or by way of other entities spread the news about this law to all indigenous communities, so they can learn of its objectives and the benefits it grants them and can help its fulfillment.

Art. 72: Be created the National Registry of Indigenous Communities dependent on the INDI, whose organization and functions shall be regulated.

Art. 73: Those cases not dealt with in this law will be ruled when pertinent by the Agrarian Statute, the Labor Code and the Social Security Laws.

Art. 74: This Law shall be regulated by the Executive Branch.

Declared into law 18 December, 1981, signed by General of the Army and President of the Republic Alfredo Stroessner

Minister of National Defense
Minister of Treasury
Marcial Samaniego
César Barrientos

From the Paraguayan Constitution of 1992: Chapter 5, About Indigenous Peoples[6]

This Constitution recognizes the existence of the indigenous peoples, groups with cultures that predate the creation and constitution of the Paraguayan state.

Article 63. On Ethnic Identity

The right of indigenous peoples to preserve and develop their ethnic identity within their respective habitats is recognized and guaranteed. They shall enjoy that right, as well as the ability to freely apply their systems of political, social, economic, cultural and religious organization, as well as the voluntary use of those norms that do not attempt against the fundamental rights established by this Constitution.

Article 64. On Communal Property

The indigenous peoples enjoy the right to own land communally, in enough extension and with sufficient quality for the preservation and development of their distinct ways of life. The State will freely provide them with these lands, which shall be inalienable, indivisible, nontransferable, not susceptible to guarantee contractual obligations nor rentable; in the same way they shall be except from

tribute. Their removal or transport from their habitat without their expressed consent is prohibited.

Article 65. On Property and Participation

The indigenous groups are guaranteed the right to participate in the economic, social, cultural and political life of the country in accordance with their common uses, the Constitution and national laws.

Article 66. On Education and Assistance

The State shall respect the cultural distinctions of the indigenous groups, especially in regards to formal education. A request from the same will lead to attention in defense against demographic regression, depredations of their habitat, environmental contamination, economic exploitation, and cultural alienation.

Article 67. On Exoneration

Members of the indigenous groups are freed from contributing social, civil or military services, as well as public duties established by law.

---

[6]*Source:* From the Paraguayan Constitution of 1992.

Suggested Sources

There have been relatively few scholarly studies about relations between the government and indigenous people in recent Paraguayan history. Most works have focused on the Jesuit missions and the bilingual heritage that resulted from extensive racial mixture during the colonial period. The best researched and written of these works is historian Barbara Ganson's book, *The Guaraní under Spanish Rule in the Rio de la Plata* (Stanford, CA: Stanford University Press, 2003). Several seminal works on nineteenth-century Paraguay include Thomas Whigham's *The Politics of River Trade: Tradition and Development in the Upper Plata, 1780–1870* (Albuquerque: University of New Mexico Press, 1991); as well as his two-volume work on the Paraguayan War, of which the first has been published as *The Paraguayan War, Volume 1: Causes and Early Conduct (Studies in War, Society, and the Military)* (Lincoln: University of Nebraska Press, 2002). For modern Paraguay, the best political analysis is Frank O. Mora and Jerry Cooney's recent book, *Paraguay and the United States, Distant Allies* (Athens: University of Georgia Press, 2007). For social policy and events during the Stroessner presidency, René Harder Horst's book, *The Stroessner Regime and Indigenous Resistance in Paraguay* (Gainesville: University Press of Florida, 2007), is the most comprehensive. Additional works on indigenous people in Paraguay and the controversy over genocide include Mark Münzel, *The Ache Indians, Genocide in Paraguay*, doc. 11 (Copenhagen: International World Group for Indigenous Affairs, 1973); and his next book, *The Ache: Genocide Continues in Paraguay* (Copenhagen: International World Group for Indigenous Affairs, 1974), in which he deepened his charges. Richard Arens, Professor of Human Rights at Temple University, supported Münzel's allegations in *Genocide in Paraguay* (Philadelphia, Temple University Press, 1976). In their book, *Aché Life History: The Ecology and Demography of a Foraging People* (New York: Aldine De Gruyter, 1996), anthropologists Kim Hill and Magdalena Hurtado offer a more objective and less politicized study of *Aché* culture based on their research among the *Aché*. To broaden the topic of recent indigenous history to the rest of Latin America, see Erick Langer and Elena Muñoz's book, *Contemporary Indigenous Movements in Latin America* (Wilmington, DE: Scholarly Resources, 2003).

For a more popular look at indigenous people in Latin America accessible to students at all levels, see Peter Winn, "Children of the Sun," in *The Americas* (Berkeley: University of California Press, 1992), chap. 7, 239–270. The best film for students on Paraguay that focuses specifically on the Stroessner regime and how it functioned is the 1992 BBC production of *Secrets of the General*. This highly recommended video shows the daily function of Stroessner's ruthless methods of control and analyzes the three support pillars of the regime. The narrative is engaging and the film is shot in Paraguay with interviews of personalities important to the regime's history. The film is available from the University of Kansas Latin American Studies Program in Lawrence, KS, Amnesty International Group 254, the Paraguayan Kansas Student Association, or from Pittsburgh State University International Programs.

Chapter 25

For Land and Dignity: Zapatista Goals in Chiapas, Mexico, in the 1990s

Erin E. O'Connor, Bridgewater State College

On January 1, 1994, the Ejército Zapatista para Liberación Nacional (the Zapatista Army for National Liberation, or EZLN) launched its first offensive, attacking army posts and taking control of several communities in the region around San Cristobal, Chiapas. The EZLN, a leftist guerrilla organization made up mostly of indigenous peoples founded in 1983, demanded land, *autonomy*, and dignity. Its leadership also opposed the North American Free Trade Agreement (NAFTA), which would disadvantage poor (mostly indigenous) farmers in the region and called for an end to corruption in Mexican politics. The Mexican government responded violently to the 1994 uprising by bombing several indigenous communities. In response to both the government and the guerrillas, Mexican citizens held demonstrations calling for peace, and in February 1994 representatives of the EZLN and the Mexican government met in San Andrés to try to come to a peace agreement. Over the next several years, alternating military clashes and peace talks in the southeastern state of Chiapas failed to produce a clear outcome. Although the *Zapatista* movement stagnated, government forces failed to defeat it. The government practice of targeting civilians, including women and children, probably won more support for the guerrillas than they might otherwise have had.

The *Zapatista* uprising in Chiapas rested on a long history of exploitation and resistance in the region.[1] Although problems began in the colonial era, it was only with the expansion of export estates in the late nineteenth century that many indigenous peoples in Chiapas fell into debt servitude. Some hope came when President Lázaro Cárdenas established land reform policies in the 1930s, but Chiapas Indians rarely received the lands they requested from the government. As Mexico modernized, most indigenous peoples in Chiapas lacked electricity and schools, and they lived on less than the legal minimum wage. When educational initiatives reached indigenous peoples, the state was mainly concerned with acculturating them into modern lifestyles rather than addressing indigenous interests or needs.

An important transformation began when Samuel Ruiz was named bishop of San Cristóbal de las Casas, a position he held from 1959 until his retirement in 2000. Ruiz had not originally intended to do any more than convert indigenous peoples, but when he saw the depth of their poverty, he knew he had to try to alleviate it. The Church officials who worked with the indigenous poor in Chiapas respected their culture and encouraged them to come to their own conclusions about what to do about their situation. Protestant churches also offered opportunities for indigenous leadership, particularly for women, and

they also contributed to the rising politicization of indigenous communities in Chiapas. Religious officials even helped to plan the First Indigenous Congress in Chiapas in 1974. Most Indians who organized around this time identified mainly as peasants, as was evident in their demands for land, labor rights, credit, and improved health care and education. However, many speakers at the Congress also argued for the need to defend indigenous cultural identity.

As indigenous peasant organizations grew, so did indigenous frustrations over the government's failure to grant them much-needed land. During the 1980s, increasing numbers of indigenous peasants either directly or indirectly supported the newly established EZLN. Several factors explain this rising indigenous support for the movement and the outbreak of violence by 1994. When the coffee market on which many poor indigenous farmers depended crashed in 1989, the government offered little assistance. Then a 1992 amendment to Article 27 of the Mexican constitution declared that land redistribution was completed, ending any hope that indigenous peasants in Chiapas had to gain land through legal means. At the same time, *neoliberal* policies, combined with discussions of a free trade agreement with the United States, threatened to further undermine indigenous subsistence in Chiapas.

When the *Zapatista* rebellion began, however, it was not a poor indigenous man or woman who became the "face" of the movement, but rather an outsider. *Subcomandante* Marcos speaks in a refined manner; discusses nuanced leftist theory and history; and conducts interviews in English, Italian, and French as well as Spanish. Though he continues to wear a mask, the Mexican government believes that Marcos is Rafael Sebastián Guillén Vicente, a Mexico City native who has a master's degree in philosophy. Marcos has skillfully used high-tech Internet and media appeals not only to get his message out to Mexican citizens, but also to gain sympathy from an international audience. The *Zapatista* leadership's use of technology stands in stark contrast with the experiences of most of the indigenous members of the EZLN, who often cannot obtain adequate utilities and resources for their villages.

The position of women within the *Zapatista* movement is complicated. Indigenous women's support was crucial to the EZLN as it worked to establish ties with indigenous communities during

---

[1]For background to the *Zapatista* uprising, see Lynn Stephen, *Zapata Lives! Histories and Cultural Politics in Southern Mexico* (Berkeley: University of California Press, 2002), chapters 4 and 5. Also see John Womack, Jr., *Rebellion in Chiapas: An Historical Reader* (New York: The New Press, 1999).

This photograph shows *Zapatista* rebels and supporters on their way to the Mexico City to demand national government support for Indian rights in Chiapas. The banner here depicts Emiliano Zapata, one of the leaders of the Mexican revolutionary conflict, in the central Mexican state of Morelos, from 1910 to 1919. Examine the photograph closely: How did the participants display their solidarity with the guerrilla movement and with poor rural peoples? Also consider their chosen namesake, Zapata—given Emiliano Zapata's place in Mexican revolutionary history: What claims were the modern guerrillas trying to make by using his name and image at the forefront of their movement?

Source: AP Wide World Photos.

the 1980s. Officially, the EZLN seeks to achieve gender equality. However, indigenous communities continue to cling to patriarchal rules, and the *Zapatista* movement itself is far more concerned with economic and political changes and the defense of indigenous cultural identity than with reforming gender relations. This tension, however, has led *Zapatista* women to speak up and demand more attention to addressing gender inequalities. In this sense, they have created a movement within a movement: They are loyal to EZLN causes, but their own focus is distinct from the male mainstream in the organization.

The *Zapatista* movement offers an excellent example of how a new focus on ethnic identity has reshaped Latin American socialism since the 1980s and 1990s. Although the core economic foundations of socialism are still present in many subaltern social protest and political movements, the tone of the movements and the relationship between leftist and indigenous organizations has changed considerably. Where indigenous concerns were once muted in leftist politics, they are now prominent. The following document reveals many of the changes, aspirations, and problems that have emerged with rising indigenous activism since the 1980s and 1990s in both Mexico and in many other parts of Latin America.

Questions to Consider:

1. At the end of this document, the *Zapatistas* called for "Freedom! Justice! Democracy!" How well do these terms reflect the *Zapatista* goals as stated in the document? How did the *Zapatistas* use these ideas to try to justify their movement?
2. How and why did economic goals overlap with cultural goals in this document?
3. Look at the section where indigenous women made demands. What were their main problems and goals? How do these compare and contrast with demands made in the rest of the document?
4. What kind of relationship did the *Zapatistas* seem to want with the Mexican national government?

Communiqué of March 1, 1994[2]

To the People of Mexico
To the peoples and governments of the world
To the national and international press

[2]*Source:* Ben Clarke and Clifton Ross, eds., *Voice of Fire: Communiqués and Interviews from the Zapatista National Liberation Army* (Berkeley, CA: New Earth Publications, 1994), 80–86; it was translated by Margi Clarke.

Brothers and sisters:

The Clandestine Revolutionary Indigenous Committee-General Command of the EZLN respectfully and honorably addresses all of you to make known the platform of demands we presented at the negotiating table during the sessions for Peace and Reconciliation in Chiapas:

"We do not ask for charity nor gifts, we ask for the right to live in dignity as human beings, with equality and justice like our forebears and grandparents."

To the People of Mexico:

The indigenous peoples of the State of Chiapas, who have taken up arms in the Zapatista Army of National Liberation against misery and corrupt government, present the reasons for our struggle and our principal demands:

The reasons and causes motivating our armed movement arise because the Government has never offered a single real solution to the following problems:

First: the hunger, misery, and marginalization that we have been suffering through forever.

Second: The total lack of land where we could work to survive.

Third: The repression, evictions, imprisonment, torture, and assassinations that the government has used against us in response to the just demands of our peoples.

Fourth: The intolerable injustices and violations of our human rights as indigenous peoples and impoverished peasants.

Fifth: The brutal exploitation that we suffer in the sale of our products, in our day's work, and in the purchase of basic necessities.

Sixth: The absence of indispensible services denied to the indigenous population.

Seventh: The lies, deceptions, promises, and impositions of the governments over the last 60 years. The lack of freedom and democracy in order to decide about our own futures.

Eighth: The constitutional laws have not yet been complied with by the governments of this nation, instead we the indigenous peoples and peasants are forced to pay for the smallest error and the full weight of laws that we have not made is thrown upon us, while those who make the laws are the first to violate them.

The EZLN came to dialogue with the word of truth. The EZLN came to speak its truth about the conditions which have given rise to its just war, and to ask the whole people of Mexico for a resolution to the political, economic, and social conditions which brought us to the point of taking up arms in defense of our very existence and our rights.

Therefore we demand . . .

First: We demand that truly free and democratic elections be held, with equality of rights and obligations for the political organizations which compete for power, with true freedom to elect one or another candidate and with respect for the will of the majority. Democracy is a fundamental right of all peoples, indigenous and non-indigenous. Without democracy, there can be neither liberty, nor justice, nor dignity. And without dignity, there is nothing.

Second: In order for there to be truly free and democratic elections, it is necessary that the holders of the Federal Executive office and the State Executive office who took power via fraudulent elections, resign from their positions. Their legitimacy comes not from respect for the will of the majority but rather from its usurpation. Therefore, a transitional government must be formed so that there may be equality and respect for all political currents. The federal and state legislative authorities, elected freely and democratically, should assume their true function of promulgating just laws for all and to be vigilant toward their compliance.

Another step toward the fulfillment of free and democratic elections would be for the great laws of the nation and of the localities to legitimize the existence and efforts of citizens and groups of citizens with no particular affiliations, which would oversee the whole electoral process, sanctioning its legality and results, and as the maximum authority, serving to guarantee the legitimacy of the whole electoral process.

Third: Recognition of the Zapatista National Liberation Army as a belligerent force and its troops as authentic combatants, and the application of all the international treaties regulating armed conflicts.

Fourth: A new pact between all the constituents of the federation to end centralization and permit the regions, the indigenous communities and the municipalities self-governance with political, economic, and cultural *autonomy*.

Fifth: General elections for the whole state of Chiapas and legal recognition of the political forces in the state.

Sixth: Producer of electricity and petroleum, the State of Chiapas pays taxes to the federation without receiving anything in return. Our communities do not have electric energy, the economic hemorrhage produced from petroleum exports and internal sales produces no benefit for the people of Chiapas. Thus, it is of primary importance that all Chiapan communities enjoy the benefits of electrical energy that a percentage of the income from the sale of Chiapas' petroleum and the industrial agriculture, commercial and social infrastructure should all benefit Chiapans.

Seventh: Reconsider the Free Trade Agreement signed with Canada and the United States since in its current form it does not take into account the indigenous populations and it sentences them to death for lack of labor skills.

Eighth: Article 27 of the Magna Carta[3] must reflect the original spirit of Emiliano Zapata: the land is for the indigenous peoples and for those *campesinos* who work it, not for the plantation owners. We want the great extensions of land which are in the hands of ranchers and [absentee] national and foreign landlords and others who occupy large plots but who are not *campesinos*, to pass into the hands of our peoples who totally lack land, as is set forth in our agrarian reform laws. Land titles must be accompanied by support services including agricultural machinery, fertilizers, insecticides, credit, technical assistance, hybrid seeds, cattle.[4] Fair prices for our products like coffee, corn, and beans. The land to be distributed should be of good quality and should be complemented with roads, transportation, and irrigation systems. The *campesinos* who already have lands also have the right to all the support services mentioned above in order to facilitate their work in the fields and to improve their productivity. New communal land structures and *ejidos* should be formed. The Salinas Administration's reforms to Article 27 must be annulled and the right to land should be returned to our constitution.[5]

Ninth: We want hospitals to be built in the municipal seats, with specialized medical personnel and sufficient medicines to treat the patients; and clinics in the rural *ejidos*, communities and hamlets, as well as training and a just wage for health workers. Where there are already hospitals, the facilities should be rehabilitated as soon as possible and they should be upgraded to include complete surgical services. In larger communities, clinics should be built, staffed

---

[3]This is a reference to Article 27 of the 1917 Constitution, which asserted the sovereignty of the Mexican nation over the country's land and resources and called for land reform. One of the important aspects of Article 27 was that it allowed for land redistribution in *ejidos* (traditional indigenous communal lands).

[4]Though President Lázaro Cárdenas redistributed enormous amounts of land in the 1930s, by the 1950s land reform had not alleviated the problems of most *campesinos*, because the government did not provide them with the products, technologies, and supports to enable them to make productive the land they now owned.

[5]When NAFTA was drafted, the Salinas government amended Article 27, allowing communal properties to be divided into individual parcels, which could then be sold, and declaring land redistribution completed. Although this did not "reverse" Article 27 as some claimed, it enabled large landowners and agribusinesses to gain lands at the expense of indigenous peasant communities.

with doctors and stocked with medicines to be closer to the people.

Tenth: We demand the right of the indigenous people to have access to accurate information about events at the local, regional, state, national, and international levels, through an indigenous radio broadcasting system, independent of the government, [led] and managed by indigenous people.

Eleventh: We want housing to be constructed in all Mexico's rural communities, equipped with the necessary services: light, potable running water, sewer drainage, telephone and transportation services, etc. And that the advantages of the city be available such as television, stoves, refrigerators, washing machines, etc. The communities should have recreational centers for the healthy enjoyment of the population: sports and culture which dignify the human condition of the indigenous peoples.

Twelfth: We want an end to illiteracy of indigenous peoples. For this we need better primary and secondary schools in our communities, with free teaching materials and supplies, and teachers with university training who put themselves at the service of the people, rather than defending the interests of the rich. We want the municipal seats to offer primary, secondary, and college-preparatory schooling, and provide students with uniforms, shoes, meals and study supplies free of cost. Outlying communities located far from municipal capitals should have secondary boarding schools. Education should be totally free, from pre-school to university level, and should be offered to all Mexicans without regard to race, creed, age, sex, and political affiliation.

Thirteenth: That all languages of the ethnic groups [in Mexico] be recognized as official languages and that their instruction be mandatory in primary, secondary, preparatory and university education.

Fourteenth: That our rights and dignity as indigenous people be respected and our culture and traditions be taken into account.

Fifteenth: We no longer want to be the object of the discrimination and contempt that we have always suffered as indigenous peoples.

Sixteenth: As indigenous people that we are, we want to be allowed to organize and govern ourselves with autonomy, because we no longer want to be submitted to the will of the national and international elites.

Seventeenth: That justice be administered by indigenous peoples according to our customs and traditions without intervention of illegitimate and corrupt governments.

Eighteenth: We want dignified jobs with just wages for all rural and urban workers of the Mexican Republic, so that our brothers and sisters do not have to turn to corrupt things, like drug trafficking, crime and prostitution in order to survive. That the federal labor laws applied to rural and urban workers include benefits, bonuses, vacations and a real right to strike.

Nineteenth: We want fair prices for our farm products, and for this we need to be able to look freely for markets where to sell and buy, and not be subject to exploitative "coyotes" or middlemen.[6]

Twentieth: We want an end to the pillage of the riches of Mexico and above all of Chiapas, one of the richest states in the republic but where hunger and misery are each day more abundant.

Twenty-first: We want the complete cancellation of all the debts from credits, loans, and high rates of interest because the great poverty of the Mexican people does not allow them to be paid.

Twenty-second: We want an end to hunger and malnutrition because they have only

---

[6]One most often sees the term "coyote" used to refer to guides for illegal Mexican migrants to the United States. However, this term also can be a general reference to a speculator, con man, or middle man.

caused the deaths of thousands of our brothers and sisters in the country[side] and in the city. In each rural community, there should be cooperatives economically supported by the federal, state or municipal government and prices should be fair. In addition, the cooperatives should own their own vehicles in order to transport their merchandise, and the government should send free food [supplements] for all children under 14 years of age.

Twenty-third: We ask for the immediate and unconditional release of all political prisoners and poor people unjustly imprisoned in the jails of Chiapas and all of Mexico.

Twenty-fourth: We request that the Federal Army and the public security forces and judicial police no longer enter the rural areas because they go only to intimidate, evict, rob, repress and bomb peasants who are organizing to defend their rights. For these reasons, our peoples are tired of the presence of the soldiers, security forces and judicial police which are so abusive and repressive. The federal government must return to the Swiss government the Pilatus airplanes used to bomb our people and the refunded money should be applied to programs to improve the lives of workers of the country[side] and the city. We also ask that the government of the United States of North America withdraw its helicopters because they are used to repress the people of Mexico.

Twenty-fifth: The indigenous, peasant people rose up in arms from nothing but their humble shacks, but then the federal army bombed the civilian population, destroying their simple homes and all the poor peoples' belongings. So we ask for and demand that the federal government compensate the families who suffered material loss caused by the bombings and by the actions of the federal troops. And we also request compensation for the widows and orphans of the war, both civilian and *Zapatista*.

Twenty-sixth: We, as indigenous peasants want to live in peace and tranquility; we want to be left to live according to our rights for freedom and dignified life.

Twenty-seventh: That the State Penal Code of Chiapas be abolished because it does not allow us to organize ourselves in any other manner than by arming ourselves because all forms of legal and peaceful struggle are punished and repressed.

Twenty-eighth: We ask for and demand the immediate cessation of the expulsions of indigenous peoples from their communities by the local *caciques*[7] supported by the State. We demand that the right to voluntary and free return of all those expelled from their lands of origin and compensation for their lost goods.

Twenty-ninth: Demands of Indigenous Women We, the peasant indigenous women, ask for immediate solutions to the most urgent needs which have never been addressed by the government:

a) Birth clinics with gynecological services for peasant women to receive necessary medical attention.

b) Child care centers for the children in the communities.

c) We ask the government to send sufficient food for the children in all the rural communities such as: milk, corn starch, rice, corn, soy, oil, beans, cheese, eggs, sugar, soup, oatmeal, etc.

d) That communal kitchens and dining halls be built for the children of the communities with all the necessary facilities.

e) That corn mills and tortilla pressing machines be set up in the communities according to the number of families in each community.

---

[7]Though originally a colonial term for local indigenous leaders, in modern Mexico the term *cacique* refers to an elite group who owned most of the privately held land in peasant villages and who traditionally controlled local government and communal lands.

f) That we get livestock projects of chickens, rabbits, lambs, pigs, etc., with the technical assistance and veterinary support services.

g) We also ask for bakery projects with ovens and supplies.

h) We want to build artisan workshops with machinery and raw materials.

i) For our craftwork, we seek markets where we can obtain fair prices.

j) That schools be built where women can receive technical training.

k) That there be pre-school and infant care in the rural communities where the children can enjoy themselves and grow up morally and physically healthy.

l) As women we need transportation available to move around as we need, and to transport our supplies and products to make our projects work.

Thirtieth: We demand judicial prosecution of the following men: Patrocinio González Blanco Garrido, Absalón Castellanos Domínguez, and Elmar Setzer M.[8]

Thirty-first: We demand respect for the lives of all the members of the EZLN and guarantees that there will be no judicial proceedings or repressive actions taken against any member of the EZLN, its combatants, sympathizers or collaborators.

Thirty-second: That all the groups and commissions working to defend human rights be independent, and non-governmental, since those of the government only hide the arbitrary actions of the government.

Thirty-third: That a National Commission of Peace with Justice and Dignity be formed with a majority of members with no relationship to the government or any political party. That this National Commission of Peace with Justice and Dignity monitor the compliance with the agreements reached by the EZLN and the Federal Government.

Thirty-fourth: That humanitarian aid for the victims of the conflict be channeled through authentic representatives of the indigenous communities.

Until these just demands of our people are met, we are willing and determined to continue our struggle until we reach our objectives.

For us, the smallest of these lands, the faceless ones left out of history, those armed with truth and fire, those of us who come from the night and mountain, true men and women the dead of yesterday, today and always . . . for us, nothing, for everyone, everything. Freedom! Justice! Democracy!

Respectfully

Subcommandante Marcos

From the southeastern mountains of Mexico

CCRI-CG of the EZLN

Suggested Sources:

Secondary works on the Chiapas uprising are plentiful. For two of the now-classic and excellent studies of the conditions that led to indigenous activism and the Chiapas rebellion, see George A. Collier and Elizabeth Lowery Quaratiello, *Basta! Land and the Zapatista Rebellion in Chiapas*, 3rd ed. (Oakland, CA: Food First Books, 2005); and Neil Harvey, *The Chiapas Rebellion: The Struggle for Land and Democracy* (Durham, NC: Duke University Press, 1998). An excellent examination of the development of Zapatismo among indigenous peoples in Chiapas is Lynn Stephen, *Viva Zapata! Histories and Cultural Politics in Southern Mexico* (Berkeley: University of California Press, 2002). For books that explore the links between women and activism in Chiapas, see Christine Eber and Christine Kovic, *Women in Chiapas: Making History in Times of Struggle and Hope* (New York: Routledge, 2003); and Shannon Speed, R. Aida Hernández Castillo, and Lynn M. Stephen, eds., *Dissident Women: Gender and*

---

[8]These three men all served as governors in the state of Chiapas from 1982 to 1994.

Cultural Politics in Chiapas (Austin: University of Texas Press, 2006). For an examination of the Chiapas Rebellion that examines its links to NAFTA, see Bill Weinberg, *Homage to Chiapas: The New Indigenous Struggles in Mexico* (New York: Verso, 2002).

There are a few important sources of primary documents on the modern *Zapatista* uprising in Chiapas. The book edited by Ben Clarke and Clifton Ross from which the document in this chapter was selected, *Voice of Fire: Communiqués and Interviews from the Zapatista National Liberation Army* (Berkeley, CA: New Earth Publications, 1994), has a good selection of EZLN documents. Also see books published by Subcomandante Marcos, such as *Our Word Is Our Weapon: Selected Writings* (New York: Seven Stories Press, 2002). Another excellent source of primary documents is John Womack, Jr., ed., *Rebellion in Chiapas: An Historical Reader* (New York: The New Press, 1999). Womack begins with a long introduction to provide context, and he then presents approximately 300 pages of document excerpts on Chiapas from the colonial period through the *Zapatista* movement of the 1990s.

Chapter 26

International Indigenous Alliances for Global Justice

Marc Becker, *Truman State University*

In 1990, Indigenous peoples[1] from across the Americas met in Quito, Ecuador, to protest planned celebrations of the quincentennial of Christopher Columbus's voyage across the Atlantic Ocean. This meeting provided an opportunity to build consensus among diverse groups and to unify around common concerns. The ability of people who had long been excluded and marginalized to gain a voice on a global stage was the result of moving from a focus on narrow, locally defined issues to much broader concerns of engaging state power. An incredibly diverse range of peoples across the Americas representing many different cultures and political

---

[1] The use of a capital "I" in reference to Indigenous peoples is intentional and based on (and in respect for) the stated preference of the board of directors of the South and Meso American Indian Rights Center (SAIIC) as a strong affirmation of their ethnic identities.

interests are included under the broad umbrella of "Indigenous," and naturally not all of them joined these organizing efforts. Nevertheless, the growing internationalization of Indigenous movements led to a much larger 2007 meeting in Guatemala that illustrated Indigenous success at linking struggles across the Americas. This chapter includes documents from both the 1990 and 2007 gatherings in order to show both the continuities in Indigenous struggles and their evolution over time.

Although Indigenous peoples long had struggled for their rights on a local level, by the 1960s they began to organize on an international level. Attitudes toward land, long one of the primary demands for many Indigenous activists, reflect this evolution. The issue of the usurpation of Indigenous lands dates back to the colonial period and gained increased importance during the nineteenth century as wealthy estate owners encroached on Indigenous communities. By the end of the twentieth century, Indigenous activists commonly framed their demands in terms of territory and *autonomy*, indicating that they viewed land as an ancestral right rather than a commodity. Their concerns extended beyond social and economic demands to the level of cosmologies, of how they perceived the world around them. The rights of self-determination and control over their own affairs gained importance in the face of government attempts to assimilate them into the dominant culture.

In the 1980s, Indigenous activists also emerged at the forefront of protests against *neoliberal* economic policies that privatized government functions and emphasized resource extraction. These austerity measures emphasized so-called free-market policies in place of government protectionism. As some of the poorest members of society, Indigenous peoples were hit the hardest by cutbacks in government subsidies. The extraction of gold, petroleum, and other precious resources from Indigenous lands left them with the negative environmental and social consequences of mining but with none of its economic benefits. Increasingly, Indigenous peoples raised their voices against these enterprises.

In addition to pressing economic demands, many Indigenous activists emphasized the importance of their unique identities with broad-reaching

political implications. They rejected previous designations as tribes, peoples, or ethnic groups as contributing to their historical marginalization from society. Instead, they demanded recognition as Indigenous nationalities. Most notably in Ecuador and Bolivia, leaders pressed for the inclusion of references to *plurinationalism* in their federal constitutions, declaring that their countries were made up of many different Indigenous nationalities. The goal was to remake the country's political structures to recognize this diversity, and to respond to the needs and concerns of common people rather than domestic elites or foreign corporations.

Anthropologists, the Catholic Church, the United Nations, and *nongovernmental organizations (NGOs)* facilitated early Indigenous networking efforts. In 1968, anthropologists founded the International Work Group for Indigenous Affairs (IWGIA) in Copenhagen to support Indigenous struggles through publications and educational campaigns. They were followed by Survival International in England and Cultural Survival at Harvard University. In 1971, eleven anthropologists gathered in Barbados to analyze the current situation of Indigenous peoples. Their "Declaration of Barbados" called for the liberation of Indians from their colonial domination.[2] Three years later, Bishop Samuel Ruiz organized an Indian Congress in Chiapas, Mexico, with the participation of hundreds of Mayas to discuss common problems of land, exploitation, and racism. At the same time, representatives of eleven South American Indigenous nationalities gathered in Paraguay to discuss similar problems and to call for a unified struggle for their rights.[3] In 1975, the IWGIA helped establish the World Council of Indigenous Peoples (WCIP) and subsequently pressured the United Nations (UN) to address Indigenous issues. At first the UN refused, claiming that such issues were domestic rather than

---

[2]International Work Group for Indigenous Affairs (IWGIA), *Declaration of Barbados*, IWGIA Document No. 1 (Copenhagen: IWGIA, 1971), http://www.nativeweb.org/papers/statements/state/barbados1.php.

[3]Yves Materne, ed., *The Indian Awakening in Latin America* (New York: Friendship Press, 1980), 49–76, http://www.nativeweb.org/papers/statements/materne/.

Women from the local Indigenous organization Pueblo Kayambi (Ecuador) participated in a 2002 protest in Ecuador's capital city of Quito against the Free Trade Area of the Americas (or Área de Libre Comercio de las Américas—ALCA in Spanish). Kayambi's Indigenous peoples have a long history of local, regional, and national political activism, dating back to the 1920s. What does this image show us about the "face" of political activism in Latin America? How does this photo capture a moment of protest that was at once local *and* hemispheric in nature?

Source: Photo by Marc Becker.

international concerns but the UN finally conceded to form a Working Group on Indigenous Populations.

Increasingly, Indigenous activists took the lead in organizing international meetings rather than relying on sympathetic outsiders for support. In the 1980s, the South American Indian Council (CISA) organized three regional conferences of Indigenous nationalities and organizations in Peru, Bolivia, and Chile. In 1983, the CISA founded the South American Indian Information Center (SAIIC) in California to support Indigenous self-determination and the unification of Indigenous rights movements on a continental level. As Indigenous organizations bridged broad geographic divides, they also reached out to environmentalists and Afro-Latin Americans.

In July 1990, the SAIIC joined the *Confederation of Indigenous Nationalities of Ecuador* (*CONAIE*) and the National Indigenous Organization of Colombia (ONIC) to organize a Continental Conference on Five Hundred Years of Indigenous Resistance in Quito, Ecuador. Hundreds of delegates from twenty countries challenged governmental plans to celebrate the upcoming anniversary of Columbus's arrival in the Americas on October 12, 1492, and instead they called for an alternative campaign of "500 years of Indigenous resistance" against European genocide. They pledged to turn October 12 into a symbol of Indigenous resistance and liberation.[4] Their "Declaration of Quito" (reprinted here) was followed by detailed resolutions on the rights of women, self-determination, education, culture, religion, communication, and territorial rights.

After the 1990 Quito conference, many Indigenous leaders returned to a focus on local struggles. A decade later, activists once again gathered at the First Indigenous Continental Summit at Teotihuacan, Mexico. Delegates from thirty-six organizations signed the Declaration of Teotihuacan, which condemned the economic policies of international lending agencies that benefited wealthy elites while increasing levels of dependence, oppression, and poverty for Indigenous peoples.[5] The Teotihuacan summit launched a decade of increased transnational organizing efforts, including a series of continent-wide summits. In 2004, the Declaration of *Kito* (so named for the Kichwa spelling of the host city of Quito) at the Second Continental Summit of the Indigenous Peoples and Nationalities of *Abya Yala* once again denounced economic policies that privatized public resources and disregarded collective rights to land.[6]

Thousands of Indigenous peoples from twenty-four countries gathered in Guatemala in 2007 for the Third Continental Summit of Indigenous Peoples and Nationalities of Abya Yala. The summit was entitled "From Resistance to Power," reflecting interest in moving beyond resistance to oppressive regimes in order to claim positions of power in government. Evo Morales's recent election to the presidency in Bolivia inspired many Indigenous activists to explore similar paths to challenge state power in their own countries. The summit concluded with a rally in Guatemala City's main plaza and the reading of the "Declaration of Iximche'" (the second document in this chapter) that called for a continued struggle for social justice and against *neoliberalism* and all forms of oppression.[7] Activists subsequently gathered in a continental summit in Peru in 2009, as well as at other venues including the World Social Forum, that brought together social movement activists around the slogan of "Another World Is Possible."[8] Not only did that world need to include Indigenous peoples, but previously marginalized and excluded peoples increasingly took the lead in defining a new world without exploitation and social injustices.

The rise of international Indigenous organizing efforts challenged and pushed governments in new directions. Rather than responding to the initiatives of outsiders, Indigenous peoples increasingly set their own agendas. They used new technologies, including the Internet, to advance their concerns. Leaders blended economic, political, and cultural demands into a unified whole that presented a new and more inclusive way of viewing the world.

Questions to Consider:

1. Reading through the documents that follow, how did Indigenous demands evolve over time? What new issues emerged, which ones disappeared, and what remained the same?

2. How did the use of rhetoric change between these two documents, particularly in the use of Indigenous words and dating? What does this language say about the politicization of Indigenous struggles and how history was used as a tool to present a particular version of Indigenous history and identity?

---

[4]Elizabeth Bobsy Draper, "Minga in Ecuador," *Z Magazine* (December 1990): 33–38.

[5]Declaration of Teotihuacan, http://www.nativeweb.org/papers/statements/state/conic1.php.

[6]Kito Declaration, http://www.nativeweb.org/papers/statements/state/kito_en.php. "Abya Yala" means "Continent of Life" in the language of the Kuna peoples of Panama and Colombia. Indigenous activists commonly use this term to refer to the Americas.

[7]Marc Becker, "Third Continental Summit of Indigenous Peoples and Nationalities of Abya Yala: From Resistance to Power," *Latin American and Caribbean Ethnic Studies* 3, no. 1 (March 2008): 85–107.

[8]The Mama Quta Titikaka Declaration, http://www.nativeweb.org/papers/statements/state/titikaka.php; Declaration of Indigenous Peoples at the World Social Forum, http://www.nativeweb.org/papers/statements/state/caoiwsf09_en.php.

Indigenous peoples from across the Americas joined a march at the conclusion of the III Continental Summit of Indigenous Nations and Pueblos of Abya Yala in Guatemala City in 2007 that is presented in the second document in this chapter. What do "Indigenous" peoples look like in this photograph, and how do they dress? What do their appearances suggest about both the unity and variety of peoples involved in international Indigenous organizations? Can you see parallels between the images in this photograph and the declaration that resulted from the meeting?

Source: Photo by Marc Becker.

3. Did these documents make primarily economic or cultural demands? What was the significance placed on different types of concerns in each document?

4. What is the value of creating international Indigenous organizations? What evidence can you find in these documents of concrete advancements on Indigenous concerns as a result of these organizing efforts?

5. How were local, regional, and global concerns reflected in these documents? What does the balance between these different levels of social protest tell us about the nature of these organizing efforts?

Indigenous Alliance of the Americas on 500 Years of Resistance: Declaration of Quito, Ecuador, July 1990[9]

The Continental Gathering "500 Years of Indian Resistance," with representatives from 120 Indian Nations, International and Fraternal organizations, meeting in Quito, July 17–20, 1990, declare before the world the following:

The Indians of America have never abandoned our constant struggle against the conditions of oppression, discrimination and exploitation which were imposed upon us as a result of the European invasion of our ancestral territories.

Our struggle is not a mere conjunctural reflection of the memory of 500 years of oppression which the invaders, in complicity with the "democratic" governments of our countries, want to turn into events of jubilation and celebration. Our Indian People, Nations and Nationalities are basing our struggle on our identity, which shall lead us to true liberation. We are responding aggressively, and commit ourselves to reject this "celebration."

The struggle of our People has acquired a new quality in recent times. This struggle is less isolated and more organized. We are now completely conscious that our total liberation can only be expressed through the complete exercise of our self-determination. Our unity is based on this fundamental right. Our self-determination is not just a simple declaration.

We must guarantee the necessary conditions that permit complete exercise of our self-determination; and this, in turn must be expressed as complete *autonomy* for our Peoples. Without Indian self-government and without control of our territories, there can be no *autonomy*.

The achievement of this objective is a principal task for Indian Peoples. Through our struggles, however, we have learned that our problems are not different, in many respects, from those of other popular sectors. We are convinced that we must march alongside the peasants, the workers, the marginalized sectors, together with intellectuals committed to our

cause, in order to destroy the dominant system of oppression and construct a new society, pluralistic, democratic and humane, in which peace is guaranteed.

The existing nation states of the Americas, their constitutions and fundamental laws are judicial/political expressions that negate our socio-economic, cultural and political rights.

From this point in our general strategy of struggle, we consider it to be a priority that we demand complete structural change, change which recognizes the inherent right to self-determination through Indians' own governments and through the control of our territories.

Our problems will not be resolved through the self-serving politics of governmental entities which seek integration and ethno-development.[10] It is necessary to have an integral transformation at the level of the state and national society, that is to say, the creation of a new nation.

In this Gathering it has been clear that territorial rights are a fundamental demand of the Indigenous Peoples of the Americas.

Based on these aforementioned reflections, the organizations united in the First Continental Gathering of Indigenous Peoples reaffirm:

1. Our emphatic rejection of the Quincentennial celebration, and the firm promise that we will turn that date into an occasion to strengthen our process of continental unity and struggle towards our liberation.[11]
2. Ratify our resolute political project of self-determination and conquest of our *autonomy*, in the framework of nation states, under a new popular order, respecting the appellation which each People determines for their struggle and project.

---

[9]*Source:* Declaration of Quito, http://www.nativeweb.org/papers/statements/quincentennial/quito.php.

[10]The Spanish and United States governments were planning large celebrations for the 500th anniversary of Christopher Columbus's October 12, 1492, arrival in the Americas.
[11]Government policies often accepted Indigenous peoples only if they integrated into the dominant population or remained an exotic curiosity that could be marketed for tourist purposes.

3. Affirm our decision to defend our culture, education, and religion as fundamental to our identity as Peoples, reclaiming and maintaining our own forms of spiritual life and communal coexistence, in an intimate relationship with our Mother Earth.

4. We reject the manipulation of organizations which are linked to the dominant sectors of society and have no Indigenous representation, who usurp our name for (their own) imperialist interests.[12] At the same time, we affirm our choice to strengthen our own organizations, without excluding or isolating ourselves from other popular struggles.

5. We recognize the important role that Indigenous women play in the struggles of our Peoples. We understand the necessity to expand women's participation in our organizations and we reaffirm that it is one struggle, men and women together, in our liberation process, and a key question in our political practices.

6. We Indian Peoples consider it vital to defend and conserve our natural resources, which right now are being attacked by transnational corporations. We are convinced that this defense will be realized if it is Indian People who administer and control the territories where we live, according to our own principles of organization and communal life.

7. We oppose national judicial structures which are the result of the process of colonization and neocolonization. We seek a New Social Order that embraces our traditional exercise of Common Law, an expression of our culture and forms of organization. We demand that we be recognized as Peoples under International Law, and that this recognition be incorporated into the respective Nation States.

8. We denounce the victimization of Indian People through violence and persecution, which constitutes a flagrant violation of human rights. We demand respect for our right to life, to land, to free organization and expression of our culture. At the same time we demand the release of our leaders who are held as political prisoners, an end to repression, and restitution for the harms caused us.

---

[12]*Indigenistas* were urban, educated, white outsiders who created policies toward Indigenous peoples, but often with little contact or history with Indigenous communities. Now, Indigenous organizations argued that they should represent their own interests to the government.

Declaration of Iximche': III Continental Summit of Indigenous Nations and Peoples of Abya Yala "From Resistance to Power" March 26–30, 2007 Iximche', Guatemala[13]

We the children of the Indigenous Nations and Peoples of the continent, self convened and gathered at the III Continental Summit of Indigenous Nations and Peoples of Abya Yala realized in Iximche', Guatemala the days of Oxlajuj Aq'abal, thirteen powers of the Spirit of the Dawn (26th of March) to Kají Kej, four powers of the Spirit of the Deer (30th of March, 2007):[14]

We hereby affirm the Declaration of Teotihuacan (Mexico, 2000), the Declaration of Kito (Ecuador, 2004) and ratify our millennial principles of complementarity, reciprocity, and duality,[15] as well as the struggle for our territories in order to preserve our Mother Nature and the *autonomy* and self-determination of our Indigenous Peoples. We

---

[13]*Source:* Declaration of Iximche', http://www.nativeweb.org/papers/statements/state/iximche.php.
[14]Iximche' is a Kaqchikel Maya ceremonial site located in the highlands two hours from the capital city. Giving the date in the Maya calendar reflects an affirmation of their long cultural history.

[15]Complementarity, reciprocity, and duality are common Indigenous values that represent the division of society along different lines, including gender, but that need to work together to function properly.

announce the continental resurgence of the Pachacu-tic (the return) along with the closure of *Oxlajuj Baq'tun* (long count of 5,200 years) and as we approach the door of the new Baq'tun, we journey together to make of Abya Yala a "land full of life."[16]

We have survived centuries of colonization and now face the imposition of the policies of *neoliberalism* that perpetuate the dispossession and sacking of our territories, the domination of all of social space and ways of life of the Indigenous Peoples, causing the degradation of our Mother Nature as well as poverty and migration by way of the sys-tematic intervention in the sovereignty of our Nations by transnational companies in complicity with the government states.

In Preparation to Face and Confront the Challenges of the New Times Upon Us, We Now Determine

To commit to the process of alliance among our Indigenous nations, and among our Indigenous nations and the movements for social justice of the continent that would allow us to collectively confront the policies of *neoliberalism* and all forms of oppression.

To make accountable the government states for the ongoing dispossession of our territories and the extinction of the Indigenous peoples of the continent, due to impunity for the transnational corporations and their genocidal practices, as well as the lack of political will on the part of the United Nations in not advancing the Declaration on the Rights of Indige-nous Peoples and failure to guarantee the full respect for the Universal Declaration of Human Rights.

To ratify the ancestral and historical rights to our territories and the common resources of Mother Nature, reaffirming the inalienable character of these rights as being non-negotiable, unquantifiable, without impediment, and unrenounceable even to the cost of our lives.

To consolidate the processes now in effect to strengthen the re-foundation of the government

states and the construction of pluri-national states and pluricultural societies via Constituent Assem-blies with direct representation of the Indigenous Peoples and Nations.

To advance in the exercise of our right of *autonomy* and self determination as Indigenous Peoples, in spite of the lack of legal recognition by the government states.

To ratify our rejection of the Free Trade Agree-ments (FTAs) that make vulnerable the sovereignty of our Peoples and to remain vigilant against similar in-tentions to implement new commercial agreements.

To reaffirm our decision to defend the nutri-tional sovereignty and struggle against the trans-genetic invasion, convoking all peoples of the world to join this struggle in order to guarantee our future.[17]

To ratify the struggle for the democratization of communication and the implementation of public policies that contemplate specific applications for Indigenous peoples and the promotion of inter-culturality.

To alert the Indigenous peoples regarding the policies of the Inter American Development Bank, the World Bank and organizations of the like that penetrate our communities with actions of assistance and cooptation whose aim is the fragmentation of au-tonomous and legitimate Indigenous organizations.

For the Well Being of the Indigenous Peoples, We Now Decide

To demand of the international financial institutions and the government states the cancellation of policies that promote concessions for the extractive industries (mining, oil, forestry, natural gas and water) from our Indigenous territories.

To condemn the policies of exclusion of Presi-dent Bush and the government of the United States demonstrated in the act of construction of the wall

---

[16]The statement combines cosmologies from across the Americas, bridging Andean (Pachacutic) and Mesoamerican (Baq'tun) notions of the closing of a cycle in order to return to a better future.

[17]Nutritional or food sovereignty is the right of people to feed themselves, something that is often challenged by genetically modified seeds that undermine traditional agricultural practices in order to ensure the profits of agrobusiness corporate giants such as Cargill, Monsanto, and Archer Daniels Midland (ADM).

along the border with Mexico while at the same time attempting to expropriate the common resources of our Mother Nature of all the peoples of Abya Yala by implementing expansionist plans and acts of war.

To condemn the intolerant attitude of the government states that do not recognize the rights of Indigenous peoples, in particular those which have not ratified nor guaranteed the application of Convention 169 of the International Labor Organization.[18]

To condemn the imposter and terrorist democracies implemented by the *neoliberal* governments, which results in the militarization of our Indigenous territories and the criminalization of our legitimate Indigenous struggle and the movements for social justice throughout Abya Yala.

In Order to Enact these Words and Realize Our Dreams, *From Resistance to Power*

We constitute ourselves as the **Continental Coordinator of Indigenous Peoples and Nations of Abya Yala**, creating a permanent vehicle of linkage and interchange, in order to converge our experiences and proposals, so that together we can confront the *neoliberal* policies of globalization and to struggle for the definitive liberation of our Indigenous Peoples and Nations, of the mother earth, of our territories, of the waters, and entirety of our natural patrimony in order that we may all live well.

In This Process We Delineated the Following Actions

To fortify the organizational processes and struggle of the Indigenous Peoples with the full participation of our women, children and young people.

To convene a Continental Summit of Indigenous Women of Abya Yala and a Continental Summit of the Children, Adolescents and Youth of the Indigenous Nations and Peoples of Abya Yala.

To convoke a continental mobilization of Indigenous Peoples to save Mother Nature from the disasters caused by capitalism, manifested by global warming, to be realized on the 12th of October of 2007.

To engage actively the diplomatic mission of the Indigenous Peoples to defend and to guarantee the rights of our Indigenous Peoples and Nations.

To endorse the candidacy for the Nobel Peace Prize of our brother Evo Morales Ayma, President of Bolivia.

To demand the decriminalization of the coca leaf.

"We have dreamt our past and we remember our future."

Iximche', Guatemala, March 30, 2007.

Suggested Sources:

Recent Indigenous movements have received a large amount of scholarly attention. A good overview by a leading scholar in the field is Alison Brysk, *From Tribal Village to Global Village: Indian Rights and International Relations in Latin America* (Stanford, CA: Stanford University Press, 2000). Donna Lee Van Cott discusses Indigenous engagement with electoral politics in *Radical Democracy in the Andes* (Cambridge: Cambridge University Press, 2008). Nancy Grey Postero and Leon Zamosc present an excellent collection of essays in *The Struggle for Indigenous Rights in Latin America* (Portland, OR: Sussex Academic Press, 2004). Also see Kay B. Warren and Jean E. Jackson, ed., *Indigenous Movements, Self-Representation, and the State in Latin America* (Austin: University of Texas Press, 2003); and Erick D. Langer and Elena Muñoz, ed., *Contemporary Indigenous Movements in Latin America* (Wilmington, DE: Scholarly Resources, 2003).

Columbus Didn't Discover Us: Native People's Perspectives on the Columbus Quincentennial (1992) is a report on the 1990 Quito conference, and it explains Indigenous opposition to the quincentennial. Several recent films portray Indigenous struggles, particularly against mining and resource extraction

---

[18]The ILO is a United Nations agency that promotes of social justice and internationally recognized human and labor rights.

that often has the strongest negative impact on marginalized peoples. In particular, see *Choropampa: The Price of Gold* (Brooklyn, NY: First Run/Icarus Films, 2000), *Tambogrande: Mangos, Murder, and Mining* (Brooklyn, NY: First Run/Icarus Films, 2007), *Ecuador: Divided Over Oil* (Princeton, NJ: Films for the Humanities & Sciences, 2004), and *Sipakapa Is Not for Sale* (Guatemala: Caracol Producciones, 2006).

NativeWeb (http://www.nativeweb.org/) is the premier Web site on Indigenous peoples around the world. It includes a resource database with links to the best Web sites on Indigenous movements, including Web sites created by Indigenous organizations. One of main Web sites on continental Indigenous organizing in the Americas is that of the Continental Summit of Indigenous Peoples and Organizations (http://www.cumbrecontinentalindigena.org/). NativeWeb also has a database of statements, declarations, and manifestos from Indigenous organizing efforts (http://www.nativeweb.org/resources/materials_hosted_on_nativeweb/). The International Work Group for Indigenous Affairs (http://www.iwgia.org/), Cultural Survival (http://www.culturalsurvival.org/), and Survival International (http://www.survival-international.org/) all have organizational Web pages. The United Nations has many of its documents online, including those from its Permanent Forum on Indigenous Issues (http://www.un.org/esa/socdev/unpfii/).

Section VII

Power and Politics in the Transition into the Twenty-First Century

Indigenous peoples, Afro-Latin Americans, and women of all classes and races in Latin America were once barred from voting or holding political office. Now, one can find representatives of these groups in the legislative halls of national governments, and sometimes even in the presidency. It would be easy to claim that because Evo Morales and Michelle Bachelet won presidential terms in Bolivia and Chile (respectively), Latin American indigenous peoples or women no longer face a political glass ceiling. However, the majority of national politicians are still wealthy white or *mestizo* men, most women still struggle with restrictive gender norms, and the poorest sectors in Latin American societies are usually non-whites in either remote rural areas or in urban slums. Therefore, it would be equally easy to assert that the ongoing problems of sexism, racism, and poverty mean that little has changed in the power dynamics of Latin American societies. Although both arguments hold some truth, each oversimplifies the complexity of Latin American politics and society in the early twenty-first century.

The ability of individuals from less-powerful groups to succeed in national politics stems in part from the rising power and influence of grassroots political organizations in Latin America. Local indigenous organizations grew and expanded in the 1980s and 1990s, enabling them to influence national-level politics and policies. Similarly, poor farmers organized to protect their lands from national and multinational corporations and to protest *neoliberal* economic policies that threatened their profits with the influx of cheap goods from other world regions. Feminist groups began to recognize the needs of poor as well as wealthy women and to win more seats for women in all levels of politics. Finally, residents of urban shantytowns, once divided against each other in the struggle for survival, started forging a sense of community and came together to demand better services and schools and greater respect. Some of their representatives, too, rose from local to national politics.

Latin American women's expanding roles in politics partly resulted from governmental commitments to address gender inequalities. Most Latin American nations today have some form of political quota system in place, typically requiring that women account for a certain percentage of candidates in any elections.[1] In some countries, police departments expanded to include women officers and to prioritize and better address the

---

[1] For a good and quick resource on the specific quotas of different world nations, as well as their impact, see http://www.quotaproject.org (last accessed September, 2008).

problem of domestic violence. Government-sponsored initiatives made it possible for women in many Latin American countries to advance into political and government-service posts more quickly than would have been possible otherwise.

All of the individuals in this section promised to transform politics and to improve the position of the marginalized. Each one of them claimed to be ideal political representatives due to their first-hand knowledge of the suffering that the poor, uneducated, and non-Europeans in their nations endure. They also believed that to address their nations' problems, it was necessary to make broad-based, structural changes in politics and the economy. Though they promised change, their methods and strategies should be familiar to students of Latin American history: They sound a great deal like a combination of *populism* and socialism, although with modern twists and features. Like the classic *populists* of the 1940s and 1950s, the activists in this section found their strongest supporters from humble working sectors of their societies, and they appealed to those groups by offering them tangible political and economic benefits. Yet whereas classic, mid-century *populists* came mainly from middle-class or elite backgrounds, *populist* leaders today often lived the poverty that they claim to understand and promise to eradicate. Furthermore, each of the leaders in this section was politicized by the death or mistreatment of close family members under previous regimes. History, they felt, thrust on them the mission to rectify the mistakes of the past that left them personally scarred. Finally, although some contemporary *populists* appear motivated to advance their personal power, many of them also support broader institutional and political changes than most early *populists* did.

Although the individuals in this section support socialist-style economic and social changes, none of them adheres strictly to Marxist dogma. In part, the shift away from classical Marxism resulted from the fall of the Soviet Union, when the Left seemed to be losing political ground around the world. Simultaneously, *neoliberal* economic policies left many former industrial and agricultural workers jobless, and they had to employ themselves in various, and mostly informal, sectors of the industrial and agrarian economies of their nations. As the nature of work changed, so did the labor movement: Self-employed poor workers collaborated to protect their interests against governments and large corporations, such as the Bolivian *cocaleros* (coca farmers) from whence Evo Morales emerged. Socialism also fused with the cultural concerns of ethnic-based activist movements that were on the rise.

New forms of *populism* and socialism raise questions about political representation: Who exactly are "the people," and who speaks for whom? None of the activists in this section represents what one would think of as a typical Indian, shantytown dweller, or woman. All of them are literate, and all possess considerable oratory and political skills. None currently lives in poverty or political exile, though most of them did at one point. Even Michelle Bachelet, born to an upper-class family with political influence, was forced into exile after the Pinochet regime assassinated her father. Following the end of Pinochet's regime, she returned to Chile to resume her medical studies and rebuild her life, eventually entering politics. Rigoberta Menchú was a poor Guatemalan indigenous woman whose parents were brutally killed by the military regime; she too spent years in exile. When she returned to Guatemala in the 1990s, however, she was a world-renowned speaker and a Nobel Peace Prize winner. Benedita da Silva maintained close ties to her shantytown beginnings, but her life as a senator was far different than her experiences as a youth. Evo Morales might lay claim to his indigenous identity and cocalero roots, but his lifestyle as Bolivian president is more luxurious and requires more nuanced strategies than his former life and activism. These individuals' lives show that, as grassroots activists gain power, the gap between leaders and commoners within political movements widens and the problems of racism and sexism remain unresolved.

Activists face new and difficult challenges as they move from the politics of protest, in which they critique governments that exclude them, to the politics of power, in which they partake in running

Venezuelan president Hugo Chavez, shown in a 2006 speech standing in front of an image of South American independence hero Simón Bolívar, is the most famous and controversial socialist-*populist* president in contemporary Latin America. Born in 1954, Chavez graduated from Venezuela's Academy of Military Science and began his political career protesting against corruption and antidemocratic practices. Early in his political career, Chavez allied with socialist forces and called upon the legacy of Venezuelan-born independence hero Simón Bolívar. After many political failures, he was elected president in 1998 and was reelected in 2006. Chavez's *populist* policies, and his willingness to alter the Venezuelan constitution to suit his own interests, generated protests and opposition, mainly from middle- and upper-class Venezuelans. However, the majority of poor Venezuelans remained loyal to him for providing socioeconomic relief. Internationally, Chavez allied with socialist Cuba and made a point of criticizing (some would say provoking) the United States. government. He helped to found the Bolivarian Alternative for the Americas, a group of eight Latin American leaders who oppose *neoliberalism* and provide alternatives to United States-backed free trade.

What message do you think is Chavez trying to convey when he calls upon Bolívar's legacy or places the independence hero's portrait in backgrounds to his speeches? Consider Bolívar's own hopes for South America—how much or how little does a leader like Chavez seem to capture the aspirations of the nineteenth-century Liberator?

Source: AP Wide World Photos.

the state. For example, although Michelle Bachelet and Evo Morales had to maintain enough of their original political platforms to continue appealing to their mass supporters, they each had to refine their stances on several issues, and seek new allies, in order to claim to represent the interests of all members of their nations. Furthermore, because she is a woman, Bachelet was accused of favoring women in her administration at the expense of appointing more qualified men. Because he is indigenous, Morales was often charged with advancing indigenous interests rather than those of all Bolivians. The two presidents had to walk a fine line between different constituencies and critics during their presidential terms.

Latin American societies are currently in the throes of tumultuous sociopolitical change, the results of which remain unclear. As readers explore these last chapters of *Documenting Latin America*, the editors encourage them to consider questions such as: How far have women, indigenous peoples, and Afro-Latin Americans come in the past two centuries? What remain their greatest limitations or challenges? How have the four individuals highlighted in this section tried to meet the complex challenges of their times? What visions and hopes have they expressed for the future, and for Latin Americans' place in the world? Studying history does not enable one to predict the future, but it can help to explain the dynamics of the present and highlight possible paths that individuals and societies might take—or hope to avoid—in years to come.

Chapter 27

Rigoberta Menchú Tum: From Indigenous Peasant to Nobel Laureate

Erin E. O'Connor, Bridgewater State College

Rigoberta Menchú Tum is the most famous indigenous woman in Latin America. Born to a poor *Quiché* Indian family in the hamlet of Chimel, Guatemala, her childhood was dominated by the struggle to subsist. She became involved in Catholic Church social reform work in her youth and lived through waves of government violence against the Guatemalan poor, particularly indigenous peoples. Menchú Tum lost much of her family to the violence: Her father was imprisoned and tortured, and he died in a fire at the Spanish embassy in Guatemala; her mother and brother were both killed by government forces. By 1981, she fled to Mexico, where she spoke out to draw attention to the state terror in Guatemala that led to the deaths of over 100,000 people, about 80 percent of them indigenous. In 1992, Menchú Tum received one of the world's most prestigious honors for her human rights work: the Nobel Peace Prize.

Menchú Tum's was more famous, however, for her life story than for her political activism. In 1983, she was in Paris trying to bring attention to state-generated violence in Guatemala, where she met Venezuelan anthropologist Elisabeth Burgos-Debray. Burgos-Debray requested an interview with Menchú Tum in order to write an article about her. The interviews lasted several days and resulted in approximately twenty-four hours of audio tapes containing Menchú Tum's rendition of her life and the story of her people. Eventually published in many different languages, *I . . . Rigoberta Menchú* became an international sensation that brought worldwide attention to the situation in Guatemala. Menchú Tum's life story reached her audience on a personal level as she described in detail the richness of indigenous cultural beliefs and traditions, the depth of poverty, and exploitation that indigenous Guatemalans experienced, and the rising government violence that eventually politicized her family. Her descriptions of the deaths of her parents and brother were particularly wrenching and alerted many readers to the necessity of speaking out against the Guatemalan military government. Her testimony became standard reading in various disciplines on many college campuses in the United States and Europe. College students identified Menchú Tum and her testimony not only with the need to end the violence in Guatemala, but many of them also looked to her as the authentic voice of Guatemalan Indians, assuming that all indigenous peoples in the country had essentially the same experiences. Some individuals even claimed that she spoke for all indigenous peoples in the Americas. Whereas these assumptions derived from concern over the suffering of the indigenous peoples of the Americas, they also homogenized "Indians" into a single category, when, in fact, indigenous experiences and cultures in the hemisphere were and are diverse.

Menchú Tum's testimony and subsequent celebrity made her a more effective political activist. She received numerous invitations to speak in locations all around the world, and she used these platforms to push for a solution to the problems in Guatemala. Still in her twenties Menchú Tum had achieved a level of influence that traditional and more experienced political activists had not. By the 1990s, when Menchú Tum won the Nobel Peace Prize, the government and the guerrilla forces in Guatemala had begun negotiations to end the civil war, and they produced a Peace Accord in March 1996. The accord called for the demobilization of guerrilla forces, the promotion of indigenous rights, and social and political reforms that would reverse many of the practices of the military governments. Since then, Menchú Tum has remained a prominent political activist and advocate of worldwide human rights. She returned to her native Guatemala after the Peace Accord was reached and added national politics to her many commitments. In 2007 she made an unsuccessful bid for the Guatemalan presidency (winning only three percent of the vote).

In the process of her political and human rights career, Menchú Tum has given many speeches and been involved in many projects in Guatemala and around the world. Yet most people still know her, or know her best, for her life story as she told it to Burgos-Debray when she was twenty-three years old. It was largely for this reason that anthropologist David Stoll prompted upheaval and controversy with his book on Menchú Tum and the civil war in Guatemala. Stoll claimed to have interviewed indigenous residents from Menchú Tum's home community and region who revealed what he claimed were contradictions and falsehoods in her life story. Menchú Tum defended her reputation and her claims while also emphasizing the importance of Burgos-Debray's role as editor of the book. Readers who are interested in this controversy might want to explore it for themselves through the sources in the bibliography at the end of this chapter.

One of the most productive results of the controversy was that it began to release Rigoberta Menchú Tum from being figuratively frozen in the early 1980s when the story she told to Burgos-Debray first appeared in print. For far too many readers, including thousands of college students, Menchú Tum was forever twenty-three years old and reeling from the violent deaths of many of her family members. They learned little about her substantial work in the United Nations on behalf of indigenous rights or about her extensive political work. They read nothing else she wrote or the other interviews she gave. The popularity of her 1983 testimony rendered this vibrant and influential *Quiché* woman and activist historically static in many minds.

This chapter offers a means of allowing Menchú Tum to reenter the flow of history. The first excerpt presented is taken from *I . . . Rigoberta Menchú*, where Menchú Tum discussed how her community became politically active in order to resist the exploitation and oppression indigenous peoples experienced at the hands of the Guatemalan state, military, and estate owners. The second excerpt contains portions of Menchú Tum's 1992 Nobel Peace Prize acceptance speech. Placing these two documents side by side should enable readers to think about Menchú Tum as a person and a political activist who, like everyone else, both remained herself and changed over the course of ten years. Like other chapters in this section, these two documents offer evidence of the considerable achievements and ongoing challenges of Latin American grassroots activists in recent years.

Questions to Consider:

1. How did Menchú Tum describe her process of politicization in "Period of Reflection on the Road to Follow?" How did she describe her commitment to political action?
2. What clues do you see in the first excerpt about the reasons that the book *I . . . Rigoberta Menchú* gained such widespread popularity?
3. How did Menchú Tum discuss Guatemala's problems in her 1992 speech in Oslo? Why did she claim that the Guatemalan situation was of global concern?
4. How did Menchú Tum describe what it meant to be an Indian in "Period of Reflection on the Road to Follow"? How did she describe what being an Indian meant in her Nobel Prize acceptance speech? What continuities and changes did you note, and what do you make of them?
5. Evaluate *how* Menchú Tum spoke about her life and about Guatemala when she was twenty-three and relatively new to politics, versus how she discussed them as a thirty-three-year-old political veteran. What do you make of similarities and differences in her tone and language over time?

Chapter XVI: Period of Reflection on the Road to Follow[2]

I'd like to say here, that I wasn't the only important one. I was part of a family, just like all my brothers and sisters. The whole community was important. We used to discuss many of the community's problems together, especially when someone was ill and we couldn't buy medicine, because we were getting poorer and poorer. We'd start discussing and heaping insults on the rich who'd made us suffer for so long. It was about then I began learning about politics. I tried to talk to people who could help me sort my ideas out. I wanted to know what the world was like on the other side. I knew the *finca*, I knew the

Altiplano.[3] But what I didn't know was about the problems of the other Indians in Guatemala. I didn't know the problems other groups had holding on to their land. I knew there were lots of other Indians in other parts of the country, because I'd been meeting them in the finca since I was a child, but although we all worked together, we didn't know the names of the towns they came from, or how they lived, or what they ate. We just imagined that they were like us. [. . .] I began making friends from other villages in Uspantán. I asked them: 'What do you eat? How

---

[2]*Source:* From Elisabeth Burgos-Debray, ed. *I . . . Rigoberta Menchú: An Indian Woman in Guatemala* (New York: Verso, 1984), trans. Ann Wright pp. 117–121.

[3]Finca is a term for a large estate geared toward export production, on which many of the indigenous poor worked, whereas the Altiplano refers to the highland regions of Guatemala where most indigenous peasants lived.

do you make your breakfast? What do you have for lunch? What do you eat for supper?' And yes, they said the same: 'Well, in the morning we eat *tortillas* with salt and a little *pinol*. At midday our mother brings tortillas and any plants she finds in the fields.' 'At night we eat tortillas with chile,' they said, 'chile with tortillas, and then we go to sleep.' So everything was the same. It gave me a lot to think about. I have to tell you that I didn't learn my politics in school. I just tried to turn my own experience into something which was common to a whole people. I was also very happy when I realized that it wasn't just my problem; that I wasn't the only little girl to have worried about not wanting to grow up. We were all worried about the harsh life awaiting us.

The CUC[4] started growing; it spread like fire among the peasants in Guatemala. We began to understand that the root of all our problems was exploitation. That there were rich and poor and that the rich exploited the poor—our sweat, our labor. That's how they got richer and richer. The fact that we were always waiting in offices, always bowing to the authorities, was part of the discrimination we Indians suffered. So was the cultural oppression which tries to divide us by taking away our traditions and prevents unity among our people. [. . .]

Later I had the opportunity of meeting other Indians. *Achi* Indians, the group that lives closest to us. And I got to know some of the *Mam* Indians too.[5] They all told me: 'The rich are bad. But not all *ladinos*[6] are bad.' And I started wondering: 'Could it be that not all *ladinos* are bad?' I used to think they were all bad. But *they* said that they lived with poor *ladinos*. There were poor *ladinos* as well as rich *ladinos*, and they were exploited as well. That's when I began recognizing exploitation. I kept on going down to the finca but now I really wanted to find

out, to prove if that was true and learn all the details. There were poor *ladinos* in the finca. They worked the same, and their children's bellies were swollen like my little brother's. So I said: 'It must be true, then, that not all *ladinos* are bad.' I was just beginning to speak a little Spanish in those days and I began to talk to them. I said to one poor *ladino*: 'You're a poor *ladino*, aren't you?' And he nearly hit me. He said: 'What do you know about it, Indian?' I wondered: 'Why is it that when I say poor *ladinos* are like us, I'm spurned?' I didn't know then the same system which tries to isolate us Indians also puts up barriers between Indians and *ladinos*. I knew that all *ladinos* rejected us but I didn't know why. I was more confused. I still thought all *ladinos* were bad. Soon afterwards, I was with the nuns and we went to a village in Uspantán where mostly *ladinos* live. The nun asked a little boy if they were poor and he said: 'Yes, we're poor but we're not Indians.' That stayed with me. [. . .]

In our village, we went on working. I still didn't have a clear idea of who exactly our enemies were. We began putting safety measures into practice in our village. We used the methods our forebears had used, and which our own grandparents told us about. Our forefathers passed them down to us. We said that if the landowners' soldiers come, we'll kill them right here. That's when we decided to use violence. I remember that it was my job to explain to the children of the community that our situation has nothing to do with fate but was something which had been imposed on us. I taught them that they had to defend themselves against it, to defend our parents' rights. I'd have a sort of political chat with the children, although I wasn't very clear about our situation politically. But my experiences told me what I needed. I didn't need speeches or courses or anything like that. [. . .]

We had a *ladino* friend in the town who gave us a little money, both for my father and us at home. But we didn't use this money for ourselves: We shared it with the community. We were now getting organized. We already had various organizations: children's groups, young peoples' groups, women's groups, catechists' groups, and we began strengthening these groups. We wanted to make plans for us

---

[4]The United Peasant Community, of which her father was one of the early members.
[5]Achi and Mam are references to other indigenous groups in Guatemala.
[6]*Ladino* is a term used frequently in Central America for all non-Indians.

Rigoberta Menchú Tum, pictured visiting the ruin of the Templo Mayor in Mexico City shortly after she won the Nobel Peace Prize. To her right is Templo Mayor Museum director Eduardo Matos, and Teresa Francom, director of Mexico's National Institute of Anthropology is on her left. Menchú Tum vowed to leave her Nobel Prize in the Templo Mayor Museum until conditions improved for Guatemalan indigenous peoples. How does this scene capture the extent to which Menchú Tum's life changed from 1980 to 1992? How does her dress differentiate her from her guides? What message did she send to the international community by choosing to leave her Nobel Prize at the site of an ancient Mesoamerican temple?

Source: AP Wide World Photos.

all to learn Spanish. I spent one afternoon teaching the children the bit of Spanish I knew. Not to write, of course, because I couldn't write. I couldn't read or write. But to teach them to speak as we spoke in our language.

At the end of 1977, I decided to join a more formal group—a group of peasants in Huehuetenango. It was a clandestine group and we'd go down to the finca and work among the workers in the finca. The *compañeros* of the CUC worked among them too. And yet, I still hadn't reached the rewarding stage of participating fully, as an Indian first, and then as a woman, a peasant, a Christian, in the struggle of all my people. That's when I started being more involved. [. . .]

I began travelling to different areas, discussing everything. I must say one thing, and it's not to denigrate them, because the priests have done a lot for us. It's not to undervalue the good things they have taught us; but they also taught us to accept many things, to be passive, to be a dormant people. Their religion told us it was a sin

to kill while we were being killed. They told us that God is up there and that God had a kingdom for the poor. This confused me because I'd been a catechist since I was a child and had had a lot of ideas put in my head. It prevents us from seeing the real truth of how our people live. I tried to get rid of my doubts by asking the nuns: 'What would happen if we rose up against the rich?' The nuns tried to avoid the question. I don't know if it was intentional or not, but in any case no-one answered my question. I was very disturbed. In my community's terms, I was already a grown woman, and I was very ashamed about being so confused, when so many of my villagers understood so much better than I. But their ideas were very pure because they had never been outside their community. *We'd* been down to the fincas, but *they* hadn't known anything different. Going to the capital in a lorry brings about a change in an Indian, which he suffers inside himself. That's why my little brothers and my brothers and sisters understood more clearly than I did.

Nobel Prize Acceptance Speech, December 10, 1992[7]

{After thanking the Nobel Peace Committee and express-ing her deep emotion and pride at receiving the award, Menchú made the following statements in her acceptance speech}

The Nobel Prize is a symbol of peace, and of the efforts to build up a real democracy. It will stimulate civil sectors so that through a solid national unity [in Guatemala], these may contribute to the process of negotiations that seek peace, reflecting the general feeling—although at times not possible to express because of fear—of the Guatemalan society: to establish political and legal grounds that will give irreversible impulses to a solution to as to what initiated the internal armed conflict. There is no doubt whatsoever that it constitutes a sign of hope in the struggle of the Indigenous people in the en-tire continent. It is also a tribute to the Centro-American people who still search for their stability, for the structuring of their future, and the path for their development and integration, based on civil democracy and mutual respect. The importance of this Nobel Prize has been demonstrated by all the congratulations received from everywhere, from heads of government—practically all the American presidents—to the organizations of the Indigenous people and human rights, from all over the world. [. . .] As a contrast, and paradoxically, it was actu-ally in my own country where I met, on the part of some people, the strongest objections, reserve and indifference for the reward of the Nobel Prize to this *Quiché* Indian. Perhaps because in Latin America, it is precisely Guatemala where the discrimination to-wards natives, towards women, and the repression of the longing for justice and peace, are more deeply rooted in certain social and political sectors. [. . .]

I would describe the meaning of this Nobel Prize, in the first place, as a tribute to the Indian peo-ple who have been sacrificed and have disappeared because they aimed at a more dignified and just life with fraternity and understanding among hu-man beings. To those who are no longer alive to keep up the hope for a change in the situation in respect to poverty, and marginalization of the Indians, of those who have been banished, of the helpless in Guatemala as well as in the entire American continent. [. . .]

It also represents a sign of the growing interna-tional interest for, and understanding of[,] the orig-inal rights of the people, of the future of more than 60 million Indians that live in our America, and their uproar because of the 500 years of oppression that they have endured; for the genocides beyond comparison that they have had to suffer all this time, and from which other countries and the elite of the Americas have profited and taken advantage.

Let there be freedom for the Indians, wherever they may be in the American continent or elsewhere in the world, because while they are alive, a glow of hope will be alive as well as the real concept of life. The expressions of great happiness by the Indian Organizations in the entire continent and the world-wide congratulations received for the award like the Nobel Peace Prize, clearly indicate the great impor-tance of this decision. It is the recognition of the European debt to the American Indigenous people; it is an appeal to the conscience of humanity so that those conditions of marginalization that condemned them to colonialism and exploitation may be eradi-cated; it is a cry for life, peace, justice, equality, and fraternity between human beings. [. . .]

At a time when the commemoration of the fifth century of the arrival of Columbus in America has repercussions all over the world, the revival of hopes for the Indian people claims that we reassert to the world our existence and the value of our cultural identity. It demands that we endeavor to actively participate in the decisions that concern our destiny, in the building-up of our countries/nations. Should we, in spite of all, not be taken into consideration, there are factors that guarantee our future: struggle and endurance; courage; the decision to maintain our traditions that have been exposed to so many perils and sufferings; solidarity towards our struggle

---

[7]*Source:* Rigobera Menchú Tum portions of the Novel Prize Acceptance Speech.

on the part of numerous countries, governments, organizations and citizens of the world.

That is why I dream of the day when the relationship between the Indigenous people and other people is strengthened; when they can join their potentialities and their capabilities and contribute to make life on this planet less unequal. [. . .]

Ladies and gentlemen, allow me to say some candid words about my country. The attention that this Nobel Peace Prize has focused on Guatemala should imply that the violation of human rights is no longer ignored internationally. It will also honor all those who have died struggling for social equality and justice n my country.

It is known throughout the world that the Guatemalan people, as a result of their struggle, succeeded in achieving, in October 1944, a period of democracy where institutionality and human rights represented the main philosophies. At that time, Guatemala was an exception in the American continent because of its struggle for complete national sovereignty. However, in 1954, a conspiracy that joined the traditional national power centers, inheritors of colonialism, with powerful foreign interests, overthrew the democratic regime as a result of armed innovations, thereby imposing the old system of oppression which has characterized the history of my country.[8] The economic, social, and political subjection that derived from that part of the Cold War, was what initiated the internal armed conflict. The repression against the organizations of the people, the democratic parties and the intellectuals, started in Guatemala long before the war started. Let us not forget that.

In the attempt to crush rebellion, dictatorships have committed the greatest atrocities. They have leveled villages, and murdered thousands of farmers, particularly Indians, hundreds of trade union workers and students, outstanding intellectuals and

politicians, priests and nuns. Throughout this systematic persecution in the name of safety of the nation, 1 million farmers were removed by force from their lands; 100,000 seek refuges in neighboring countries. In Guatemala there are today almost 100,000 orphans and more than 40,000 widows. The practice of 'mission' politicians was invented in Guatemala, as a government policy. As you know, I myself am a survivor of a massacred family. [. . .]

It is necessary to point out, here in Oslo, that the issue of the human rights in Guatemala constitutes the most urgent problem that has to be solved. My statement is neither incidental nor unjustified. As has been ascertained by international institutions, such as the United National Commission of Human Rights, the Inter-American Commission of Human Rights and many other humanitarian organizations, Guatemala is one of the countries in America with the largest number of violations of these rights, the largest number of cases of impunity where security forces are generally involved. It is imperative that the repression and persecution of the people and the Indians be stopped. The compulsory mobilization and integration of young people into the Patrols of Civil Self-Defense, which to a great extent affects the Indian people, must also be stopped.

Democracy in Guatemala must be built up as soon as possible. It is necessary that human rights be fully complied with. We must put an end to racism, guarantee freedom to organize and to move within all sectors of the country. In short, it is imperative to open the fields to the multi-ethnic civil society with all its rights, to demilitarize the country and establish the basis for its development, so that it can be pulled out of today's underdevelopment and poverty. [. . .]

In Guatemala it is just as important to recognize the identity and the rights of the Indigenous people, that have been ignored and despised not only during the colonial period, but also in the republican one. It is not possible to conceive a democratic Guatemala, free and independent, without the Indigenous identity shaping its character in all aspects of national existence. [. . .]

I call upon the social and ethnic sectors that constitute the people of Guatemala to participate actively in the efforts to find a peaceful solution to the armed conflict, to build-up a sound unity between

---

[8]Menchú Tum was referring to the 1954 United States-backed overthrow of the Arbenz government in Guatemala. Labor and land reform laws under the Arévalo and Arbenz governments gave land and hope to the indigenous majority, but they threatened to undermine the power and profits of Boston-based United Fruit Company, the single largest landowner in Guatemala. The coup resulted in the reversal of these reforms and decades of military dictatorship.

the '*ladinos*', the blacks and the Indians, all of whom must create within their diversity, their [Guatemalan identity]. Along these same lines, I invite the international community to contribute with specific actions so that the parties involved may overcome the differences that at this stage keep negotiations in a wait-and-see state, and thereby succeed, first of all, in signing an agreement on human rights. And then, re-initiate the rounds of negotiation and find those issues on which to compromise, allowing for the Peace Agreement to be signed and immediately verified, because I have no doubt that this will bring about a great relief to the prevailing situation in Guatemala.

Ladies and gentlemen, the fact that I have given preference to the American continent, and in particular to my country, does not mean that I do not have an important place in my mind and in my heart for the concern of other people of the world and their constant struggle for the defense of peace, of the rights to a life and all its inalienable rights. The majority of us, who are gathered here today, constitute an example of the above, and along these lines I would humbly extend to you my gratitude. [. . .]

A world at peace that could provide consistency, interrelation and concordance in respect of the economic, social and cultural structures of the societies. That could have deep roots and sound influence. We have in our mind the deepest felt demands of entire humanity, when we strive for a peaceful coexistence and the preservation of the environment. The struggle we fight purifies and shapes the future. Our history is a live history that has throbbed, withstood and survived many centuries of sacrifice, now it comes forward again with strength. The seeds, dormant for such a long time, break out today with some uncertainty, although they germinate in a world that is at present characterized by confusion and vagueness.

There is no doubt that this process will be long and complex, but it is no Utopia and we, the Indians, we have no confidence in its implementation.

The people of Guatemala will mobilize and will be aware of their strength to build up a worthy future. It is preparing itself to sow the future, to free itself from atavisms, to rediscover itself. To build up a country with a genuine national identity. To start

a new life. By combining all the shades and nuances of the '*ladinos*,' the 'garifunas' and Indians in the Guatemalan ethnic mosaic, we must interlace a number of colors without arising contradictions, without them becoming grotesque or antagonistic, but we must give them brightness and a spirit of superior quality, just the way our weavers weave. A typical 'guipil' shirt. Thank you very much.

Suggested Sources:

A superb account of the historical foundations of racial conflicts in Guatemala is Greg Grandin's *The Blood of Guatemala: A History of Race and Nation* (Durham, NC: Duke University Press, 2000). For an account that questions the veracity of Menchú Tum's testimony, see David Stoll, *Rigoberta Menchú and the Story of All Poor Guatemalans* (New York: Harper Collins, 2000). For a different evaluation of the controversy, see Arturio Arias, ed., *The Rigoberta Menchú Controversy* (Minneapolis: University of Minnesota Press, 2001). Included is Larry Rohter's original *New York Times* exposé based on Stoll's book, along with other newspaper responses to Stoll's claims, and scholarly evaluations of the controversy and its relevance in both international and Guatemalan politics and society.

There are a number of interesting primary sources on Menchú Tum and the situation in Guatemala. Menchú Tum herself wrote a book titled *Crossing Borders*, trans. Ann Wright (New York: Verso, 1998). For an early documentary made on Guatemala that has since been redistributed, see *When Mountains Tremble* (New York: New Video Group, 2004 [1983]). For other primary sources on the situation in Guatemala, consult either the Web site for the Foundation for Human Rights in Guatemala (http://www.fhrg.org), which has both current and archived information. Also see an abridged version of the 1998 Human Rights Report on Guatemala printed by the Archdiocese of Guatemala, *Guatemala: Never Again!* (New York: Orbis Books, 1999).

Chapter 28

An Afro-Brazilian Woman Activist Advances from the Favela to the Senate

Leo J. Garofalo, Connecticut College

Afro-Brazilian politician Benedita da Silva's life story offers an inside look at how her politics emerged from growing up poor in a *favela* (shantytown) and engaging in community politics as a young woman during the waning years of Brazil's military dictatorship. Born in 1943 to a big family of poor rural migrants, Benedita da Silva seemed an unlikely candidate for the distinctions of being the first black woman to enter congress and the first woman of any race or class to enter the Brazilian senate. However, her life in Rio de Janeiro's *favelas* gave her precisely the organizing skills and the political base needed to take her long-ignored constituents' message, and her own brand of Brazilian optimism, to the halls of power. Growing up poor, black, and female immediately conjures up images of abject poverty and hopelessness.[1] Nevertheless, when interviewed for her life story, da Silva explained that, even in the *favela*, she enjoyed working with others and excelled in politics. She achieved personal, political, and economic success, and her star was still rising as her party claimed a second presidential term. The excerpts presented here introduce her youth, rise to power, and political views.

Benedita da Silva's rise in politics is linked to the explosion of Brazil's poor urban population and to military rule (1964–1984). Devastating droughts and the lack of land reform forced a rural exodus to southern coastal cities, but urban centers proved poorly equipped to house or employ migrants. Consequently, they occupied undeveloped lands and steep hillsides close to where they worked. Informal employment in the service sector and manual labor denied them health care, pensions, and the protection of labor laws. With meager earnings and no affordable housing, migrants' squatter settlements became permanent. Even after residents built brick houses, municipal governments provided no electricity, running water, sewer systems, garbage collection, or police protection. Therefore, residents organized neighborhood associations to demand services and legal title to their homes. During the democratic governments between 1955 and 1964, politicians listened to demands and made promises.

With the 1964 overthrow of a popularly elected government, the whole country felt the far-reaching impact of military rule. The military brutally stifled dissent and imposed an economic development model that depended on massive borrowing and infrastructure projects to exploit the resources of the interior. The generals and their allies hoped to divert attention away from cities and toward colonizing the Amazon and enjoying the "Economic Miracle" that benefited the middle classes and made Brazil's economy one of the world's ten largest. They stressed nationalistic and patriotic themes, such as soccer, while denying the existence of class and racial divisions. With the coup, *favelas* went from bad to worse. The military were hostile toward *favelados*

Favelas ring Brazil's famed Rio de Janeiro. A street-level view of residents' front doors shows electrical and telephone cables overhead and a *favela* women's association's open door in the lower right corner with local artists' artwork displayed inside. Benedita da Silva literally helped build this world and win its residents a political voice. How does this *favela* resemble or differ from photos of other shantytowns, or what people in the United States imagine about shantytowns? What evidence suggests gains in infrastructure and the community's capacity to meet its needs? What still seems lacking?

Source: Photograph by Leo J. Garofalo.

(*favela* dwellers) and suppressed attempts to organize or discuss social problems. Not surprisingly, the gradual return to democracy in the late 1970s and the 1980s left many battles still to be fought for social justice.

During the dictatorship, Benedita da Silva rose as a neighborhood association leader. As the military loosened its hold on power beginning in 1978, civil society responded by forming new parties and pressing for attention to illiteracy, malnourishment, triple-digit

---

[1]Carolina Maria de Jesus (1914–1977) provided the most famous portrait of the *favela* in her dairy of life in a São Paulo slum. See Carolina Maria de Jesus, *Child of the Dark: The Diary of Carolina Maria de Jesus*, trans. David St. Clair (New York: Penguin, 1963).

Rio's modern high-rises stand juxtaposed with the poverty and precariousness of the *favela* just blocks away. Rich and poor live virtually alongside one another. Proximity to wealthy employers initially induced people to settle in these gullies and steep hillsides. How might this "geography of class" affect politics in Rio and Brazil? Would the rural poor develop different views of the wealthy and the political system than *favelados*?

Source: Photograph by Leo J. Garofalo.

inflation, and limited political participation. During this political opening, da Silva was elected to Rio de Janeiro's City Council in 1982 as a candidate of the new Worker's Party (PT), which was looking for candidates with a grassroots base. Launched officially in 1980, the PT grew out of a 1979 meeting of metalworkers, mechanics, and electricians in São Paulo, and it enjoyed the support of the progressive wing of the Catholic Church. Benedita da Silva, an evangelical, found the PT more appealing than other left-wing parties because it welcomed both atheists and believers, included intellectuals and grassroots organizers, and

offered women new opportunities. She credited union organizer and PT founder Luis Inácio Lula da Silva, who later became a two-term president of Brazil, for much of the party's internal diversity. Benedita da Silva and others fought within the PT to establish a system of quotas to guarantee a percentage of female candidates each election; they prevailed over the objections of those who argued that time and merit would eventually allow women to rise in the party ranks.

After the end of the dictatorship, Benedita da Silva was elected federal deputy for the National Assembly in 1986 (reelected in 1990). She was one of 26 women out of a total of 599 deputies in 1986; and she was one of only 7 black deputies. In 1994, Benedita da Silva made history by winning the first senate seat ever held by a Brazilian woman. After the publication of her testimonial, she went on to serve as a state governor and a government minister in President Lula da Silva's administration. Her life spans a momentous 65 years of Brazilian history.

Questions to Consider:

1. What was da Silva's childhood like, and how did it influence her politics?
2. How did da Silva's gender shape her youth and her views?
3. How did da Silva define democracy? How similar or different is her definition from the term's use and definition in the United States? What accounts for differences?
4. How do her discussions of democracy and socialism—and her life more generally—help to explain why socialism enjoys support in Latin America?

Benedita da Silva's Story of Politics and Love in Brazil (1997)[2]

[. . .]

When I look back at my life, I first think of my parents. . . . [M]y mother's family didn't let them get

---

[2]*Source:* Benedita da Silva, *An Afro-Brazilian Woman's Story of Politics and Love*, ed. Medea Benjamin and Maisa Mendonça (Monroe, OR: Food First Books, 1997), 4–5, 7–8, 18–21, 33–35, 42–45, 176–178, 197–201.

married because he was a peasant and had nothing. When my mother was 13, she had to marry a man named Benjamin, who was 40 years old and had his own farm. She invited her girlfriends over to her house all the time and all she wanted to do was play—after all, she was just a girl. She didn't know anything about getting pregnant and giving birth, and her first two daughters, Luarita and Sindoca, almost died.

Her marriage didn't last very long because Benjamin got sick and died. His family didn't allow my mother to inherit anything. [*Her mother remarried a few years later.*]

Since my father had no land and my mother was left with nothing, they had to work as day laborers on *fazenda* (landed estate) in Minas Gerais. They were treated like slaves—they worked in exchange for food and they weren't free to leave. The working conditions on the *fazenda* were horrible, and the food they received wasn't enough to feed all the children. So after many years my mother decided to take all 12 of her children and run away to Rio de Janeiro.

My father, José, stayed in Minas. He told my mother that she was crazy. She didn't have any money, she didn't know anyone in Rio, she had 12 children and was pregnant. But my mother said, "No, José, I'm not crazy. You'll see. We're going to get a house and when it's all set up, I'll send for you." And that's just what she did.

It was 1936 when my mother moved to Rio and set up a shack in a *favela*, a shantytown, called Praia do Pinto.[3] To make money she opened a *birosca*—a little store front—and washed clothes. As soon as she managed to get a bigger shack, she sent for my father. As you can see, my family is very matriarchal. It's the women who are the risk-takers and the ones who make the decisions—the women in my family are fearless.

[. . .]

My mother had 13 children in all, but I only knew eight of them. The others died of different diseases like measles and tuberculosis, which used to kill a lot of children in those days. . . . Today, there are only five of us left—Sindoca, Roserval and Tonho died of cancer.

My father worked in construction and he also washed cars. My mother washed clothes, but with the invention of washing machines and dry cleaners, she began to get less and less work.

One of the people my mother washed clothes for was Juselino Kubitschek, who later became President of Brazil.[4] Their relationship was like that of master and slave. There was not much dialogue—one gave orders and the other obeyed. I used to go to his house to deliver the laundry and Juselino's wife would feel sorry for me and give me old clothes and toys that belonged to their daughter Marcia. Actually, the first doll I ever had was Marcia's old doll. I never imagined that I would become a Federal Deputy and meet up with her in Congress—the daughter of the former president and the daughter of the laundry woman!

[. . .]

Even though we were poor, my mother understood the importance of education. She wanted me to be a teacher and I wanted to be a doctor. I was better off than my older brother and sisters because they grew up in the *fazenda* and couldn't go to school. I was the only one in my family who learned how to read and write. At least I was able to go to elementary school, but I couldn't afford to continue until I was much older.

I remember that when I was in school I only had one outfit and I wore it every day. . . .

[. . .]

By the time I was seven, I was already out working. I shined shoes, and I sold candy, peanuts, and fruit in the marketplace. I learned early on the prejudices against girls. The market venders didn't want to hire us because they said we weren't as strong as boys and it would take us twice as long to carry the boxes to and from the market. I insisted on proving that I could work as hard as the boys did. That's when they started calling me macho woman—a reputation I have to this day.

[. . .]

I also had a strong sense of morality. For example, no matter how bad things got, I would never sell my body. . . .

I was good at doing domestic work, but during that time it was very difficult work because maids had no rights. The women of the house dealt directly

---

[3]They later moved to another *favela*, Chapéu Mangueira.

[4]Following the populist politics of Gétulio Vargas (1946–1951), President Juselino Kubitschek (1956–1961) promoted heavy industry, built roads, and constructed a new capital in the interior (Brásilia) to alleviate the coastal cities' overpopulation, unemployment, and poverty. Kubitschek's policies brought rapid inflation. Fearful of his populist policies and popularity, the military forced Kubitschek into exile in 1964.

with the maids, and this was one of the things that gave these rich or middle-class women some power. They wanted to show their husbands that their maids worked hard for little money. The needs of the workers were rarely taken into consideration.

When I was single I'd work as a live-in maid and only come home once every two weeks. It was terrible work because there were no set hours. When you worked as a live-in maid, you had to work all day and night. My bosses would always tell me that I was part of the family. What a joke! I don't know what family member would agree to be treated like a slave.

After I got married and had children, I stopped working as a live-in maid and only cleaned the house during the day. . . . It was very humiliating work. Sometimes my boss would say that she forgot to go to the bank and couldn't pay me. I'd leave the house with a piece of hard bread to give to my children and I'd have to go home and make bread soup.

[. . .]

For a long time, I worked as a domestic servant, but then I got really tired of it and looked for other work. I worked as a street vendor, selling food, clothes, cosmetics, everything you can imagine. I worked at a leather belt factory and as a janitor at a school. In 1975, when I was in my early thirties, I landed a government job in the Department of Transportation, working as a clerk. And in 1979, I took a nurse's aide course and supplemented my income by getting a part-time job in the Miguel Couto Hospital.

I always felt insecure because I never had a chance to finish high school. So I decided that I would study at home and then take the high school equivalency exam. I borrowed textbooks from Danilo, one of the neighborhood kids, and studied in the early hours of the morning. [. . .]

With a lot of sacrifice, I managed to get my high school diploma in 1980, and I enrolled in the University to study social work. In fact, my daughter Nilcea and I went to college at the same time—great—they always encouraged me to continue my studies.

In that sense, my husband was very good to me. He adored me and supported my efforts to study and get a better job. And during all the years we were together, he always supported my community work. Other women's husbands would give them a hard time when they wanted to go out to neighborhood

meetings at night, but not Mansinho. Whether it was organizing in the community or studying to get ahead, Mansinho encouraged me.

[. . .]

Let me take you on a little tour of Chapéu Mangueira, where I have been living all of my life. . . . The history of *favelas* goes back to the quilombos where the blacks, Indians and some poor whites formed independent republics on the hillsides as a way to resist slavery. The *favelas* are also a result of the rural exodus, with people streaming out of the countryside to the city in search of a better life—just like my parents did. These rural folk, mostly small farmers and their families, are expelled from the land by the big landowners or are already landless and have no way to survive. So they come to the city, look for a piece of empty land, and then occupy it and set up their shacks. Little by little, others join them and form communities. There are now about 480 *favelas* in Rio, which are home to some 2.5 million people. . . . They don't get any government help, they have no infrastructure or public services such as sewage, water and electricity.

Conditions in Chapéu Mangueira are different because we've had a strong neighborhood association that's been fighting for years to improve the living conditions. I've been working with the association since I was 16. I've been president of the association two times. During all these years, we've managed to turn Chapéu Mangueira into a model *favela*. Look at the houses. They have poor sanitation and people are crowded together, but about 95 percent of the houses are made of brick. In other *favelas* you'll see houses made of everything—plywood, stucco, tin, even cardboard. And here we have running water and electricity in our homes.

[. . .] [T]he government saw the *favelas* as a hotbed of subversives, and when the military coup took place in 1964, they unleashed a massive wave of repression against us. Many *favelas* were physically destroyed. The military would come in and raze whole neighborhoods. Then they'd move the people to remote areas that were far from where they worked. It was difficult for children to get to their schools. Women who did laundry for a living lost their jobs because there was no room to wash clothes in the new neighborhoods. Men would often start second families because they were unable to return home after work every day.

[. . .]

The repression touched every part of our lives. We didn't have the same visibility as the intellectuals or middle class activists who went abroad into exile. We were exiled in our own country. We weren't allowed to sing our religious hymns or celebrate our festivals. We dug holes in our houses to hide our books and notepads. We couldn't keep minutes of our meetings because it was considered subversive to demand better living conditions like electricity, plumbing or paved roads.

[. . .]

There were not many avenues open for us to organize during the dictatorship, but I started to work with the Catholic Church and the underground left parties that organized in the *favelas* through literacy programs. We began a literacy campaign here in Chapéu Mangueira and used methods developed by the great educator Paulo Freire, which not only taught people to read, but raised their consciousness at the same time. It was a highly revolutionary way of teaching compared to the official teaching methods, which were very traditional. Brazilian education assumed that there were no inequalities in our society, that there was no class or ethnic consciousness.

[. . .]

One of the positive changes that happened during the dictatorship was that the women's movement in the *favelas* gained strength. Before the coup, women played a backstage role within the neighborhood associations. We would usually do the administrative work, make the food for the parties, and work on health and education. But when it came to decision-making, the men were in charge.

During the years of military rule, women were forced to take over many of their roles since the men in the *favelas* who were community organizers were persecuted. Many women leaders, myself included, emerged during this period. I became so active that in 1978 the women put me forward as a candidate for president of our association, and I won. It was a first for Chapéu Mangueira.

[*Benedita da Silva's account continues for several chapters to explain leadership during military rule, her election to city government as a candidate with the Worker's Party, and her congressional victories. She concludes with Brazil's problems at the time she wrote this book.*]

But you don't have to be an expert to understand the real reason for the increasing impoverishment of the Brazilian people: the present economic model.

This model, called *neoliberalism*, is based on blind faith in the free market. It believes that the market will automatically solve our economic and social ills, and calls for minimum levels of government intervention. Enterprises like telecommunications and the oil industry that have been in the hands of the state should be sold off to private owners. Regulations that protect national companies, as well as tariffs that make it more difficult for foreign products to enter Brazil, should be lifted. And social programs should be cut in order to balance the budget and pay back the huge loans we owe to foreign banks.

This packet of economic policies is imposed on Third World countries by international financial institutions like the International Monetary Fund, the World Bank, and the Club of Paris. They tell poor countries like Brazil that we can only get loans if we follow those policies.

It is an economic model that reverses the efforts made by many Third World nations during the 1960s and 1970s to create domestic industries. . . .

In the *neoliberal* system, the market is supposed to resolve everything, but it certainly doesn't solve the biggest problem we face, which is how to bridge the enormous gap between the haves and have nots. In Brazil we have the super-rich, who live better than the rich in wealthy countries. They have their sumptuous mansions, country clubs, and beach houses, where they are waited on hand and foot by an army of maids and butlers. They go on weekend shopping sprees to Miami, they send their children to the best European schools, and they have chummy relationships with top government officials. On the other side of paradise are Brazilians who can't feed their children, who have no access to the halls of power, and for whom the capitalist dream is a cruel joke.

According to the United Nations, Brazil has the worst income gap between the rich and poor in the entire world! How shameful it is to be the world champions of inequality. The entire bottom half of

Brazilian society receives less than four percent of the national income, while the richest 10 percent get over 50 percent of the income! Compare this to countries like Sweden, Belgium and Holland, where the richest 10 percent of the population receives only 20 percent of the income.

. . . That's because our governments have always been unwilling to touch the colossal appetites of the bankers, the financial speculators, the landowners, or the big businessmen. In Brazil, governments come and go, but the social divisions remain intact. When times are bad, it's the poor who have to tighten their belts. When times are good, it's the rich who profit.

During the military dictatorship, the generals tried to justify this social injustice by saying, . . . first the pie has to grow so we can divide it later. After 20 years of military rule, Brazil emerged in the 1980s as one of the world's top 10 economics, a success story among Third World nations. But the pie was never divided. The "economic miracle" benefited the few at the expense of the many.[5]

The new civilian governments have maintained strong ties with the same economic elites. With all their blah-blah-blah about social justice, the only concrete social programs they have implemented follow a paternalistic, populist formula that gives charity to the poor as a way to keep them quiet and submissive.

[. . .] Growing up poor, black, and female, I know what it means to live at the margin of society. I know what it's like to be a second class citizen. I learned early in life that the "service entrance" was my point of entry. I learned that the place for women was the kitchen. And I rebelled against all of this. Today I'm proud to be a black woman from a poor family. My origins provide me with a reference point that I will never reject. And it gives me the passion I need to keep fighting.

But fighting for what? After nearly 30 years of military rule, Brazil now has an elected government and is seen by the rest of the world as a democratic nation. But in a country where millions go hungry and justice is on the side of the rich, we have to question what democracy really means.

For me, democracy has many components. It means freedom to express your thoughts. It means freedom to practice your own religion. It means respect for racial and cultural differences. On the political front, democracy means the right to elect your own representatives, regardless of their race, sex, religion or class. It means one person, one vote, and the freedom to vote for whomever you want.

Most people would agree with these elements of democracy. But they leave out another dimension that is equally critical. When we talk about democracy, we have to incorporate rights like the right to a job at a decent wage, the right to a clean environment and the right to a more equitable form of development. These issues are as much a part of democracy as the right to free speech and free elections.

In Brazil, millions are denied their economic rights, and real power lies in the hands of a small minority. Decisions are made at the top, without the effective participation of the majority. And in this era of globalization, decisions by banks located thousands of miles away often have more impact on the daily lives of Brazilians than our own representatives do.

That's why I believe we need something radically different. We need to transform our society into one where human relations take precedence over material things. Socialism, in theory, could do that. Unfortunately, it has been distorted in almost all the places it has been tried. But I think we must keep on trying, since the poorer countries of the world are in desperate need of new social experiments. I think we need to try a version of socialism that respects our culture and works from the bottom-up.

For me, ideology is not the key issue. Whether you believe in capitalism or socialism as the best social system is really irrelevant. The most important thing is what you do in your everyday life to make the world better. The most important thing is your actions. You may believe that in theory, people shouldn't go hungry, but if you don't do anything to stop hunger, then your thoughts are meaningless. I've already been hungry, so it's not just an intellectual exercise for me. It's a question of doing something so that others don't have to suffer like I did.

In the 1960s, people dreamed the impossible. After all, the world context was propitious to thinking big. It was a time of euphoria when the students were

---

[5] Civil and human rights were also casualties of military rule. See, for example, *Vala comum* [Mass Grave], dir. Juan Godoy (Brazil, 1996).

taking to the streets of Paris demanding fraternity and equality. It was the time of the Prague Spring when there were hopes of political reform in the Eastern bloc. It was the time of the Watts uprising in Los Angeles that reshaped the civil rights laws in the United States. It was the time of the student struggles in Mexico that were violently crushed by the Tlatelolco massacre. It was the time of the worldwide movement against the war in Vietnam.

[. . .]

In some ways, we've lost that sense of euphoria, that sense of making the impossible possible. The ensuing years have been difficult ones, with wages and living conditions declining all over the world. We still see outrageous forms of resistance, but today it's more difficult to envision radical change. Somehow, we have to regain the momentum. Somehow, we have to be able to dream again.

I want to see more working people and poor people in power. I want to see the PT win the presidency. I want to see respect for children's rights, a better distribution of wealth, and jobs for all. I want to see the business community take pride in building a more equitable economic system. I want to see a society that does not separate rich and poor, black and white, men and women.

. . . No matter our race, nationality or religion, we are brothers and sisters if we are united by the same longing for justice.

[. . .]

Suggested Sources:

The documentary film *Benedita da Silva,* dir. Eunice Gutman, covers her 1990 reelection campaign (New York: Cinema Guild, 1990). "Capital Sins: Authoritarianism and Democratization," dir. Rachel Field, *Americas,* part 2 (South Burlington, VT: Annenberg/CPB Collection, 1993) explores how Brazil's union movement and the Church ended military rule. Rachel Field and Juan Mandelbaum show parallels with da Silva in Chile: "In Women's Hands: The Changing Roles of Women," *Americas,* part 5 (South Burlington, VT: Annenberg/CPB Collection, 1993). Democracy also opened space for native peoples. Seth Garfield, "Mario Juruna: Brazil's First Indigenous Congressman," in *The Human Tradition in Modern Brazil,* ed. Peter M. Beattie (Wilmington, DE: Scholarly Resources, 2004), 287–304. Democracy and urbanization helped black candidates elsewhere. See María Elena Moyano, *The Autobiography of María Elena Moyano: The Life and Death of a Peruvian Activist,* ed. Diana Miloslavich Túpac, trans. Patricia S. Taylor Edmisten (Gainesville: University Press of Florida, 2000); and *Coraje* [Courage], dir. Alberto Durant (New York: Latin American Video Archives, 1998).

Da Silva condemns the violence of drug trafficking, and Robert Gay offers an inside look at this problem in *Lucia: Testimonies of a Brazilian Drug Dealer's Woman* (Philadelphia: Temple University Press, 2005); and *Cidade de Deus* [City of God], dir. Fernando Meirelles (Miramax Films, Burbank, CA; O2 Filmes and Videofilmes, Brazil, 2003) dramatizes the same issue. Carolina Maria de Jesus provided the classic account of *favela* life a generation earlier in *Child of the Dark: The Diary of Carolina Maria de Jesus,* trans. David St. Clair (New York: Penguin, 1963). Robert M. Levine and José Carlos Sebe Bom Meihy study Carolina de Jesus as a writer and a public figure in *The Life and Death of Carolina Maria de Jesus* (Albuquerque: University of New Mexico Press, 1995).

Chapter 29

Verónica Michelle Bachelet Jeria: A Woman President

Karin Alejandra Rosemblatt, University of Maryland

Chile

Michelle Bachelet became the first woman president of Chile on March 11, 2006. A physician by profession, she served as minister of health in the government of Ricardo Lagos Escobar (2000–2006) and later as President Lagos's minister of defense. As a woman in a male-defined political culture, Bachelet struggled to make a place for herself while expressing her vision as a woman. Like Evo Morales, who confronted the challenge of expressing his Native American identity and being the president of all Bolivians, Bachelet struggled to lead Chile as a whole while representing women and other marginalized groups. This chapter presents two speeches that address different audiences. The first is Bachelet's speech from the night of her electoral victory at an open-air rally. In the second, she spoke before the Tenth Regional Conference on Women in Latin America and the Caribbean, sponsored by the United Nations' Economic Commission on Latin America.

Bachelet's life was decisively shaped by a military coup that overthrew the democratically elected government of Salvador Allende in 1973, when Bachelet was a twenty-two-year-old medical student. Allende had come to power in 1970 as the representative of a left-wing coalition, the Popular Unity (PU).[1] Rather than advocating violence, the parties that joined the PU had long used elected office to seek reforms, and the PU coalition sought social transformation within the democratic system. The PU was overthrown, with United States support, by a military dictatorship that suspended elections and the institutions of representative government, suppressed dissident political activity, and brutally repressed opponents. It also implemented free-market policies that caused intense social and economic dislocation.

Bachelet's father, Air Force General Alberto Bachelet Martínez, had served in the Allende government and like many PU activists, he was detained immediately following the coup and was tortured. Later, Bachelet Martínez died of a heart attack. Subsequently, Bachelet's mother, Ángela Jeria Gómez, became active in groups made up of family members of victims of human rights abuses. Bachelet, who had participated in the youth branch of the Socialist Party during the Allende government, worked clandestinely for the Socialist Party. Because of these activities, Bachelet and her mother were detained and tortured. In 1975, they fled Chile for the German Democratic Republic, where Bachelet lived until returning to Chile and resuming her medical studies in 1979.

In 1990, after strident public protest and seventeen years of military rule, the authoritarian government of Augusto Pinochet Ugarte ceded power. Many Chileans hoped that a new, democratically elected government would not only restore democracy but also undo the economic inequities generated by Pinochet's *neoliberal* economic policies. Patricio Aylwin Azócar, a member of the centrist Christian Democrat Party who represented an electoral coalition of center-left political parties that included Bachelet's Socialist Party, became the new elected president of Chile. Aylwin was succeeded by two representatives of the same center-left Concertación coalition.[2] These governments substantially increased government spending on social programs but retained Pinochet-era free-market economic policies. The Chilean economy grew at a fast pace (except for a severe recession in 1999), and the average income of Chileans rose notably. Yet the gap between rich and poor widened.

Concertación leaders began to see Bachelet as a promising candidate after December 2002, when Chileans responded to an open-ended poll question by naming Bachelet as one of the five people in Chile with the most promising political future. By December 2004, Bachelet topped that list.[3] Potential voters saw her as warm and caring, qualities she had demonstrated as minister of health. They also saw her as competent. Many remembered her swift response to flooding in Santiago in June 2002, when Minister of Defense Bachelet ordered troops out into the streets for civil protection and rode around in a tank to oversee the efforts. Potential voters responded as well to her stance as a victim of human rights abuses who spoke out repeatedly about the need to recognize past abuses but who also worked, as a daughter of a military leader, to reconcile Chilean citizens and the armed forces.

Public opinion polls indicated that Bachelet was the Concertación candidate most likely to defeat the right-wing candidate in general elections. As a result, Bachelet, who had never aspired to the presidency, accepted the Concertación's nomination. Her campaign focused on the theme of "change" as a way of dispelling fatigue with Concertación politics. Bachelet was a credible agent of transformation: She

---

[1] The PU was made up of Allende's Socialist Party, the Communist Party, and a number of smaller left-wing and center-left parties.

[2] The Party for Democracy (Partido por la Democracia) was an offshoot of the Socialist Party. The Christian Democrats, a centrist party that initially opposed Allende, later actively opposed Pinochet. Together, these and other smaller center and center-left parties ran common presidential candidates in elections in 1990, 1994, 2000, and 2006. They also ran slates of candidates for congressional and municipal elections. The Concertación did not include the Communist Party or parties to the left of the Communists.

[3] Centro de Estudios de la Realidad Chilena (CERC), "Informe de prensa: Encuesta nacional septiembre 2002" and "Informe de prensa: Encuesta nacional diciembre 2004," http://www.cerc.cl/Encuestas.htm (accessed May 21, 2008).

was the first Concertación presidential nominee who was not old enough to have held an important political position before the military coup of 1973. Moreover, Bachelet promised a new, more participatory style of government. Her televised campaign spots featured Chileans of all walks of life wearing the presidential sash—the young, the old, indigenous peoples, the disabled, artists, fishermen, a pregnant woman.[4] Her campaign slogan "*Estoy Contigo*" ("I'm with you") replaced hierarchical notions of leadership with more horizontal ones, raising the question of the proper relation between represented and representative. Was it the citizens who were with the candidate? Or the candidate who was with the citizens? Bachelet also introduced a new, more inclusive political language and emphasized her own feminine as well as masculine qualities. "I speak to you from the heart," she said at the end of a campaign spot, "I speak to you from the head. We must be one so that we can be all of us."[5] Bachelet won handily in a second round of voting. Perhaps most surprising, in a country where women had consistently voted to the right of men, she was the first presidential candidate ever on the left not to win a smaller proportion of votes among women than among men.

Bachelet advocated policies aimed at gender equality, and one of her first measures as president was to ensure parity between men and women in her government appointments at all levels. The second speech details some of Bachelet's goals and achievements related to gender. But Bachelet was wary of being labeled a feminist and was careful to argue that equality—whether between men and women or between people of different ethnicities or social classes—benefited everyone.[6]

After taking office, Bachelet came under attack from supporters as well as opponents of the Concertación who questioned not only her decisions but also her political style. From the start, many blamed Bachelet's insistence on gender parity in ministerial appointments for the perceived weaknesses of her government. Criticisms of Bachelet often had a gendered subtext. She was commonly referred to as "Chanchelet," a play on the Spanish word for pig ("*chancho*"). Commentators on YouTube referred to the president as a "lesbian hungry for power," not qualified enough to be even "director of a girl's school in the provinces." "Bachellet [*sic*] go back to the kitchen," added another. "Let me remind you," read one post, "that to govern you need to be strong, and I'm not being sexist."[7] These themes were picked up by the more polite press, with *The Economist* reporting that one of Bachelet's advisors, José Antonio Viera-Gallo had the "intellectual weight Bachelet lacks." The article quoted Christian Democrat Jaime Ravinet, who reportedly said that "people want results and not just empathy and a smile."[8]

Despite these criticisms and a consistently hostile press, Bachelet's popularity rebounded. Divergent assessments of Bachelet and her government are yet another expression of the diversity of Chilean society. They are a reminder of how challenging it can be to govern amidst expressed differences—the very differences Bachelet herself promoted and celebrated.

Questions to Consider:

1. Did Bachelet's treatment of gender issues vary in these speeches and, if so, how? To what would you attribute any differences?
2. What did Bachelet suggest about the impact of women entering politics? To what extent, and how, did Bachelet believe her gender shapes her perspective?
3. In what ways did Bachelet address critics of her government?
4. Why did Bachelet say that equality is not just a dream? What are the implications of this statement?
5. How did Bachelet portray the Chilean nation?

---

[4] http://www.youtube.com/watch?v=am1L8sOfpYc (accessed May 21, 2008).

[5] Ibid.

[6] See, for example, her interview on United States television with Charlie Rose, available online at: http://www.youtube.com/watch?v=lsJaqd9TlcE (accessed May 21, 2008).

[7] http://www.youtube.com/watch?v=am1L8sOfpYc; http://www.youtube.com/watch?v=7UTbLuB3rmk&feature=related (accessed May 21, 2008).

[8] "Bachelet Tries Again," *The Economist* (March 31, 2007): 66.

Victory Speech, Santiago, Chile, 15 January 2006

Who would have thought, *amigos y amigas* [friends][9], who would have thought? Who would have thought twenty, ten, or five years ago that Chile would elect a woman as president? It seemed difficult, but it was possible, it is possible, because the citizens wanted it, because democracy allowed it.

Thanks, amigas and amigos, thanks, Chile! Thanks for the votes that millions of you gave to me. Thanks for the confidence you had in me. Thanks for inviting me to walk with you along the path of liberty, equality, prosperity.

This is not the triumph of one person, or one party, or one coalition. It is the triumph of us all. It is Chile's triumph. Chile won again, like always, as it always will. [. . .]

We Chileans are proud of what we have achieved, and we are going to continue on this path. We are once again going to astonish the world. We will demonstrate that a country can become more prosperous without losing its soul, that we can create wealth without polluting the air we breathe or the water we drink, that we can encourage those who show entrepreneurship and progress, but at the same time lend a hand to those who are left behind, that we can build a country with room for everybody, women and men, from the capital city and from all the regions of the country. People of all colors, creeds and convictions.

That is the path we are all going to walk along together, friends. That is the path. Thanks for choosing me to lead Chile on that journey!

To get to this place tonight, I too went down a long road. You all know it. I have not had an easy life. But who among you has? Violence entered my life destroying what I loved. Because I was a victim of hatred, I have consecrated my life to overturning that hatred, turning it into understanding, into tolerance and, why not say it, love.

You can love justice and at the same time be generous.[10]

Chile is reuniting. We have advanced much along this path. My government will be a government of unity. I will be the President of all Chileans. . . .

At this moment, I remember the faces and voices of so many Chilean women and men who I spent time with during these past months, hard-working people who work from sunup to sundown. Over and over they said to me: "We believe in you, doctor." The faith deposited in me by so many women and men makes me feel responsible and humbles me. Faith in others has been at the center of my life and work. I know it will be the motor of this new Chile that we will all build together. [. . .]

Today we have witnessed the magic of democracy, amigos and amigas. Today we're all equal. The vote of the most humble person is worth the same as the vote of the most powerful. Democracy can help untangle the wishes and hopes of the people. . . .

Starting right now, your hopes are my hopes, your wishes mine. To all the people who welcomed me into their homes, all the men and women who gave me the gift of a hug and a kiss, above all so many women who gave me my victory today, on this night. To all the people from the provinces, I send my greetings and my assurance that I will fulfill the vow I took in the last days of my campaign, that we would remember them when we were here celebrating and surely they are all celebrating in each of their cities our great triumph tonight.

Amigos y amigas, starting March 11, Chile will have a woman president, but it will also be the start of a new phase where we will make sure that the successes we achieve in this great country make their way into the homes of all Chileans, because I want people to remember my government as a government of all, for all. Ours is a dynamic country, with the desire to be successful, that is becoming more

---

[9]Bachelet consistently jettisoned the traditional use, in Spanish, of the masculine form to refer to both men and women. Instead, she referred to *"Chilenas y Chilenos,"* or *"amigos y amigas,"* referring specifically to men (generally signaled in Spanish by words ending in the letter "o") and women (generally signaled in Spanish by words ending in the letter "a").

[10]Bachelet here spoke out in favor of legally prosecuting perpetrators of human rights abuses during the Pinochet era who were still shielded by laws passed before Pinochet left office. She also argued for forgiveness rather than retribution. Both ideas were the subject of continued and often passionate public debate in Chile.

and more integrated into the world, a country of entrepreneurs who create prosperity with their ingenuity and creativity. But for Chilean men and women to dare to be entrepreneurial and to innovate, they must also know that the society they live in protects them.

I promise that by 2010 we will have consolidated a system of social protection that will give Chileans and their families peace of mind: the peace of mind that comes from knowing they will have a decent, dignified job; the peace of mind that comes from knowing their children will be able to study and develop themselves; the peace of mind that comes from knowing that illness can't destroy years of effort; the peace of mind that comes from knowing they will have a dignified old age. That is what we all aspire to. That is what my government will guarantee.

March 11 will mark the start of a new style in our national politics, a style of governing that is more open to dialogue, more participatory. I was the candidate of the citizens. Now I will be the president of the citizens. Chile needs a new politics for a new kind of citizen, amigos y amigas, because the fact that I am standing here tonight is a symbol of the changes that we have lived through.

Many fears and prejudices have been left behind. Chilean society is today more tolerant and open. People not only want the right to vote but also the right to speak. They want to be heard; they want to forge their destiny. In my government, we will channel the desire to participate. We will forge a grand alliance between the world of politics and society, between representatives and represented. [. . .]

Michelle Bachelet, surrounded by supporters when she arrived in Santiago, Chile, for a campaign rally one week before a runoff election against her opponent, conservative Sebastián Pinera. The sign in the background reads: "Michelle: Chile is with you." How might one of Bachelet's supporters have interpreted this photograph? How might one of her opponents have used it to critique her campaign?
Source: AP Wide World Photos.

My government will be a government of parity, of the best men and best women. It will be a government of excellence, a government of talent, of new faces and new experiences. I will choose the best people because Chile deserves it.

Chilenas and Chilenos, the tasks we have ahead of us are so beautiful: to build a more prosperous, more just country, with more solidarity, a country of all and for all. That is what I've dreamed about my whole life. [. . .]

Her Excellency, President of the Republic Michelle Bachelet, Speech before the Tenth Regional Conference on Women in Latin America and the Caribbean (CEPAL), Quito, Ecuador, 6 August 2007

It is a real honor for me to participate in this Tenth Regional Conference on Women in Latin America and the Caribbean. . . .

I want to take special note of the effort being made to open spaces for discussion and work on a topic that I place at the very heart of our policies for achieving greater equity, that is to say women's issues. . . .

Because thanks to this effort we can . . . place the diverse dimensions of gender equity policies on the public agenda of Latin America as a region. [. . .]

266 Section VII Power and Politics in the Transition into the Twenty-First Century

[When] we speak here about the situation of women what we are talking about is equity in our societies. We are talking about all the peoples of Latin America working together for societies that are more just, have more humane relations, where there is no longer room for inequality, arbitrariness, abuse, abuse of power, where all people, men and women, have equal opportunity. . . .

Because many forms of exclusion persist in Latin America, and there are many forms of exclusion in my own country, Chile. But my election as president is precisely that: a defeat of exclusion, a defeat for those who believe there is an imminent and untouchable order in our societies that sanctions exclusion.

My presence here today as the first woman president of Chile symbolizes our having won a victory for inclusion. "We are all Chile" was my campaign slogan.

That is why I say, dear amigas y amigos: Let us never lose that ethical horizon before us: a more inclusive, and therefore more just, society is possible if we work for it. . . .

Let me also share with you something that is a bit more personal, some general reflections on women, politics, and public policy that are also based on practice. And let me do so based on my own experience as the first woman president of Chile.

Every day, and I insist every day, I see even in the smallest details how my country faces a new and different experience—from etiquette and protocol, where people don't know whether to call me *Presidente* or *Presidenta,* to the notorious discomfort of some people who don't know whether to shake my hand or give me a peck on the cheek.

From the sexist criticisms of some to the differential treatment that the press gives us. The press worries about the color of my dress, shoes or purse. I never heard them making any comments about my predecessors at all. At most you might hear something like this about the men presidents: "The blue suit looks better on him than the gray." But the press is concerned even about my haircut.

But, well, I knew it would be like that, and if I bring it up it's not to complain, because it's in our power to work to change those prejudices and to create a more open and more democratic culture, more accepting of difference.

But there is much more. There is a whole symbolic and semiotic load behind all this. A woman holding the reins of a country, with her style, signs and forms, is serving I think as a catalyst to the cultural changes that move us toward greater equality and toward the more horizontal relations which we are already seeing in our countries. [. . .]

And I notice this every day in Chile, when I visit schools and girls say with all naturalness that they want to be like me when they grow up. Before they used to say that they wanted to be a doctor like me; now they say "Presidenta" of course.

I don't mean this as an anecdote, because when I was eight years old, at a time when power was essentially masculine in its form, gestures and style, I probably would not have even have thought about that.

The symbolism of being able to reach the highest rung is very powerful, and it's changing Chilean society. When I celebrated International Women's Day for the first time as president, I said, "Equality is no longer a dream."

But there's more. How does being a woman translate into the public arena? Is it the same as being a man but with a skirt? No. I have always believed that being a woman also adds something.

How do you translate a woman's rich interior world—full of ways of seeing and reflecting that allow her to understand the worth of human beings and of life—into public?

To be a woman is to love life and to express it as we vibrate, laugh, cry, love, with all the richness those emotions bring. To be a woman is to relate to others with the tremendous ability of putting yourself in the place of others. And those feelings express themselves naturally and in all their intensity in private.

To break through that boundary and deploy them in public is a new adventure I am fully committed to, at times hard and difficult but tremendously gratifying.

Without doubt there are different ways of seeing, and for modern societies where women are in all walks of life for good, I insist that the challenge is to be able to integrate masculine and feminine ways of seeing into a harmonious whole.

That more properly masculine *ethics of results,* in which what you achieve is what matters most and not how you get there, can be virtuously combined with women's *ethics of process,* where it also matters what path you take, the costs, how much involuntary damage you inflict, how many disturbances you occasion.

Now, it is hard to break those barriers and sometimes you are forced to play with what we might call the masculine within each woman. I have had to do it many times, to be sure. It's tempting, easier, just to stay in the same place, relate to others using codes that have been the tonic of the patriarchal world. That is clearly not the choice I want to make.

Still, I am convinced that our people want a greater integration of those worlds. I believe that men as well as women want to leave behind a daily existence that endlessly repeats meaningless routines that seem necessary for reasons we can't figure out, and that we don't know how to change. . . .

When a woman enters politics alone, she changes. When many women enter politics, politics changes. And, clearly, improving the quality of political life is one of the greatest challenges of our democracy, one of the most urgent necessities.

That is why I celebrate the fact that this Conference is discussing and recommending affirmative action measures that can ensure the full participation of women in public office and in elected positions. [. . .]

If we think, and we do think, that we want equity, that minorities should be respected and properly represented, then it is even more evident that majorities, and in this case women, are underrepresented in politics.

And this is not just a question of numbers. It's a question of democratic principles, of noting shortcomings in representative government and therefore justifiably putting in place measures, even if they are temporary, to overcome those shortcomings. [. . .]

And, in this regard, I want to . . . announce that in September I will send to Congress a law that modifies the Electoral Law and the Law of Political Parties, so that we can establish a minimum number of women candidates that political groups must put forward as candidates in congressional and municipal elections.

We know that women candidates encounter a series of difficulties. That's why I will propose that women candidates get additional public financing. . . . And we'll also propose less state financing for groups that put fewer women on the ballot.

And I will propose that we provide incentives for political parties that provide equal opportunity for men and women in the exercise of internal democracy and in the selection of party authorities, and that secure gender balance in party members' access to, and exercise of, positions of authority within the party and in public service.[11]

And this will be, without doubt, an important step forward for Chilean democracy.

The incorporation of women into politics is valuable in and of itself because it helps make our institutions more representative.

But that's not all. It also contributes to a better "delivery"[12] of our policies, better results. It allows us to incorporate a gender perspective in our public policies. . . .

We want to incorporate that perspective in every public policy. Let me give some examples:

In Chile, one of the great reforms we are initiating is a reform of the pension system. . . . Among the many measures we are putting in place, we are putting in place several measures to give women a subsidy equivalent to one year of pension contributions for each child they give birth to, so as to compensate them for the time they are out of the workforce because they are caring for their children.

Another measure we are proposing is a basic solidarity pension for the poorest 60 percent of citizens who have not contributed enough to their pensions to fund their retirement.

What does this mean? Often women work at home without pay and because of that women are going to receive this pension in greater proportion than men. That will mean growing old with fewer fears, but also greater dignity for women.

And I want to tell you that when I was a candidate, I did not propose this because I looked at all the countries in the world and none of them gave housewives a pension. The cost was very high. . . .

---

[11]Bachelet introduced a bill proposing such measures on October 29, 2007. It affirms that no sex should control more than seventy percent of elected offices or of positions within political parties.

[12]In English in original.

But having said that I couldn't guarantee this, I formed a multidisciplinary commission made up of politicians, experts, representatives of unions and trade associations [*gremios*] and asked them, although I had not seen this problem solved anywhere else, "Find a solution so we can give housewives a pension."

And today I'm satisfied because I didn't promise it, since I wasn't sure we could achieve it, but now we are going to achieve it, and we expect that next year we'll be paying out pensions to a large number of people.[13]

Or take what we are doing in the worlds of work and education. We have the most ambitious plan ever to build daycare centers in Chile. In the first year of my presidency, we built more nurseries than in all of our country's history. I am talking about free, public nurseries.

Why this concern? Because we know that inequality starts at birth, and from that very moment we need to provide girls and boys with more opportunities. Because we also know that only twenty percent of women who have small children work for wages, because they don't have a place to leave their children.

And so this is how we are setting in place public policies by incorporating women's perspectives.

In education, we promote programs of study that avoid prejudices and stereotypes regarding the domestic roles of boys and girls; as a way of preventing violence and abuse, we promote respect between the sexes in our educational programs starting in preschool. And we've launched a strong offensive against violence against women.

And I am not going to ignore this sad reality. In what goes of this year, already 32 women have been killed by their partners. Some say *sexism kills.*

And I cannot accept this. So in Congress we are proposing stiffer penalties for those who attack or kill women.

In addition, with the Minister of Women, we are creating a network of shelters throughout the country, to help and house victims of severe cases of violence or threats. [. . .]

But wait: all this concern for women is not just the feminist outburst of a president. It's not just

that, to be sure. It's not just an ethical imperative. It's not just a political imperative. It's also crucial to the development of our countries.

How is it possible for our countries not to take advantage of the talents of more than half of their population? If we are serious about developing, developing integrally, we have to take advantage of all our potential. . . .

We are not yet a society of free men and women with equal rights and opportunities. To reach that goal, we have to deepen the cultural changes already underway. [. . .]

Because equality cannot be only a dream: we have to build it with women's stubbornness and perseverance.

The writer Isabel Allende used to say that the masculine elite is pessimistic. I am not. If I weren't optimistic—historically optimistic, I should add—I would certainly not be president of Chile.

So: more women, more democracy, more justice, more humanity, more progress, more equality. Equality is not a dream.

Thank you.

Suggested Sources:

There are no book-length treatments of Bachelet in English. Susan Franceschet contextualizes Bachelet's rise in "Bachelet's Victory and the Political Advance of Women," *Nueva Sociedad* 202 (March–April, 2006): 13–22. Marcelo Ríos Tobar's short piece on Bachelet, "Chilean Feminism and Social Democracy from the Democratic Transition to Bachelet" in NACLA's *Report on the Americas* 40, no. 2 (March/April 2007) is part of an issue devoted to gender issues in Latin America. Another article by Ríos Tobar, on second-wave Chilean feminism, provides context on women' s organizing in "'Feminism Is Socialism, Liberty, and Much More:' Second-Wave Chilean Feminism and Its Contentious Relationship with Socialism," *Journal of Women's History* 15, no. 3 (Autumn 2003): 129–134. Good sources on gender and politics in Chile include Lisa Baldez's *Why Women Protest: Women's Movements in Chile* (Cambridge: Cambridge University Press, 2002); and Susan Franceschet's *Women and Politics in Chile*

---

[13]The first new pensions were paid in June 2008.

(Boulder, CO: Lynne Rienner, 2005). A readable account of Chile during the years of military rule can be found in Pamela Constable and Arturo Valenzuela, *A Nation of Enemies: Chile Under Pinochet* (New York: W. W. Norton, 1993). The third edition of Lois Hecht Oppenheim's *Politics in Chile: Socialism, Authoritarianism, and Market Democracy* (Boulder, CO: Westview Press, 2007) goes over some of the same ground but also covers the Concertación governments.

A wealth of excellent films document Allende's years in power, the Pinochet dictatorship, and issues of historical memory and human rights in post-dictatorship Chile. The fictional film *Machuca*, dir. Andrés Wood (Venice, CA: Menemsha Entertainment, 2004) uses the story of two boys to illuminate the conflicts raging during Allende's years in power. Two documentaries that look at how Chileans have dealt with the legacy of the dictatorship are Patricio Guzmán's moving *Chile, Obstinate Memory* (New York: First Run Films, 1997) and *The Judge and the General*, dir. Elizabeth Farnsworth and Patricio Lanfranco (San Francisco: West Wind Productions, 2008), which chronicles judge Juan Guzmán's personal transformation as he investigated crimes committed during the Pinochet era. The diverse nature of women's involvement in politics from 1989 through the early 1990s and the changing use of ideas about gender in political mobilizations are well documented in *In Women's Hands*, dir. Rachel Field and Juan Mandelbaum (South Burlington, VT: Annenberg/CPB Collection, 1993).

Chapter 30

❦

We Are All Presidents: Evo Morales and the Challenges of an Indigenous-Popular Government in Bolivia

José Antonio Lucero, University of Washington

On December 18, 2005, Evo Morales Ayma, known as "Evo" in Bolivia, became the first self-identified indigenous person to become president of Bolivia, where indigenous people make up a majority of the population. Morales was born in a mining village and served in the military as a youth. He worked most of his life as a farmer, and his crops included *coca*—the leaf from which cocaine is derived, but which has also been (in its plant form) a staple of Andean diets and rituals for centuries. Morales became an active member and leader of the coca-growers union, and he helped to found the leftist Movement toward Socialism (*Movimiento al Socialismo,* or MAS). It was through MAS that he became a prominent political figure, serving in the Bolivian legislature and coming in a close second in his 2002 presidential bid. The two following inaugural statements, the first delivered at the pre-Inca ruins of Tiwanaku and the second in the National Congress, give a sense of the historic importance of this victory.

To understand Evo's rise and the challenges his government faces, it is important to situate his victory within the centuries-long history of indigenous resistance in Bolivia. In every century, Bolivia has seen major indigenous uprisings. These conflicts have left deep imprints on Bolivian politics, as these two speeches amply demonstrate. Even the seemingly far-away rebellion of Tupaj Katari, whose eighteenth-century *Aymara* armies surrounded the city of La Paz, is present across a wide spectrum of contemporary Bolivian political discourses. In the twentieth century, there were early attempts to provide greater rights to indigenous people who were, as these documents mention, once legally prohibited from even entering the public plazas of La Paz. In 1945, President Gualberto Villaroel convoked an unprecedented Indigenous Congress that fueled the hopes of many rural populations as well as the fears of conservatives. For this and other reasons, Villaroel was overthrown and killed in 1946.[1] In 1952, a social revolution, fought largely by miners and *campesino* militias, finally established universal suffrage in Bolivia, and land reforms (although limited) also changed much of the neocolonial power structures of the country. Over the next several decades, civilian and military governments sought to incorporate indigenous people, identifying them mainly as peasants, through a network of state-sanctioned rural unions.

In the 1970s, an independent union movement arose that began to blend class and ethnic discourses in a movement known as *katarismo,* taking its name

from the fallen eighteenth-century rebel. A wide spectrum of katarista leaders emerged: some, like Felipe Quispe, advocated armed struggle, whereas others, like Victor Hugo Cárdenas, advocated working through the political system. As military rule gave way to democracy in the early 1980s, a Left-leaning government found itself facing unprecedented hyperinflation and severe economic crisis. This crisis undermined many parts of the indigenous and nonindigenous Left and opened the door to dramatic *neoliberal* economic reforms. Along with Chile, Bolivia was one of Latin America's earliest and most aggressive cases of free-market *neoliberal* reform.

In 1993, the architect of the earlier *neoliberal* reforms, Gonzalo Sánchez de Lozada (a United States–trained technocrat universally known as Goni) successfully ran for president in a surprising alliance with katarista leader Victor Hugo Cárdenas. While many of his fellow *Aymaras* labeled Cárdenas as a traitor, he led the effort to institutionalize a series of reforms that would further incorporate indigenous people into public life. New land, education, and decentralization laws recognized indigenous people as indigenous (rather than only as peasants), and the revised constitution defined the Bolivian nation as pluricultural and multiethnic. Yet many derided these reforms as governmental "divide and conquer" strategies, because they favored indigenous organizations that negotiated with *neoliberal* policy-makers and excluded organizations seeking more radical anti-*neoliberal* alternatives.

Conflict increased in the late 1990s when former military dictator Hugo Bánzer was democratically elected to office (1997–2001). Tensions mounted when Bánzer attempted to privatize water and increase Bolivia's role in the United States–supported "war on drugs" by eradicating coca plants. In 2000, a major social conflict, known as the "Water War," erupted in Cochabamba and signaled the first of several major anti-*neoliberal* protests that would soon bring the period of so-called *neoliberal* multiculturalism to an end. In the 2002 election, Goni won a narrow victory over a surprisingly strong Evo Morales. During the campaign, the United States ambassador to Bolivia claimed that a vote for Evo would put United States aid in jeopardy, comments

---

[1]Evo Morales alludes to the death of both Tupaj Katari and Villaroel in these documents.

that fueled nationalist anti-United States sentiment among Bolivians. This, along with Evo's expulsion from the Congress (also for reasons related to United States drug policies) made Evo an anti-imperial celebrity virtually overnight. With anti-United States sentiment already running high, Goni announced a plan to export natural gas to the United States through a pipeline that ran through Chile, another of Bolivia's historic enemies. In bloody clashes between protesters and state forces, the 2003 "Gas War" forced Goni, and later Vice-President Carlos Mesa, out of office.

In the 2005 elections, Evo Morales and his MAS party won a stunning victory. The MAS "political instrument" emphasized a broad national-popular coalition, which articulated both indigenous and nonindigenous themes. The growing strength of the MAS was mirrored by the weakness of traditional parties that were increasingly seen as corrupt, elitist, and unrepresentative. In 2005, for the first time since the return of democracy, a presidential candidate won an election with a majority of votes (fifty-four percent voted for Evo).

The first year of Evo's government brought important victories as well as setbacks. As promised, he nationalized the hydrocarbon sector in order to recover much of the gas, oil, and mineral income that had previously gone to transnational corporations. Yet, critics on the Left saw this as a false nationalization because Evo had simply, if aggressively, renegotiated contracts with foreign companies rather than expropriating any property. Despite increased revenues, a drop in foreign investment and a decrease in demand for natural gas had severely challenged Bolivia's capacity to export its natural gas.[2]

The government also convoked a Constituent Assembly, presided over by an indigenous woman, Silvia Lazarte, to consider questions of **autonomy,** (indigenous self-governance) and the restructuring of the Bolivian state. However, many indigenous MAS allies criticized the government decision to elect assembly members through traditional

western rather than indigenous forms of election. Additionally, calls for regional *autonomy*, especially from the economically more affluent and ethnically less indigenous lowland region, increased fear of national disintegration and inter-regional violence.

Even with all these tensions, there is no doubt that a historic change has taken place in Bolivia as a new set of popular and indigenous leaders enjoy widespread support and challenge the nation's long history of exclusion and racism. Additionally, Bolivia has avoided the large-scale violence that engulfed neighbors like Peru and Colombia. Anthropologist Xavier Albó characterized Bolivian politics with the following image: an entire country running toward an abyss, stopping just in the nick of time, and then looking for another abyss to run toward.[3] Yet, as Albó likes to say, "despite all the despites," there exists hope that once again this abyss can be avoided and perhaps, with some luck, bridges, not barricades, may finally be built over the fractured terrain of Bolivian society.

Questions to Consider:

1. How did Morales's understanding of history inform his political project? How did he seek to change the historical relationship between Bolivia and the world?

2. Morales often referred to "sisters and brothers" and to "*compañeros and compañeras*" (roughly: comrades). Is there any difference in the meaning of these two kinds of terms?

3. How did Evo Morales see indigenous and social struggles in Bolivia as representative of themes in Latin America more generally? How do his views compare with Rigoberta Menchú's?

4. What were Morales's proclaimed goals? Can you see hints in his speeches about why these might be difficult to carry out?

5. Why did Morales claim that Bolivia is still a "colonial state"?

---

[2]"Bolivia debilita su liderazgo energético y afecta a la región," *La Razón*, 25 jun. 07, Special Section: Crisis Energética, C2.

[3]Personal communication, February 11, 2007.

Remarks of Evo Morales Ayma at the Presidential Investiture Ceremony, Tiwanaku, Bolivia, 21 January 2006[4]

Thank you very much for the support you have given me during the campaign, sisters and brothers, *Aymaras, Quechuas, Mojeños.*[5]

I was saying, sisters and brothers from the provinces of La Paz, the departments of Bolivia, the countries of Latin America, today begins a new year for the indigenous peoples of the world, a new life in which we search for equality and justice, a new era, a new millennium for all the peoples of the world, beginning here in *Tiwanaku,*[6] here in La Paz, Bolivia. I am very excited, convinced that only with the strength of the people, with the unity of the people, can we end this colonial state and *neoliberal* model.

This commitment, in this most sacred space of Tiwanaku, this commitment to defend Bolivians, to defend indigenous people not only from Bolivia, but as we were told last night, to defend all the indigenous peoples of America,[7] the land once called Abya Yala . . . But I also want to say, with great respect to our indigenous authorities, our organizations, our

President Evo Morales kicks off Carnival festivities in Oruro, Bolivia, in traditional indigenous garments. Compare this dress with his outfit in the next photograph: What do the differences between the two images reveal about the nature of Morales's different (sometimes conflicting) commitments as president of Bolivia?

Source: CORBIS – NY/ © Martin Alipaz/EPA/ CORBIS. All Rights Reserved.

Bolivian president Evo Morales, photographed with Venezuelan president Hugo Chávez, on Morales's first day in office (January 23, 2006). That day, Morales signed trade agreements with Venezuela and discussed literacy projects with representatives of the Cuban government. What message did Morales convey about his presidency with these actions?

Source: Newscom.

---

[4]*Source:* Palabras de Evo Morales Ayma en la ceremonia de investidura presidencial en Tiwanaku, Bolivia, 21 de enero 2006. Full Spanish-language text available at http://www.**bolivia-usa**.org/noticias/**2006/DISCURSO**%20DE%20**EVO**%20**MORALES**%20AYMA.doc.

[5]These are three of the largest indigenous groups in Bolivia.

---

[6]Pre-Incan ruins and an important *Aymara* spiritual site located on the Bolivian altiplano, close to La Paz.

[7]"America" is used in the continental sense to include North and South America.

amautas,[8] to watch over me, if I don't advance, push me, sisters and brothers, correct me always. It is possible that I may make mistakes, I can make mistakes, we can all make mistakes, but I will never betray the struggle of the Bolivian people and the liberation struggles of the peoples of Latin America. The triumph of 18 December [2005] is not only the triumph of Evo Morales, it is the triumph of all Bolivians, the triumph of democracy; it is an exceptional triumph of the democratic and cultural revolution of Bolivia.

But I also want to tell you that many sisters and brothers who are [non-indigenous] professionals, intellectuals, and middle class joined the political instrument of liberation, today the political instrument of the people. I want to say that, as an *Aymara,* I am proud of those middle class professionals, those intellectuals. But I also remind my sisters and brothers of the middle class, of the professional, intellectual, and business classes, that you too should be proud of these indigenous peoples. We search for the unity of all the sectors, respecting diversity, respecting our differences, that we all have a right to life. Yet, if we speak of Bolivia, the *Aymara, Quechua,* Mojeño, Chapaco, Valluno, Chiquitanos, Yuracaré, Chipaya, Murato peoples, are the absolute owners of this immense land.[9] [. . .]

For this reason, because of your invitation, because of the initiative of our indigenous authorities, we give a special greeting to the red ponchos, our *jilakata* brothers, the *mallkus,* the *jiliri mallkus,* the *mamatallas.*[10] Thanks to the indigenous authorities for the realization of this event, so indigenous, so our own, for inviting me to commit myself to governing well. I only want to say in this sacred place that with the help of the *Quechua, Aymara, Guaraní* sisters and brothers, we seek to govern with honesty, with the responsibility of changing the economic situation of the Bolivian people.

We also have the responsibility, of the upcoming Constituent Assembly . . . Indigenous participation in

the founding of Bolivia was marginalized in 1825, and this is why the indigenous people demand the refounding of Bolivia through a Constituent Assembly. I ask the new National Parliament that by February or March a law be approved to convoke the Constituent Assembly . . . so that on August 6 [2006] in the historic capital of Bolivia, Sucre, Chuquisaca, where Bolivia was founded, we may initiate a Constituent Assembly to bring an end to the colonial state.

Sisters and brothers, I want to ask you all for unity above all. You have seen last night, the indigenous movement of all America concentrated in Bolivia, saluting and greeting us, sending resolutions of support and strength to this political movement that seeks to change our history. And they have not only been the social movements of America, of Europe, or Asia. You have seen, sisters and brothers how this political movement has raised up our Bolivia in the international community. You have also seen sisters and brothers, that we are not alone on the world stage, governments, presidents support Bolivia and this government. [. . .]

We *Aymaras* and *Quechuas* are not resentful, and if we have won now, it is not to take vengeance on anyone, it is not to seek to subordinate anyone, we only seek unity, equality, sisters and brothers. Sisters and brothers, I want to say something again about that international campaign started by the [indigenous] leaders of America, the campaign called 500 years of indigenous and popular resistance. In . . . 1992, we concluded 500 years of resistance of indigenous peoples again the policies of internal colonialism. . . . And I want to say something about the move from resistance to governance to all the indigenous leaders gathered here. We are done resisting just to resist. We have seen that if we are organized and united with the social movements of the city and of the countryside, along with social conscience, with intellectual capacity, it is possible to defeat democratically external interests. This happened in Bolivia. This is why I say to the sisters and brothers of America, of the entire world: united and organized we can change the economic policies that do not improve the economic situation of the majority of nations. By now, we are convinced that concentrating capital in the hands of a few is no solution for humanity . . . it is no solution for the poor of the world.

---

[8]*Quechua* and *Aymara* terms for traditional indigenous intellectuals.
[9]These are a various indigenous peoples in Bolivia.
[10]Jilakata, mallkus, and jiliiri mallkus are, in ascending order of importance, traditional indigenous male authorities. Mamatallas are women community leaders who co-govern with their husbands.

This is why we have the obligation to remedy those economic problems of privatization, of selling to the highest bidder. That must end, and we are starting here together. All of us in America, the social movements, want to keep moving forward, to liberate our Bolivia, our America. That struggle that Tupaj Katari left us continues, sisters and brothers, and we will keep recuperating territory. The struggle that Che Guevara left us, we are going to fulfill it, sisters and brothers. . . .[11]

This is so exciting, sisters and brothers. We are not used to being in these kinds of gatherings. In the moment that I came out here, I understood that the people are truly organizing and mobilizing. This great concentration, in this place, I would compare with the Plaza of the Revolution in Cuba. When I left there, where thousands of *compañeros* were gathered, I thought that this is never seen in Bolivia. A campaign rally is one thing, but these acts of support and strength are another. This gathering is totally different, and for that, on behalf of the Movimiento Al Socialismo (MAS), of the parliamentary MAS block, and above all, in the name of all the indigenous peoples of Bolivia, I thank you.

Thank you, sisters and brothers. This struggle does not end, in this world either the rich will govern or the poor will govern. We have the obligation and task to create greater consciousness in the whole world so that national majorities, the poor of the world, will move their countries toward changing their economic situations. From here, we advance the idea that the poor also have a right to govern ourselves, and in Bolivia, that indigenous people also have the right to be presidents.

This is why, sisters and brothers, thanks to your votes, for the first time in Bolivian history, *Aymaras*, *Quechuas*, Mojeños, we are presidents, it is not only Evo who is president, sisters and brothers.

Thank you very much.

---

[11]Ernesto "Che" Guevara tried to take the foco theory of revolution, the idea that a small group of revolutionaries could light a broad revolutionary fire from Cuba to Bolivia. By his own admission, he failed to recruit a single *campesino* and was captured and killed by the Bolivian military in 1967. Although Che's military failure says much about the limited knowledge that the Left had about the cultural and political complexities of Bolivia, he has become an iconic figure for a wide range of popular movements.

Inauguration Speech of the Constitutional President of the Republic, Evo Morales Ayma, La Paz, 22 January 2006[12]

Thank you:

In order to remember our ancestors, Mr. President of the National Congress, I ask for a minute of silence for Manco Inca, Tupaj Katari, Tupac Amaru, Bartolina Sisa, Zárate Villca, Atihuaiqui Tumpa, Andrés Ibañez, Ché Guevara, Marcelo Quiroga Santa Cruz, Luis Espinal,[13] and many more fallen brothers, cocaleros of the tropics of Cochabamba, for the brothers who fell in defense of the dignity of El Alto,[14] the miners, the thousands, the millions of human beings who have fallen throughout America, for them, Mr. President, I ask for a moment of silence.

Glory to the martyrs of liberation!

Mr. President of the Congress, Mr. Alvaro García Linera; Presidents, Heads of State present here, thank you for your presence. International

---

[12]*Source:* Palabras de Evo Morales Ayma en la transmisión de mando presidencial en el Congreso Nacional, La Paz, Bolivia, 22 de enero de 2006. Full Spanish-language text available at http://www.presidencia.gov.bo.

[13]This pantheon of heroes reflect anticolonial indigenous figures as well as fallen figures from the Marxist Left.

[14]*El Alto* is the indigenous-majority "satellite city" of La Paz that is made largely of migrants from the countryside and their children and grandchildren. With a dense organizational landscape, various neighborhood organizations played leading roles in the conflicts over water and gas that forced Presidents Sánchez de Lozada and Mesa out of office.

organizations, former presidents, [members of] the National Congress, the Supreme Court of Justice, sisters and brothers of the indigenous peoples of America, thank you for your presence.

To all the Bolivian people, I greet and salute you, I am grateful for the life I have been given, I am thankful for my parents, may they rest in peace, convinced that that they are still with me, helping me. I thank God, the *Pachamama*,[15] for giving me this opportunity to guide this country. Thanks to all of them, I am where I am, and thanks to the popular movement, the indigenous movement of Bolivia and America.

Certainly, we are obliged to acknowledge greatly the indigenous movement, the challenges of the colonial period, the republican period, and the *neoliberal* period. The indigenous people—who are a majority of the population—for the international press here, you should know that according to the last census in 2001, 62.2 percent of the population are *Aymaras*, *Quechuas*, Mojeños, Chipayas, *Mulatos*, *Guaraníes*. These peoples have historically been marginalized, humiliated, hated, held in contempt, condemned to extinction. This is our history, our peoples were never recognized as human beings, though these peoples are the absolute owners of this noble land, of our natural resources.

This morning, it gave me great joy to see some sisters and brothers singing in the historic Plaza Murillo which, like Plaza San Francisco, not 40 or 50 years ago we would have not been able to enter. Some 40 or 50 year ago, our ancestors didn't have the right to walk these sidewalks.[16] That is our history, our life.

Bolivia seems like South Africa. We were threatened, condemned to extermination, but we are here today. I want to tell you that still there are remnants of those enemies of indigenous peoples, but we want to live in a condition of equality with them, and that is whey we are here to change our history. This indigenous movement is not anyone's concession, nothing has been given to us . . .

I want to tell you, tell the international press, that the first *Aymaras*, *Quechuas*, who learned to read and write, had their eyes removed, had their hands cut off so that they would never again learn to read or write. We have been subordinated, but today, we seek to resolve these historic problems, not with vengeance. We are not resentful. [. . .]

I want to say to that popular movement, to those honest Andean people of the cities, of the indigenous movement, that we are not alone, the social movements and governments of America, Europe, Asia and Africa are with us. Though unfortunately, even recently, there has been a dirty war, a war of lies that does not go away. This has to change, its wounds are real. Based on lies, they want to humiliate us. Remember, last year, in Plaza Murillo, they wanted to hang Evo Morales, they wanted to draw and quarter Evo Morales.[17] That kind of thing can't happen anymore, *compañeras y compañeros*.

Evo is not important, we are no longer in the campaign. I only want us to remember our history, that dark history. . . . It is true that it hurt, but we are not ones to cry for 500 years, we are no longer in that epoch, we are in an epoch of triumph, joy, celebration. That is why it is important to change our Bolivia, our Latin America. . . .

And why do we speak of changing that colonial state? We must bring that colonial state to an end. Imagine: after 180 years of republican democratic life, it is only recently that we can be here, in the parliament, in the presidency, in the municipalities. Before we had no rights.

Imagine. Universal suffrage in 1952 cost us blood. Peasants and miners rose up in arms so that we could all vote, it is not a gift from any party, they organized and conquered, it was a struggle of the people. [. . .]

There was the colonial state, it is still there today. Imagine. Is it possible that in the national army there is not one General Condori, General Villca, General Mamani, General Ayma.[18] There are none. It is still a colonial state. For this to change, there must be

---

[15]Mother Earth.
[16]Referring to an Andean form of apartheid, Morales refers to the recent past when indigenous people were banned from certain public spaces.

[17]A reference to the hanging of President Villaroel.
[18]These are all common indigenous last names.

spaces of debate and dialogues. We have a duty as Bolivians, to understand each other and to change those forms of discrimination that have existed among our peoples.

Before, we heard talk of democracy, about pacts for democracy, pacts for governability. In 1997, the year I came to Parliament, I saw this personally, but I didn't see any pact of democracy or pact of governability, I saw pacts of corruption, pacts of how and where to extract money. Thanks to the conscience of the Bolivian people, that is all over . . . If there had really been responsible people who governed loving this country, Bolivia would be better off that Switzerland. Switzerland, a developed country without natural resources, and Bolivia with such natural resources and such poverty. That must change, and that is why we are here to remedy those injustices, and end the constant sacking of our resources.

After hearing the reports of the transition commission, I have been able to see how the State does not control the State, does not control its institutions. As in economics, we are in total dependency, this is a transnationalized country. With the excuse of capitalization,[19] the country has been decapitalized. I thought the capitalization was to import capital rather than export it. Not only is capital exported as a result of these policies but human beings are also exported. . . .

Politics is the science of serving the people, and we must serve the people not live off of the people. We have to live for politics and not live off of politics. I understand that politics is a way to resolve the economic problems of the country . . . [Yet politics should not be used] to privatize basic services. I cannot understand how the former rulers privatized basic services like water. Water is a natural resource without which we could not live, thus it cannot be a private commodity, once it becomes that human rights are violated. Water is a public good.

The wars of water, coca, natural gas have brought us here, sisters and brothers. We have to recognize that these policies were wrong, mistaken,

driven by particular interests, sold to the highest bidder. All this called out to the conscience of the Bolivian people. We must change these policies. . . .

At the same time, we must also guarantee a referendum on *autonomy*. Historically, indigenous people have wanted *autonomy*, even before the republican period we fought for self-determination. *Autonomy* is not anyone's invention, it is the struggle of indigenous people throughout America. We want *autonomy* with solidarity, with reciprocity, where there is a redistribution of wealth, *autonomy* for indigenous peoples, for the provinces, for the regions. We search for this through the Constituent Assembly. . . .

I am sure that this is great support among the Bolivian people for these changes. It is also true that we need the support of the international community. We don't want a beggar-State, sadly they have made us that. We don't want Bolivia, its government, its economic teams to go begging for help from the United States, Europe or Asia. I would like that to end, and for this to end we must nationalize our natural resources. The new economic regime will be based on our natural resources and this too will pass through the Constituent Assembly. And we will not nationalize for the sake of nationalizing. In the case of natural gas, oil, mineral, or timber, we have the duty to industrialize . . .

In the world, there are large and small countries, rich and poor countries, but we are all equal in our rights to our dignity and sovereignty, and above all I value a message of our ancestor *Tupac Yupanqui* who said: a people that oppresses another people cannot be free. . . .[20]

Finally, to conclude my remarks, I wish to express my profound respect for the indigenous movements of Bolivia and America, for the social movements, and for the leaders, professionals, and intellectuals that joined in the effort to change our history. I salute my native land, Orinoca, Sur Carangas, Department of Oruro, which witnessed my birth and taught me to be honest, thank you people from Oruro and Orinoca. And I also salute and thank the [Cocalero] Union San Francisco

---

[19]Capitalization was one of President Sánchez de Lozada's economic reforms that privatized many sectors in hopes of bringing in greater foreign investment.

[20]Yupanqui, a descendant of Inca nobility who was educated in Madrid, was reported to have said these words as the representative of the Viceroyalty of Peru at the Cadiz Court in 1811.

Bajo of the Central Villa, 14 of September zone, the Federation of the Tropics, the Six Federations of the Cochabamba Tropics, Cochabamba, which was the birthplace of my union and political life. Thank you people of Cochabamba for allowing me to live with and learn from you. These two lands taught me about life, surely now it will be the land of Bolivia that will teach me to govern well.

I will fulfill my obligation, as Sub-Commander Marcos[21] says, to govern obeying the people. I will govern Bolivia obeying the Bolivian people.

Thank you very much.

---

[21]Marcos is the spokesperson for the Ejercito Zapatista de Liberación Nacional (EZLN) in Chiapas, Mexico—another important and largely indigenous movement in Latin America.

Suggested Sources:

An excellent overview of Bolivian history is Forrest Hylton and Sinclair Thomson, *Revolutionary Horizons: Past and Present in Bolivian Politics* (London: Verso, 2007). The seemingly paradoxical combination of *neoliberal* policies and multiculturalism has received some superb treatments, including Bret Gustafson, "Paradoxes of Liberal Indigenism: Indigenous Movements, State Processes, and Intercultural Reform in Bolivia," in *The Politics of Ethnicity: Indigenous Peoples and Latin American States,* ed. David Maybury-Lewis (Cambridge, MA: Harvard University Press, 2002), 267–306; and Charles Hale, "Rethinking Indigenous Politics in the Era of the 'Indio Permitido,'" *NACLA Report on the Americas* 38, no. 2 (2004): 16–22. The transition for *neoliberal* multicultural Bolivia to the post-multicultural, anti-*neoliberal* backlash has been chronicled by Benjamin Kohl and Linda Farthing in *Impasse in Bolivia: Neoliberal Hegemony and Popular Resistance* (London: Zed, 2006); and Nancy Postero, *Now We Are Citizens: Indigenous Politics in Postmulticultural Bolivia* (Stanford, CA: Stanford University Press, 2006). For an excellent, region-wide account of the evolution of indigenous movements to indigenous political parties, see Donna Lee Van Cott, *From Movements to Parties: The Evolution of Ethnic Politics* (Cambridge: Cambridge University Press, 2005).

In addition to being able to find many of Evo Morales's speeches online, there are several excellent video resources on Bolivia. For a good introduction to the history of race in Bolivia (compared with the Dominican Republic), see *Mirrors of the Heart* (South Burlington, VT: Annenberg/CPB Collection, Volume 4 of *Americas* Series, 1993). A good account of the breakdown of the Washington Consensus in Bolivia is the documentary on the water war, *Leasing the Rain* (Alexandria, VA: PBS, Frontline), http://www.pbs.org/frontlineworld/stories/bolivia, 2002. One of the leaders of the "water war" protests, Oscar Olivera (with Tom Lewis), gives his own account of events in *Cochabamba: Water War in Bolivia* (Cambridge, MA: South End Press, 2004). An excellent account of the rise and fall of Gonzalo Sánchez de Lozada (and the role played by United States "democracy promoters" in Bolivia) is Rachel Boyton's documentary, *Our Brand is Crisis* (Port Washington, NY: Koch Lober Films, 2005).

Glossary

Aché: A hunter-gatherer indigenous group living in Paraguay. They have often been targets of private and state oppression and exploitation. They were particularly persecuted during the Stroessner dictatorship of 1954–1989.

Alcabala: The alcabala was the sales tax collected under the Spanish colonial state. It was one of the taxes from which indigenous peoples were theoretically exempt (see Two Republics, System of).

Anarchism: A political theory, anarchism considers all forms of governmental authority unnecessary and undesirable; advocating a society based on voluntary cooperation and free association of individuals and groups.

Autóctono: This is the Spanish term for *autochthonous*, meaning "indigenous" or "native."

Autonomy: Questions of "autonomy" have been prominent in many Latin American indigenous movements since the 1980s. Debates over indigenous autonomy have revolved around the question of greater self-governance for indigenous communities as well as greater economic and political independence for local and regional governments. One finds many autonomy adherents, for example, in the eastern parts of nations such as Bolivia, where Morales's central government is most concentrated.

Ayllu: Defined by sharing common ancestry, the allyu constituted the basic kin group and organizational unit in the Andes.

Aymara: This term refers to both a spoken language and a large ethnic group in the southern highlands of Peru and Bolivia (see Quechua).

Bourbon Reforms: Eighteenth-century economic and administrative measures imposed by the Spanish and eventually the Portuguese Crowns to strengthen royal control over colonial tax collection, commerce, and colonial courts and officials. The tightening of royal control made the reforms unpopular.

Brazilian Federation for the Progress of Women (FBPF): Founded by Bertha Lutz in 1922, the FBPF was a national umbrella organization to campaign for female suffrage, civil rights, educational and occupational opportunities, and labor rights for women.

Cacique: Under Spanish rule, cacique became the general term for indigenous leader of all levels, often hereditary. Cacica referred to female ethnic chiefs. (See Kuraka.) In some regions of Latin America caciques gradually lost their association with indigenous identity. In Mexico, caciques had little to do with ethnic structures by the nineteenth and twentieth centuries and were instead political bosses who exploited the indigenous and mestizo peasantry.

Campesinos: This term refers to members of the rural poor, typically either peasants who till their own land or workers on large estates.

Castas: A Spanish term identifying a variety of people of mixed racial heritage (i.e., some combination of Spanish, indigenous, and African ancestry). Casta labels functioned as legal designations of ethno-racial status and sometimes determined official rights and obligations.

Caudillo: A reference to politico-military strongmen who dominated regional, and occasionally national, politics in nineteenth-century Latin America. Traditionally, most caudillos came from the upper- or at least middle classes, and they exercised some military experience before their rise to national power. Although caudillos often bent laws to suit them, many of them worked within constitutional frameworks and established organized systems of government administration. Caudillos often enjoyed broad-based popular support due to their charisma, personal connections, and willingness to offer tangible benefits to the poor majority in times of turmoil and need.

Chicha: Chicha is a traditional fermented drink among indigenous Andean peoples. Sometimes referred to as "corn beer," the drink is occasionally made from other plants, such as barley that came to the Americas from Europe.

Ciudadano: Literally translating to "citizen," the term ciudadano has strong class, race, and gender implications in modern Latin American history. During the nineteenth and early twentieth centuries, all women were excluded from full participatory rights in national politics, and property or literacy requirements kept most poor peoples of non-European or mixed racial descent from enjoying citizenship rights.

Compañero/a: Though it can mean "companion" more generally, the term compañero is most often used to refer to a comrade, particularly during times of revolution or among leftists.

CONAIE: The Confederación de Nacionalidades Indígenas del Ecuador (the Confederation of Ecuadorian Indigenous Nationalities), or CONAIE, is an umbrella organization established by various regional indigenous activist organizations in Ecuador. CONAIE was one of the earliest indigenous organizations in Latin America to have a significant impact on national politics, and its leaders played a pivotal role in establishing meetings for indigenous organizations throughout the western hemisphere (the Americas).

Conservative: Conservatism was one of two dominant political ideologies in nineteenth-century Latin America. Though many versions of conservatism did (and do) exist, most Latin American conservatives advocated high protective tariffs, strong central government, and a strong role for the Catholic Church in state and society. Many conservatives also supported a corporatist model that gave particular rights and obligations to different social groups (such as clergy, military, or indigenous peoples).

Creole (criollo/crioulo): In Spanish, criollo distinguished non-native Americans born in the Americas from those born in Europe or Africa. In Mexico, for instance, criollo described an American-born person of Spanish parentage. In plantation-based societies, in the Caribbean, for example, creole or criollo more often referred to American-born blacks. In Brazil, people used the Portuguese crioulo in the same ways.

Department of Indigenous Affairs (DAI): The DAI was a Paraguayan government institution, dependent on the Ministry of National Defense, created under the Stroessner regime in 1958 to further integrate the indigenous population into national society and markets.

Descamisados: Literally meaning "the shirtless ones," Juan Perón used this phrase to refer to the Argentine workers who provided the base support for his rise to power as a populist leader in the 1940s (See populism).

Divorcio: Though a cognate of the English-language term "divorce," historically a divorcio in Latin America referred only to a formal, ecclesiastical separation of a married couple, with the goal of eventual reconciliation, and not to the permanent termination of the marriage.

Ejido: Ejidos referred to traditional indigenous communal lands, commonly used in Mexico. Ejidos survived under the colonial political system (see Two Republics) and after the Mexican Revolution of 1910–1940, some of the land that was redistributed to the rural poor was in the form of communal grants called ejidos.

Eugenics: Eugenics was a popular theory (particularly in western societies) in the early twentieth century. Eugenicists held that certain racial or social groups (usually wealthy people of western European descent) were biologically superior to other groups. Eugenicists in the United States and western Europe believed that racial intermixing would weaken the dominant race and, ultimately, the nation. Conversely, proponents of eugenics in Latin America proposed that racial intermixing would improve the "inferior" group and they often advocated racial intermixing and intermarriage as a way of strengthening their nations.

Favela: This is a Portuguese term referring to a shantytown that grows on the outskirts of a city or hilly and inaccessible locations within the city. Favelas in Brazil were first established with Afro-Brazilians' flight to cities following the 1888 abolition of slavery, where few of them found adequate jobs or housing. Favelas grew rapidly with industrialization and the collapse of small-scale agriculture in the northeast, beginning with ramshackle home-made structures and eventually evolving into more permanent buildings, alley-like streets, and businesses where the poor live on the margins in large and wealthy cities like São Paulo.

Guaraní: A South American indigenous group whose largest population is in Paraguay. In fact, more Paraguayans speak Guaraní than Spanish.

Hacienda (fazenda in Portuguese): Latin America's elite owned large estates, with large workforces of poor rural workers, typically of indigenous, African, or mixed racial descent. Hacienda owners (*hacendados*) wielded both economic and social power over the men and women working on their estates.

Indígena: Translated loosely as the rarely used term "Indigene" in English, Indígena emerged as an alternative to using the pejorative term "indio" in nineteenth-century Latin America. Indígena marked indigenous peoples as members and potential citizens of the nation, but the reference was rife with interethnic paternalism in which political and economic elites continued to view indigenous peoples as childlike and incapable of self-rule.

Indigenism/*Indigenismo*: This was a set of legislative policies enacted by many Latin American nations following the first Interamerica Indigenous Congress in Mexico in 1940. The policies tended to integrate indigenous people into national life by guaranteeing them civic, property, and labor rights and valuing their cultural contributions and history. Although the legislation usually lauded the native heritage and promised respect for indigenous cultures, it often imposed guidelines for Indians' cultural change and incorporation into mainstream national ways of life.

Indio: The term "Indian" (indio) is one of the most powerful negative racial epithets one can use in Latin America. Some indigenous activists in Latin America today are using the term with a more positive sociopolitical emphasis, but it remains a controversial and highly charged term.

Kuraka: Native Andeans called their local ethnic lords kurakas, or they used the term *cacique* that the Spanish adopted in the Carribbean and Mexico (see Cacique).

Ladino: This is a general reference to a non-Indian, whether a person of European or mixed indigenous-European (mestizo) descent. Though used throughout many parts of Latin America, it is used more commonly in Central rather than South America.

Liberals: Liberalism was one of two dominant political ideologies in nineteenth-century Latin America. Though liberalism was complex, there were some core principles that most liberals shared. Most advocated free trade (or at least reduced tariffs), a central state that did not dominate regional politics, secular government, and individual rights.

Liberation Theology: Liberation Theologians believe in studying the Bible through the perspective of the poor, and they believe that in order to do God's work, one must join the struggle to eradicate poverty and injustice. Latin America became one of the main centers of Liberation Theology as it emerged in the 1960s and 1970s. Liberation Theologians are diverse: Some focus on gradual change through existing systems, whereas others advocate more radical means such as overthrowing the state (some even suggest that violence is justified in the struggle against oppressive regimes).

Libertos: This term refers to an African, Afro-Latin American, or mulato who was born to slavery but manumitted during the course of his or her lifetime. A liberto's status and rights were often unclear, particularly after independence, when constitutional conventions sought to identify citizens and their rights.

Mapuche: An indigenous people living in the southern cone of South America, with their largest populations in Chile, making up about ten percent of the Chilean population. The Mapuche have a long history of resistance to foreign invasion. It was only in the 1880s that Chilean military forces defeated the Mapuche and subjected them to an inferior position at the margins of the Chilean nation.

Mestizaje (Cult of Mestizaje): Mestizaje refers to cultural as well as biological intermixing. Many Latin American nations not only have a majority of mestizos, but they also promote national cultural values that (purportedly) draw on both indigenous and European backgrounds. In practice, cultural blending often gave greater value to European heritage, and government officials frequently pressured indigenous peoples to give up their own language and customs. Though in most countries mestizaje was a term to discuss the intermixing of European and indigenous peoples and cultures, peoples of African descent were also included in the term—particularly in areas of Latin America (such as the Caribbean) where there were large African-descended populations and only small indigenous populations.

Mestizo (mestiço): Someone with both European and indigenous ancestry.

Modernism: This was an international movement of artists and intellectuals who broke from traditional styles and pioneered new forms of expression during the late nineteenth and early twentieth century.

Mulato: A person of mixed European and African heritage.

Neocolonialism: Although colonial regimes collapsed by the 1820s in most parts of Ibero-America (except for Cuba and Puerto Rico), many Latin American nations continued to rely on foreign assistance, through loans and trade, in order to keep their economies and governments afloat. These foreign interests often received preferential treatment and had a great deal of political influence within Latin American nations, often reinforced by military actions. Colonial-style social, economic, and political relationships also continued within the independent nations, albeit informally, between elites and subalterns.

Neoliberalism: Neoliberalism refers to a set of economic policies that reflect classically liberal economic ideas of thinkers like John Locke and Adam Smith, especially the belief in the protection of individual property rights, the importance of trade, and a relatively small state. Neoliberal policies, therefore, reduced the state role in the economy, opened markets to United States and other imported goods, and relied on exports and foreign investment to create economic growth. In the late twentieth century, these policies—referred to as the "Washington Consensus"—were often aggressively encouraged by the United States Treasury Department and international (though Washington-based) actors like the International Monetary Fund and the World Bank.

Nongovernmental Organization (NGO): According to the UN, a "Nongovernmental Organization" is any private organization that is independent from government control, nonprofit, noncriminal, nonviolent, and does not seek to challenge any governments. In practice, there can be indirect government influence in NGOs, particularly those that seek contracts or grants from a given government. The nature of NGOs varies dramatically, but in general they are created to carry out small-scale development projects.

Parcialidad: This Spanish term refers to a faction or group. In Paraguay, it is often used to designate an indigenous tribe or people.

Pardos: People with some African ancestry. In places like Caracas, they made up the majority of the mixed-race populace (see Casta).

Patria: Meaning homeland or fatherland, patria is a term often called upon in Latin American nationalist rhetoric across a wide political spectrum.

Patria Potestad: Meaning "paternal power," the patria potestad was a legal term that gave the father of the family (the patriarch) legal rights and obligations with regard to his children. While the children were minors, or if they were in some way unfit to govern themselves as adults, their father maintained control of their persons, assets, and actions. Historically, if a couple separated, the father would maintain control over the children in his household.

Peninsulares: Persons born on the Iberian Peninsula, that is, in Portugal or Spain. They enjoyed considerable social and political prestige under colonial rule, especially with the Bourbon Reforms (see Bourbon Reforms).

Plurinationalism: Proponents of plurinationalism hold that many different nations, or peoples, make up the members of a particular state, and they want central state governments to recognize the existence of different cultures or nations and design policies and institutions that are sensitive to different cultures and worldviews. Many indigenous activists use plurinationalist concepts to demand the right to control territory and construct local or regional laws and the right of different cultural groups to enjoy equal representation within the central government. Opponents of plurinationalism charge that it threatens to create a "state within a state" and undermine national sovereignty and security.

Populism: A major part of Latin American political history, populism is a style of government in which a particular (often charismatic) leader rises to power through nationalist rhetoric and promises and policies to offer tangible benefits to the poor majority.

Pueblo: Though "pueblo" can mean a village, in Latin America it often refers to "the people."

Quechua (Quichua): Quechua was the language of the Inca ethnic group, which they spread as they conquered a vast empire in South America in the mid- to late fifteenth century, requiring that their subjects learn the language. Spanish colonizers and missionaries seized upon this "common language" to help establish their rule, and both promoted it at the expense of other local languages and extended its use east into the Amazon region. Quechua remains one of the two predominant indigenous languages in the Andes today. Quichua is a dialect of the language spoken in the northern Andes, particularly in Ecuador (see Aymara).

Quiché Maya: The Quiché are the largest of the Mayan linguistic groups in Central America. Though they are not socially or politically unified, the various Quiché Maya groups share many of the same cultural foundations and customs. In Guatemala, many Quiché (like other indigenous groups) suffered at the hands of state officials and large landowners, particularly during the civil war that raged from the 1960s through the 1990s.

Racial Democracy: Made famous by Brazilian scholar Gilberto Freyre, the notion of racial democracy appealed to many Latin American intellectuals and political elites in the early to mid-twentieth century. Adherents to the idea of racial democracy insisted that no barriers existed to keep peoples of mixed, indigenous, or African backgrounds from advancing in society, the economy, or politics. Thus, racism *per se* did not exist. Over time, the theory of racial democracy was proven to be a myth: Systematic and institutionalized racial inequalities existed and persisted in Latin American nations.

Social Darwinism: The term Social Darwinism first appeared in the late nineteenth century to suggest that humans, like animals and plants, struggle with each other for survival and the "most fit" come to dominate society, the economy, and politics. Social Darwinism was used to justify racism, imperialism, and capitalism. In the early twentieth century, it was closely associated with eugenics (see Eugenics).

Soldadera: Soldaderas were women who followed armies and sometimes participated in combat. Usually, these women were of poor, non-European backgrounds who followed their male family members into war. Though one can find evidence of soldaderas in the wars of independence in Latin America, they are (now) most famous for their significant contributions to the Mexican revolutionary conflict from 1910 to 1920.

Tarahumara: The Tarahumara are an indigenous group in northwest Mexico. Unlike the large indigenous populations of central and southern Mexico, the Tarahumara were not incorporated fully into the Spanish colonial or Mexican states. However, because their home territory was the location of valuable mineral deposits, they came into increasing conflict with nonindigenous groups from the nineteenth century forward. The government that resulted from the Mexican Revolution (1910–1940) attempted to incorporate the Tarahumara and acculturate them into white-mestizo ways.

Testimonio/Testimonial Literature: This refers to autobiographical accounts, either written by the narrator or told to a second party (usually a scholar or political activist). Written in the first person, the accounts are typically moving accounts of warfare, violence, or oppression inflicted by the narrator's own national government or economic system. These sources are often aimed at bringing a particular cause or problem to international attention. In the United States and Europe, some of these accounts were taken as "the authentic story of a people," rather than as the constructed story of an individual, and a few of them became very controversial.

Tribute: A head tax paid exclusively by indigenous men between the ages of eighteen and sixty, tribute was the lynchpin of the colonial system of Two Republics (see next), and it continued to be collected in the independent Andean nations of Bolivia, Ecuador, and Peru until the 1850s under the name *contribución de indígenas* (contribution of indigenous peoples).

Two Republics (System of): The Spanish colonial state divided subjects into two groups, or "republics." Members of the Republic of Indians held an inferior position: They paid a head tax (tribute) to the colonial state, and they provided rotating labor drafts for the state. To meet their tribute requirements, the colonial state allowed them access to land (both individual and communal) and exempted them from most other taxes and fees. Members of the Republic of Spaniards enjoyed a privileged social and legal position, and they paid no tribute nor served in labor drafts. They did have to pay other taxes, such as sales taxes, and provide military service should the state require it. Throughout Latin America, the legacy of the Two Republic system could be found in nineteenth-century struggles over indigenous rights to communal lands as well as in lingering elite stereotypes about Indians' inferiority.

Zapatistas: Within the Mexican revolutionary war from 1910 to 1920, a Zapatista was a supporter of Emiliano Zapata, who led a revolutionary army in the central Mexican state of Morelos. Zapata promised "land to the tillers" and his forces were made up primarily of peasants and estate workers. In the 1990s, Marxist guerrillas in the southeastern Mexican state of Chiapas invoked this radical revolutionary hero when they named their army the *Ejercito Zapatista para Liberación Nacional* (The Zapatista Army for National Liberation, or EZLN). Associating their demands for economic and cultural change in Chiapas, and throughout Mexico, with Emiliano Zapata suggested that they viewed themselves as completing the unfinished work and promises of the revolution.